Essay Strategies for Canadian S

MW00826498

Refining
Reading Writing

Essay Strategies for Canadian Students

Refining
Reading Writing

Geri Dasgupta
Centennial College

Jennifer Jianghai Mei
Centennial College

THOMSON

NELSON

Australia   Canada   Mexico   Singapore   Spain   United Kingdom   United States

THOMSON

NELSON

Refining Reading Writing: Essay Strategies for Canadian Students
by Geri Dasgupta, Jennifer Jianghai Mei

Associate Vice President,
Editorial Director:
Evelyn Veitch

Editor-in-Chief,
Higher Education:
Anne Williams

Executive Editor:
Laura Macleod

Marketing Manager:
Shelley Collacutt Miller

Developmental Editor:
Theresa Fitzgerald

Photo Researcher/Permissions
Coordinator:
Sheila Hall

Content Production Manager:
Tannys Williams

Production Service:
ICC Macmillan Inc.

Copy Editor:
Wendy Thomas

Proofreader:
Dianne Fowlie

Indexer:
Maura Brown

Production Coordinator:
Ferial Suleman

Design Director:
Ken Phipps

Interior Design:
ICC Macmillan Inc.

Cover Design:
Dianna Little

Cover Image:
Erik Rank/Getty Images

Compositor:
ICC Macmillan Inc.

Printer:
Thomson/West

COPYRIGHT © 2008 by Nelson,
a division of Thomson Canada Limited.

Printed and bound in the United States
1 2 3 4 10 09 08 07

For more information contact
Nelson, 1120 Birchmount Road,
Toronto, Ontario, M1K 5G4. Or
you can visit our Internet site at
http://www.nelson.com

Statistics Canada information is used
with the permission of Statistics Canada.
Users are forbidden to copy this material
and/or redisseminate the data, in an
original or modified form, for commercial
purposes, without the expressed
permissions of Statistics Canada.
Information on the availability of the
wide range of data from Statistics Canada
can be obtained from Statistics Canada's
Regional Offices, its World Wide Web
site at <http://www.statcan.ca>, and its
toll-free access number 1-800-263-1136.

ALL RIGHTS RESERVED. No part of this
work covered by the copyright herein
may be reproduced, transcribed, or used
in any form or by any means—graphic,
electronic, or mechanical, including
photocopying, recording, taping, Web
distribution, or information storage and
retrieval systems—without the written
permission of the publisher.

For permission to use material from this
text or product, submit a request online
at www.thomsonrights.com

Every effort has been made to trace
ownership of all copyrighted material
and to secure permission from copyright
holders. In the event of any question
arising as to the use of any material, we
will be pleased to make the necessary
corrections in future printings.

Library and Archives Canada
Cataloguing in Publication

Dasgupta, Geri, 1949–
  Refining reading writing: essay strategies
for Canadian students / Geri Dasgupta,
Jennifer Jiang-hai Mei.

ISBN 978-0-17-610353-8

  1. Essay—Authorship—Textbooks.
2. English language—Rhetoric—
Textbooks. 3. Readers—Essays—
Textbooks. I. Mei, Jennifer Jiang-hai
II. Title.

PE1408.D2344 2007   808.84
C2007-900795-3

Table of Contents

Unit Three

Unit Five

Unit Six

Appendix

Alternative Table of Contents: Readings by Author

Student Essays

Preface

All writers, by the way they use the language, reveal something of their spirits, their habits, their capacities, and their biases. This is inevitable as well as enjoyable.

(William Strunk Jr. and E.B. White)

Refining Reading Writing is a textbook designed for college or university students who are studying English composition and honing their communication skills. As its title suggests, the book aims to refine the students' abilities in both reading and writing that are essential to their success in their future career as well as at school. The emphasis in this text is to encourage and cultivate lifelong interest in critical reading and effective writing.

Units 1 and 2 focus on the interrelated capabilities of comprehending what one reads and creating meaning in one's own writing, and the emphasis is also on the enhancement of critical thinking skills through analysis of the readings. Unit 3 examines the writing process more systematically as it introduces, explains, and exemplifies the composition of the formula five-paragraph essay.

Units 4 and 5 provide further models for various patterns in reading and writing. We have chosen to divide these units into two categories: expository and affective discourse respectively. We realize that such a division can be interpreted as an arbitrary distinction because expository writing attempts ultimately to affect or persuade readers whereas affective writing also seeks to educate through explanation and clarification of ideas. In addition, descriptive and narrative prose, as distinct from fictional writing, is often a component of other patterns of development. While the two units are organized by rhetorical modes, we do not intend to prescribe such patterns of development for the student writer, *the writer in training*. Rather, this organization serves to teach the usefulness of recognizing patterns in what one reads and of the incorporation of such patterns into one's own writing. Unit 6, on writing the research paper and documentation, provides guidelines and models of research techniques and documentation principles in the MLA and APA styles. Finally, the appendix offers proofreading and editing tips, as well as a basic review of English grammar.

Throughout *Refining Reading Writing,* new terms are not only bolded and explained when they are first introduced, but they are also defined in the Glossary of Terms (see page 323).

Each reading in this book is followed by *Comprehension* and *Analysis* questions. The *Comprehension* questions are designed to ensure the ideas and organization of the reading have been understood; the *Analysis* questions require the reader to reflect on the content and development of what has been understood. Each reading is also followed by *Suggestions for Discussion or Writing.* In addition, each reading is carefully related to other selections in the book that offer a similar approach or that reflect on a similar subject or theme. In these ways, we have attempted to integrate all the readings in this textbook into a common framework for refining reading and writing skills.

Finally, perhaps as befits a text for Canadian college and university students, the book features a range of writings by Canadian authors, which constitute two-thirds of our selections. We hope that the book's Canadian content will make the teaching and the learning of reading and writing skills more enjoyable and enriching.

Acknowledgements

First and foremost, this text is for our students, and we thank them for their inspiration. We owe a debt to Jon Redfern, whose support, advice, and acumen have been invaluable. The thoughtful feedback from our reviewers has also helped to refine this book, so we are grateful to the following people: Tannys Williams for her calm guidance, Wendy Thomas for her thoughtful editing, and Dianne Fowlie for the careful proofreading. We also thank Andrea Nelson for her patient technical help. Finally, we thank Yang Yang for her adept secretarial skills and help, Kieran for the interesting discussions, and John for his unfailing support in our search and research.

Reading the Writings

*Active reading—reading from context, skimming, scanning,
and reading for purpose and audience*

"I do not understand; I pause; I examine." (Michel de Montaigne 1533–1592)

Active Reading

Active reading is a process by which you ask yourself *critical questions* about the text in order to draw your own conclusions. Critical questions include the following: asking what the main idea is and what the supporting details are; considering how a writer supports his or her ideas through the inclusion and order of details; distinguishing between fact and opinion; thinking about purpose as you notice how ideas and facts are used and positioned for effect; becoming aware of the author's attitude, tone, and audience as you examine such things as the use of language, humour, or **irony.** The conclusions you draw about the text are, therefore, based on and supported by your responses to the critical questions you ask.

Based on rereading and thinking, active reading enables you to come to a deeper understanding of a text. Active reading is a slower and more careful process than the cursory reading you do to get an overview of the news, or the story you skip through for relaxation. This careful reading helps you develop vocabulary and equips you with a knowledge of sentence structures and organizational patterns, such as comparison and contrast or classification. Active reading is an important step to becoming a good writer. The critical questions you ask while reading actively encourage you to consider your own writing style, your intended reader, and your response to the subject.

This book focuses on reading and writing **expository prose,** a type of writing that explains ideas and concepts by presenting information in an organized manner. The author's main idea is most often stated in a thesis statement. The **thesis statement** expresses the central idea of the essay and directs its development, so identifying it is of vital importance. Occasionally, the thesis is implied by the author.

Nearly everything you read in college and will read in your professional life is expository prose of some sort, so you need to learn how such texts work and how to read them actively and effectively. Expository prose takes the form of such things as essays, articles, textbooks, speeches, reports on lab procedures, journals, government documents, newspaper and magazine articles, manuals, and directions.

Reading from Context

Context refers to the verbal surroundings of a word or idea; the words that come before and after a new concept help to define its specific meaning.

- Careful readers can guess or give a temporary meaning to new or difficult words as they read because nearby words (the context) supply enough information to make the ideas reasonably clear. You grasp the general meaning of an unfamiliar word, make a quick guess, and continue reading. Here is an example:

  > When I see our **bickering** politicians stirring up trouble and hatred where there is no need or cause for either, I remember Clarendon's comment on England after the Puritan **agitators** had talked the public into a terrible civil war. (MacLennan, p. 6)

  In the quotation above, the highlighted words—bickering, agitators—might have made you pause, but you probably read on because you had a general sense of the content. In fact, both words are defined by their contexts: "bickering" stirs up trouble between people, and "agitators" create civil unrest.
- Many words in English have more than one meaning, so reading from context can guide you as to which definition in the dictionary is the most fitting one. When words are taken *out of context,* their precise meanings may get lost.
- If you are a second-language reader, you will face a more difficult task in reading from context when you come across an **idiomatic** expression. Such groups of words cannot be interpreted (or defined) literally—that is, they cannot be understood by defining the individual words, but by knowing the meaning of the set phrase (e.g., *open a can of worms*). Consequently, the meaning of an idiom must be understood from the context. Most good English dictionaries include the definitions of idiomatic phrases.
- You may also have wondered about the allusions to "Clarendon" and "Puritan" in the quote above. An **allusion** is a reference to a thing, person, concept, quotation, or character—something that is familiar to readers and so creates a mental connection to the subject. An allusion can be taken from history, as most of MacLennan's are, and also from the fields of popular culture, literature, science, mythology, politics, religion, and so on. If you are not sure of a term or reference, use a pencil to underline it or put a question mark in the margin, but keep on reading; you can check the precise meaning later. In doing this, you are reading from context.

Skimming

When you **skim,** you read a text rapidly in order to get a general understanding of its content.

- Skimming can be used to familiarize yourself with the style of a piece of writing, its format, and its key ideas.
- It should be a fast process, a speedy reading or "overview" reading of content; you want only a glance at the more obvious features of a piece of writing to get a general understanding of the shape and extent of its content.
- Once you have completed a first read-through, you will know the important points. Next, you will begin to ask yourself some questions about the text: What main ideas, vital facts, or organizational pattern must you understand? What words must you look up in the dictionary? What key terms must you grasp?

  In many texts, key terms are identified by the use of italics or boldface; these are visual clues that help you when skimming a text. Sometimes key words are defined either in a vocabulary list or by an explanation following the term, and, the context often explains their meaning.

  In this book, for example, a number of rhetorical and literary devices are discussed; they are bolded the first time they are used and are often defined in the text, making it easy to understand while skimming. Another way to recognize and appreciate the use of those devices is to become familiar with their definitions and major functions by using the Glossary of Terms on page 321.

- You can skim a textbook by going through the table of contents and noticing what is included and how it is organized; familiarizing yourself with the book enables you to use it more efficiently.
- Skimming is also a very useful technique for reviewing familiar material when you are preparing for a test or a meeting.

Scanning

Scanning is selective reading. When you **scan,** you are deliberately searching for a detail or fact. The purpose of scanning, then, is to locate a specified item or information.

- Think about how you use the telephone book. You do not sit down for an hour to study names and numbers. Instead, like most people, you run your eyes over the columns on the pages to find one single name or number. Locating information in a telephone book is a form of scanning.
- To help make scanning a more efficient reading skill, examine how the material you are reading is organized. Your skimming skills come into play here because understanding the structure of a piece of information can save time in your search.
  —Use the table of contents to guide you to pages in a book that you can also scan for material you need.

—An index at the end of a book or a report will refer you to a page that you can scan for the details you need. An index is arranged alphabetically, making it easy to locate the terms or concepts you want to find.

—Reports often list statistics in a separate section. If you were looking for a specific number or percentage, it would help to know where the statistics are placed.

—Manuals and lab reports often present information in a series of step-by-step instructions.

—A research article is often preceded by an abstract, which will offer you an overview of the key points of the paper.

—Often a thesis statement in a long essay will specify the order in which information, broken down into sections, will be discussed. Clearly, identifying the thesis and knowing how the essay is set up would help you quickly locate any data you are looking for.

Purpose

The **purpose** is the reason for writing the essay. An author writes to inform, to persuade, to entertain, or to attain some combination of two or all of the three.

Style

Essentially, writing style refers to *how* a writer presents ideas. When we think of a writer's style, we consider the **syntax** (the order of words in individual sentences), the **diction** (the words chosen), and the **tone**. The tone is the writer's expressed attitude or feelings toward both subject matter and audience through the choice of words.

• Writing style is a matter of personal expression just as, for example, the clothes you choose to wear make a personal statement about who you are.

• The writer's attitude can be stated directly, conveyed by word choice, and suggested by the arrangement of ideas or information—all of which can be defined as tone. It is important to keep in mind that as a writer, you are your own "first reader"; the tone you choose should be one that is right for you and your feelings about the subject.

Audience

The **audience** is the intended reader whom the writer has in mind when composing an essay.

• Purpose and audience are closely linked. We all adjust our communication style depending on our audience and the situation; for example, you speak differently with a five-year-old than you do with a parent, a manager, or a close friend. Everything changes, often unconsciously, from the tone of voice to the sentence structure and vocabulary as you communicate with your listener. For the same reasons, a good writer also takes the needs of the intended readers into account; an essay's *tone* and *style* are in many ways determined by its audience and purpose.

Read the following essay by Hugh MacLennan all the way through without stopping, but be aware of words, terms, or ideas you may need to reconsider after this first reading. An asterisk (*) marks names and events explained in the Notes section following the reading; a small circle (°) indicates a word that is defined in the Vocabulary section. Notice the title before you begin to read: what do you suppose this essay will be about?

No Nation So Favoured

Hugh MacLennan

Hugh MacLennan (1907–1990) was born in Glace Bay, Nova Scotia, and moved with his family to Halifax, Nova Scotia, in 1914. MacLennan was a Canadian author and professor of English at McGill University. He won five Governor General's Awards and a Royal Bank Award for his writing. He was educated at Dalhousie University, Oxford University, and Princeton University before accepting a teaching position at Lower Canada College in Montreal, Quebec. MacLennan wrote Barometer Rising *(1941) about the social class structure of Nova Scotia and the Halifax Explosion of 1917. His most famous novel,* Two Solitudes, *a literary allegory for the tensions between English and French Canada, was published in 1945. In 1967, he was made a Companion of the Order of Canada. In 1985, he was made a Knight of the National Order of Quebec*

MacLennan was passionately concerned with national themes, as can be seen in this short essay. This essay is taken from My Canada *(1984).*

1 Until my twenty-eighth year, I knew virtually nothing of Canada. Having been born in Cape Breton, Nova Scotia, within half a mile of the Atlantic, having grown up in Halifax, I then studied in England, travelled over most of Europe, and later lived for three years in the United States. Finally in my twenty-eighth year I came to Montreal for a Depression* job and have lived there ever since. So it happened that most of my adult life has been occupied in the adventure of discovering for myself the Canadian land and—more important by far—the nature of the Canadian people and the Canadian society. Therefore, what Canada means to me comes close to being the meaning of my entire professional life.

2 Canada is a country unlike any other I have ever encountered in history. Her population is derived almost entirely from people whose causes had been lost elsewhere. The Québecois were abandoned by their motherland more than two centuries ago. The Loyalists* were driven out of the thirteen American colonies by their own brothers. The Scottish Highlanders were enclosed and forced overseas in starvation ships by their own chiefs. Most of the Irish were starved out of their ancient home, and, since World War II, a flood of immigrants have come in from

the wreckages of Europe and Asia. Canada has given all of us a home, and her true nature is all the more mysterious because none of the stereotypes come near to her human reality.

3   We are more respected by others, I believe, than we are respected by ourselves. Students who have travelled in Europe tell me they have encountered American students with Canadian flags stitched onto their backpacks. "These Europeans hate our guts," one of them said, "but you guys they really like."

4   Yes, as Pericles* said of Athens, Canada is certainly better than the report she gives of herself. When I see our bickering° politicians stirring up trouble and hatred where there is no need or cause for either, I remember Clarendon's* comment on England after the Puritan* agitators had talked the public into a terrible civil war. "Oh too fortunate, if only they had understood how fortunate they were!"

Notes

1 Depression (n): a period of economic hardship during the 1930s

2 Loyalists (n): supporters of the British monarchy in Canada

4 Pericles (n): a leader of the Athenian democracy in 5th century B.C.E.

4 Clarendon (n): 17th-century English statesman and historian

4 Puritan (n): member of a religious group in England; many emigrated to North America to escape persecution in the 17th century

Vocabulary

4 bickering (adj): arguing (verb – to bicker)

In the Notes and Vocabulary lists above are answers to questions you may have had as you read through the essay. However, you probably understood the gist of the essay as MacLennan's vocabulary is not difficult although it is by no means informal.

On the first read, you could mark unfamiliar words or terms like these with your pencil, and then check their dictionary definitions and contextual significance when you reread the passage.

After each reading in this book, you will encounter a section called "Responding to the Reading." It presents a series of questions. Let's work through the questions and some possible answers for the Hugh MacLennan essay.

 ## RESPONDING TO THE READING

1. What was your first impression of this reading?

What is the reading about and how is its subject presented? The answer to this question is based on your first read-through.

Did you like or dislike this essay? Whatever your opinion, it is valid, but you must be prepared to back it up with a reason or two. You probably also noticed the essay is quite short, but MacLennan manages to make a lot of social and historical allusions. Scan to check them over. Why do you think he includes them? How do the allusions and examples support MacLennan's view of Canada as a favoured nation?

You probably will have noticed the following features:

- MacLennan uses very simple, accessible, personal examples to explain his feelings. How would you characterize his feelings?
- MacLennan presents a number of examples to show that Canada has welcomed those "whose causes had been lost elsewhere" (page 5). Why do you think this is important to him?
- One example offers an indirect comparison to the United States. Why do you think MacLennan included that anecdote?
- MacLennan's allusions refer to great figures in the history of democracy. What does this suggest about his view of Canada?
- MacLennan's tone is appreciative of Canada; look for examples that show this attitude. How does he convey his love for Canada?

2. What is the main idea of this reading? State it in your own words in one or two sentences.

- What idea is most significant to you in MacLennan's essay?
- Look at the title; which nation does MacLennan refer to? Clearly it is Canada; think about the reasons he provides to prove that Canada is "so favoured."

3. What do you think is the purpose of this essay?

- In other words, try to figure out why the author, in this case Hugh MacLennan, has chosen to write about the subject and what response the author is expecting to the essay.
- How has the writer set about accomplishing that purpose? The information, ideas, and organization—the *what* and *how* of the text—are determined by its purpose. The author's purpose is usually stated in the introduction, most often in the thesis statement. How did you determine what Hugh MacLennan's purpose is? Give reasons for your opinion.

In answering this question, you are probably influenced, though perhaps unconsciously, by MacLennan's style and tone. MacLennan has a tone of admiration for Canada. How else could you describe his tone?

Your response to the previous questions will guide you here:

- MacLennan wants to show that Canada is a "favoured" nation; that is, Canada offers many benefits (favours) to its citizens and is well regarded (well favoured) internationally. It is his "favourite" nation.
- His purpose is to praise Canada and to present clear reasons for why this praise is justified.

4. Who do you think is the intended audience of this essay?

How did you determine who the audience is? Give your reasons for your answer.

Once again, you will find a key clue to your answer by recalling your previous responses. Now you are asking who is willing to share MacLennan's praise for Canada and who will likely understand the allusions he makes.

The answer is other Canadians—those who truly favour (prefer and love) Canada. So this essay is intended for Canadians to read with pride. Notice that MacLennan says at the end of Paragraph 2, "Canada has given all of *us* a home"; the italicized pronoun is further proof that his intended audience is Canadian.

He continues to address his readers in Paragraph 3: "*We* are more respected by others."

When you work through the Comprehension and Analysis questions following each of the essays in this book, you are engaged in active reading.

Reread MacLennan's essay and then answer the following questions.

Comprehension

Comprehension questions test what you have understood about the ideas and organization of the essay. Generally, the Comprehension questions will take you through the essay sequentially, from beginning to end. Support your answers with an example from the essay; scan to locate it.

1. What reasons does Hugh MacLennan give for knowing very little about Canada before he turned 28?
2. What does he say Canada has come to mean to him?
3. What sort of details does he give for Canada being "a country unlike any other"?
4. How many examples does he give of "people whose causes have been lost elsewhere"?
5. Why did American students in Europe sew Canadian flags onto their backpacks?
6. Why does MacLennan end with a quote about being fortunate?

Analysis

Analysis questions ask you to reflect on the information you have understood. When you consider the implications and evaluate the ideas, you are formulating your own informed position on a given subject.

1. Do you agree with MacLennan that Canadians "have come in from the wreckages of Europe and Asia"? Why or why not?
2. What do you think he means when he says, "[N]one of the stereotypes come near to her human reality"?
3. Why do you think he includes the political examples in Paragraph 4?
4. Do you agree or disagree with Hugh MacLennan's vision of Canada? Why or why not?
5. How useful is the introductory information about MacLennan in analyzing this essay?

Discussion/Writing Suggestions

1. What does Canada mean to you? Be specific.
2. This essay originally appeared in an anthology intended to promote Canadian unity. Do you think it would be successful in that attempt? Why or why not?

Levels of Language: Guidelines

Standard written English has different levels of language, which can be put into broad categories of formal, general, and informal. Formal English is typically used for documents in business, law, government, international affairs, etc., as well as academic publications in all fields of arts and sciences. It characteristically follows the strict rules of grammar and uses an elevated and specialized vocabulary and complex syntax. At the other end of the spectrum is the informal level of language, which is characterized by short sentences (including some sentence fragments), short paragraphs, conversational tone, and casual words (including some colloquial and slang expressions and contractions). Informal language is normally used in personal letters, works of fiction, some newspaper articles, and so on.

General language, which falls between the two extremes, refers to the language that uses non-specialized and common words readily understood by an educated audience. Composed of complete sentences of varying lengths and well-structured paragraphs, it represents the kind of language we read mostly in newspapers, magazines, and many other types of fiction and non-fiction writings. MacLennan's essay uses the general level of language as you can tell by its vocabulary and sentence and paragraph structure. This is also the level of language you should adopt for your writing in College English. When choosing the level of language, keep in mind the intended audience and your purpose. As the poet Ezra Pound reminds us, "Good writers are those who keep the language efficient."

Think about an article on a good meal and how it would vary depending on the publication it appears in. For a gourmet dining magazine, the writer would emphasize the appeal of the presentation and delicacy of the flavours and would no doubt recommend fine wines to accompany each course; the vocabulary would probably be elaborate, embellished with adjectives and foreign terms. An article on the same topic in the weekend edition of a newspaper would be intended for a different audience, so it would adopt a different tone and vocabulary as well as a different approach to the subject. In this case, while taste and flair are important, cost and service would also be stressed. The article would be more practical in tone and approach. In a cookery book, the same subject would be presented as a recipe that contains concise and precise directions written in simple words. Again, it is the audience and purpose that influence all aspects of the writing: the approach to subject, background details, pattern of organization, variety of sentences, choice of words, tone, and level of language.

READINGS

The next three selections all reflect on reading in some way. Charles Dickens writes about the validity of education, but perhaps he could advance the same argument for reading. Bill Bryson comically presents a reading challenge we have all experienced—the "how to" manual. Malcolm X's poignant account specifically discusses reading and the power it had in his life. However, each reading is quite different: Dickens has written a literary account, Bryson a set of instructions, and Malcolm X a personal memoir. Remember to consider not only *what* the essay is about, but *why,* for *whom,* and *how* each writer writes: what is the purpose, audience, style, and tone of each essay?

Murdering The Innocents

Charles Dickens

Charles Dickens (1812–1870) is a world-famous novelist. His characters live on in people's imaginations more than a century after his death. The adjective "Dickensian" is used to describe his work and also poor social conditions; it also alludes to characters that are larger than life in an old-fashioned and often humorous fashion.

"Murdering the Innocents" is an excerpt from Dickens's novel Hard Times *and thus is not really expository prose. However, his novels were always works of social commentary. He was a fierce social reformer, critical of poverty and in particular the plight of children. His fiction was widely read and so influential that he was able to force real changes in the law and social conditions of Victorian England.*

"Murdering the Innocents" focuses on children, and the novel from which it is taken is also in part a campaign to create changes in the factories of industrial Britain and the school system of the time. Read this excerpt as a narrative essay designed to encourage social reform. Dickens's diction, or word choice, makes his style seem quite formal to us today. In part, that is because he wrote this passage in the 1850s, and English vocabulary and syntax have undergone changes since that time. Any difficulties you may experience with his vocabulary are probably caused by this unfamiliarity. In his time, Dickens was one of the world's most popular writers and very widely read, so his style must have been very accessible to his intended audience. Hard Times *was published in 1854.*

1   Thomas Gradgrind, sir. A man of realities. A man of facts and calculations. A man who proceeds upon the principle that two and two are four, and nothing over, and who is not to be talked into allowing for anything over. Thomas Gradgrind, sir— peremptorily° Thomas—Thomas Gradgrind. With a rule and a pair of scales, and the multiplication table always in his pocket, sir, ready to weigh and measure any parcel of human nature, and tell you exactly what it comes to. It is a mere question of figures, a case of simple arithmetic. You might hope to get some nonsensical

belief into the head of George Gradgrind, or Augustus Gradgrind, or John Gradgrind, or Joseph Gradgrind (all suppositions, non-existent persons), but into the head of Thomas Gradgrind—no, sir!

2   In such terms Mr. Gradgrind always mentally introduced himself, whether to his private circle of acquaintance, or to the public in general. In such terms, no doubt, substituting the words "boys and girls" for "sir," Thomas Gradgrind now presented Thomas Gradgrind to the little pitchers° before him, who were to be filled so full of facts.

3   Indeed, as he eagerly sparkled at them from the cellarage° before mentioned, he seemed a kind of cannon loaded to the muzzle° with facts, and prepared to blow them clean out of the regions of childhood at one discharge. He seemed a galvanizing° apparatus, too, charged with a grim mechanical substitute for the tender young imaginations that were to be stormed away.

4   "Girl number twenty," said Mr. Gradgrind, squarely pointing with his square forefinger, "I don't know that girl. Who is that girl?"

5   "Sissy Jupe, sir," explained number twenty, blushing, standing up, and curtseying°.

6   "Sissy is not a name," said Mr. Gradgrind. "Don't call yourself Sissy. Call yourself Cecilia."

7   "It's father as calls me Sissy, sir," returned the young girl in a trembling voice, and with another curtsey.

8   "Then he has no business to do it," said Mr. Gradgrind. "Tell him he mustn't. Cecilia Jupe. Let me see. What is your father?"

9   "He belongs to the horse-riding, if you please sir."

10   Mr. Gradgrind frowned, and waved off the objectionable calling with his hand.

11   "We don't want to know anything about that, here. You mustn't tell us about that, here. Your father breaks horses°, don't he?"

12   "If you please, sir, when they can get any to break, they do break horses in the ring, sir."

13   "You mustn't tell us about the ring, here. Very well, then. Describe your father as a horsebreaker. He doctors sick horses, I dare say?"

14   "Oh yes, sir."

15   "Very well, then. He is a veterinary surgeon, a farrier°, and horsebreaker. Give me your definition of a horse."

16   (Sissy Jupe thrown into the greatest alarm by this demand.)

17   "Girl number twenty unable to define a horse!" said Mr. Gradgrind, for the general behoof of all the little pitchers. "Girl number twenty possessed of no facts, in reference to one of the commonest of animals! Some boy's definition of a horse. Bitzer, yours."

18   The square finger, moving here and there, lighted suddenly on Bitzer, perhaps because he chanced to sit in the same ray of sunlight which, darting in at one of the bare windows of the intensely whitewashed room, irradiated° Sissy. For the boys and girls sat on the face of the inclined plane in two compact bodies, divided up the centre by a narrow interval; and Sissy, being at the corner of a row on the sunny side, came in for the beginning of a sunbeam, of which Bitzer, being at the corner

of a row on the other side, a few rows in advance, caught the end. But whereas the girl was so dark-eyed and dark-haired that she seemed to receive a deeper and more lustrous° colour from the sun when it shone upon her, the boy was so light-eyed and light-haired that the selfsame rays appeared to draw out of him what little colour his eyes possessed. His cold eyes would hardly have been eyes but for the short ends of lashes which, by bringing them into immediate contrast with something paler than themselves, expressed their form. His short-cropped hair might have been a mere continuation of the sandy freckles on his forehead and face. His skin was so unwholesomely deficient in the natural tinge, that he looked as though, if he were cut, he would bleed white.

19   "Bitzer," said Thomas Gradgrind. "Your definition of a horse."

20   "Quadruped°. Graminivorous°. Forty teeth, namely, twenty-four grinders°, four eye-teeth, and twelve incisive°. Sheds° coat in the spring; in marshy° countries, sheds hoofs, too. Hoofs hard, but requiring to be shod with iron. Age known by marks in mouth." Thus (and much more) Bitzer.

21   "Now, girl number twenty," said Mr. Gradgrind. "You know what a horse is."

22   She curtseyed again, and would have blushed deeper if she could have blushed deeper than she had blushed all this time. Bitzer, after rapidly blinking at Thomas Gradgrind with both eyes at once, and so catching the light upon his quivering° ends of lashes that they looked like the antennae° of busy insects, put his knuckles to his freckled forehead and sat down again.

Vocabulary

1 peremptorily (adv): in a decisive manner, like a command

2 pitchers (n): large jug

3 cellarage (n): storage, stock

3 muzzle (n): open end of the gun

3 galvanizing (adj): a forceful means of stimulation (like an electric shock)

5 curtsey (n): a bending of the knees in respectful greeting

11 to break horses (idiom): to train horses

15 farrier (n): a person who shoes horses

18 irradiated (v): shine upon, light up

18 lustrous (adj): shining, brilliant

20 quadruped (adj): having four feet

20 graminivorous (adj): feeding on grass and cereal

20 grinders (n): back teeth that grind

20 incisive (adj): biting

20 sheds (v): to let or cause to fall off

20 marshy (adj): as watery land

22 quivering (adj): moving with rapid motion, trembling

22 antennae (n): pair of feelers on an insect's head

RESPONDING TO THE READING

- What is your first impression of this reading?
- What is the main idea of this reading? State it in one or two sentences in your own words.

- What do you think is the purpose of this essay? Give reasons for your opinion.
- Who do you think is the intended audience of this essay? Give your reasons for your opinion.

Levels of Language: Word Use

You can increase your reading speed and comprehension rate by identifying a prefix or suffix. You can also use prefixes and suffixes in your own writing to improve your style.

Recognizing Prefixes and Suffixes

- Words in English often begin with a word part that changes the meaning of the word. That word part is a prefix, and the meanings of prefixes remain consistent. When you encounter two words starting with the same prefix, you know the words are related in meaning. For example, let's look at the words *prearrange*. Pre- means "before" or "ahead of time." Thus, *prearrange* means to organize or set up something beforehand.
- **Suffixes,** or word endings, indicate the part of speech of a word. For example, you are familiar with regular verb endings: -*ing* for the present participle, with which we make the progressive tense, participial adjectives, and gerunds; -*ed* for the past participle, with which we make the past tense, passive voice, and participial adjectives. You also recognize -*ly,* which is most often a suffix that turns an adjective into an adverb.

Look at these two words from the list above: *lustrous* and *graminivorous.* Their function in the sentences and the suffix -*ous* tell you they are adjectives. You will find a list of the most commonly used prefixes and suffixes in Appendix A (page 304). Try to become familiar with them as recognizing word parts will develop your vocabulary and improve your reading rate.

Comprehension

1. There is enough information in this excerpt for you to be able to draw a floor plan of Gradgrind's classroom and to include with it such details as lighting and probable class size. Scan to find the related information and then draw up the floor plan.
2. Scan "Murdering the Innocents" to locate the statements about Thomas Gradgrind. Using this information, determine what sort of man he is. Is he a teacher whose class you would enjoy? Why or why not?
3. What do you think is meant by "He seemed a galvanizing apparatus, too, charged with a grim mechanical substitute for the tender young imaginations that were to be stormed away"?
4. What could be the possible meanings of Mr. Gradgrind's name?

5. In what way is Mr. Gradgrind's name reflective of his character?
6. Does Charles Dickens approve of Thomas Gradgrind? Scan, if necessary, to find details in the reading to support your opinion.
7. What details inform you how Thomas Gradgrind views boys and girls? What conclusions do you draw from these details?
8. Look at the words Dickens uses to describe Bitzer and then those he uses for Sissy. What impression does Dickens give you of each child by the words he chooses? What, for example, does each child's name suggest to you?
9. What does Bitzer's definition of a horse sound like to you?
10. Based on their suffixes, identify the part of speech of the following words taken from the reading: multiplication, nonsensical, non-existent, acquaintance, squarely, objectionable, veterinary, horsebreaker, reference, unwholesomely.

Analysis

1. You know from the introductory notes that Dickens was a social reformer and educational activist. How is his interest in education reflected in this excerpt?
2. What changes do you think Dickens would have wanted to see in Gradgrind's classroom?
3. Dickens wrote *Hard Times* in the middle of the 19th century. What details can you find in the passage that illustrate the differences between our system of education and that of Victorian England?
4. How does Dickens show you which of the two children he sympathizes with?
5. What do you make of the fact that Thomas Gradgrind thoroughly approves of Bitzer and is dismissive of Sissy?
6. Given that Sissy lives with horses (her father is a horse trainer in a circus), what do you think Dickens intended his reader to understand when Gradgrind says, "Girl number twenty . . . Give me your definition of a horse."
7. Do you think Dickens gave this passage an appropriate title? Why or why not?

Discussion/Writing Suggestions

1. Are there any aspects of Gradgrind's classroom that you think ought to be incorporated into today's education system? Why or why not?
2. Do you believe that education is more than being "filled so full of facts"? Why or why not?

Your New Computer

Bill Bryson

Bill Bryson (1951–) is an American author of many best-selling humorous books. He lives mostly in England, but his travels underlie many of his books, including his first, The Lost Continent *(1989), about driving his mother's car around America;* Notes from a Small Island *(1996), an affectionate and amusing analysis of the British; and* A Walk in the Woods *(1998), an entertaining account of his attempt to hike the Appalachian Trail. In addition, he has written books on the English language and on scientific subjects, including* A Short History of Nearly Everything, *which is an award-winning book on general science, and* Mother Tongue, *which is a light-hearted history of the English language.*

In this essay (taken from Notes from a Big Country *[1998]), Bryson confronts both technology and language with his trademark sense of humour.*

1 Congratulations. You have purchased an Anthrax/2000 Multimedia 615X Personal Computer with Digital Doo-Dah Enhancer. It will give years of faithful service, if you ever get it up and running. Also included with your PC is a bonus pack of preinstalled software—Lawn Mowing Planner, Mr. Arty-Farty, Blank Screen Saver, and Antarctica Route Finder—which will provide hours of pointless diversion° while using up most of your computer's spare memory.

2 So turn the page and let's get started!

Getting Ready

3 Congratulations. You have successfully turned the page and are ready to proceed.

4 Important meaningless note: The Anthrax/2000 is configured° to use 80386, 214J10, or higher processors running at 2472 Herz on variable speed spin cycle. Check your electrical installations and insurance policies before proceeding. Do not machine wash.

5 To prevent internal heat build-up, select a cool, dry environment for your computer. The bottom shelf of a refrigerator is ideal.

6 Unpack the box and examine its contents. (Warning: Do not open box if contents are missing or faulty, as this will invalidate° your warranty. Return all missing contents in their original packaging with a note explaining where they have gone and a replacement will be sent within twelve working months.)

7 The contents of the box should include some of the following: monitor with mysterious De Gauss button; keyboard; computer unit; miscellaneous wires and cables not necessarily designed for this model; 2,000-page Owner's Manual; Short Guide to the Owner's Manual; Quick Guide to the Short Guide to the Owner's Manual; Laminated Super-Kwik Set-Up Guide for People Who Are Exceptionally Impatient or Stupid; 1,167 pages of warranties, vouchers°, notices in Spanish, and other loose pieces of paper; 292 cubic feet of Styrofoam packing material.

Something They Didn't Tell You at the Store

8 Because of the additional power needs of the preinstalled bonus software, you will need to acquire an Anthrax/2000 auxiliary° software upgrade pack, a 900-volt memory capacitor for the auxiliary software pack, a 50-megaherz oscillator unit for the memory capacitor, 2,500 mega-gigabytes of additional memory for the oscillator, and an electrical substation.

Setting Up

9 Congratulations. You are ready to set up. If you have not yet acquired a degree in electrical engineering, now is the time to do so.

10 Connect the monitor cable (A) to the portside outlet unit (D); attach power offload unit suborbiter (Xii) to the coaxial AC/DC servo channel (G); plug three-pin mouse cable into keyboard housing unit (make extra hole if necessary); connect modem (B2) to offside parallel audio/video lineout jack. Alternatively, plug the cables into the most likely looking holes, switch on, and see what happens.

11 Additional important meaningless note: The wires in the ampule modulator unit are marked as follows according to international convention: blue = neutral or live; yellow = live or blue; blue and live = neutral and green; black instant death. (Except where prohibited by law.)

12 Switch the computer on. Your hard drive will automatically download. (Allow three to five days.) When downloading is complete, your screen will say: "Yeah, what?"

13 Now it is time to install your software. Insert Disc A (marked "Disc D" or "Disc G") into Drive Slot B or J, and type: "Hello! Anybody home?" At the DOS command prompt, enter your License Verification° Number. Your License Verification Number can be found by entering your Certified User Number, which can be found by entering your License Verification Number. If you are unable to find your License Verification or Certified User numbers, call the Software Support Line for assistance. (Please have your License Verification and Certified User numbers handy as the support staff cannot otherwise assist you.)

14 If you have not yet committed suicide, then insert Installation Diskette 1 in drive slot 2 (or vice versa) and follow the instructions on your screen. (Note: Owing to a software modification, some instructions will appear in Turkish.) At each prompt, reconfigure the specified file path, double-click on the button launch icon, select a single equation default file from the macro selection register, insert the VGA graphics card in the rear aerofoil, and type "C:\>" followed by the birthdates of all the people you have ever known.

15 Your screen will now say: "Invalid file path. Whoa! Abort or continue?" Warning: Selecting "Continue" may result in irreversible file compression and a default overload in the hard drive. Selecting "Abort," on the other hand, will require you to start the installation process all over again. Your choice.

16 When the smoke has cleared, insert disc A2 (marked "Disc A1") and repeat as directed with each of the 187 other discs.

17 When installation is complete, return to file path, and type your name, address, and credit card numbers and press "SEND." This will automatically register you for our free software prize, "Blank Screensaver IV: Nighttime in Deep Space," and allow us to pass your name to lots and lots of computer magazines, online services, and other commercial enterprises, who will be getting in touch shortly.

18 Congratulations. You are now ready to use your computer. Here are some simple exercises to get you off to a flying start.

Writing a Letter

19 Type "Dear _____ "and follow it with a name of someone you know. Write a few lines about yourself, and then write, "Sincerely yours" followed by your own name. Congratulations.

Saving a File

20 To save your letter, select File Menu. Choose Retrieve from SubDirectory A, enter a backup file number, and place an insertion point beside the macro dialogue button. Select secondary text box from the merge menu, and double-click on the supplementary cleared document window. Assign the tile cascade to a merge file and insert in a text equation box. Alternatively, write the letter out longhand and put it in a drawer.

Advice on Using the Spreadsheet Facility

21 Don't.

Vocabulary

1 diversion (n): distraction

4 configured (v): set up for use

6 invalidate (v): cause to be cancelled

7 vouchers (n): coupons for future purchases

8 auxiliary (adj): extra

13 verification (n): testing the truth or accuracy

Levels of Language: Jargon

Many of the words and phrases in this essay are **jargon**—specialized language that is associated with a particular area of work or study. For people working in a particular trade or profession, using jargon can be an efficient and exact means of communication. However, jargon is not always readily understood by those outside the field, so you must be careful with its use in your own writing. You should use it mainly when you're writing in your field of study, but if you believe a specialized term needs an explanation, provide one for your intended reader. For example, English teachers will talk about *dangling modifiers* and *pronoun-antecedent agreement* to the complete mystification of people who don't share their professional knowledge. Clearly, a definition of each of those terms with one or two examples attached would help to clarify any confusion.

In "Your New Computer," Bryson has written a **parody** (copying a characteristic style for comic effect or ridicule) of an assembly manual by making fun of the abuse of jargon. He intends to confuse and mystify the reader to create the sense of frustration he feels when reading such "goobledygook"—language that is wordy and pretentious and obscures meaning. Bryson is playing with the fact that most of us have been baffled by the jargon-ridden instructions that come with a piece of electronics.

What was most confusing about the instructions—our ignorance or the bad writing? Bryson makes fun of both. By parodying the style of a computer manual, he provides an amusing series of instructions to explain *how to*; this essay falls into the general category of **process analysis,** exposition that explains a procedure or gives directions.

RESPONDING TO THE READING

- What is your first impression of this reading?
- What is the main idea of this reading? State it in your own words in one or two sentences.
- What do you think is the purpose of this essay? Give reasons for your opinion.
- Who do you think is the intended audience of this essay? Give reasons for your opinion.

Comprehension

1. Skim to determine how Bill Bryson has organized his instructions.
2. Scan the headings. What do you notice about their language? What is the purpose of the headings?
3. How many times does Bryson repeat the word "Congratulations"? How does the repetition help to organize this essay?
4. What problem will you encounter by following the instructions in Paragraph 6?
5. What will your computer screen say when you have completed down-loading your hard drive?
6. Explain the relationship between the help offered and the parenthetical advice in Paragraph 13: "If you are unable to find your License Verification or Certified User numbers, call the Software Support Line for assistance. (Please have your License Verification and Certified User numbers handy as the support staff cannot otherwise assist you.)."
7. In Paragraph 17, what will happen if you register for the prize?
8. What alternative to saving a letter does Bryson give? Is it appropriate?
9. Explain the following terms in your own words: multimedia, processors, capacitator, oscillator, gigabytes, coaxial, servo, ampule, aerofoil.

Analysis

1. What is implied by the name Bryson gives to his computer: The Anthrax/2000 Multimedia 615X Personal Computer with Digital Doo-Dah Enhancer?
2. What is Bryson suggesting with the names of the preinstalled software in Paragraph 1?
3. After a set of complicated instructions, Bryson frequently adds a final comment that is simple and easily understood: for example, "Do not machine wash" and "The bottom shelf of the refrigerator is ideal." What is the effect of these inclusions?
4. In Paragraph 7 there is a list of contents. Which one stands out as especially unlikely to you and why? Why does Bryson include it?

5. In Paragraph 14, you are told: "At each prompt, reconfigure the specified file path, double-click on the button launch icon, select a single equation default file from the macro selection register, insert the VGA graphics card in the rear aerofoil, and type 'C:\>' followed by the birthdates of all the people you have ever known." What point is Bryson making?

6. Is the last section (from Paragraph 18) an effective conclusion? Why or why not?

7. Bryson uses a lot jargon in his essay. Why do you think he has introduced so many technical terms into this essay? What is the effect?

8. What do you think of Bryson's style in this essay?

Discussion/Writing Suggestions

1. Do you agree with Bryson that manuals for the assembly of machines or furniture are often poorly written? Why or why not? How should these manuals be written?

2. Do you think Bryson is successful in presenting the level of stress often felt by people when they are following a set of seemingly contradictory instructions? Why is humour a useful stylistic technique?

Prison Studies

Malcolm X

Malcolm X (1925–1964) was born Malcolm Little in Omaha, Nebraska. His father, Earl Little, a prominent Baptist minister and civil rights activist, was murdered in 1932. In 1946, Malcolm Little was convicted on burglary charges, and while in jail, he converted to Islam. He became a Muslim minister and was for a time national spokesperson for the Nation of Islam. During his life, Malcolm X changed from a barely educated petty criminal to one of the most articulate and passionate black leaders of his generation. A champion of his people, Malcolm X advocated black pride, economic self-reliance, and equality. After breaking with the Nation of Islam in 1964, he was assassinated by three of its members.

In the following essay excerpted from his famous autobiography Malcolm X *(1964), he presents the many causes that led to his becoming an educated man and the arduous process by which he learned to read. Although it is also a narrative like the Dickens passage, this is a personal account.*

1   Many who today hear me somewhere in person, or on television, or those who read something I've said, will think I went to school far beyond the eighth grade. This impression is due entirely to my prison studies.

2   It had really begun back in the Charlestown Prison, when Bimbi [another prisoner] first made me feel envy of his stock of knowledge. Bimbi had always taken charge of any conversation he was in, and I had tried to emulate° him. But every book I picked up had few sentences which didn't contain anywhere from one to

nearly all of the words that might as well have been in Chinese. When I just skipped those words, of course, I really ended up with little idea of what the book said. So I had come to the Norfolk Prison Colony still going through only bookreading motions. Pretty soon, I would have quit even these motions, unless I had received the motivation that I did.

3   I saw that the best thing I could do was get hold of a dictionary—to study, to learn some words. I was lucky enough to reason also that I should try to improve my penmanship. It was sad. I couldn't even write in a straight line. It was both ideas together that moved me to request a dictionary along with some tablets and pencils from the Norfolk Prison Colony school.

4   I spent two days just riffling° uncertainly through the dictionary's pages. I'd never realized so many words existed! I didn't know which words I needed to learn. Finally, to start some kind of action, I began copying.

5   In my slow, painstaking, ragged° handwriting, I copied into my tablet everything printed on that first page, down to the punctuation marks.

6   I believe it took me a day. Then, aloud, I read back, to myself, everything I'd written on the tablet. Over and over, aloud, to myself, I read my own handwriting.

7   I woke up the next morning, thinking about those words—immensely proud to realize that not only had I written so much at one time, but I'd written words that I never knew were in the world. Moreover, with a little effort, I also could remember what many of these words meant. I reviewed the words whose meanings I didn't remember. Funny thing, from the dictionary first page right now, that "aardvark" springs to my mind. The dictionary had a picture of it, a long-tailed, long-eared, burrowing African mammal, which lives off termites caught by sticking out its tongue as an anteater does for ants.

8   I was so fascinated that I went on—I copied the dictionary's next page. And the same experience came when I studied that. With every succeeding page, I also learned of people and places and events from history. Actually the dictionary is like a miniature encyclopedia. Finally the dictionary's A section had filled a whole tablet—and I went on into the B's. That was the way I started copying what eventually became the entire dictionary. It went a lot faster after so much practice helped me to pick up handwriting speed. Between what I wrote in my tablet, and writing letters, during the rest of my time in prison I would guess I wrote a million words.

9   I suppose it was inevitable that as my word-base broadened, I could for the first time pick up a book and read and now begin to understand what the book was saying. Anyone who has read a great deal can imagine the new world that opened. Let me tell you something; from then until I left that prison, in every free moment I had, if I was not reading in the library, I was reading on my bunk. You couldn't have gotten me out of books with a wedge. Between Mr. Muhammad's teachings, my correspondence, my visitors, . . . and my reading of books, months passed without my even thinking about being imprisoned. In fact, up to then, I never had been so truly free in my life. . . .

10   As you can imagine, especially in a prison where there was heavy emphasis on rehabilitation°, an inmate was smiled upon if he demonstrated an unusually intense interest in books. There was a sizable number of well-read inmates, especially the popular debaters. Some were said by many to be practically walking

encyclopedias. They were almost celebrities. No university would ask any student to devour° literature as I did when this new world opened to me, of being able to read and understand.

11   I read more in my room than in the library itself. An inmate who was known to read a lot could check out more than the permitted maximum number of books. I preferred reading in the total isolation of my own room.

12   When I had progressed to really serious reading, every night at about ten p.m. I would be outraged with the "lights out." It always seemed to catch me right in the middle of something engrossing°.

13   Fortunately, right outside my door was a corridor light that cast a glow into my room. The glow was enough to read by, once my eyes adjusted to it. So when "lights out" came, I would sit on the floor where I could continue reading in that glow.

14   At one-hour intervals the night guards paced past every room. Each time I heard the approaching footsteps, I jumped into bed and feigned° sleep. And as soon as the guard passed, I got back out of bed onto the floor area of that light-glow, where I would read for another fifty-eight minutes—until the guard approached again. That went on until three or four every morning. Three or four hours of sleep a night was enough for me. Often in the years in the streets I had slept less than that.

15   I have often reflected upon the new vistas° that reading opened to me. I knew right there in prison that reading had changed forever the course of my life. As I see it today, the ability to read awoke inside me some long dormant° craving° to be men-tally alive. I certainly wasn't seeking any degree, the way a college confers° a status symbol upon its students. My homemade education gave me, with every additional book that I read, a little bit more sensitivity to the deafness, dumbness, and blind-ness that was afflicting° the black race in America. Not long ago, an English writer telephoned me from London, asking questions. One was, "What's your alma mater°?" I told him, "Books." You will never catch me with a free fifteen minutes in which I'm not studying something I feel might be able to help the black man. . . .

16   Every time I catch a plane, I have with me a book that I want to read—and that's a lot of books these days. If I weren't out here every day battling the white man, I could spend the rest of my life reading, just satisfying my curiosity—because you can hardly mention anything I'm not curious about. I don't think anybody ever got more out of going to prison than I did. In fact, prison enabled me to study far more intensively than I would have if my life had gone differently and I had attended some college. I imagine that one of the biggest troubles with colleges is there are too many distractions, too much panty-raiding, fraternities°, and boola-boola° and all of that. Where else but in prison could I have attacked my ignorance by being able to study intensely sometimes as much as fifteen hours a day?

Vocabulary

2 emulate (v): try to equal or excel, to imitate

4 riffling (v): turning pages in quick succession

5 ragged (adj): faulty, not uniform

10 rehabilitation (n): restoration, returned to proper condition

10 devour (v): eat hungrily, take in eagerly

12 engrossing (adj): demanding full attention

14 feign (v): pretend

15 vistas (n): long views

15 dormant (adj): sleeping

15 craving (n): desire

15 confer (v): grant, bestow, give as a right

15 afflicting (v): distressing physically or mentally

15 alma mater (Latin term): one's university or college

16 fraternities (n): male student societies, brotherhoods

16 boola-boola (slang, no longer current): silliness

 # RESPONDING TO THE READING

- What is your first impression of this reading?
- What is the main idea of this reading? State it in your own words in one or two sentences.
- What do you think is the purpose of this essay? Give reasons for your opinion.
- Who do you think is the intended audience of this essay? Give reasons for your opinion.

Levels of Language: Slang

The most creative form of language is slang. Slang has an ability to regenerate meanings, but this type of language is very short-lived. Look at Macolm X's deliberate use of "boola-boola," for instance. Slang frequently changes the dictionary definitions of words and originates within a specific social group: teenagers, for example, invent slang as a kind of private language separate from their parents'. Slang is the most informal level of language and is generally used only in speech, unless you are writing a chatty letter to a friend. In some instances, slang is used in journalistic articles to add liveliness to the writing, particularly when the articles talk about such things as movies or rock music. The problem with slang is not only that it quickly loses its meaning and vitality, but that it also restricts your audience. If it is current, only the peer group knows its meanings, so you need to be careful with its use. The occasional use, like Malcolm X's "boola-boola," creates the impact you may need, but overuse of slang expressions may make your general audience feel excluded.

Denotation and Connotation

The **denotation** of a word is its literal or dictionary definition. **Connotation,** on the other hand, refers to the emotional responses a word can create in the reader's mind.

What is the denotation of "prison"? The dictionary tells you that a prison is "a building in which persons are kept while awaiting trial or for punishment." Connotatively, the word "prison" creates an imaginative response of confinement, isolation, discipline, anger, violence, despair, and so on.

Now that you understand the differences between denotation and connotation, think of Malcolm X's claim that he had never been so free as when he learned to read while he was in prison.

As you look over the list of defined words, you will notice how varied Malcolm X's language is. It ranges from sophisticated vocabulary to simple words used in fresh ways; he incorporates a well-known Latin term—alma mater—as well as slang such as "boola-boola."

The English language borrows extensively from other languages and introduces many slang terms. About a quarter of the words commonly in use in English are new, borrowed, or adapted from other languages. For example, do you know in which language any of the following everyday words originate?

sugar, pizza, gumbo, law, barbecue, salsa, squash, pyjamas, garage, ketchup, diesel, sputnik, booze, giraffe, power, cookie, hamburger, cotton, die.

Comprehension

1. How did Bimbi inspire Malcolm X to become better educated?
2. Malcolm X outlines the process by which he taught himself to read. List the steps he gives.
3. What was the effect of Malcolm's copying the dictionary?
4. What caused Malcolm X to feel so "truly free" in prison?
5. To what use did Malcolm X put his newly gained ability to read?
6. On what grounds does Malcolm X compare his prison studies with a college education?
7. What caused those who met Malcolm X to believe he was university educated?
8. Paraphrase the following sentences taken from Malcolm X's essay:
   So I had come to the Norfolk Prison Colony still going through only bookreading motions. (paragraph 2)
   You couldn't have gotten me out of books with a wedge. (paragraph 9)
   I have often reflected upon the new vistas that reading opened to me. (paragraph 15)

Analysis

1. How does Malcolm X end the story of his life in prison? How effective is this ending?
2. For whom did Malcolm X write this essay? What assumptions did he make about his audience? How well do you think he addressed this audience?
3. In what ways do you identify with Malcolm X's self-improvement process? Have you ever taught yourself to do something difficult? If you have, outline the process and compare it with the attitude Malcolm X expressed in his essay.
4. Malcolm X claims that prison allowed him to be free. In what ways was that true?

5. How would you characterize Malcolm X's style?
6. Is the title "Prison Studies" effective? Why or why not?

Discussion/Writing Suggestions

1. In what ways did Malcolm X show his belief in the dignity of humankind—white or black? Do you think he was a revolutionary humanist?
2. Have you ever experienced a limitation that helped you to grow and change?

2

Writing from Readings

Responding in Writing: Critique and Summary

"The greatest part of a writer's time is spent in reading, in order to write. . . ."
(Samuel Johnson 1709–1784)

Responding in Writing

Most of what you write in any postsecondary course or at work is based on what you have read, observed, or discussed, and what you write is intended either to inform the reader or to encourage the reader to act in a certain way. Clearly, the ability to record the details you have encountered in readings and present them in an organized and coherent manner in your own writing is crucial to your success in any sort of written communication.

Often you are asked to respond to or give your opinion on what you have read. In order to validate your opinion, you need to support it with an analysis of and details from your reading; in other words, you need to write a critical response, or a critique.

Critique

A critique is an organized evaluation of a set of ideas or a work of art or literature, usually in written form. The word *critique* is clearly related to *criticism* although *critique* is used more in a neutral sense. Generally, we think of *criticism* as a negative response to a person, a situation, or an object; this is the word's current connotation. However, while we now frequently hold a pejorative view of the word *criticism,* and *critique* for that matter, a critique is actually a reasoned assessment of good and bad qualities in order to arrive at a sound judgment; this is its denotation.

For example, we are all familiar with movie criticism (or critique); in fact, you may choose to see a movie because a criticism of it rates it as worthwhile. In essence, a *critique* in this context is nothing more or less than an analytical appraisal or commentary on a piece of writing.

Whenever you consider a writer's vocabulary, style, organization, details, ideas, and so on, you are engaged in *critiquing*. Active reading enables you to create your response to a text. If you write a paragraph or an essay about what you have read and your response to it, you are writing a critique.

After each essay in Units 1 and 2 of *Refining Reading Writing,* you are asked for your impression of it in the "Responding to the Essay" section. Your answers to the questions in the Comprehension and Analysis sections provide you with the means to organize, support, and develop a critique of the essay you have read. That is, your answers provide you with *reasons for your opinions.* A good argument requires solid support. It is not enough to state an opinion; your position has to be validated with specific and accurate references to your reading in order to avoid unsupported opinions.

You can use several methods to support your evaluation of a reading. These methods include summary, paraphrase, and citation.

Summary

A **summary** is a shortened version of a piece of writing. Its aim is to condense but not to refashion an author's work; a summary normally follows the pattern of information and development found in the original piece.

- Active reading is a necessary component of summary writing as you must identify the key facts and ideas first so that you can reword them. You do not include supporting details and examples, but you must present information in the same order as in the original. A summary is not analysis, so you cannot add to or change the author's facts or ideas, nor do you comment on or redesign the information in the source text.
- In the opening sentence of a summary, you must state the name of the author, the title of the piece, the source (i.e., publication details, if any), and the main idea of the piece.
- Summary writing can be time-consuming. You may need to rewrite a number of times, changing unclear phrases, correcting verb tenses, combining sentences, and revising paragraphs, in order to represent the original in a condensed form.

Generally speaking, there are three types of summaries:

1. *A single-sentence summary:* Although very short, this must state the key content and focus of the original passage.
   - For example, if you had to write a single-sentence summary of a paragraph, you could simply reword the topic sentence. However, if you combined the reworded topic sentence with the major supporting

details, your single-sentence summary would be more effective and comprehensive. In effect, the thesis statement of an essay is its single-sentence summary.

- In textbooks and in business and technical reports, single-sentence summaries often function as headings. Although it is seldom in a complete sentence, a newspaper headline offers a "single-sentence" summary of the article that follows.

2. *A selective summary:* This is a shortened version of specific information taken from the original piece.
   - When writing a selective summary, you choose only the facts and ideas you need for your purposes. You scan for the relevant information and record it in point form. These points are then reworded into your summary.
   - A selective summary can be used in writing research papers, recording significant details from articles or textbooks, and preparing the texts for oral presentations.

3. *Point-by-point summary:* This is a shorter, reworded version of an entire passage.
   - In this kind of summary, you identify main ideas and major supporting details, reword them, and then put them in the same order as in the original. You omit most examples.
   - This type of summary is mainly used in year-end reports, minutes in meetings, outlines of technical data, and abstracts of formal company reports.

Paraphrase

When you read a passage and discuss it, or write an essay in response to a reading, it is important to make specific and relevant references to the reading in order to support your thesis. You can summarize to present the main ideas. Use a **quotation**—borrowing words from the original writing—in order to provide a detail, support a point, show readers the tone and wording of an author, or build a stronger argument in your own writing. An indirect form of quoting is **paraphrase.** When you paraphrase, you express the ideas or facts of another in your own words; other terms for paraphrase are "rephrase" and "reword."

Having a store of synonyms and antonyms is a definite asset when paraphrasing and summarizing. A **synonym** is a word that means the same or almost the same as another (e.g., big, large, huge, massive, gigantic). An **antonym** is a word with an opposite meaning to another word (e.g., tall vs. short, shallow vs. deep, and happy vs. sad).

A note about two important words: infer and imply. These two verbs do not mean the same thing.

Infer means to deduce, conclude, figure out (noun—inference)
Imply means to strongly suggest, without actually stating, to hint, to insinuate (noun—implication)

You can infer meaning from the context. If you didn't know the meaning of the word "lubricated," it is explained contextually in the last line of Paragraph 2 of Ralph Nader's essay "The Real McCoy" (p. 28): "so that the moving parts could be oiled or lubricated." In fact, *oil* (v.) is a synonym for *lubricate* (v.) here.

Citation

Whenever you summarize, quote, or paraphrase, the specific references made to the source in question must be properly documented in each case; this sort of documentation is known as citation.

- For specific rules that prescribe how to quote from or make references to your readings (your source texts), read Unit 6 (p. 256), which is devoted to the writing of documented essays and research papers.

Writing a critical essay on a reading in *Refining Reading Writing* involves specific and accurate documentation; such an essay is called a **documented essay.** Sang Il Lee's essay "Our Earthly Fate" on page 233 is a documented essay.

Failure to acknowledge your sources according to the required documentation style whenever you have incorporated other people's ideas and findings into your own writing means you are committing **plagiarism**, which is also known as "academic theft" and is considered a serious offence, possibly leading to expulsion or receiving a zero for your paper.

The first essay in this unit is by Ralph Nader. "The Real McCoy" is a brief biography of a very influential man, Elijah McCoy. Not only did he invent a product that was used worldwide, but this invention also gave rise to the expression "the real McCoy," which was widely used from the late 1800s to the mid-1900s and may still be heard today. This expression means that something is the genuine article, the best you can get. A 19th-century invention led to the expression "the real McCoy." How did it happen? Nader researched the life story of the inventor, a Canadian, Elijah McCoy, and recounts it here.

The Real McCoy

Ralph Nader

Ralph Nader (1934–) is an American attorney and political activist. He is a powerful advocate for consumer rights, feminism, humanitarianism, environmentalism, and democratic government. Nader has also been a strong critic of American foreign policy in recent decades, and he has been active in many government and non-governmental organizations. Nader has run for the presidency of the United States three times (1996, 2000, and 2004). In 1996 and 2000, he was the nominee of the Green Party, and in 2004, he ran as an independent.

The essay is organized chronologically, by the significant dates of Elijah McCoy's life, and offers little analysis of the facts it presents. The title plays with the famous expression and the fact that this essay is a biographical account of Elijah McCoy. It is taken from Nader's book, Canada Firsts *(1992).*

1 On May 2, 1844, Elijah McCoy was born in Colchester, Upper Canada (now the province of Ontario, Canada). The son of fugitive° slaves George and Mildred McCoy, who escaped from Kentucky through the Underground Railroad*, Elijah would go on to revolutionize the operation of machinery with his inventions. After raising Elijah on a farm in Colchester, the McCoy family left Canada and moved back to the United States after the Civil War, settling in a place about one mile from Ypsilanti, Michigan. George McCoy opened a cigar manufacturing firm and used the profits to send Elijah to Edinburgh, Scotland, to complete an apprenticeship in mechanical engineering. Since he was a young boy Elijah had shown an interest in machines and things mechanical.

2 In 1870, Elijah returned to Ypsilanti as a full-fledged mechanical engineer, but met with racial prejudice and was forced to take a job as a fireman for the Michigan Central Railroad. He operated a small machine shop on the side, but his main job involved shovelling coal for the trains' steam engines, and oiling all the moving parts of the trains. At that time, trains and all other machinery had to be shut down periodically so that the moving parts could be oiled or lubricated.

3 McCoy became interested in the problems of lubricating machinery, as he saw the frequent shutting down of engines and other machines for oiling and lubricating as a waste of both time and money. In his machine shop he began working on various devices that would lubricate machines as they worked. The idea was to build into the machine canals to carry lubricant to the parts of the machine that needed it. On July 12, 1872, McCoy received the patent for his first invention, an automatic lubricator for steam engines, patent #129,843. The lubricator consisted of a cup that held oil that was built in as part of the steam cylinder; the bottom of the cup was attached to a hollow rod and the opening closed off by a valve; the cup released oil into the cylinder automatically when the engine's steam pressure pushed a piston up through the rod opening the valve. A year later, McCoy improved upon his original design so that the lubricator oiled the cylinder at the most important time, when the steam was exhausted.

4 In 1873, he married Mary Delaney, and they moved to Detroit in 1882. He opened up Elijah McCoy Manufacturing Co. in Detroit with white friends and promoters and acted as Vice-President for the company. Further improvements patented by McCoy in later years numbered fifty-seven in all for lubricating systems for heavy machinery used in locomotives, steamboats and ocean liners. He also invented an ironing board, a lawn sprinkler, a wagon tongue support, and a rubber heel for shoes—eighty-seven inventions in total. By 1892, his lubricating cups were used in factories everywhere, on all railroads in the West and on steamers on the Great Lakes. Eventually, no piece of heavy machinery was considered complete unless it had the "McCoy system." Buyers of machinery would always inspect to make sure McCoy's lubricators were part of the deal. From this concern for quality in automatic lubricators comes the now widely known saying, "the real McCoy."

5   Unfortunately for Elijah McCoy, this fame did not prevent him from losing control of his investment and inventions. While others made millions from his lubricating systems, McCoy lost his business and his home after his wife's death in 1923 and was committed to Wayne County (Eloise) Hospital in 1928, where he died penniless on October 10, 1929.

Note

1 Underground Railroad: a secret organization that helped slaves escape from the southern United States to Canada

Vocabulary

1 fugitive (n): a person who is running away, fleeing

RESPONDING TO THE READING

- What is your first impression of this reading?
- What is the main idea of this reading? State it in one or two sentences in your own words.
- What do you think is the purpose of this essay? Give reasons for your opinion.
- Who do you think is the intended audience of this essay? Give reasons for your opinion.

Comprehension

1. The following words are taken from the reading:
   revolutionize, apprenticeship, prejudice, periodically, devices, canals, patent, valve, promoters, committed
   For practice in using synonyms, find other words to use in place of each of them. Scan the reading to locate them and check their meanings in this context. To make sure your replacement word is appropriate, use a dictionary.
2. Paragraph 3 uses "lubricate" in many different forms. Identify the part of speech of each of the following and explain the different meanings of the nouns:
   lubricate: lubricating, lubrication, lubricant, lubricator
   Refer to the suffix chart in the Appendix (p. 305) if necessary.
3. Paraphrase the following sentences taken from the essay:
   a. The son of fugitive slaves George and Mildred McCoy, who escaped from Kentucky through the Underground Railroad, Elijah would go on to revolutionize the operation of machinery with his inventions.

b. At that time, trains and all other machinery had to be shut down periodically so that the moving parts could be oiled or lubricated.

c. The idea was to build into the machine canals to carry lubricant to the parts of the machine that needed it.

d. The lubricator consisted of a cup that held oil that was built in as part of the steam cylinder; the bottom of the cup was attached to a hollow rod and the opening closed off by a valve; the cup released oil into the cylinder automatically when the engine's steam pressure pushed a piston up through the rod opening the valve.

e. Eventually, no piece of heavy machinery was considered complete unless it had the "McCoy system."

3. In a one-paragraph selective summary, write Elijah McCoy's biography using the dates in the essay to organize your answer.

4. Using either MLA or APA style (see pp. 265–295), quote the sentence that gives the reasons Elijah McCoy decided to invent his lubricating cup. Introduce the quotation appropriately by giving it a brief context.

5. In your own words, explain why Elijah McCoy invented his lubricating cup.

6. What was the Underground Railroad? Explain its significance to McCoy's life.

7. Besides industrial tools, what domestic items did McCoy invent or improve?

8. In your own words, explain how the expression "the Real McCoy" came into being.

Analysis

1. Given that McCoy's parents were once slaves, what impresses you about their achievements?

2. What can you infer about Elijah McCoy's character based on this essay? Remember to support each claim about him with details from the essay.

3. Did anything in this historical essay surprise you? What was it, and why or why not?

4. In a paragraph, summarize Elijah McCoy's achievements in life. Briefly state why Ralph Nader finds McCoy's life and many accomplishments worth writing about.

Discussion/Writing Suggestions

1. Only a few proper nouns become everyday words or expressions. Here are some: Braille, Dickensian, Diesel, Lynch, Pasteurize, Quixotic, Scrooge. Also, some products became so well known that their names or the names of their producers are now identified with the generic type of these products. Some typical examples are Aspirin, Kleenex, Xerox, and Scotch tape. What do you know about any of them?

2. Write a one-paragraph critique of this essay.

Before you move on to the main essay section of this unit, there are a few more literary terms and conventions you should be aware of.

Point of View

Point of view in exposition means the "voice" that is used for writing. There are three points of view to choose from:

1. The first-person point of view or *I/we;* using the first person tends to make the essay subjective and personal.
2. *You* is the second-person point of view; it is frequently used for giving instructions or a procedure.
3. The third-person point of view or *he/she/it/one/they;* the third-person point of view frequently gives the essay an objective and sometimes more formal tone.

Think of the essays you have read so far. In Unit One, MacLennan and Malcolm X adopted the first-person point of view, while Dickens used the third-person approach, and Bryson used the second person to give how- to advice. In Unit Two, Nader wrote using the third person. In the following essays, Ginsburg writes in the first person; Epstein moves from third to first (we); and Ingram uses third person for the most part, but also addresses his reader (you) and speaks for his reader (I/we).

Is the point of view appropriate for each essay? Why or why not?

Irony

Irony is a method of essentially saying one thing while meaning something different, usually the opposite of what you said or wrote. Irony is a useful technique because it forces readers to look at what is incongruous and to attempt to relate what is said and what is meant. In this way, irony is used by writers to make their writings more thought-provoking. To fully appreciate the value of irony in a piece of expository writing, the reader has to be active and alert to the author's tone by paying close attention to his or her choice of words and expressions.

Expository writing is at its best when it presents its ideas in the simplest form possible. The intended audience and the intended purpose help the writer determine not only the development, organization, and syntax, but also the diction and tone of a piece of writing. When you read the first essay in the Readings section, it is clear that David Ginsburg has succeeded in keeping his audience and purpose in mind as he wrote and revised this essay.

By the end of the essay, we know that Ginsburg is vehemently opposed to smoking because of its devastating impact on public health. Here, he is an authority because he is a doctor and more, he is a specialist—an oncologist. Referring to himself, Ginsburg writes, "I am a cancer specialist and I look after patients with lung cancer." It is simple, direct language. He uses familiar words, normal word order, and conversational phrasing. There is no possibility of confusion here.

As you read this essay, you will see that several times Ginsburg asks questions that start the same way: "Would it have been more acceptable . . .?" There are two things to notice about this technique:

1. First, it is *a **rhetorical question,** a statement that is presented in the form of a question and requires no answer.* The assumption is that only one answer is possible—the writer's opinion. These rhetorical questions are posed as part of Ginsburg's strategy in building his argument to convince the reader that he is right.

2. Second, these sentences demonstrate Ginsburg's *effective use of repetition to form **parallel structure.*** As you read the essay, notice how many different sorts of repetition Ginsberg employs.

Repetition for stylistic impact is very different from the type of repetition caused by lack of new information and interesting ideas. Notice that each time Ginsburg begins with this rhetorical question, he follows it with a forceful example in response. And later, in Paragraph 18, he turns the question into a declarative statement that now has acquired more force because it echoes that series of questions: "I am filled with rage and not at all concerned that smoking is good for my business." This is the conclusion of the essay. Notice how it reflects the introductory conversation.

As you read each essay in this unit and in this book, be aware of how different authors use a variety of techniques to make their points and convey opinion and emotion.

READINGS

Each of the following three essays in this unit is based on careful and organized research. Epstein's "The Virtues of Ambition" is a philosophical essay, yet it makes its subject very accessible to the reader. Ingram's "The Atom's Image Problem" contains a historical account organized by the dates of great breakthroughs in science. Ginsburg's "Smoking Is Good for My Business" derives from personal and social data.

Ginsburg's essay demonstrates that it is possible to write an essay that is personal and subjective in tone, but inclusive and objective in content. His point of view is first person. This is clearly an essay that initially adopts an ironic tone and slowly moves through sadness to the rage he expresses at the end.

Smoking Is Good for My Business

David Ginsburg

David Ginsburg is a Canadian oncologist and professor of Oncology and Medicine at Queen's University, Kingston, Ontario. This essay was first published in the Globe and Mail *(1997).*

1   "Do you mind if I smoke?" my travelling companion asked me.

2   "Not at all," I replied. "In fact, I should be most pleased if you would. It would be good for my business."

3   "What do you do?"

4   "I am a cancer specialist and I look after patients with lung cancer."

5   He seemed utterly taken aback°.

6   This is a most tasteless anecdote. Would it be any less crass° were I to have said that I was a heart surgeon repairing vessels damaged by cigarettes? Or an undertaker?

7   Or would it have been more acceptable if the pleasure that I took in his smoking being good for my business had related to my work as a tobacco farmer in southwestern Ontario, to my work as a tobacconist, a tobacco company executive, the receiver of revenue benefiting from a tobacco tax, or a social agency anticipating a reduced payout on his old-age-security pension because of his early death?

8   Would it have been more acceptable were I an organizer of a sporting event or an arts festival dependent on a tobacco sponsorship°?

9   When 350 people died in a plane crash last summer, there was appropriate concern and consternation. The police were involved, government agencies were involved, CNN provided 24-hour coverage, and the company may yet be in serious trouble as a result.

10   Three hundred and fifty people died yesterday, another 350 people the day before and 350 the day before that. Three hundred and fifty people will die today and tomorrow and the day after tomorrow—all from the same cause and all involving the same industry. Does anybody care?

11   There seems to be a remarkable lack of concern for the deadly implications of tobacco smoking that does not apply to other areas. Were an aircraft company to build airplanes with the sole problem that one plane each day, filled with 350 people, crashed killing all aboard, this would undoubtedly evoke° a response. There would be concern even if the company could justify its existence on the basis that jobs are provided building the plane, flying the plane, servicing the plane, taxing ticket sales and gasoline sales and generally supporting the economy.

12   It would not be acceptable if the company were to claim that there was no proof that the planes, or the pilots, or maintenance policies were in any way at fault; or if it were able to show that many other planes fly without any problems at all. It would not be acceptable if the company promised to build a lighter plane with possibly fewer consequences of the crash.

13   The equivalent toll on human life consequent on cigarette sales is ignored—seemingly on the basis that we need the tax money, need the tobacco sponsorship to promote the arts or sporting events, need the jobs the industry provides, need the conviviality° of smoking in bars and restaurants.

14   Do these people know that they are riding on the backs of the three or four hundred people who die each day as a result of smoking? Do they care? Are we blind to the connection between the economic benefits on one side and the human suffering on the other side of this equation?

15   I recently consulted on a mother of three young girls. She had begun smoking when she was 12. Now she had a large lump in her neck, her liver was enlarged, her abdomen swollen, her breathing gasping. She had lung cancer. Could I justify this to her 12-year-old daughter on the basis that her mother was dying for the economic good of society, for a tennis tournament, for a concert?

16   Today I saw a man of 39 who had smoked 25 cigarettes a day since his early teens. He is paralyzed from the spread of lung cancer to his spinal cord. Can I reassure him that his cigarette smoking has benefited farmers and tobacco company employees?

17   My mother died a few years ago with evidence of widespread lung cancer. Should I feel comforted that over time she spent a lot of money at the local drug store where she bought her daily packet of cigarettes; that she had a short-lived illness which cost the health-care system very little and that she no longer needs her old-age-security payments?

18   In my view, nothing justifies the growing of tobacco, the making, advertising and selling of cigarettes and the exploitation of the people who smoke them. When I see one patient after another dying of lung cancer, of heart disease, of chronic° lung disease, I am filled with rage and not at all concerned that smoking is good for my business.

Vocabulary

5 taken aback (idiom): surprised

6 crass (adj): insensitive

8 sponsorship (n): paying for a project or activity

11 evoke (v): to inspire or bring forth memories

13 conviviality (n): sociability, friendliness

18 chronic (adj): of long duration

RESPONDING TO THE READING

- What is your first impression of this reading?
- What is the main idea of this reading? State it in one or two sentences in your own words.
- What do you think is the purpose of this essay? Give reasons for your opinion.
- Who do you think is the intended audience of this essay? Give reasons for your opinion.

Comprehension

1. "This is a most tasteless anecdote." What is Ginsburg referring to and do you think the anecdote is tasteless?
2. Ginsburg gives a number of occupations he could be in rather than that of oncologist. What are they?
3. Two significant associations are connected with the number 350. What are they?
4. Ginsburg presents three anecdotes of cancer patients. What is the purpose of each?

5. Ginsburg ends his essay saying he is "filled with rage." What reasons does he have for being enraged?

6. This essay provides many examples of the impact of cancer. How many are there? What is the effect of these examples on the reader?

Analysis

1. What are the benefits Ginsburg cites that derive from cigarette sales? Does he convince you that the suffering outweighs the benefits?

2. Ginsburg presents two examples of dramatic numbers of deaths in this article caused by plane crashes and by smoking. What is the difference between how each is treated by the media and society in general? Why do you think this difference exists?

3. Explain the irony of the title and how the title relates to the cause-and-effect structure of Ginsburg's argument.

4. Throughout his essay, Ginsburg offers no proof that smoking actually causes cancer. Why do you think that is?

5. How would you feel if you had been the travelling companion of Ginsburg referred to in the opening of the essay?

6. Irony is often used to convey the unpleasant reality in a subtle manner. What is the harsh truth that Ginsburg reveals in his essay?

Summary Writing

1. Write the main idea of this essay in a sentence.
2. Summarize what Ginsburg says about tobacco sponsorship.
3. Summarize this essay in about 80 words.

Discussion/Writing Suggestions

1. Has Ginsburg's essay affected your attitude to smoking in any way? Why or why not?

2. Would this essay be more or less effective if it were written in the third person? Explain your response.

3. Write a one-paragraph critique of this essay.

The Virtues of Ambition

Joseph Epstein

Joseph Epstein (1937–) is a noted American essayist who has published several collections of essays. He is a regular contributor to Commentary, The New Yorker, Harper's, New Republic, New York Review of Books, *and* The Weekly Standard. *He has also written short fiction as well as a number of works of literary criticism and is the former editor of* The American Scholar. *Epstein teaches writing and literature at Northwestern University. He is also a member of the Hudson Institute, a think tank focusing on social science issues.*

This essay, taken from his book Ambition *(1980), reflects his continuing interest in society.*

1 It may seem an exaggeration to say that ambition is the linchpin° of society, holding many of its disparate elements together, but it is not an exaggeration by much. Remove ambition and the essential elements of society seem to fly apart. Ambition, as opposed to mere fantasizing about desires, implies work and discipline to achieve goals, personal and social, of a kind society cannot survive without. Ambition is intimately connected with family, for men and women not only work partly for their families; husbands and wives are often ambitious for each other, but harbor some of their most ardent° ambitions for their children. Yet to have a family nowadays—with birth control readily available, and inflation a good economic argument against having children—is nearly an expression of ambition in itself. Finally, though ambition was once the domain chiefly of monarchs and aristocrats, it has, in more recent times, increasingly become the domain of the middle classes. Ambition and futurity—a sense of building for tomorrow—are inextricable°. Working, saving, planning—these, the daily aspects of ambition—have always been the distinguishing marks of a rising middle class. The attack against ambition is not incidentally an attack on the middle class and what it stands for. Like it or not, the middle class has done much of society's work in America; and it, the middle class, has from the beginning run on ambition.

2 It is not difficult to imagine a world shorn° of ambition. It would probably be a kinder world: without demands, without abrasions°, without disappointments. People would have time for reflection. Such work as they did would not be for themselves but for the collectivity. Competition would never enter in. Conflict would be eliminated, tension become a thing of the past. The stress of creation would be at an end. Art would no longer be troubling, but purely celebratory in its functions. The family would become superfluous° as a social unit, with all its former power for bringing about neurosis° drained away. Longevity would be increased, for fewer people would die of heart attack or stroke caused by tumultuous° endeavor. Anxiety would be extinct. Time would stretch on and on, with ambition long departed from the human heart.

3 Ah, how unrelievedly boring life would be!

4 There is a strong view that holds that success is a myth, and ambition therefore a sham°. Does this mean that success does not really exist? That achievement is at bottom empty? That the efforts of men and women are of no significance alongside the force of movements and events? Now not all success, obviously, is worth esteeming, nor all ambition worth cultivating. Which are and which are not is something one soon enough learns on one's own. But even the most cynical° secretly admit that success exists; that achievement counts for a great deal; and that the true myth is that the actions of men and women are useless. To believe otherwise is to take on a point of view that is likely to be deranging. It is, in its implications, to remove all motive for competence, interest in attainment°, and regard for posterity°.

5   We do not choose to be born. We do not choose our parents. We do not choose our historical epoch°, the country of our birth or the immediate circumstances of our upbringing. We do not, most of us, choose to die; nor do we choose the time or conditions of our death. But within all this realm° of choicelessness, we do choose how we shall live: courageously or in cowardice, honorably or dishonorably, with purpose or in drift. We decide what is important and what is trivial in life. We decide that what makes us significant is either what we do or what we refuse to do. But no matter how indifferent the universe may be to our choices and decisions, these choices and decisions are ours to make. We decide. We choose. And as we decide and choose, so are our lives formed. In the end, forming our own destiny is what ambition is about.

Vocabulary

1 linchpin (n): a person or thing vital to the organization or structure

1 ardent (adj): eager, passionate

1 inextricable (adj): cannot be separated

2 shorn (v, past part.): clipped, cut off

2 abrasions (n): scrapes, damage caused by scraping

2 superfluous (adj): more than is needed

2 neurosis (n): irrational or disturbed behaviour

2 tumultuous (adj): noisy, turbulent

4 sham (n): imposture, pretence

4 cynical (adj): doubting the existence of sincerity or motives other than self-interest, pessimistic

4 attainment (n): achievement, accomplishment

4 posterity (n): future generations

5 epoch (n): period of history marked by significant event

5 realm (n): kingdom, domain

 ## RESPONDING TO THE READING

- What is your first impression of this reading?
- What is the main idea of this reading? State it in one or two sentences in your own words.
- What do you think is the purpose of this essay? Give reasons for your opinion.
- Who do you think is the intended audience of this essay? Give reasons for your opinion.

Comprehension

1. Find Epstein's definition of ambition. Write your own one-sentence definition of ambition.
2. Explain the connotation of *harbor* in Paragraph 1.

3. Scan the reading to locate the following words, check their meanings in context, and replace each with synonyms. Make sure your replacement word is appropriate both in meaning and part of speech:
    exaggeration, fantasizing, attack, reflection, endeavour, cultivating, extinct, trivial, upbringing

4. Paraphrase the following three quotations:
    a. "[A]mbition is the linchpin of society, holding many of its disparate elements together."
    b. "[A]mbition implies work and discipline to achieve goals."
    c. "[H]usbands and wives . . . harbor some of their most ardent ambitions for their children."

5. In Paragraph 1, Epstein gives a number of examples to prove that ambition keeps society functioning. What are they?

6. What do "success is a myth" and "ambition is a sham" mean? How does Epstein argue against the meaning of these two statements in Paragraph 4?

7. Epstein indicates that we choose few things in life. What are we able to choose?

Analysis

1. How would you describe Epstein's tone? Use examples to support your description.

2. In Paragraph 2, Epstein imagines what life would be like without ambition. Why does he then say, "[H]ow unrelievedly boring life would be without ambition"?

3. Do you agree with Epstein that "ambition is the linchpin of society"? Write a paragraph explaining why you do or do not agree. Use your own examples.

4. What do you think Epstein means in his concluding sentence?

5. Epstein talks about society and the individual. What is the relationship between them in Epstein's opinion? Do you agree or disagree and why?

Summary Writing

1. State the main idea of this essay in a sentence.

2. Summarize what Epstein says about the middle class in this essay.

3. Summarize this essay in about 50 words.

Discussion/Writing Suggestions

1. What does ambition mean to you and how important is it in your life?

2. Has this essay made you reconsider your concept of ambition? How and why?

3. Write a one-paragraph critique of this essay.

The Atom's Image Problem

Jay Ingram

Jay Ingram (1945–) is a science broadcaster and writer. He is the co-host and producer of Daily Planet *on Discovery Channel, which he joined in 1994. Before that, he was the host of* Quirks and Quarks *on CBC Radio from 1979 to 1992. For 10 years, Jay Ingram wrote articles for the popular children's publication* Owl Magazine, *and he has written a weekly science column for the* Toronto Star *since 1993. He is the author of several popular books on science, three of which have won a Canadian Science Writers' Award. His most recent book is* Theatre of the Mind: Raising the Curtain on Consciousness *(2005). Ingram has won many awards for his efforts to popularize science, including honorary doctorates from Carleton University and McGill University. In 1984, he was awarded the Sandford Fleming Medal from the Royal Canadian Institute, and he also earned the Royal Society of Canada's McNeil Medal for the Public Awareness of Science in 1997. His* The Talk Show *for the CBC won a Science in Society Journalism Award. Jay Ingram is able to make complex scientific theories and knowledge comprehensible to the non-scientist.*

This essay first appeared in Equinox *in 1996.*

1   What do you envision° when you hear the word *atom?* I bet if you see anything at all it is a miniature solar system, with the nucleus of the atom as the sun, and tiny electrons whirling° planetlike around it. And why not? A stylized version of this has long been synonymous with atomic power. It's probably the atom you saw in public school and is, indeed, a model rooted in science. The science is, however, a little out of date—by at least 70 years. If you try to redraw the atom as scientists imagine it today, it is transformed. What was solid becomes wispy° and foggy, what was compact becomes vast, and, most important of all, what was predictable is not.

2   This revolution in the concept of the atom was largely accomplished in a few years of incredible scientific progress during the 1920s. So why are we non-scientists so out of date in our mental image of the atom? Is it because atomic science is so incompatible° with everyday experience that we simply can't form and hold an image of it?

3   In his 1928 book *The Nature of the Physical World,* the great English astrophysicist Sir Arthur Eddington cast his eye back to the nineteenth century and said, "It was the boast of the Victorian physicist that he would not claim to understand a thing until he could make a model of it; and by a model he meant something constructed of levers, geared wheels, squirts, or other appliances familiar to an engineer." I suspect that most of us, if we are physicists at all, are Victorian. And I wonder if the Victorian physicists Eddington described weren't revealing something about human psychology that holds for most of us today.

4   By the time Eddington published his book, the solar-system model of the atom had already been out of favour for two years, replaced by the infinitely more challenging imagery of quantum mechanics. In fact, the solar-system atom, for all its hold on the popular imagination, held sway among scientists for little more than a

decade. In that sense, it takes its place beside the cowboy: the Wild West has had much greater staying power in popular culture than it did in reality.

5   However brief the scientific reign of the solar-system atom, its beginnings were honest. In 1911 Ernest Rutherford made public the experiment that set the stage for its appearance. When he aimed highly energized subatomic particles at thin sheets of gold foil, he was shocked to see that in some cases the particles bounced right back. Rutherford said, "It was almost as incredible as if you had fired a 15-inch shell at a piece of tissue paper and it came back and hit you." Rutherford concluded that the atoms of gold in the sheet couldn't be likened (as had been suggested) to minia-ture raisin buns—blobs° of positive electrical charge stuffed with tiny negative charges. Instead, the positive charge had to be intensely concentrated at a point inside the atom. Only such a compact object could deflect° the particles Rutherford had aimed at it. He didn't go so far as to limit the outer negative charges (the elec-trons) to precise orbits, and in that sense he was more in tune with the modern vision of the atom.

6   However, in 1912, shortly after this experiment, the Danish physicist Niels Bohr came to work with Rutherford, and by 1913 he put the electrons firmly in orbits about the nucleus. In doing so, Bohr solved what had been a major problem in pre-vious theories: classical physics had predicted that as electrons circled in orbits, they would steadily radiate away their energy; as this happened, their orbits would decay and they would eventually spiral° into the nucleus like satellites reentering the earth's atmosphere. In one scientist's words, "matter would incandesce° and collapse." Bohr argued that continuous processes such as radiating energy and decaying orbits were out-of-date concepts, failing to capture the inner workings of the atom. He suggested that electrons were restricted to certain stable orbits, in which they could move without loss of energy, and could only jump from one to another by emitting or absorbing a packet, or quantum, of energy.

7   So by the beginning of World War I, the solar-system atom was in place, but by the mid-1920s, it was gone. It couldn't withstand the brilliant onslaught° of experi-mentation and thought that swept through physics in Europe during that decade. A who's who of science repainted our portrait of the atom, even if we haven't noticed. Perhaps the most radical change was that, as seen from the quantum-theory point of view, such particles as electrons could behave as waves. So Erwin Schrödinger, an Austrian-born Irish physicist, was able to dispense with° the precise orbits of the electrons, filling the same space with waves radiating outward from the nucleus, the peaks of which corresponded to the now-defunct° orbits. Max Born, a theoret-ical physicist, altered that idea slightly by claiming that the waves' peaks didn't really show where electrons were but, rather, where they might be.

8   In 1927 German physicist Werner Heisenberg elevated that sense of uncertainty into a principle, called (guess what?) Heisenberg's Uncertainty Principle. He estab-lished that it was not just difficult but literally impossible to pinpoint both the posi-tion and the momentum (or velocity) of an electron at the same time—the very act of measurement would inevitably disturb the object being measured. In physics, the relationship has mathematical precision: you can know where the electron is, but then you don't know where it's going; if you endeavour to detect where it's going, you lose track of where it is. Is it any wonder that the solar-system model of

the atom was trashed? It was replaced by a dissonant° sort of picture—in tune with physicists' thinking but out of tune with the rest of us.

9   In today's atom, the electrons are still there outside the nucleus (although they often venture° perilously close to it), but they are represented not by mini-planets but by probabilities, clouds of likelihood that suggest, "this is where you might find it." Sometimes there are gaps in those clouds—places forbidden to electrons, yet these seem to present no barrier to the electrons' ability to materialize, first on one side of the gap, then on the other.

10   There's also the nucleus, the image of which has evolved from a tightly bound cluster° of protons and neutrons to something that might be like a drop of liquid, spinning, pulsating°, and quivering° with the movements of the particles inside. Or it might be more like a series of Russian doll-like shells, nestled° one inside the other. And as important as the nucleus is, it occupies only a minuscule fraction of the total size of the atom.

11   It has always struck me that physicists and chemists are, for the most part, perfectly happy to think of and talk about the atom as the sum of a set of equations. I'm sure they all believe these equations represent something in the real world, but it is probably not possible any more to say exactly what. The indeterminate and unknowable have replaced precision and prediction.

12   That's fine if you're a physicist—it's necessary—but it doesn't work very well for the rest of us. We don't have the language and skills to understand the atom as math; we need a model that squares with° intuition. Clouds of probability don't; balls moving in orbits do.

13   Much is made these days of the idea that we are coping with the twentieth century equipped with only a Stone Age hunter-gatherer brain. It follows, then, that the brain should be particularly skilled at doing things useful for hunter-gatherers. Imagination is certainly one of those skills, but imagination of what? Of solid, substantial objects moving around each other in regular fashion? Or of pointlike particles that can't be localized and that behave like waves and move in strange and unpredictable ways?

14   And why should you care what the atom is like? If you are at all interested in the natural world, you have to care. The atom isn't just another feature of nature—it is nature. Unfortunately, the solar-system atom was likely about as much as we could handle in concrete conceptual terms. When scientists left the concept behind forever in the 1920s, it seems they left the rest of us behind too. They have their mathematical atom to contemplate. We have only our mental pictures.

Vocabulary

1 envision (v): imagine, picture

1 whirling (v): rotating, turning rapidly

1 wispy (adj): delicate, translucent

2 incompatible (adj): not able to be matched, unsuitable

5 blobs (n): soft lumps or drops

5 deflect (v): turn away from

6 spiral (v): wind around a centre point in a continuous curve

6 incandesce (v): flame, shine

7 onslaught (n): attack, assault

7 dispense with (v): do without

7 now-defunct (adj) :out of date, obsolete

8 dissonant (adj): not in agreement, inharmonious

9 venture (v): try, set off on

10 cluster (n): group, gathering

10 pulsating (v): throbbing with a regular beat

10 quivering (v): shaking rapidly with small movements, trembling

10 nestled (v): settled in a safe, comfortable position

12 squares with (v): agree with, correspond to

RESPONDING TO THE READING

- What is your first impression of this reading?
- What is the main idea of this reading? State it in one or two sentences in your own words.
- What do you think is the purpose of this essay? Give reasons for your opinion.
- Who do you think is the intended audience of this essay? Give reasons for your opinion.

Comprehension

1. Look at this list of words taken from the reading:
   atom, nucleus, quantum, subatomic, electrons, protons, orbit, matter, momentum, velocity
   Although you may not know the exact definition of all of them, it is likely that you recognize these words and know that they all relate to the field of physics. Each of these words gained its current definition about a hundred years ago, and now they are readily recognizable words. Use a dictionary to check their meanings.

2. Look at these words: input, download, interface, printout. Where did they originate? They did not exist 25 years ago and now they are commonly used. What does this tell you about language?

3. What does Ingram describe in Paragraph 1?

4. What does Ingram describe in Paragraph 10?

5. Look at all the dates and names of famous physicists:
   1928 Sir Arthur Eddington, 1911 Ernest Rutherford, 1912–1913 Niels Bohr, mid-1920s Erwin Schrodinger, mid-1920s Max Born, and 1927 Werner Heisenberg
   They are listed in the order in which they appear in the essay. What does that tell you about the essay's organization?

6. Why does Ingram select the particular date for each of the famous physicists?

7. What do the following quotations imply about Ingram's intended audience and his point of view?
   - "So why are we non-scientists so out of date in our mental image of the atom?"
   - ". . . it doesn't work very well for the rest of us."

- "We don't have the language and skills to understand the atom as math; we need a model that squares with intuition."
- "When scientists left the concept behind forever in the 1920s, it seems they left the rest of us behind."

8. What examples does Ingram give to show how physicists are different from us?
9. Explain the allusions to the Wild West and the cowboy in Paragraph 4.
10. Why do we have to care about what the atom looks like according to Jay Ingram? Do you agree with him?

Analysis

1. How would you describe Ingram's tone? Support your answer with details from the essay.
2. Do you think it is true that we can't understand something unless we can make a model of it as Sir Arthur Eddington claims in Paragraph 3?
3. In Paragraph 3, what does Ingram mean when he says, "I suspect that most of us, if we are physicists at all, are Victorian"?
4. Throughout the essay, Ingram identifies himself with "us," the readers, rather than with the physicists by referring to the scientists as "they" and the non-scientists as "we" and "the rest of us." Is this approach effective for his purpose? Why or why not?
5. One of Ingram's purposes in this essay is to explore the analogy of the atom as a solar system. Is it ironic that he wants to erase the image used by atomic power?
6. In his attempt to replace the commonly held solar-system image, Ingram uses a number of images, analogies, metaphors, and similes, such as "clouds of likelihood," "like a drop of liquid, spinning, pulsating, and quivering," and "like a series of Russian doll-like shells." Are these effective? Can you envision an atom from this imagery?
7. Explain Ingram's allusion to "the hunter-gatherer" in Paragraph 13. How effective is it?
8. What sort of essay do you think Jay Ingram has written? To which field of study do you think it belongs?

Summary Writing

1. Write the main idea of this essay in a sentence.
2. Summarize Heisenberg's Uncertainty Principle.
3. Summarize this essay in no more than 80 words.

Discussion/Writing Suggestions

1. What is your image of the atom? Is it the "solar system" one and has it been challenged by Ingram's essay? Why or why not?
2. Is our world defined by our power of imagination as Ingram suggests in Paragraph 13?
3. Write a one-paragraph critique of this essay.

Organized Writing

Composing a Formula Five-Paragraph Essay

"True ease in writing comes from art, not chance." (Alexander Pope 1688–1744)

Writing is a form of art that can be learned, refined, and perfected. To write effectively requires good knowledge about and skillful use of certain conventions and formulas. For both experienced writers and *writers-in-training* like you, the five-paragraph essay structure is an established and proven formula in writing although, once mastered, it is open to adaptation and refinement.

As a standard essay formula, the five-paragraph structure enables you to select, arrange, and present your thoughts and supporting information in a clear and logical fashion. Furthermore, this format, which epitomizes well-structured non-fictional prose, can be adapted to all types of writing tasks, ranging from an expository essay or a documented essay to a business letter, and from a project proposal to a research report. As you will see in Unit Four, the five-paragraph essay structure can be used to suit the varied purposes of writers and patterns of essay development.

The five-paragraph essay is made up of an introductory paragraph that presents a thesis statement, three body paragraphs, and a concluding paragraph that reiterates the thesis statement. Because it resembles a hamburger in shape, the five-paragraph essay structure is frequently referred to as "the hamburger structure." In order to make the "hamburger" inviting and satisfying, the writer needs to select, organize, and present well-supported ideas as clearly and succinctly as possible. There are essentially four steps to writing a five-paragraph essay:

1. Generate information
2. Select and arrange the information
3. Present the information
4. Edit the information

Step one: Generate Information

Choose a Manageable Subject

First of all, an essay must have a **subject**, an idea you find worth writing about. For instance, a five-paragraph student essay may be about the importance of friendship, personal opinion on a certain sport, or major reasons that renewable energy sources should be used. When you are not given a subject, how do you come up with one? If you are deciding on your own subject, always choose one that you are interested in and have something to write about.

Often student writers take on a subject that is too broad and therefore unmanageable. Their subject has so many aspects to cover and requires so much information that it is impossible to discuss it in five paragraphs. With an overwhelming amount of information and ideas to choose from, student writers frequently find writing an essay a frustrating experience. Thus it is important to narrow down your subject.

One effective way to narrow down your subject is to ask questions using *who, what, when, where, why,* and *how.* Normally these questions could help you find the specific aspect(s) of the subject you want to focus on in the essay. Suppose your subject is driving, something of interest to many of us. You will soon find that this general topic branches out into too many aspects for you to cover in five paragraphs. For example, you could write about the costs of driving, its hazards, joys, frustrations, driving for one age group in one part of the world, or for the general public across the world—these are simply a few of the numerous aspects of driving you might examine. To decide exactly what your essay will be about, you may want to ask yourself questions, such as "Who drives?" "What makes an effective driver?" "When should a person learn to drive?" "Where is the best place to learn to drive?" "Why do people drive as they do?" "How can one reduce driving hazards?" "How does one learn to drive a car well?"

How you answer any one of these questions will depend on what you know and how many facts you can come up with for a five-paragraph essay. You may find that just one question will be sufficient to activate your imagination and lead you to a narrowed-down and better-focused subject. For instance, "how to become an effective driver" is a lot narrower than the blanket term "driving." Once you have chosen your focus, you need to generate enough ideas to form both the main idea and the supporting details in your essay.

Brainstorm

One way to generate ideas on your chosen subject is to **brainstorm**, an activity that involves thinking freely about ideas related to the subject. To achieve the most effective results in brainstorming, first find yourself a quiet spot (normally no brainstorming is possible when distractions are present). Then write down the subject—for example, "importance of friendship"—at the top of a blank sheet of paper. Your mind will then be able to respond to the subject while your eyes are focused on the words. Set yourself a firm time limit—a maximum of ten minutes is a good guideline—and jot down everything that comes to you within that time, without worrying about grammar, sentence structure, or spelling. If you can't seem to put anything worth pursuing down on paper, search for another topic. However, brainstorming usually produces valuable "raw material" that can be shaped and moulded into useful components for your essay.

Using the subject "how to become an effective driver" as an example, you might start by jotting down the things you like about driving. For example:

sense of control
freedom of movement
showing off my car (Porsche, fully loaded)
status
convenience
changing gears
washing and maintaining the car

For each item in such a list, you would then brainstorm to generate more specific details to support the precise focus you wish to write about. For "sense of control," you might list the following:

- Feeling more capable behind the wheel (sense of skilled accomplishment)
- Coming and going at any hour I wish (independence)
- Getting to work or school on time (no waiting for a bus)
- Getting away for a weekend whenever I want to (convenience)

These lists can be presented as a map or a web of ideas on a piece of paper if you find graphic presentation makes things clearer to you.

Driving: I hate

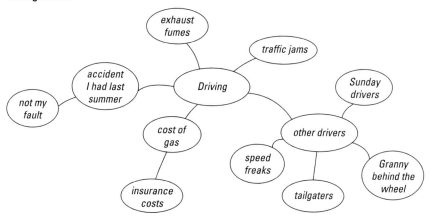

Step Two: Select and Arrange the Information

Select

Now that you have generated sufficient ideas on your chosen topic, carefully sort through your brainstorming notes or chart to decide which ideas to include or exclude and how to connect the remaining ideas. This is a crucial step to composing a well-organized and effective essay. Sorting out and selecting ideas that will interest both you and your reader can lead to new ideas about the aspect of the subject you want to focus on and the way you develop and support that idea. The prewriting process, in fact, requires you to make constant decisions and choices.

This selection step can be difficult but must be undertaken with care. Label or number items on your brainstorming notes and circle or cluster them into groups to see if you can find a valid topic and a sufficient number of supporting details to write into paragraphs. Check to make sure that you haven't repeated yourself in your selection and that all the chosen points are *separate* and *supportable*. Once you feel confident in your chosen subject, you are ready to decide how to present your ideas to your readers.

Organize

Readers appreciate clarity. As a writer, you must choose and organize your ideas in a way that best suits your subject, your intended audience, and your purpose. There are four basic ways to arrange information:

1. *Chronological order:* Present details in a series of steps or events, following a clear time sequence.
2. *Climactic or emphatic order:* Arrange your details from the least important to the most important point. In other words, to reach the climax, save the most difficult, complex, or convincing ideas for the last.
3. *Logical order:* Organize your supporting details to show logical reasoning, either **inductively** (from specific to general) or **deductively** (from general to specific), or to demonstrate how one idea leads to another or how one idea causes another to occur.
4. *Equivalent or random order:* Arrange details in any order when they are of equal importance and do not have chronological or logical connection.

As a test for yourself, identify the specific ways in which each student essay collected in this unit is organized and figure out why a certain order is better than the others. For example, did Marcelo Olenewa choose to organize his information in an order different from Rosemary Afriye and Jeff Haas? Why?

Outline

An outline is a working plan for your essay, although not everybody needs to make one before writing. You can write the outline in point form or draw a diagram. Its purpose is to give you a preliminary overview of the scope and layout of your essay. It helps you to try out ways to shape your essay and "see" its structure before it is produced. Write out your selected ideas and details in a brief format. Use subheadings, abbreviated in point form, as in this model outline based on Jeff Haas's essay in this unit (p. 56).

> Subject: The importance of a common stone
> Audience: The general reader
> Purpose: Mainly to inform and partly to entertain
>
> Pattern—Key Ideas:
> 1. Introduction—stone's contributions in three areas
> 2. Point 1: its contributions to technology—from past to present
> 3. Point 2: its contributions to science—from past to present
> 4. Point 3: its contributions to politics—from past to present
> 5. Conclusion

Notice how few specific details were included. The outline serves only as a foundation upon which to build up details in a first draft. For a longer essay, such as the research paper, a fuller outline may be required, but the basic procedure remains the same.

Step Three: Present the Information

Craft the Thesis Statement

A thesis statement is normally one or more sentences that tell your readers what your essay is about. It acts as a brief guide to what will follow and is valuable both for helping the writer to remain focused on the purpose and organization of the essay and for guiding readers by informing them from the start about the essay's subject and focus. For example, after generating and selecting enough information for his essay on effective driving, Marcelo Olenewa eventually decided to present his thesis statement as this:

> Effective driving involves the mastery of vehicle management, interaction with the driving environment, and courtesy to other drivers.

Notice how Olenewa uses three key ideas to shape and develop his thesis in the five-paragraph essay structure:

- Mastery of vehicle management
- Interaction with the driving environment
- Courtesy to other drivers

Also notice that each of Olenewa's three key ideas is written as a noun phrase, forming a carefully constructed parallel structure. The thesis statement, being the anchor of an essay, deserves not only clear thinking but also meticulous crafting. Many of us find it takes time to formulate an idea or to choose an interesting angle to approach a subject. Frequently, it requires special efforts to compose a well-crafted thesis statement. Be patient and persistent while working on your thesis statement.

Now read "Effective Driving," a sample essay composed by the student writer Marcelo Olenewa, and get a concrete idea of how information generated through brainstorming is selected, organized, and outlined and how the thesis statement functions in a five-paragraph essay.

SAMPLE STUDENT ESSAY I

Effective Driving

Marcelo Olenewa

1   When I was growing up, I had an absolute trust in my parents' driving ability. This trust grew out of my prolonged daydreams while my mother or father slalomed through the congested city streets. It seemed to me they were automatically in control. The first time I drove my parents' car, however, fear overcame me. I simply did not own the same sense of confidence as my parents did when trying to pilot the four-wheeled monster. Nonetheless, with plenty of practice, I learned to be confident and become an effective driver. In my opinion, effective driving involves the mastery of vehicle management, interaction with the driving environment, and courtesy to other drivers.

2   First of all, an effective driver should know how to control the vehicle he/she is driving. When I became a member of the driver's licence club, I had to learn how to drive a car with a manual transmission. After watching my friends drive manual transmission for years, I felt like a seasoned professional, yet all my confidence in handling this form of driving quickly dissipated when I was told to put the car in first gear and roll away. The car began bucking like a wild stallion due to the fact that I let the clutch out too fast. Then forgetting I was supposed to be the driver of the car, I tried to squeeze myself into the passenger seat. My poor father was not impressed although I had assured him that I could manage a manual transmission car with the greatest of ease. With a great deal of practice, I gradually learned to master the fundamentals of driving a car with a manual transmission, everything from up-shifting to down-shifting, speeding up to slowing down. Eventually vehicle management became second nature to me. This, however, was only a part of my driving experience. Now it was time to move from empty parking lots to the open road and put my driving abilities to the test.

transition sentence →

3   Similarly, interacting with the driving environment seemed daunting to me at first, but became easier with practice. The perspective of the pedestrian is quite different from that of the driver in terms of having to negotiate the road with other cars around and, sometimes, with ominous weather. Rain, sleet, and snow often spell chaos to many drivers, and I was no different; treacherous weather conditions frightened me. In times of poor weather, extra caution needs to be exercised. I learned quickly not to follow the vehicle ahead too closely, to signal my intentions to change lanes well in advance, and to begin slowing down a good distance from

where I wanted to stop the car. What strikes me as crucial is how much I have to be aware of the position of my car in relation to other cars. This reminds me of the time I was on a slight incline and my car began to roll backwards, almost into a Rolls-Royce. After that incident, I make sure always to check for other cars before making any sort of move. Interaction with the environment, however, goes beyond just being aware of traffic lights and weather.

4   Regardless of how a driver has mastered the vehicle and regardless of the skill with which he/she negotiates driving with other vehicles, effective driving has a philosophical dimension to it, which transcends mechanical aptitude, and that is courtesy. Courtesy is the aspect of driving that is not taught in the classroom, but learnt on the road. I learned that I must abide by the notion that driving is a privilege rather than a right, and that every privilege has a responsibility attached to it. All drivers have to show respect for the laws that are made to ensure safety of road conditions. Driving involves more than mechanical skill; it requires common sense, something most of us seem to lack when driving a car. How often have I been frustrated by the person who insists on being a road hog and not letting me change lanes? I in fact learnt a lesson in the etiquette of driving in a most horrifying incident. I was in the express lanes and wanted to merge onto the collector lanes when another car was blocking the lane. I almost ended up as part of the guardrail.

5   The key to effective driving, then, is to be familiar with the car you are operating, be attentive while on the road, and always be polite to other drivers. There needs to be a greater recognition of the skill required of a driver. This skill is acquired mainly through the driver's experience on the road. However, there are also basic guidelines that can be followed. It is therefore important to master the fundamentals—that is what makes an effective driver. My experiences throughout the years have allowed me to gain a true appreciation for what my parents were doing in the car while I was chasing rainbows or flying to the moon. Now I am the one who slaloms through the congested streets of the city with confidence and ease.

Working with the Essay: Paragraphs

The Introduction

As you see in Olenewa's essay, the **introduction** or the introductory paragraph in a five-paragraph essay typically begins with an "attention grabber" that leads readers to the thesis statement. It is true that in many essays the thesis is implied rather than stated. However, for writers-in-training it is important to form the habit of stating the thesis in the introductory paragraph because it helps you to focus. Also, you may notice later that some writers, such as Bertrand Russell, choose to begin their essays with the thesis statement instead of using it as an introductory link to the body paragraphs. Theoretically the thesis statement can be placed anywhere you see fit in the essay. However, the "straitjacket" of a five-paragraph essay structure is meant to assist you with the organization and presentation of your thoughts. Uncomfortable and confining as this "training suit" seems, in due course it will make organized writing second nature to you.

Effective writers always try to attract the readers' attention and interest by using certain proven strategies at the beginning of the essay. How can you effectively attract readers and make them spend time reading your writing in an increasingly busy world? The frequently used attention grabbers include the following:

- Relating an **anecdote** (a short interesting or amusing story about a real person or event; Olenewa includes one in his essay)
- Making a strong statement (as Rosemary Afriye does)
- Raising one or more questions (as Jeff Haas does)
- Using a quotation
- Presenting background information about the subject

These techniques, when used effectively, help to attract readers and lead them first to the thesis statement and then to the essay itself. As demonstrated in Olenewa's essay, the introduction should not use details that belong in the essay's body paragraphs. Yet it is advisable and helpful to present the supporting details succinctly both to remind yourself of your chosen direction and to provide the reader with an overview of your essay.

Examine Olenewa's introductory paragraph to find out how the two-part structure (attention grabber + thesis statement) works to fulfill its purpose. By relating personal anecdotes from the viewpoint of a passenger and a learner-driver, he first "hooks" the readers and then leads them to the point he intends to make—his thesis statement.

The Conclusion

The **conclusion** or concluding paragraph of an essay is essential. Readers expect an ending that is not abrupt or dismissive. The conclusion to a five-paragraph essay commonly provides a short summary of the essay's key ideas, often with the thesis restated in different words. As Olenewa's concluding paragraph exemplifies, the writer's focus on the subject is reinforced when the thesis statement is reiterated in a different way. Writers-in-training will find it easier to begin the concluding paragraph with the restatement of the thesis, so that the content in the paragraphs of the body is coherently funnelled into the final remarks. As you become more experienced and more comfortable with the structure, you may want to restate the thesis at a later point or at the end of the concluding paragraph.

Writers use the conclusion to provide a closing to their discussion, or, if we return to the metaphor of a hamburger, to hold all the nutritious components together on the "bottom piece of bun." As you see in Olenewa's essay, the conclusion contains more than a concise restatement of the thesis. Rather, most writers like to end their writings with some thought-provoking statements, mostly to strike a mental "click" before the door is finally shut. Occasionally, a conclusion can also present one final related detail or idea that may stimulate readers to think beyond the scope of the essay, to inspire readers to explore the subject further, or to reflect on it in a more open and pleasurable manner. Now have a closer look at Olenewa's conclusion and see how sentences and ideas evolve from, but are by no means strictly restricted to, the succinctly restated thesis. Also, a comparison of Olenewa's conclusion and those in the essays collected in this unit will reveal to you the varied approaches to composing the concluding paragraph for a similar purpose.

The Body Paragraphs

Ideally you should incorporate the three key points into your thesis statement as Marcelo Olenewa does. That way your thesis statement, which is normally presented in the introductory paragraph, serves to "cut" the body of your essay "into three separate slices," so your job of "building the body" becomes much easier. To support the thesis, you simply need to explain each key idea in one of the three body paragraphs without needless repetition. Unnecessary repetition will give your readers the impression that you don't really know enough about your subject.

By definition, a **paragraph** is a series of related sentences that develop or explain one key idea. For that reason, the standard paragraph contains a **topic sentence** and a body, which presents the supporting details. The topic sentence states *what* the key idea of the paragraph will be and indicates *how* and *why* the idea will unfold. The body is made up of supporting details. Each detail explains an aspect of the key idea (by using an example, say, or giving a reason). Details must be separate, strong, and singular, and they must support or explain what the topic sentence conveys to readers. Frequently whether a statement is valid or strong enough depends entirely on the strength and appropriateness of supporting details.

As you see in Olenewa's essay, each of his three body paragraphs begins with the topic sentence, which refers back to one of the three aspects enumerated in the thesis statement in the same order that they are introduced in the first paragraph. After the main idea is articulated in the topic sentence, all the other sentences in that paragraph are composed to support the main idea.

To take Olenewa's first body paragraph as an example, the topic sentence "an effective driver should know how to control the vehicle he/she is driving" opens the discussion of the first aspect of the subject, providing the whole paragraph with a clear focus. Specific and interesting details based on the writer's personal experience in learning to operate a car with a manual transmission then form a solid body.

First Body Paragraph: Reread Olenewa's first paragraph, underline the topic sentence, and then identify and number the supporting details in the margin.

After presenting sufficient evidence to prove the first point, Olenewa brings the paragraph to a close and proceeds to elaborate on his second point—interaction with the driving environment—in a new paragraph. The second body paragraph shares a similar structure to the first one with selected and organized details backing up the topic sentence, and so does the third. Below, analyze Olenewa's structure of the second and third body paragraphs and find out how each topic sentence controls every word in the paragraph.

Second Body Paragraph: First, locate the topic sentence and underline it; then identify and number the supporting details in the margin.

Third Body Paragraph: First, locate the topic sentence and underline it; then identify and number the supporting details in the margin.

Graphically, each of the three middle layers of ingredients in the "hamburger essay" forms a well-structured entity on its own; together they all contribute to the "organic whole" that an effective essay is designed to achieve. Although in your reading you may find slight variations in the paragraph structure of some organized essays, your training in effective writing requires plenty of practice with structured writing. It is therefore important that you follow the formula carefully until it becomes an integral part of your thinking and writing process.

With a good command of the five-paragraph structure, you are guaranteed to find essay writing and writing in general much easier and thus more enjoyable. Returning to the hamburger analogy again, the top half of the bun (the introduction) and the bottom half of the bun (the conclusion) should always be in place to hold the delicious and nutritious hamburger together. The number of middle layers and toppings (the body paragraphs), on the other hand, could be flexible and varied. The hamburger formula can be adapted to compose an essay of six or eight paragraphs or a research paper of any length. All you need to adjust is the substantiality (number of body paragraphs) of the "hamburger" by using your knowledge and skills. In many ways, learning to master the five-paragraph structure is an effective method to liberate you from anxiety about writing or "writer's block" of any sort rather than to confine you to a mechanical pattern.

In order to help you reinforce your knowledge of the five-paragraph essay structure, we present below two more student essays, "My True Love Is Reading" by Rosemary Afriye and "The Common Stone" by Jeff Haas. Read these essays carefully. You should be able to figure out how they each are structured using what you have learned about the thesis statement, the introduction, the conclusion, the body paragraphs, and the topic sentence in each body paragraph. You should also be able to notice the slight stylistic variations between these two essays. How is each of them similar to and different from the essay by Olenewa?

SAMPLE STUDENT ESSAY II

My True Love Is Reading

Rosemary Afriye

1 I love to read. I'll read anything that I set my eyes on. It could be a package, a newspaper, a juicy novel or a dry textbook. I'll read anywhere: at the table, on my computer, on the bus or curled up in a comfortable chair. Right now I'm a student, so my love of reading is useful, but apart from its utility, reading offers me the means of self-improvement, and it gives me pleasure as a way of escaping the stress or banality of my life.

2 Never underestimate the usefulness of reading. Even when I read to pass the time, it is never time wasted. For example, just yesterday at different meals, I was reading all sorts of interesting things. My breakfast cereal box lists the daily recommended intake of various nutrients, and for some reason I focused on the fact that mine contains 20% of the daily recommendation for folic acid. I wondered if that is a good thing, whether the body stores folic acid and I could perhaps overdose on folic acid if I ate something else that contained it. I had to check it out, so

that sent me to my computer to research. This all took less than half an hour, but I left home with more knowledge than I would have if I weren't an incurable reader. And guess what: I also made sure I had green leafy food at lunch time! Apart from adding to my knowledge, my love of reading means I do have a definite edge. From experience, I know how to figure out the direction that a chapter in a textbook is going, how to recognize its key points and so eliminate extraneous details when I skim on a reread for a quiz. For example, during my break, I "reread" the chapter for a quiz because I was feeling anxious about it and managed to do this in the time it takes to drink a very hot, large tea. I am so lucky also that my inveterate reading habit means I have increased my reading rate. I know many others in my classes spend longer reading an individual piece than I do. Sadly, they don't enjoy the activity and probably find it either boring or so difficult that they want to give up on it. Clearly, for me, reading is a very practical love.

3   Reading is not only useful, but it also enhances my self-esteem. For example, what do you think of my vocabulary? I am actually quite proud of it. It's not that I am flashing fancy, polysyllabic words around all the time, but I do feel at ease about using words correctly and can readily find synonyms for frequently used words. This is just one small example of how reading has improved me. This morning on the bus, I was given a valuable reading opportunity because someone had left a newspaper. Who can resist a freebie? Of course, I checked out the comics first and enjoyed a few smiles at presentations of human silliness. Fortified with good humour, I moved on to the news sections covering the horrors of foreign wars, local problems with violence and the promises of politicians. By the time I got to college, I was more knowledgeable about what is going on in the world and my city, and so I felt comfortable chatting about various issues in an informed manner rather than just blurting out opinions. This relates to what I am writing now because we know a good essay has to support its main points with details. Reading gives me the confidence to state and develop my ideas when I write as well as when I am talking. It doesn't matter if I'm in a class or hanging out with my friends, I am confident in my ability to express myself. I do think that reading has given me a better sense of myself.

4   I don't love reading just because it is useful and builds character; I love reading mainly because it is exciting and truly recreational. When we read stories, we develop feelings for the characters because of how we relate to them. We share their experiences so intimately that they can seem like our own. In fact, reading lets me be someone I am not, so I can be Elizabeth Bennet* in *Pride and Prejudice* and flirt with Mr. Darcy*, or I can be a detective on the trail of a psychopathic murderer. Reading makes me more imaginative, showing me the world and placing me in another time and place. For example, I hear the voices from Ghana in stories by Ama Ata Aidoo*, travel to nineteenth-century Russia with Chekhov* or else visit the U.S. with Stephen King*. When I am tired from the day, I can read a book and be energized emotionally. While a good read is like recharging your battery, ironically, it also helps me unwind and relax, so I usually read part of a novel before I go to sleep. When reading takes me into another life, my own doesn't seem as arduous or demanding, and I benefit from this different perspective on myself. A good book is my friend; reading is an enriching part of my life.

5   My love of reading is personally useful, builds my self-confidence, and gives me a fuller experience of life. Reading is enriching because it stimulates my imagination and encourages my curiosity about the world and the people in it. Although reading is something I do by myself, in a strange way it makes me part of the whole world. This is what I love about reading.

Notes

4 Elizabeth Bennet and Mr. Darcy: two of the main characters in *Pride and Prejudice* by Jane Austen (1775–1817)

4 Ama Ata Aidoo (1942–): a woman writer from Ghana

4 Chekhov (1860–1904): a celebrated Russian writer

4 Stephen King (1947–): one the most prolific writers in the world, best known for his horror stories about macabre and supernatural events that happen to ordinary people

Now answer the following questions:

1.   Underline the thesis statement in the first paragraph and its restatement in the last paragraph.
2.   Identify the topic sentences in the three body paragraphs.
3.   How has Afriye organized the examples and anecdotes she uses?
4.   Do you think Rosemary Afriye is successful in supporting her thesis? Why or why not?
5.   How do you feel about reading? Be prepared to share an example that shows your attitude.

SAMPLE STUDENT ESSAY III

The Common Stone

Jeff Haas

Attention-grabber; series of questions

Thesis statement subject + focus : common stone and its historical influence

3 key points : technology, science, politics

1 topic sentence: technology

Supporting detail 1— hammer

Supporting detail 2—chisel

1   Have you ever walked along a path and kicked aside a small stone? It is insignificant, seemingly ubiquitous and rarely given a second thought. Like many things that are familiar and ordinary, we take it for granted. It is, after all, just a stone. However, little do we realize that the common stone has actually made uncommon contributions to human life, both in the past and at present. The common stone, despite its simplicity, has guided the design and use of many tools and institutions in technology, science, and politics from ancestral times to the present.

2   Technology involves tool making, and tools are a human construction used to make living easier. While the stone-age hammer has been replaced by ones made of steel, their general design does not differ. Basic similarities can be found among many tools. The primitive stone chisel is much the same as its modern counterpart. But even though the stone chisel is inferior, it helped create the

Supporting detail 3—drill

Concluding sentence

2 topic sentence: **3**
science

Supporting detail 1—
trajectories

Supporting detail 2—
kinetics

Supporting detail 3—
geology

Concluding sentence

3 topic sentence: politics **4**

Supporting detail 1—
arrowheads

Supporting detail 2—
knives

Supporting detail 3—
missiles

Concluding sentence

Concluding paragraph **5**
Restatement of thesis

Thought-provoking
statements and related
details to stimulate
readers

pyramids and the statues of Easter Island, feats that are still wondered at. While the stone drill, powered by a wooden bow, has been replaced in workshops by electric powered steel drills, it's not uncommon to find stone drills and cutters in the modern world. Diamond-studded drills are used to cut through rock to get at oil, the staple of modern technology. Without the stone, we would not have our modern technology.

Stone, while not normally considered a part of science, has actually played a major role in scientific development. Ancient humans, without knowing it, discovered many important scientific facts. They learned trajectories from throwing rocks and spears at animals. They learned kinetic energy from observing what the rock did to the target. They learned stress factors and gravity from standing too close to the edge of a cliff. Modern science has also developed geology to study how the earth developed. Stones have taught us the shifts in the magnetic poles, and where to look for oil and metals. Thus the simple stone with its aspects of metallurgy is not so simple after all.

Most amazingly, the influence of the stone has shown itself in many odd places, such as politics. Was it not common to settle the first disputes by bashing in the head of the opposition? Since that time little has changed except the method of delivery and the composition of that which is delivered. Stone arrowheads were in use in Europe long after the introduction of bronze or steel. This is because stone was sharper and cheaper. Obsidian, for example, can be made into knives sharper than surgical steel. The common hand-thrown stone, settler of ancient disputes, has become the hand-grenade, settler of modern disputes. Where we once made catapults to hurl boulders at opponents' castles, we now make rockets and artillery to fire on the cities of our enemies. Thus, the lowly stone has helped create our most frightening and climactic form of politics: war.

The common stone, still as simple as ever, continues in its service to humankind in technology, science, and politics. In fact, the stone has yet to leave the arsenal. Its deployment can still be seen alongside modern weapons in Korea, Ireland, and the U.S.A. where it is being thrown at the police or any other likely target. Next time you come across a stone on your path, stop and think about its vital contribution to your life. Then you can kick it aside. After all, that's probably how football was invented!

Working with the Essay

From the marginal notes accompanying this essay you can see that Jeff Haas's essay shows good mastery of the "hamburger essay" formula. After using a question to catch his readers' attention, he further appeals to them by sharing some common feelings about his unusual subject—the ordinary stone. Then in the last sentence of the introductory paragraph he presents his thesis statement, both to inform the reader about the point he is making and to organize his thoughts in the five-paragraph essay structure. Notice how in the thesis statement Haas places *technology, science,* and *politics,* the three specific aspects of his thesis, in the order he will discuss them later. Also notice how by using phrases like *the design and use of many tools and institutions* and *from ancestral times to the present,* Haas indicates the particular type of examples he will cite as well as the historical perspective he adopts. Once again, we are reminded that in a carefully crafted thesis statement every word counts.

Once the focus and framework are thus established, Haas proceeds to expand on the three aspects with well-chosen examples in his body paragraphs. As the thesis statement proclaims, Haas's discussion focuses on the use of the stone as tools and institutions in technology, science, and politics, and the subject is also approached from a historical angle through a comparison between the stone's use in the past and present. Notice how each body paragraph begins with a topic sentence and develops the discussion with focus on one of the key areas mentioned in the thesis statement.

Finally, the concluding paragraph opens with a slightly rephrased statement of the thesis. By changing *The common stone, despite its simplicity, has guided . . .* to *The common stone, still as simple as ever, continues in its service to humankind,* Haas redirects the reader's attention from the past (and the present) to the future. After placing the reader in a forward-looking mood, Haas completes his essay by making thought-provoking references to the special uses of the stone in Korea, Ireland, and the United States. His final words serve to bring the reader back to the light-hearted tone in which the attention-grabber is presented, leaving an enjoyable echo in the reader's mind.

Now give some thought to the following questions:

1. Is the title for Haas's essay "The Common Stone" appropriate? Why or why not?
2. Using Paragraph 2 as a model, analyze how Jeff Haas compares examples from ancestral times and those in the present.
3. Is Haas's concluding paragraph effective? Why or why not?

Step Four: Edit the Information

Once you have written a draft of your essay, you need to read it over carefully before you hand it in. **Editing** or **revision** is the final and crucial step in composing an essay. Keep in mind the advice of the great essayist and creator of the first dictionary, Samuel Johnson: "What is written without effort is in general read without pleasure."

To edit or revise involves restructuring, rewriting, rephrasing, and refining. In taking this step, you may need to rearrange your thoughts according to your approach to the thesis, move sentences around in your paragraphs to achieve clarity, check facts, add or delete information, and change words or expressions to be more precise or more concise. Compared with the earlier stages of writing, revision is sometimes more difficult for writers in training because most of them tend to be protective of their own writing once words are put on the page. As a result, they often feel reluctant to make changes when they don't see the need to do so. It is thus advisable to put your writing aside, if possible, after the first draft is completed. Even a few hours away from the piece could find you somewhat detached from it and allow you to view it with a pair of fresh eyes and a refreshed mind. With a bit of distance, you will be more willing to find faults with your own writing and to make changes. If you are writing an in-class essay, try to leave yourself time to reread, and ensure you have at least a five-minute break before you look over what you have written. Consult the Writing Checklist on the inside cover of this book to review the structure of an essay.

How do you revise an essay effectively? Many authors find their own methods that work well for them, but here are a few suggestions:

1. Since it can be difficult to be objective about your own writing, have a friend read your essay out loud to you so you can *listen* to your own words. Do they make sense? Or read the essay aloud to yourself, pretending it was written by someone else. Is it clear? How can you make it better?

2. Read your essay at least twice in the revision stage. Try reading it from the conclusion back to the thesis. Does it hold together as an organic whole? Does the thesis relate to the body paragraphs? If you find your essay lacks unity, coherence, or clarity, rewrite the parts that are questionable, rephrase your sentences, and change, add, or delete the unsatisfactory supporting details.

3. Once you feel that the facts and format are sufficiently polished, check the grammar, mechanics, and spelling. Use your dictionary or the spell-check on your computer and your grammar handbook.

You may also want to read over the points presented in the Appendix (p. 297).

Unity and Coherence

Unity and coherence are the two vital principles that every writer should incorporate in any composition. Along with the audience and purpose, unity and coherence determine the level of language and style of a piece of writing.

Unity

As the first key principle in writing, unity requires *oneness* or *singleness* in content. To ensure unity, you should present a single and specific point in the topic sentence (of a paragraph) and in the thesis statement (of an essay). Also, you should make sure that *every* sentence in your paragraph or essay supports your controlling idea. No sentence should contain any idea unrelated to the point made in the topic sentence or the thesis statement.

With this principle in mind, examine the essays by Olenewa, Afriye, and Haas (again) and find out how their paragraphs and essays pass or fail the unity test. When a writer wanders "off topic" by allowing unrelated information to intrude into his or her writing, the paragraph or essay will lack unity and lose its focus and strength. One method for checking unity in your own writing is to begin with the final sentence of a paragraph or an essay and then read each preceding sentence all the way back to the topic sentence or thesis statement while constantly asking yourself if each sentence relates.

Coherence

As the second key principle in writing, coherence, which means "sticking together," requires an *organic whole* in structure. Sentences and paragraphs should lead smoothly from one to the other as if they are organically linked. To achieve coherence, you should

1. arrange your ideas in a suitable order (see "Organize" earlier in this unit), and
2. use transitions to glue sentences together.

Transitions refer to verbal cues that show the relationship between one idea and the next. They are essential to coherence in writing. Transitions can either be implied or stated.

Implied transitions can be achieved by

1. repeating a key word,
2. using synonyms, and
3. using pronoun references.

Transitions are stated when words and phrases are used to bind sentences together.

There is a whole family of transitional expressions, many of which you may have been using without knowing it. In order to help you gain better familiarity with this group, you will find in the Appendix (p. 297) a list of the most commonly used transitional words and phrases under the different categories of their usage.

To sum up, effective writing requires effective use of transitions, either implied or stated with the help of transitional expressions, to turn every piece of writing into an *organic whole*.

Exercises for Coherence

Exercise I

The following sentences are adapted from an essay titled "Unwritten Laws Which Rule Our Lives," by Bob Greene, an award-winning American journalist and columnist. All linking and transition words and phrases have been removed to illustrate how disjointed a piece of writing would be without any glue to hold individual ideas and sentences together.

After reading the disconnected sentences, you will read two more coherent versions of the same passage. We have written the passage in two different ways to demonstrate the variations that are available to you. Which version do you prefer? Can you say why?

Last week I was sitting in a restaurant with a friend.
A steady hum of conversation hung over the room.
The man sitting next to me started shouting at the top of his voice.

His face was red.

He yelled at the woman sitting opposite him for about 15 seconds.

In the crowded restaurant it seemed like an hour.

All other conversation in the room stopped.

He must have realized this. He stopped abruptly.

He lowered his voice.

He finished whatever it was he had to say.

He spoke in a low tone.

The rest of us could not hear.

It was startling.

It almost never happens.

There are no laws against such an outburst.

With the pressure of our modern world you would almost expect to run
   into such a thing on a regular basis.

You don't.

I had never thought about it before.

It was the first time I had witnessed such a demonstration.

I have eaten many meals in restaurants.

I have never seen a person start screaming at the top of his lungs.

When you are eating among other people, you do not raise your voice.

This is just an example of the unwritten rules we live by.

I have been thinking about it.

These rules probably govern our lives on a more absolute basis than the
   ones we could find if we looked in the law books.

There would be chaos without them.

For some reason we still obey these rules.

Version A

Last week I was eating dinner in a restaurant with a friend; a steady hum
of conversation hung over the room. Suddenly, the man sitting next to me
started shouting at the top of his voice. His face was red, and he yelled at
the woman sitting opposite him for about 15 seconds. In the crowded
restaurant, it seemed like an hour. All other conversation in the room
stopped, and everyone looked at the man. He must have realized this,
because as abruptly as he had started, he stopped; he lowered his voice
and finished whatever it was he had to say in a tone the rest of us could
not hear.

It was startling because it almost never happens. There are no laws
against such an outburst, and yet with the pressures of our modern world,
you would almost expect to run into such a thing on a regular basis. But
you don't; as a matter of fact, when I thought about it, I realized that it was
the first time in my life I had witnessed such a demonstration. In all the
meals I have had in all the restaurants, I had never seen a person start
screaming at the top of his lungs.

When you are eating among other people, you do not raise your
voice; it is just an example of the unwritten rules we live by. When you

consider it, you recognize that these rules probably govern our lives on a more absolute basis than the ones you could find if you looked in the law books. The customs that govern us are what make a civilization; there would be chaos without them, and yet for some reason, we obey them.

Version B

Last week while I was sitting in a restaurant with a friend, a steady hum of conversation hung over the room. Abruptly, the man sitting next to me started shouting at the top of his voice; his face was red. He yelled at the woman sitting opposite him for about 15 seconds, although in the crowded restaurant it seemed like an hour. He must have realized this, for as abruptly as he had started he stopped. Lowering his voice, he finished whatever it was he had to say in a tone the rest of us could not hear.

It was startling because it almost never happens, yet there are no laws against such an outburst. With the pressures of our modern world, you would almost expect to run into such a thing on a regular basis, but you don't. As a matter of fact, when I thought about it, I realized that it was the first time in my life I had witnessed such a demonstration. Even though I have eaten many meals in restaurants, I had never seen a person start screaming at the top of his lungs.

When you are eating among other people, you do not raise your voice. This is just an example of the unwritten rules we live by. When I think about it, these rules probably govern our lives on a more absolute basis than the ones you could find if you looked in the law books; there would be chaos without them. Oddly enough, for some reason we still obey these rules.

Exercise 2

Rewrite the following passages of disconnected sentences into more coherent paragraphs. Vary your sentence structure using **complex sentences** (an independent clause plus a subordinate clause) as well as **compound sentences** (two independent clauses joined by coordinate conjunctions).

1. In restaurants and coffee shops, people pay their bills.
   This is a simple enough concept.
   It would be remarkably easy to wander away from a meal without paying at the end.
   In these difficult economic times, you might expect that to become a common form of cheating.
   It doesn't happen very often.
   There are unwritten rules of human conduct.
   People automatically pay for their meals.
   They would no sooner walk out on a bill than start screaming.
2. Restrooms are marked "Men" and "Women."
   Often there are long lines at one or another of them.
   Males wait to enter their own washrooms.

Women enter theirs.

This is an era of sexual equality.

You would expect impatient people to violate this rule on occasion.

There are private stalls inside.

It would be less inconvenient to use them than to wait.

It just isn't done.

People obey these signs.

3. I know a man.

When he pulls his car up to a parking meter, he will put change in the meter.

He does this even if there is time left on it.

He regards this as the right thing to do.

He says he is not doing it just to extend the time remaining.

Even if there is sufficient time on the meter to cover whichever task he has to perform at the location, he will pay his own way.

He believes that you are supposed to purchase your own time.

The fellow before him purchased only his.

Exercise 3

Write a thesis statement for a five-paragraph essay that would have the three sets of sentences in Exercise 2 as its body paragraphs.

Exercise 4

Reread "Effective Driving" by Marcelo Olenewa and "My True Love Is Reading" by Rosemary Afriye along with "The Common Stone" by Jeff Haas. Find out how each author achieves coherence in his or her essay. Is it by repeating the key word(s) or by using synonyms and pronouns, or by a combination of both?

READINGS

Three essays by professional writers are presented below to further illustrate the formula five-paragraph essay writing and writing in general. Bertrand Russell's essay "What I Have Lived for" is considered a classic example of a five-paragraph essay. Using his own life as the subject, the Nobel Prize winner skillfully uses the five-paragraph structure to describe his three lifelong passions in highly poetic language. Now that you are equipped with the knowledge of how to construct a five-paragraph essay, you will doubly appreciate this essay as your enjoyment of Russell's pithy poetic prose is enhanced by your insight into the essay's seamless structure. "Writing and Its Rewards" by Richard Marius is also a carefully crafted five-paragraph essay; "How to Write with Style" by Kurt Vonnegut varies the formula of the five-paragraph essay. Using different essay structures, both Marius and Vonnegut write about the same subject—writing, with which they are very familiar. When you are studying these two essays, pay special attention not only to *what* these two accomplished writers offer on writing, but also to *how* they deliver their messages.

What I Have Lived For

Bertrand Russell

Bertrand Russell (1872–1970), an English philosopher and mathematician, made great contributions to mankind during his nearly century-long life. As his biographer, Alan Wood, commented, Russell "started by asking questions about mathematics and religion and philosophy, and he went on to question accepted ideas about war and politics and sex and education. . . . The world was never again the same once Russell had set the minds of men on the march." On the world stage Russell was a controversial character. Because of his caustic criticism of British involvement in World War I and his radical campaigning for nuclear disarmament, Russell was put in jail twice. However, his writings on a variety of social issues earned him many awards, including the Nobel Prize for Literature in 1950. As a writer, Russell was not only noted for the profundity of his ideas, but he was also celebrated for his pithy style. He once joked, "I'm paid by the word so I always use the shortest words possible."

This essay was originally written as the prologue to his autobiography, which was published in three volumes in 1967, 1968, and 1969 respectively.

1   Three passions, simple but overwhelmingly strong, have governed my life: the longing for love, the search for knowledge, and unbearable pity for the suffering of mankind. These passions, like great winds, have blown me hither and thither°, in a wayward° course, over a deep ocean of anguish°, reaching to the very verge of despair.

2   I have sought love, first, because it brings ecstasy°—ecstasy so great that I would often have sacrificed all the rest of life for a few hours of this joy. I have sought it, next, because it relieves loneliness—that terrible loneliness in which one shivering consciousness looks over the rim of the world into the cold unfathomable° lifeless abyss°. I have sought it, finally, because in the union of love I have seen, in a mystic miniature, the prefiguring vision of the heaven that saints and poets have imagined. This is what I sought, and though it might seem too good for human life, this is what—at last—I have found.

3   With equal passion I have sought knowledge. I have wished to understand the hearts of men. I have wished to know why the stars shine. And I have tried to apprehend the Pythagorean° power by which number holds sway above° the flux°. A little of this, but not much, I have achieved.

4   Love and knowledge, so far as they were possible, led upward toward the heavens. But always pity brought me back to earth. Echoes of cries of pain reverberate° in my heart. Children in famine, victims tortured by oppressors, helpless old people a hated burden to their sons, and the whole world of loneliness, poverty, and pain make a mockery of° what human life should be. I long to alleviate° the evil, but I cannot, and I too suffer.

5   This has been my life. I have found it worth living, and would gladly live it again if the chance were offered me.

Vocabulary

1 hither and thither (adv, archaic): to this place and to that place

1 wayward (adj): difficult to control

1 anguish (n): severe pain, mental suffering

2 ecstasy (n): a feeling of very great joy

2 unfathomable (adj): too deep to measure, too difficult to be understood

2 abyss (n, formal or literary): a bottomless hole

3 Pythagorean (adj): relating to the Greek philosopher Pythagoras (c.582–c.507 B.C.E.), who believed that the essence of things was number, and that all relationships—even abstract ethical concepts like justice—could be expressed numerically

3 hold sway above (literary): hold power over

3 flux (n): continuous movement and change

4 reverberate (v): echo

4 make a mockery of (v): to make ridiculous and useless

4 alleviate (v): to make less severe

Working with Words

Russell's remarkable vocabulary astonishes most readers because his simple words are made to express deep feelings and complex ideas. He wrote the essay to address readers with a similar philosophical background, yet a person not familiar with his background could also readily grasp his profound thoughts.

Exercise 1

Read over the following quotations from Russell's essay and try to rephrase them in more ordinary language:

1. "[O]ne shivering consciousness looks over the rim of the world into the cold unfathomable lifeless abyss."
2. "Love and knowledge, so far as they were possible, led upward toward the heavens."
3. "Echoes of cries of pain reverberate in my heart."

Exercise 2

Read these quotations from Russell's essay and answer the questions that follow each.

1. "Three passions . . . have governed my life." What part of speech is *passion*? What is the adjective form of the word? Write a sentence using the adjective form.
2. One of Russell's governing passions was his "unbearable pity for the suffering of mankind." *Pity* here is used as a noun, but it can also be a verb, and it has adjectival forms. Write two sentences, using *pity* as a verb in one and an adjectival form of *pity* in the other.
3. The author's passions pushed him "to the very verge of despair." Use *despair* as a verb in a sentence.
4. "[L]ove . . . brings ecstasy." What is the adjectival form of *ecstasy*? Is there a verb form for *ecstasy*?

5. Love gave Russell a consciousness of relationships. The verbal phrase of *consciousness* is *to be conscious of*. Use this verbal phrase in a sentence.
6. "[I]n the union of love I have seen, in mystic miniature, the prefiguring vision of the heaven that saints and poets have imagined." Write a sentence using the word *miniature* as an adjective.
7. Russell tried to apprehend mathematics, the power of numbers, spoken of by the philosopher Pythagoras. There is a noun form for *apprehend*. Write a sentence using its noun form. There is also an adjectival form. Use it in a sentence.
8. *Reverberate* is used as a verb by Russell. Change it to its noun form and use the noun in a sentence.
9. Pain makes a mockery of human life. Use the verb form of *mockery* in a sentence. What is the adjectival form of *mockery*? What is a synonym for *mockery*?
10. "I long to alleviate the evil." Here, *alleviate* is a verb. Use the noun form in a sentence. What is a synonym of *alleviate*? Use it in a sentence.

Exercise 3

Write in the missing words, but do not use the same ones that are in the Russell essay. Instead, find synonyms for Russell's words.

Three _____ that have _____ Bertrand Russell are the _____ for love and _____ and the resulting _____ for all life. The desire for _____ brings him much _____ and gives him a sense of his own special place in the world. The _____ for _____ helps him _____ the physical universe and human beings. Finally, _____ allows him to care deeply for _____. His _____ to achieve this adds to his own suffering.

Working with the Essay

Simply looking up words in the dictionary cannot always convey the full meaning of language as poetic as that found in this essay by Bertrand Russell, a master of the English language. For example, the power and charm of Russell's last sentence in Paragraph 1 arise from his combined use of **simile** (comparing two different things using the words *like* or *as*) in *like great winds* and **metaphor** (comparing one thing to another in an imaginative way without using *like* or *as*) in *have blown me hither and thither. . . .* By comparing his passions to the *great winds* over *a deep ocean* blowing a ship and pushing it to an extreme, to *the very verge* of an emotional limit, Russell illustrates his uncontrollable feelings using **imagery,** a device mostly used by poets.

Thanks to Russell's skillful use of these literary devices, the abstract objects in his life—*passions, anguish,* and *despair*—are turned into a series of concrete images, which together form a vivid picture in writing, making it easier for readers to comprehend, to relate, and to appreciate.

RESPONDING TO THE READING

- If the thesis is stated, identify it; if it is implied, write it in your own words.
- What do you think is the purpose of this essay? Give reasons for your opinion.
- Who do you think is the intended audience of this essay? Give reasons for your opinion.

Comprehension

1. What does Russell mean by his title, "What I Have Lived For"?
2. For Russell, in what way is pity different from love and knowledge?
3. What do you think Russell means when he claims he was driven to the *verge of despair* by his passions?
4. What three reasons does Russell give for seeking love?
5. What types of knowledge did Russell seek?
6. Why does Russell mention Pythagoras?
7. Is the first sentence in Paragraph 4 necessary? Why or why not?
8. What reasons does Russell give for pity's bringing him back to earth?

Analysis

1. How is the thesis statement supported in the essay?
2. How is coherence achieved in Paragraph 2?
3. Is Russell's concluding paragraph too short to be effective? Why or why not?
4. How does the concluding paragraph relate to Russell's thesis statement?
5. How is unity achieved in Russell's essay?
6. In what order does Russell arrange his supporting details—is it chronological, climactic, logical, or random order? Do you think it is appropriate for the essay? Why or why not?

Discussion/Writing Suggestions

1. What has made your life worth living? Start by identifying the three most important things in your life and then, using reasons and examples, show readers in a paragraph why *one* of them is important.
2. Would you, like Russell, choose to live your life again? Why or why not? Explain your answer, using reasons and references to actual experiences in your life.

   - Other essays in this book that discuss life's significance include those by Timothy Findley (p. 92), Pico Iyer (p. 96), Nicola Bleasby (p. 109), Stephen L. Carter (p. 132), Judith Viorst (p. 142), Charlie Angus (p. 180), Margaret Laurence (p. 202), Michael Dorris (p. 208), and Rosie DiManno (p. 211).

Writing and Its Rewards

Richard Marius

Richard Marius (1933–1999) was an American historian, educator, and author of novels and non-fiction. He was a newspaper reporter while attending college. After earning M.A. and Ph.D. degrees at Yale University, he taught history at a number of American universities and was the director of the expository writing program at Harvard University for many years. He was well known for his biographies of Thomas More and Martin Luther. In 1969, his novel The Coming of Rain *was designated the best novel of the year by Friends of American Writers. His books on writing, such as* The McGraw-Hill College Handbook, *co-authored with Harvey Wiener, and textbooks on writing are praised for their commonsensical approach to writing and their readable and humorous style. In the Dictionary of* Literary Biography Yearbook, 1985, *Marius is called "a memorable novelist" and "a good historian with a love of language."*

"Writing and Its Rewards" appeared in A Writer's Companion *(1985), a guide meant for both experienced and developing writers.*

1   Writing is hard work, and although it may become easier with practice it is seldom easy. Most of us have to write and rewrite to write anything well. We try to write well so people will read our work. Readers nowadays will seldom struggle to understand difficult writing unless someone—a teacher perhaps—forces them to do so. Samuel Johnson, the great eighteenth-century English writer, conversationalist, and lexicographer°, said, "What is written without effort is in general read without pleasure." Today what is written without effort is seldom read at all.

2   Writing takes time—lots of time. Good writers do not dash off° a piece in an hour and get on to other things. They do not wait until the night before a dead-line to begin to write. Instead they plan. They write a first draft. They revise it. They may then think through that second draft and write it once again. Even small writing tasks may require enormous investments of time. If you want to become a writer, you must be serious about the job, willing to spend hours dedicated to your work.

3   Most writers require some kind of solitude°. That does not mean the extreme of the cork-lined room where the great French writer Marcel Proust composed his huge works in profound silence. It does mean mental isolation—shutting yourself off from the distractions around you even if you happen to be pounding a computer keyboard in a noisy newspaper office. You choose to write rather than do other things, and you must concentrate on what you are doing.

4   In a busy world like ours, we take a risk when we isolate ourselves and give up other pursuits to write. We don't know how our writing will come out. All writers fail sometimes. Successful writers pick themselves up° after failure and try again. As you write, you must read your work again and again, thinking of your purpose,

weighing your words°, testing your organization, examining your evidence, checking for clarity. You must pay attention to the thousands and thousands of details embodied in° words and experience. You must trust your intuitions°; if something does not sound right, do it again. And again. And again.

5   Finally you present your work to readers as the best you can do. After you submit a final draft, it is too late to make excuses, and you should not do so. Not everybody will like your final version. You may feel insecure about it even when you have done your best. You may like your work at first and hate it later. Writers wobble° back and forth in their judgments. Chaucer, Tolstoy and Auden are all on record for rejecting some of their works others have found enduring° and grand. Writing is a parable° of life itself.

Vocabulary

1 lexicographer (n): writer of a dictionary

2 dash off (v): to write or draw something very quickly

3 solitude (n): the state of being alone, especially when you find it pleasant

4 pick up (v): to make someone feel better

4 weigh your words (idiom): to choose your words carefully so that you say exactly what you mean

4 (to be) embodied in (v): to be expressed in

4 intuition (n): the ability to know something by using your feelings rather than your mind

5 wobble (v): to move from side to side in an unsteady way

5 enduring (adj): lasting for a long time

5 parable (n): story with a moral or spiritual lesson, especially one of those recorded in the Bible

Working with Words

Phrasal Verbs

Phrasal verbs (sometimes called multi-word verbs) are verbs that consist of two, or sometimes three, words. The first word is a verb, and it is followed by an adverb (e.g., *turn down*) or a preposition (e.g., *eat into*) or both (*put up with*). These adverbs or prepositions are sometimes called particles.

The meaning of some phrasal verbs, such as *sit down*, is easy to guess because the verb and the particle keep their usual meaning. However, many phrasal verbs have idiomatic meanings that you need to learn. The separate meanings of *put, up, with*, for example, do not add up to the meaning of *put up with* (= tolerate).

The meaning of a phrasal verb can sometimes be explained with a one-word verb. However, phrasal verbs are frequently used in spoken English and, if there is a one-word equivalent, it is usually more formal in style. For example, in the sentence "I wish my car didn't *stick out* so much," the style will be much more formal if *stick out* is changed to *protrude*, although both mean "to extend beyond a surface."

Here you have a chance to have some personal experience with phrasal verbs by completing the following tasks:

1. Find the contextual meanings of the following phrasal verbs that Marius uses in his essay:
   dash off (2)
   shut off from (3)
   give up (4)
   come out (4)
   pick up (4)
2. Replace each of the phrasal verbs above with a synonymous phrase, preferably a verb.
3. Comment on the differences in style when phrasal verbs are replaced.
4. In his essay, Marius uses a number of abstract nouns, which follow:
   pleasure (1)
   solitude (3)
   silence (3)
   isolation (3)
   distraction (3)
   failure (4)
   intuition (4)
   Find the verb and/or adjective(s) for each of the listed words.

Working with the Essay

In this essay Richard Marius practises the simple and direct style he advocated as both a professional writer and a coach for writers-in-training. Not only do most of his words belong to the common core of the English language, but his sentence structure also strives to be simple and clear. Because the piece was written as part of a writing handbook, many sentences, especially in Paragraphs 4 and 5, are imperative sentences that prescribe *do's and don'ts* to the target group of readers.

In spite of its simple and direct style, however, the essay could not be fully understood if the reader missed the numerous references Marius made to names like Samuel Johnson (English writer, 1709–1784), Marcel Proust (French writer, 1871–1922), Geoffrey Chaucer (English poet, c.1345–1400), Leo Nikolaevich Tolstoy (Russian writer, 1828–1910), and W. H. Auden (English poet, 1907–1973). When he makes these references, Marius is alluding to some "big names" in world literature. As we learned in Unit One, an allusion is usually an implicit reference to another work of literature or art or to a well-known person or event. When using allusions, a writer expects the reader to "pick up" the references. An allusion may enrich a piece of writing and give it depth. Yet, when missed, allusions would have little or no effect. It is the reader's responsibility, then, to find out the full meaning hidden under certain proper names and unfamiliar references.

To be an active and analytical reader, you should learn how to find different types of information from a variety of sources. Today, the wide use of the Internet has made our life much easier. However, the most reliable reference tools for researching any allusion remain such reputable volumes as *The Encyclopaedia Britannica* and *The Oxford Companion to Literature* (volumes for specific national literature, such as Canadian literature, are available).

RESPONDING TO THE READING

- If the thesis is stated, identify it; if it is implied, write it in your own words.
- What do you think is the purpose of this essay? Give reasons for your opinion.
- Who do you think is the intended audience of this essay? Give reasons for your opinion.

Comprehension

1. What could Marius mean when he writes, "Today what is written without effort is seldom read at all"?
2. In what way does writing take "lots of time"?
3. How can writers concentrate on writing, in Marius's opinion?
4. Marius addresses his readers directly. Find two examples where he talks directly to his readers.
5. What is the topic sentence of the second paragraph? How is it supported?
6. What is the key point made in the third paragraph? How does Marius support it?
7. In Paragraph 4, find the two sentence fragments Marius wrote.
8. What point does Marius make in Paragraph 4? State it in your own words.
9. In what order does Marius arrange his supporting details—is it chronological, climactic, logical, or random? Do you think it is appropriate for the essay? Why or why not?
10. How is coherence achieved in the essay? Is it by means of implied or stated transitional devices?

Analysis

1. What is the meaning of Marius's last sentence—"Writing is a parable of life itself"?
2. How does the concluding paragraph relate to Marius's thesis statement?
3. If you were to change the title of Marius's essay, what would it be?
4. How does Marius's essay, also written in five paragraphs, differ from the essays by Olenewa, Afriye, Haas, and Russell?

Discussion/Writing Suggestions

1. What is your experience as a writer-in-training? Write a five-paragraph essay to share with your fellow students your experience in writing, revising, and editing.

2. If you don't agree with Marius on some points he makes in the essay, write one or two paragraphs to voice your different opinion.

3. Marius's essay contains some proven and practical advice for new writers. Write an essay to discuss in what ways this essay has changed your thoughts about writing.

- Other essays in this book that focus on communication are by Charles Dickens (p. 10), Kurt Vonnegut (p. 72), Margaret Atwood (p. 85), Pico Iyer (p. 96), Stuart Johns (p. 103), Peggy Lampotang (p. 129), Dan Zollmann (p. 166), and Russell Baker (p. 316).

How to Write with Style

Kurt Vonnegut

Kurt Vonnegut (1922–) is one of America's most respected novelists. He is noted for his thematic interest in showing that though humans may live in a purposeless universe full of self-seeking manipulations, there is hope for something better. He began his writing career as an editor for Cornell Daily Sun *in his university years and taught at high schools and universities before becoming a full-time writer. As an award-winning writer, Vonnegut is best known for his science fiction masterpieces, such as* Slaughterhouse Five *(1969). As the* Dictionary of Literary Biography *comments, Kurt Vonnegut's contribution to American literature is "twofold: through his artistry (and persistence) he has helped to elevate the pulp genre of science fiction to the level of critical recognition, and through his philosophy he offers a mixture of wistful humanism and cynical existentialism."*

This essay first appeared as an advertisement sponsored by a paper company that claimed in a sidebar to "believe in the power of the printed word" in 1996.

1 Newspaper reporters and technical writers are trained to reveal almost nothing about themselves in their writings. This makes them freaks° in the world of writers, since almost all of the other ink-stained wretches in that world reveal a lot about themselves to readers. We call these revelations, accidental and intentional, elements of style.

2 These revelations tell us as readers what sort of person it is with whom we are spending time. Does the writer sound ignorant or informed, stupid or bright, crooked or honest, humorless or playful—? And on and on.

3 Why should you examine your writing style with the idea of improving it? Do so as a mark of respect for your readers, whatever you're writing. If you scribble your thoughts any which way, your readers will surely feel that you care nothing about them. They will mark you down as an egomaniac° or a chowderhead°—or, worse, they will stop reading you.

4 The most damning revelation you can make about yourself is that you do not know what is interesting and what is not. Don't you yourself like or dislike writers

mainly for what they choose to show you or make you think about? Did you ever admire an empty-headed writer for his or her mastery of the language? No.

5   So your own winning style must begin with ideas in your head.

1. Find a Subject You Care About

6   Find a subject you care about and which you in your heart feel others should care about. It is this genuine caring, and not your games with language, which will be the most compelling and seductive° element in your style.

7   I am not urging you to write a novel, by the way—although I would not be sorry if you wrote one, provided you genuinely cared about something. A petition to the mayor about a pothole in front of your house or a love letter to the girl next door will do.

2. Do Not Ramble, Though

8   I won't ramble° on about that.

3. Keep It Simple

9   As for your use of language: Remember that two great masters of language, William Shakespeare and James Joyce, wrote sentences which were almost child-like when their subjects were most profound. "To be or not to be?" asks Shakespeare's Hamlet. The longest word is three letters long. Joyce, when he was frisky°, could put together a sentence as intricate and as glittering as a necklace for Cleopatra, but my favorite sentence in his short story "Eveline" is this one: "She was tired." At that point in the story, no other words could break the heart of a reader as those three words do.

10   Simplicity of language is not only reputable°, but perhaps even sacred. The Bible opens with a sentence well within the writing skills of a lively fourteen-year-old: "In the beginning God created the heaven and the earth."

4. Have the Guts to Cut

11   It may be that you, too, are capable of making necklaces for Cleopatra, so to speak. But your eloquence should be the servant of the ideas in your head. Your rule might be this: If a sentence, no matter how excellent, does not illuminate your subject in some new and useful way, scratch it out.

5. Sound Like Yourself

12   The writing style which is most natural for you is bound to echo the speech you heard when a child. English was the novelist Joseph Conrad's third language, and much that seems piquant° in his use of English was no doubt colored by his first language, which was Polish. And lucky indeed is the writer who has grown up in Ireland, for the English spoken there is so amusing and musical. I myself grew up in Indianapolis, where common speech sounds like a band saw cutting galvanized tin, and employs a vocabulary as unornamental as a monkey wrench.

13   In some of the more remote hollows of Appalachia, children still grow up hearing songs and locutions of Elizabethan times. Yes, and many Americans grow up hearing a language other than English, or an English dialect a majority of Americans cannot understand.

14   All these varieties of speech are beautiful, just as the varieties of butterflies are beautiful. No matter what your first language, you should treasure it all your life. If

it happens not to be standard English, and if it shows itself when you write standard English, the result is usually delightful, like a very pretty girl with one eye that is green and one that is blue.

15   I myself find that I trust my own writing most, and others seem to trust it most, too, when I sound most like a person from Indianapolis, which is what I am. What alternatives do I have? The one most vehemently recommended by teachers has no doubt been pressed on you, as well: to write like cultivated Englishmen of a century or more ago.

6. Say What You Mean to Say

16   I used to be exasperated° by such teachers, but am no more. I understand now that all those antique essays and stories with which I was to compare my own work were not magnificent for their datedness or foreignness, but for saying precisely what their authors meant them to say. My teachers wished me to write accurately, always selecting the most effective words, and relating the words to one another unambiguously, rigidly, like parts of a machine. The teachers did not want to turn me into an Englishman after all. They hoped that I would become understandable—and therefore understood. And there went my dream of doing with words what Pablo Picasso did with paint or what any number of jazz idols did with music. If I broke all the rules of punctuation, had words mean whatever I wanted them to mean, and strung them together higgledy-piggledy°, I would simply not be understood. So you, too, had better avoid Picasso-style or jazz-style writing, if you have something worth saying and wish to be understood.

17   Readers want our pages to look very much like pages they have seen before. Why? This is because they themselves have a tough job to do, and they need all the help they can get from us.

7. Pity the Readers

18   They have to identify thousands of little marks on paper, and make sense of them immediately. They have to *read,* an art so difficult that most people don't really master it even after having studied it all through grade school and high school—twelve long years.

19   So this discussion must finally acknowledge that our stylistic options as writers are neither numerous nor glamorous, since our readers are bound to be such imperfect artists. Our audience requires us to be sympathetic and patient teachers, ever willing to simplify and clarify—whereas we would rather soar high above the crowd, singing like nightingales.

20   That is the bad news. The good news is that we Americans are governed under a unique Constitution, which allows us to write whatever we please without fear of punishment. So the most meaningful aspect of our styles, which is what we choose to write about, is utterly unlimited.

8. For Really Detailed Advice

21   For a discussion of literary style in a narrower sense, in a more technical sense, I commend to your attention *The Elements of Style,* by William Strunk, Jr., and E. B. White (Macmillan, 1979). E. B. White is, of course, one of the most admirable literary stylists this country has so far produced.

22   You should realize, too, that no one would care how well or badly Mr. White
expressed himself, if he did not have perfectly enchanting° things to say.

Vocabulary

1 freak (n, slang): a person who is considered unusual because of his/her behaviour

3 egomaniac (n): a person who has a psychologically abnormal egotism (thinking he/she is better or more important than others)

3 chowderhead (n, slang): a stupid person

6 seductive (adj): attractive, tempting

8 ramble (v): talk about something in a confused way for a long time

9 frisky (adj): full of energy

10 reputable (adj): considered honest and to provide a good service

12 piquant (adj): when describing writing—exciting and interesting

16 exasperate (v): annoy or irritate very much

16 higgledy-piggledy (adv, informal): in an untidy way that lacks any order

22 enchanting (adj): attractive and pleasing

Working with Words

To test your ability to read from context, look at some of the idiomatic expressions Kurt Vonnegut uses. Once you have read over these expressions in the context of their sentences, try to explain the meaning of each in your own words.

1. If you scribble your thoughts *any which way,* your readers will surely feel that you care nothing about them.
2. They will *mark you down* as an egomaniac or a chowderhead—or, worse, they will stop reading you.
3. I won't *ramble on* about that.
4. At that point in the story, no other words could *break the heart* of a reader as those three words do.
5. *Have the guts* to cut.
6. It may be that you, too, are capable of making necklaces for Cleopatra, *so to speak.*
7. English was the novelist Joseph Conrad's third language, and much that seems piquant in his use of English was no doubt *colored by* his first language, which was Polish.
8. The one most vehemently recommended by teachers has no doubt *been pressed on you,* as well.
9. Our audience requires us to be sympathetic and patient teachers, ever willing to simplify and clarify—whereas we would rather *soar high above the crowd,* singing like nightingales.
10. A love letter to the girl next door *will do.*

In the following brief summary of the Vonnegut essay, write in the missing words. Do not use the same words the author wrote; instead, use synonyms—words that are different but convey the same meaning.

Kurt Vonnegut provides eight _____ to improve your writing style so that readers will not only _____ but also _____ you. First, find a _____ that you _____ but keep your discussion short. Make your language _____ and direct and be willing to _____ unnecessary words. Try to write so that you sound natural; however, you must follow the rules of _____ English to communicate effectively. A good writer is aware of the _____ readers often have. For more _____ advice, Vonnegut suggests consulting *The Elements of Style*.

Working with the Essay

Like Richard Marius, Kurt Vonnegut addresses his audience directly in this essay. In fact, Vonnegut goes much further than Marius as he practically conducts a conversational workshop on how to write with style with new writers. What is noticeable in the essay are not only the structure of this "writing workshop," but also the personal style of this master writer.

First of all, his essay is organized differently from the other essays collected in this unit. The most obvious difference lies in the fact that it is not composed in the five-paragraph structure. Also, instead of presenting his supporting details in the body paragraphs arranged according to his purpose and connected by stated or implied transitional devices, he divides the body into eight sections, each beginning with a numbered subheading, which in many cases act as the "topic sentence" of that section. This "point-form" structure greatly facilitates and enhances the clarity of Vonnegut's presentation, which falls into the general category of process analysis (see p. 100).

As Vonnegut himself puts it in the first paragraph, this essay contains quite a few "revelations, accidental and intentional, elements of style." As readers, we find these revelations both entertaining and instructive. In spite of the serious nature of his subject, Vonnegut's essay is by no means heavy or boring. On the contrary, it is filled with interesting autobiographical details and teeming with his delightful sense of humour. Have a look at the second section. "Do Not Ramble, Though," states the heading. "I won't ramble on about that," writes Vonnegut. In these two short simple sentences much is revealed about what the author believes and advocates, how he practises his own principle, and why he is a popular writer.

You may also spot many allusions in Vonnegut's essay. Scan for Cleopatra and Pablo Picasso. Who are these people and why does Vonnegut choose to allude to them in support of his argument?

RESPONDING TO THE READING

- If the thesis is stated, identify it; if it is implied, write it in your own words.
- What do you think is the purpose of this essay? Give reasons for your opinion.
- Who do you think is the intended audience of this essay? Give reasons for your opinion.

Comprehension

1. In Vonnegut's opinion, how should you choose the subject you write about?
2. What kind of language should you use when you write?
3. What is the best way to say what you mean?
4. What approach to your readers should you take?
5. Why is it important to edit your work?
6. In what order does Vonnegut arrange his suggestions, chronologically, climactically, logically, or in random order? Do you think the chosen order is appropriate for the essay? Why or why not?
7. Why is Paragraph 8 only one sentence long?

Analysis

1. What does Vonnegut mean by saying "your eloquence should be the servant of the ideas in your head"?
2. What is Vonnegut suggesting when he reminds us the "readers want our pages to look very much like pages they have seen before"?
3. Find some examples of Vonnegut's sense of humour. What is the effect of his humour on the reader?
4. How is coherence achieved in this essay?
5. Does Section Eight "For Really Detailed Advice" form the conclusion of the essay, or is it just the final suggestion Vonnegut has for the reader?
6. In what ways is Vonnegut's essay different from the other essays in this unit?

Discussion/Writing Suggestions

1. Do you like or dislike Vonnegut's style? Write an essay of five paragraphs to express your opinion on Vonnegut's essay structure, choice of words, and humorous approach to the subject.
2. What have you learned from Vonnegut's "talk" on writing? Write a letter to a friend about this essay, either to recommend it or to advise him or her to avoid it.

    • Other essays that focus on communication are by Charles Dickens (p. 10), Richard Marius (p. 68), Margaret Atwood (p. 85), Pico Iyer (p. 96), Stuart Johns (p. 103), Peggy Lampotang (p. 129), Dan Zollmann (p. 166), and Russell Baker (p. 316).

4

Writing That Informs the Reader

Example, Process Analysis, Comparison and Contrast,
Classification, and Cause and Effect

"The pen is the tongue of the mind." (Miguel de Cervantes 1547–1616)

Analyzing Patterns in Reading and Writing

Rhetoric is the study of the various ways to write effectively either to inform or to affect your reader. Traditionally, there are four major **rhetorical modes**: exposition, narration, description, and argument or persuasion. Rhetoric is the art of using language to impress the reader—to inform, explain, amuse, entertain, affect, or move. This unit focuses on exposition and the variety of **organizational patterns** that can be used to explain information and ideas to the reader.

The reading and writing techniques you have practised so far in this textbook form the basis of all good communication—the purpose of any writing is to share information or ideas. As a reader, your ability to recognize and follow a writer's pattern of thought and the structure chosen by the writer to express ideas will help you read more efficiently and understand what you read more easily. As a writer, having control of those patterns and rhetorical modes will enable you to organize and structure your own writing effectively. Once you have determined your subject and attitude, you will be able to choose the most appropriate pattern of development. Additionally, organizing your writing into distinct patterns not only enables you to express yourself more clearly but also allows your readers to follow you more easily. Reading works by both student and professional writers can show you the value of learning basic techniques and applying them to your own compositions.

What you will notice is that writers rarely adhere strictly to one pattern of organization. Although an essay may be structured mainly by one pattern of development, it is often necessary for the writer to explain what something means (*definition*), or to give an example to show an aspect of the subject (*example*), or make a comparison to develop the subject effectively (*comparison and contrast*).

Writers mix and match the patterns of organization according to their purpose and audience, so recognizing a particular pattern helps you to analyze and evaluate the quality of an argument and the impact of its presentation.

Major Patterns of Organization

EXAMPLE	Explains through illustrations or specific instances
PROCESS	Illustrates how to do something or how something happened
COMPARISON/CONTRAST	Draws similarities and differences between two subjects
CLASSIFICATION	Sorts subjects into categories based on an organizing principle
CAUSE AND EFFECT	Shows how subjects can be related through conditions (causes) and consequences (effects)

Other Patterns of Development: Analogy and Definition

Using an Analogy

"Life is like a bowl of cherries; sometimes it's the pits." When you use an analogy, you compare two apparently unlike terms (life and the bowl of cherries). An analogy allows you to explain a complex or abstract idea by stating it in different terms. This is probably why it is so popular with science writers like Jay Ingram, Maureen Littlejohn, and James Rettie. The analogy is established to explain the idea to the reader. Whereas a comparison examines similar things and a contrast focuses on their differences, an analogy shows how things that seem to bear no relationship to one another are alike (life and cherries).

The purpose of the comparison made in an analogy is to explain the subject in question—*life*—by means of another item—*a bowl of cherries*. The comparison, because it is a surprising one, forces the reader to think about life in a new way and to gain insight into it. Frequently, an abstract idea is compared to a concrete object as with life and cherries. J. Anthony Lukas's essay "Pinball" contains such an analogy; in fact, it is a typical essay of analogy.

Analogy is used to explain something that is complex or unfamiliar by establishing an imaginative comparison to something simple and well-known. For example, a business organization can be analogous to a beehive—a hive of industry. Essays of analogy are rare because this pattern of organization is more often used as supporting detail. In fact, many of the essays in this book use analogies to support their arguments: an atom is analogous to the solar system, and a person is analogous to a banana. In addition to illustrating a point, an analogy is often used to create a stylistic or dramatic effect, so analogy is a literary device found frequently in poetry, novels, and short stories.

Using a Definition

A definition explains the meaning of a term. When you define a word, term, or concept in depth, you are either providing a personal commentary on what the specific subject means or giving facts and information to support your definition. Writers tend to use a definition or a paragraph of definition within an essay organized by another pattern of development rather than compose an entire essay of definition.

You need to understand a term before you can define it for others. You will probably turn to the dictionary to be sure of the term's exact denotation. By all means read the dictionary, but don't just copy the definition. Instead, paraphrase the meaning of the term briefly in your own words. A word can have several dictionary definitions, and not all of them will be appropriate for the development of your essay.

In addition, it is important to limit your term before you start defining it. Some terms such as *snow, marriage,* or *beer* have definite, concrete meanings or specific physical properties that most people can agree on. However, abstract terms such as *honesty, freedom,* or *love* are more dependent on a person's point of view because such terms play on people's feelings more than their physical senses. For example, you could fill several library shelves writing about the term *love.* To limit your definition, you could write about a particular love such as *mother's love, romantic love, first love, platonic love,* and so on.

A definition is a practical tool whether you are explaining a medical procedure to a patient or giving advice about installing a new muffler in a car. You will find definitions included in articles, memos, letters, talks, or all kinds of information sessions. Whatever the occasion, try to avoid sounding like an encyclopedia entry when you are using a definition.

Essay of Example

An **example** is a verbal snapshot, either written or spoken. It helps the reader "see" what you are explaining. A written example, or a set of examples, works like a photograph in a magazine or a diagram in a textbook. It helps readers see, experience, or feel an idea. An example is an explanatory group of words in one or more sentences that makes an idea "come alive" by using concrete details. The details can be descriptions, anecdotes, definitions, analogies, references, data, facts, allusions, and citations.

We use examples in all sorts of communication, whether formal reports, essays, e-mail, or informal conversations. Most essays, regardless of their pattern of development, will incorporate some examples to illustrate a point. Most essays organized by a particular pattern, say process analysis, will incorporate an example or two in their supporting details. Writing effective examples is a useful technique for you to master. In Units 1, 2, and 3 you have read some essays of example: "No Nation So Favoured," "Effective Driving," "Reading Is My True Love," and "The Common Stone" are all organized by this pattern. MacLennan cites examples to demonstrate how Canada is favoured; Olenewa and Afriye provide personal examples of effective driving and enjoyable reading respectively, while Haas collects examples to show the usefulness of the stone. Other writers like Ginsburg, Ingram, Russell, and Vonnegut also make extensive use of examples and anecdotes within the organizational patterns of their choice; however, Ginsburg's essay is mainly a persuasive *cause and effect* essay, Ingram's an *informational process analysis,* Russell's a *classification* essay, and Vonnegut's a *directional process analysis.*

Using an Anecdote

An anecdote is a useful form of example; it is in essence a short story or incident that illustrates a particular point about a person or an object. It can be used as a very effective example, as shown in this brief anecdote from novelist Robertson Davies:

> Another learned professor I know, who would scorn to settle a problem by tossing a coin (which is a humble appeal to Fate to declare itself), told me quite seriously that he had resolved a matter related to university affairs by consulting the I Ching. And why not? (p. 151)

An anecdote may be extended and more developed as you can see in this one taken from author Timothy Findley's essay "Remembrance":

> I am my Aunt Marg, for instance, telling me not to lean into the cemetery over the fence at Foxbar Road. I am not me leaning over the fence, I am her voice—because that is what I remember. And I am all the gravestones I was looking at when she called me. And the fence boards that supported me. And the sun on my back. But I am not that little boy. I don't remember him at all. I remember him falling and being picked up—but I am the distance he fell and the hands that lifted him, not the bump in between. I remember the sound of my own voice crying—but not the feel of it. That voice is gone. (p. 93)

An anecdote could also act as a sure-fire attention-grabber as David Ginsburg demonstrates in his essay:

> "Do you mind if I smoke?" my travelling companion asked me.
> "Not at all," I replied. "In fact, I should be most pleased if you would. It would be good for my business."
> "What do you do?"
> "I am a cancer specialist and I look after patients with lung cancer."
> He seemed utterly taken aback.
> This is a most tasteless anecdote. Would it be any less crass were I to have said that I was a heart surgeon repairing vessels damaged by cigarettes? Or an undertaker? (pp. 33–4)

Writing Strategy

In an essay of example, the content is the development of a series of illustrations that support the thesis by showing the reader various aspects of its subject; the development is based on your need to explain and clarify the subject.

In your introduction, discuss the subject in general terms. You can provide some general background information about your chosen subject or explain why this subject appeals to you. You can refer to the traditional definition of your term. However, no matter what you decide to do, begin your essay with an attention-grabber. Here is student author Victoria Santiago's playful opening:

Winter! Does the very word strike a chill in your heart? Does the thought of winter send shivers down your spine?

Your thesis statement identifies the subject and establishes your focus. Look at how Victoria Santiago introduces her thesis. She first provides a brief, basic approach to her subject:

We have to put more effort into enjoying this season than any of the others.

Then she continues by stating what the term means to her, presenting the key points for her essay, and sending signals to the reader in her thesis statement:

Clearly, winter is the season that receives most attention from us through our scientific explanation, our mythological ideas and our personal determination.

In your body paragraphs, you need to present clear and strong information using interesting and relevant facts, examples, or anecdotes to support the key points presented in the thesis statement. Do not use any examples that will not support the subject. One sure method for determining the validity of your thesis statement in an essay developed by the use of examples is to ascertain that your key examples are accurate and relevant and that you present them clearly and coherently.

It is always worthwhile to work out an outline before you begin to write. This outline could be a list of points that will chart your introduction, conclusion, and body paragraphs and assign concrete examples to each paragraph in the order you have chosen to develop your essay.

SAMPLE STUDENT ESSAY OF EXAMPLE

Thoughts of Winter

Victoria Santiago

1   Winter! Does the very word strike a chill in your heart? Does the thought of winter send shivers down your spine? In my parents' homeland, the Philippines, winter is a very different season compared with what we experience here in Canada. With the prospect of the next winter looming, it is time to think about winter here in Canada. There are scientific explanations for the seasonal changes, but they seem to focus on why winter happens. There are more famous myths about winter than any other season. We have to put more effort into enjoying this season than any of the others. Clearly, winter is the season that receives most attention from us

through our scientific explanation, our mythological ideas and our personal determination.

2   Winter happens inevitably every year around the same time. It brings us colder and darker days, and with the falling temperatures we have snow, ice and even blizzards. Scientific explanations of the seasons are about why winter happens, not why summer, spring or fall occurs. There is a popular modern idea that winter is caused by the fact that the earth is farther from the sun in winter than in summer. This is not true. In fact, winter occurs in the Northern Hemisphere when the earth is closest to the sun. Winter is caused by the tilt of the earth in relation to the sun. In winter, the sunlight hits our hemisphere at an oblique angle, so the same amount of solar radiation is spread over a larger area. In addition, the oblique angle to the sun means the sunlight must travel further through the earth's atmosphere and this decreases the already limited heat from the sun. Precisely when winter begins and ends varies depending on geography and culture, but for us in southern Canada, it has always begun by December and it ends sometime in April. However, our calendar dictates that the season begins with the winter solstice which is the shortest day of the year, December 21, and it ends with the spring equinox, which occurs on March 21. Strangely, December 21 is also known as midwinter, but that probably comes from the tradition of the winter solstice.

3   As you can see, the real cause of our winter is hardly romantic, but there are lots of myths about winter. A lot of them are about death and rebirth on the winter solstice. There was the birthday of Osiris, an ancient Egyptian god of fertility and death; the ancient Romans celebrated the Unconquered Sun in their Saturnalia festival; and greatest festival for the Celts and Vikings was the winter celebration of Yule which is also about death and new life. The winter myth I know best is a Greek one that explains the origins of winter and it has associations with death and rebirth. In that myth, the God of the Underworld and the Dead, Hades, kidnaps Persephone to be his wife. Demeter her mother, the Goddess of the Earth, tries to make him return Persephone to her; however, because Persephone has eaten the food of the dead, it is decided that Persephone would spend six months with Demeter and six months with Hades. During the time when her daughter is Queen of the Underworld, Demeter becomes depressed and causes winter. Everything seems to be dead; the days are short and dark and the weather is so cold that many animals hibernate or migrate and many plants and trees die back until spring.

4   That myth might also have started as an explanation of the psychological response to winter many people actually have. Our long, harsh winters can change the habits and moods of people. From the end of November on, many people have a sense of melancholy. This sense of sadness has lots of nicknames: "winter blues," "February blahs," "Holiday depression," or the doldrums. The worst cases of this depression are diagnosed as seasonal affective disorder (SAD), and the symptoms include excessive sleep, fatigue, depression, and physical aches. It is caused by decreased exposure to sunlight and vitamin D because of winter. There is hardly this amount of attention paid to people who dislike heat in summer or rain in spring. This is how winter is the most interesting season; it is the season that requires more of our effort. In winter, we have to pay extra attention to what we wear, it takes longer to get ready each morning and just going outside can be a

difficult task. In winter, visiting friends takes more planning and energy. There are lots of winter activities if we can make the effort to enjoy them. Skiing, snowboarding and sledding make us zoom over the snow while making snow-angels, building snow-men and having snow-ball fights bring out our sense of play. There are lots of things to do on the ice besides enjoying our national game of hockey; we can skate, fish and create ice sculptures. There is more to winter than gloom and freezing cold.

5   Science and mythology can explain the natural environment to us and help us deal with it. Winter has a significant impact on our society. In winter our bright, colourful world becomes white and grey, and we have to make an effort to venture outside, so for lots of Canadians, winter brings out our best qualities. We don't despair. As Canadians, we are not defeated by winter. We are the world's greatest hockey players after all.

Comprehension

1. Underline the thesis statement and its restatement.
2. Victoria Santiago introduces her subject in the first paragraph in three ways. What are they?
3. Identify the topic sentences in the body paragraphs. Does Santiago follow her thesis?
4. How does Santiago explain the period of winter? Find her separate examples, reasons, and explanations.
5. Santiago presents two versions of the cause of winter. What are they?
6. What is the difference between the two causes of winter as Santiago describes them?
7. What transitional technique does Santiago employ when she moves from the cause of winter to discuss people's psychological responses to it?
8. What types of supporting details does Santiago provide in Paragraph 5? Are they descriptions, references, data, facts, allusions, citations, or anecdotes?
9. Examine Santiago's conclusion. Is it effective? Why or why not?

Analysis

1. Do the facts, examples, or the anecdotes seem convincing to you? Why might that be?
2. What is your opinion of this essay? Be prepared to support your response.
3. How do you feel about winter? Be prepared to explain your attitude.

READINGS: ESSAYS OF EXAMPLE

The four essays that follow make use of very different types of examples. In "The Great Communicator," Margaret Atwood chooses anecdotes for her very personal tribute to Northrop Frye. David Suzuki makes extensive use of statistics and data as well as allusion and anecdote to create a powerful argument of social concern in his essay "Overpopulation Is Bad, But Overconsumption Is Worse." Timothy

Findley reflects on the power of memory in his essay "Remembrance" through personal anecdotes; his reflection on these remembrances allows him to claim that we are all defined by our memories. Finally, Pico Iyer's witty and sophisticated essay "In Praise of the Humble Comma" uses many allusions while vividly exemplifying the very thing he is advocating.

The Great Communicator

Margaret Atwood

Margaret Atwood (1939–) is an internationally acclaimed poet, novelist, and critic as well as one of Canada's most successful novelists. Her novels are varied in genre and theme although women's issues are always a central focus for her. Among her many novels are The Handmaid's Tale *(1985), which won the Arthur C. Clarke Award and has been made into a movie and an opera.* The Blind Assassin *(2000) won the prestigious Booker Prize. Atwood has also written extensively on Canadian identity, human rights, and environmental issues and has edited many literary anthologies. She has been vice-chairman of the Writers' Union of Canada, and from 1984 to 1986 she was president of P.E.N. International, a pressure group committed to freeing writers who are political prisoners. Elected a senior fellow of Massey College of the University of Toronto, she has 16 honorary degrees, including a doctorate from Victoria College (1987) and was inducted into Canada's Walk of Fame in 2001.*

This essay first appeared in the Globe and Mail *on the occasion of Northrop Frye's death in 1999. Atwood first met Northrop Frye at the University of Toronto where she was a student. In "The Great Communicator," she pays tribute to Frye, praising his many accomplishments, so it is a* **eulogy** *that reflects on his importance in her life. To demonstrate that Northrop Frye was "the great communicator," she uses a series of examples, which are mostly anecdotes.*

1   I first encountered Northrop Frye where so many did: in a lecture room, at Victoria College in the University of Toronto, where he taught for five decades. It was his famous "Bible" course, considered *de rigueur*° for any serious literature student at the time. I don't know what I was expecting: thunder, perhaps, or a larger-than-life talking statue. What actually appeared was an unassuming, slightly plump and rumpled figure, with distracted hair and extremely sharp eyes behind Dickensian spectacles. This person placed one hand on the desk in front of him, took a step forward, took another step forward, took a step back, took another step back. While repeating this small dance pattern, he proceeded to speak, without benefit of notes or text, in pure, lucid°, eloquent°, funny and engaging prose, for the space of an hour. This was not a fluke°. He did it every week.

2   Teaching was not something Northrop Frye engaged in as an unimportant and tedious° academic duty. Despite his reputation as the foremost literary critic of his

own and many another generation, both nationally and internationally, he always spoke of himself as an educator. He did not lock literature into an ivory tower°; instead he emphasized its centrality to the development of a civilized and humane society. As a critic, he did not write for other critics, in an esoteric° jargon only a few could comprehend; he wrote instead for the intelligent general reader. His early experiences as a divinity student and preacher stood him in good stead: pick up any of his books and what you will hear (not *see,* for he was enormously conscious of the oral and even the musical values of the word) is a personal voice, speaking to you directly. Because of its style, flexibility and formal elegance, its broad range and systematic structure, his literary criticism takes its place easily within the body of literature itself.

3   That sounds fairly intimidating, and a lot of people were intimidated by Frye. I suppose it's difficult not to be intimidated by someone so brilliant. But intimidation was not something Frye did on purpose. He didn't suffer fools gladly, it's true, and he could be devastatingly ironic when confronted with malicious or willed stupidity; but he was surprisingly gentle with youthful *naiveté°* and simple ignorance. In contrast to the image of austerity and superhuman power others projected on him, he could be quite impish. His students were often startled to find references to current pop songs, comic books or off-colour jokes injected dead-pan° into an otherwise serious-minded lecture on *King Lear* or *Paradise Lost,* which probably intimidated them more: Was there anything this man hadn't read? Apparently not; but since one of his major themes was the way in which plots resemble other plots—whether they are found in fairy tales, epic poems or soap operas—there was nothing he refused to consider. He knew also that the way in which we understand ourselves is less through theory than through story. In the life of any individual, as in the lives of communities and nations, stories are primary.

4   So now I will tell a couple: because, when anyone dies one of the first things we do is tell stories about them. What to choose from? The apocryphal° one about how he first came to Toronto by winning a speed-typing contest? (Actually, he didn't win; but he *was* a very swift typist.) The one about the adulating° woman who said to him, "Oh, Dr. Frye, is there *anything* you don't know?" Norrie, gazing characteristically at his shoes, mumbled that he didn't really know very much about Japanese flower arranging and proceeded to deliver an informed page or two on the subject. Or, from M.T. Kelly, a writer friend with whom he discussed northern-exploration journals: "He came to my book-launch at the Rivoli! Can you picture it? Queen Street West, with the black leather? The man was spiritually generous!"

5   Or the time we had him to dinner and something burnt in the kitchen and the fire alarm went off, waking our young daughter. She wandered downstairs and got into a conversation with Norrie. Despite his well-known social shyness, he had no difficulty talking with a six-year-old, and she herself was enchanted by him. That interlude, not the high-powered adult conversation that surrounded it, was the high point of the evening to him.

6   I think one of the sadnesses of his life was that he never had children. But there are many people, including some who never knew him personally, who will feel orphaned by his death.

Vocabulary

1 *de rigueur* (adj, French): necessary, required

1 lucid (adj): clear to the understanding

1 eloquent (adj): fluent use of language

1 fluke (n): accidental success

2 tedious (adj): dull, boring

2 ivory tower (idiom): academic world

2 esoteric (adj): understood by or restricted to a small group

3 *naiveté* (n, French): lack of sophistication, simplicity

3 dead-pan (adj): without feeling or expression

4 apocryphal (adj): a story probably not based on reality or fact

4 adulating (adj): admiring, praising

RESPONDING TO THE READING

- If the thesis is stated, identify it; if it is implied, write it in your own words.
- What do you think is the purpose of this essay? Give reasons for your opinion.
- Who do you think is the intended audience of this essay? Give reasons for your opinion.

Comprehension

1. Notice how Atwood organizes her examples. Is the chronological sequence appropriate for her essay? Why or why not?
   a. What is the first anecdote she tells? When did it happen and what clues assist you in determining the time?
   b. What is the final anecdote she tells? When did it happen and what clues assist you in determining the time?
2. In both of these anecdotes, Atwood also presents Frye as an endearing human being. What examples help to achieve this effect?
3. In her second paragraph, Atwood stresses that Frye "always spoke of himself as an educator."
   a. How many examples of his role as educator does she present?
   b. What does Atwood identify as Frye's most powerful qualities as an educator?
4. In the third paragraph, Atwood concentrates on Frye's personality. Identify the ways in which she supports her contention that Frye was brilliant as a communicator.
5. In the fourth paragraph, notice how well Atwood has established the transition from her third paragraph. What is the connection?

Analysis

1. In both the first and last anecdotes in the essay, how does Atwood show that Frye was "the great communicator"? Based on these anecdotes, what qualities are essential to a great communicator, according to Atwood?
2. What is the purpose of each of the anecdotes told in Paragraph 4?
3. What does Atwood mean when she says "stories are primary"? Do you agree with her?
4. What is your response to Atwood's essay? Provide examples from the essay to support your point of view.

Discussion/Writing Suggestions

1. Have you been inspired by a teacher or mentor? How and why has this person played an important role in your life?
2. Read Frye's essay "Don't You Think It's Time to Start Thinking?" in Unit 5 on page 19. Would you agree with Atwood that Frye was a great communicator?

   • Other essays that provide personal anecdotes are by Malcolm X (p. 19), David Ginsburg (p. 33), Timothy Findley (p. 92), Pat Capponi (p. 158), Wayson Choy (p. 169), Michael Dorris (p. 208), Rosie DiManno (p. 211), and Almas Zakiuddin (p. 240). And in its own way, Charles Dickens's "Murdering the Innocents" (p. 10) also focuses on good teaching.

Overpopulation Is Bad but Overconsumption Is Worse

David Suzuki

Dr. David Suzuki (1936–) is a world-renowned geneticist. He is a distinguished Canadian professor emeritus, writer, broadcaster, and leading analyst of social and environmental issues. He hosted the radio program Quirks and Quarks *on CBC Radio from 1975 to 1979. Since 1979, Suzuki has hosted* The Nature of Things, *a popular CBC TV science magazine, seen in syndication in over 40 nations. He is also co-founder of the David Suzuki Foundation. In recognition of his work popularizing science and environmental issues, he has been presented with honorary doctorates from universities in Canada, the United States, and Australia. He is also the recipient of many distinguished Canadian and international awards, including the Order of Canada and the UNESCO Kalinga Prize (1986). This statement from his 1985 TV series,* A Planet for the Taking, *sums up his environmental concern: "We have both a sense of the importance of the wilderness and space in our culture and an attitude that it is limitless and therefore we needn't worry." He asks that we make a major "perceptual shift" in our relationship with nature and the wild.*

As this essay demonstrates, Suzuki is a master at explaining the complexities of science and ecological issues in a way that is easily understood. His many examples include statistics, data, and authorities after his opening anecdote. This essay first appeared in the BC Environmental Report *in 1993.*

1 After a recent lecture, two people objected vehemently° to my suggestion that we in industrialized countries are the major cause of global ecological degradation° and pollution. They blamed overpopulation in the Third World. I countered by pointing out that the great disparity° in wealth and consumption between rich and poor countries has to be addressed. Excess population does lead to ecological destruction and it's made worse in the Third World by their access to little of the planet's resources.

2 But each Canadian consumes 16 to 20 times as much as a person in India or China and 60 to 70 times more than someone in Bangladesh. Thus we 1.1 billion people in industrialized nations have the same ecological impact as 17 billion to 77 billion Third World people. The planet certainly could not take 5.5 billion people living as we do. But if we don't cut back consumption and pollution, poorer nations can rightfully aim to emulate° us. My disputants weren't convinced and retorted°: "You're crazy if you expect people in Canada or the U.S. to cut back on consumption. It's natural to want more."

3 More than 2,000 years ago, Aristotle had come to the same conclusion: "The avarice° of mankind is insatiable°." Last century, Leo Tolstoy had backed him up: "Seek among men, from beggar to millionaire, one who is contented with his lot and you will not find one such in a thousand." Alan Durning of the Worldwatch Institute raises the issue in his book *How Much Is Enough?* (W.W. Norton & Co., New York) which opens: "Consumption: the neglected god in the trinity° of issues the world must address if we are to get on a path of development that does not lead to ruin. The other two—population growth and technological change—receive attention; but with consumption, there is often only silence."

4 So is it human nature to want more? Durning suggests that today's appetite for more consumer goods was a deliberate goal of American business and government. Retailing analyst Victor Lebow stated shortly after World War II: "Our enormously productive economy . . . demands that we make consumption our way of life, that we convert the buying and use of goods into rituals, that we seek our spiritual satisfaction, our ego satisfaction, in consumption. . . . We need things consumed, burned up, worn out, replaced, and discarded° at an ever increasing rate."

5 The chairman of the U.S. Council of Economic Advisers in 1953 pronounced the ultimate goal of the American economy was "to produce more consumer goods." And they were immensely successful. The contents of the average North American home today would be the envy of kings and emperors of the past. We now classify cars, televisions, telephones, refrigerators, microwave ovens and stereos as necessities.

6 We even think of ourselves as "consumers" and "shopping" is a recreation. Consumption has become so crucial for the economy that in periods of recession, the consumer is often blamed for not spending enough while business and government seek ways to increase consumer confidence to stimulate spending. Media propaganda° pounds home° the message that consumption brings happiness. But possessions can't fill the emotional and spiritual needs for human relationships, community and some purpose beyond accumulation of wealth and goods.

7   Durning quotes a psychologist who finds "there is very little difference in the levels of reported happiness found in rich and very poor countries." In spite of the steep rise in consumption, the fraction of people who feel happy with life has not changed during the past 40 years. And continued escalation in consumption is not sustainable. Durning says, "In constant dollars, the world's people have consumed as many goods and services since 1950 as all previous generations put together. Since 1940, Americans alone have used up as large a share of the Earth's mineral resources as did everyone before them combined."

8   It is a fact that everything on Earth is limited. So endless increase in consumption cannot continue and will fall. But that does not mean the future must be a bleak° life of denial and sacrifice. Much of our consumption is based on inefficiency and waste. We can reduce our ecological impact severalfold simply by improving our efficiency.

9   Overconsumption is not a goal that society must maintain at all costs; it has become a symptom that something is wrong because no matter how much we possess, we are not fulfilled or satisfied. Our lifestyle exacts a heavy price: violence, alcoholism, burglary, vandalism, drug abuse, alienation, loneliness, pollution and disruption of family and neighbourhood. Making do with less and designing a future that is based in communities with greater self-reliance and self-sufficiency makes ecological and social sense. But we won't get started until we stop trying to shift the responsibility elsewhere.

Vocabulary

1 vehemently (adv): with intensity, expressed forcibly

1 degradation (n): loss of quality or deterioration in performance

1 disparity (n): difference or inequality

2 emulate (v): imitate, especially in order to equal

2 retorted (v) reply in a quick, direct manner

3 avarice (n): greed

3 insatiable (adj): not able to be satisfied

3 trinity (n): a group of three closely related people or things; in Christianity, the unity of Father, Son, and Holy Spirit in one godhead

4 discarded (v): to get rid of

6 propaganda (n): organized spreading of ideas, information or rumour in order to promote or damage an institution or movement

6 pounds home (idiom): to emphasize

8 bleak (adj): not hopeful, discouraging

RESPONDING TO THE READING

- If the thesis is stated, identify it; if it is implied, write it in your own words.
- What do you think is the purpose of this essay? Give reasons for your opinion.
- Who do you think is the intended audience of this essay? Give reasons for your opinion.

Comprehension

1. Suzuki begins with an anecdote in Paragraph 1. What is it?
2. What sorts of examples does Suzuki list in Paragraph 2, and why does he use them?
3. Suzuki introduces different sorts of examples in Paragraph 3. What type of examples are they?
4. In Paragraphs 4 to 7, Suzuki provides many examples of consumption. Identify them.
5. In Paragraphs 4 to 7, Suzuki also considers the reasons that our society is so eager to consume. What are the causes he examines?
6. Paragraph 8 begins, "It is a fact." In your own words, what fact does Suzuki refer to?
7. What ideas does Suzuki present in his conclusion?

Analysis

1. What is the effect of the anecdotes Suzuki presents in this essay?
2. Why does he supply so many statistics and facts in his argument?
3. What is your response to Suzuki's "appeal to authorities" on society in Paragraph 3?
4. Does Suzuki succeed in integrating the data into his conversational style? Why or why not?
5. Does this essay provide an answer to the disputants mentioned in Paragraph 1? Why or why not?
6. How is the tone in Paragraph 8 different from Paragraph 9?
7. Does Suzuki convince you that overconsumption is a grave social and environmental problem? Why or why not?

Discussion/Writing Suggestions

1. The basis of Suzuki's argument is that we in North America are irresponsible in our attitude and behaviour when it comes to the environment. Do you agree with him? Why or why not?
2. What is your response to Suzuki's essay? Use examples from the essay to support your point of view.

   - Other essays that examine social obligation are by Joseph Epstein (p. 36), Rachel Carson (p. 123), Stephen L. Carter (p. 132), James C. Rettie (p. 221), Amartya Sen (p. 252), Derek Cohen (p. 172), Charlie Angus (p. 180), Sang Il Lee (p. 233), and Pat Capponi (p. 158).

Remembrance

Timothy Findley

Timothy Findley (1930–2002) was born in Toronto. As a young man, he studied dance and acting, and he had a successful career as an actor before turning to writing. His third novel, The Wars *(1977), gained Findley both recognition as a major Canadian writer and the Governor General's Literary Award. Findley wrote scripts for television, radio, film, and theatre. While Timothy Findley is best known as the author of novels, such as* Famous Last Words *(1981),* Not Wanted on the Voyage *(1986), and* The Pianoman's Daughter *(1995), he was also a playwright and short-story writer. Very active in the Canadian writing community, Findley helped to found the Writers' Union of Canada and served as its chairperson. He was also president of the Canadian chapter of P.E.N. International. Findley's work has been widely translated and he achieved an international reputation. He received numerous awards and honours, including the Canadian Authors Association Award, the Order of Ontario, the Ontario Trillium Award, and was appointed an Officer of the Order of Canada. Findley believed that a writer had the responsibility to speak out about what was wrong with society.*

This essay comes from his personal memoir, Inside Memory: Pages from a Writer's Workbook *(1990), a collection of articles, journal entries, and reminiscences.*

1   In the plays of Anton Chekhov, there is always a moment of profound silence, broken by the words: "I remember. . . ." What follows inevitably° breaks your heart. A woman will stand there and others will sit and listen and she will say: "I remember the band playing and the firing at the cemetery as they carried the coffin. Though he was a general, in command of a brigade, yet, there weren't many people there. It was raining. Heavy rain and snow."

2   Or some such thing. And she is transformed, this woman, by her memories—absolutely transformed. And as you watch her and listen to her, you are transformed, too—or something inside you is. You change. Your attitude changes. In a way—if it has been well done—your life changes. Why should this be?

3   I think one reason must be that Chekhov discovered the dramatic value of memory—that a woman in tears remembers happiness; that a smiling, laughing man remembers pain. This gives you two views in one: depth and contrast. But, there's more to it than that. Memory, Chekhov also discovered, is the means by which most of us retain our sanity°. The act of remembrance is good for people. Cathartic°. Memory is the purgative° by which we rid ourselves of the present.

4   Because memory is what it is, the first thing we tend to "remember" is that time passes. In going back, we recognize that we've survived the passage of time—and if we've survived what we remember, then it's likely we'll survive the present. Memory is a form of hope.

5   If the memory is a bad one, say of pain or of a death—then it's clouded. The sharpness is blunted. We remember that we were in pain. But the pain itself cannot

be recalled exactly. Not as it was. Because, if we could recall it, then we'd have to be in pain again—and that, except where there's psychological disorder, is a physical and mental impossibility. If you've ever had a bad accident, then you'll remember that you can't remember what happened. But you can recall joy. You can make yourself laugh again and feel again something joyous that happened before.

6   Of course, you can make yourself cry again, too. But the tears aren't as valid as the laughter, because the tears you conjure° have as much to do with the passage of time as with the sadness you remember. Still, a sad memory is better than none. It reminds you of survival.

7   Most of the activity in your brain relies on memory. That takes energy. Have you ever noticed that when you're tired and there's silence in your brain, you begin to sing? That's good health taking over. The tensions of serious thought are being released through play.

8   Today is Remembrance Day, and it's a strange thing to me that we confine° ourselves to remembering only the dead—and only the war dead, at that. If they were able, what would *they* be remembering? Us. And we're alive. Here we are. Maybe it's sad—I suppose it is—that the dead should be remembering the living and the living remembering the dead. But the main thing is, we all remember when we were together. We remember what we were in another time. Not now, but *then.* Memory is making peace with time.

9   They say that loss of memory is not to know who you are. Then, I suppose, it has to follow that we *are* what we remember. I can believe that. I mean, it's very easy for me to imagine forgetting my name. That wouldn't worry me. And it wouldn't worry me to forget how old I am (I wish I could!) or to forget the colour of my eyes and have to go look in a mirror to remind myself. None of that would worry me. Because I can skip all of that. None of those things are who I am.

10   But it would worry the hell out of me if I couldn't remember the smell of the house where I grew up, or the sound of my father playing the piano, or the tune of his favourite song. I remember my brother, Michael, as a child. And the child I remember being myself is as much a remembrance of him as it is of me. More, in fact—because I saw him every day and did not see myself. I heard him every day—and did not hear myself (except singing). So, to be a child in memory means that I conjure Michael, not the child in photographs who bears my name.

11   I am my Aunt Marg, for instance, telling me not to lean into the cemetery over the fence at Foxbar Road. I am not me leaning over the fence, I am her voice—because that is what I remember. And I am all the gravestones I was looking at when she called me. And the fence boards that supported me. And the sun on my back. But I am not that little boy. I don't remember him at all. I remember him falling and being picked up—but I am the distance he fell and the hands that lifted him, not the bump in between. I remember the sound of my own voice crying—but not the feel of it. That voice is gone. And I am the gloves my mother wore when she held my hand and the tones of her laughter. And I remember and will move forever, as all children do, to the heartbeats of my mother. That remembrance is the rhythm of my life. So memory is other people—it is little of ourselves.

12   I like Remembrance Day. I'm fond of memory. I wish it was a day of happiness. I have many dead in my past, but only one of them died from the wars. And I think very fondly of him. He was my uncle. He didn't die in the War, but because of it. This was the First World War and so I don't remember the event itself. I just remember him. But what I remember of my uncle is not the least bit sad.

13   I was just a child—in the classic sense—a burbling, few-worded, looking-up-at-everything child. Uncle Tif—who died at home—was always in a great tall bed—high up—and the bed was white. I would go into his room, supported by my father's hands, and lean against the lower edge of the mattress. There was a white sheet over everything, and I can smell that sheet to this day. It smelled of soap and talcum powder°. To me, Uncle Tif was a hand that came down from a great way off and tapped me on the head. He smoked a pipe. And there was something blue in the room—I don't know whether it was a chair or a table or my father's pant legs—but there was something blue and that has always been one of my favourite colours.

14   And high above my head, there was a tall glass jar on a table and the jar was full of hard French candies. They had shiny jackets and were many colours. And Uncle Tif's hand would go out, waving in the air above my gaze and lift up the lid of the jar and take out a candy and slowly—it was always slowly—he would pass the candy down into my open mouth. Then I would lean against the bed, or fall on the floor, and taste the candy for about two hours—or what, to a kid, just seemed two hours—while the adult voices buzzed above my head.

15   I know he sacrificed his youth, his health, his leg and finally his life for his country. But I'd be a fool if I just said *thanks—I'm grateful.* I might as well hit him in the mouth as say that. Because my being grateful has nothing to do with what he died for or why he died. That was part of his own life and what I am grateful for is that he had his own life. I am grateful he was there in that little bit of my life. And I am grateful, above all, that he is in my memory. I am his namesake. He is mine.

16   Remembrance is more than honouring the dead. Remembrance is joining them—being one with them in memory. Memory is survival.

Vocabulary

1 inevitably (adv): unavoidably

3 sanity (n): the state of having a sound and healthy mind, rational behaviour

3 cathartic (adj): expressing emotions through literature or drama

3 purgative (n): the means of getting rid of impurities or give relief

6 conjure (v): to produce from imagination or by using creative powers

8 confine (v): limit

13 talcum powder (n): used for dusting the body

RESPONDING TO THE READING

- If the thesis is stated, identify it; if it is implied, write it in your own words.
- What do you think is the purpose of this essay? Give reasons for your opinion.
- Who do you think is the intended audience of this essay? Give reasons for your opinion.

Comprehension

1. "Memory . . . is the means by which most of us retain our sanity." Explain what Findley means in this quote from Paragraph 3.
2. With what example does Findley support the definition of memory quoted above?
3. What reason does Findley give for saying, "Memory is a form of hope" (Paragraph 4)?
4. Why is a sad memory better than no memory according to Findley?
5. In what ways does the essay's tone change in Paragraph 8?
6. In Paragraph 8, Findley states, "Memory is making peace with time." How does he support this remark on memory?
7. What is the main idea of Paragraph 9?
8. How many examples of childhood memories does Findley provide in Paragraph 10?
9. What sort of example is given in Paragraph 11?
10. What is your impression of Findley's memory of his uncle Tif?
11. Why does Findley say he is grateful for his uncle Tif?
12. Findley ends his essay with these words: "Memory is survival." How has he supported this statement?

Analysis

1. Do you agree with Timothy Findley that remembrance is good for people? Why or why not?
2. Does Findley succeed in making you reflect on the significance of Remembrance Day (November 11)?
3. In Paragraph 9, Timothy Findley makes an extraordinary claim: "We are what we remember." Do you agree with him on that idea? Why or why not?
4. Look over all the definitions of memory Findley gives. How many are there? Why does Findley give so many? Can memory be so many different things?
5. How effective is the title of this essay? Explain.

Discussion/Writing Suggestions

1. What is your strongest childhood memory and why do you think it is so significant to you?
2. Are you, like Findley, "fond of memory"? Explain your response.

   • Other essays that reflect on memories in some way include those by Hugh MacLennan (p. 5), Malcolm X (p. 19), David Ginsburg (p. 33), Bertrand Russell (p. 64), Margaret Atwood (p. 85), Wayson Choy (p. 169), Derek Cohen (p. 173), Margaret Laurence (p. 202), Michael Dorris (p. 208), Rosie DiManno (p. 211), and Almas Zakiuddin (p. 240).

In Praise of the Humble Comma

Pico Iyer

Pico Iyer (1957–) is an Indian journalist and author. He was born in Oxford, England, and was raised there. He attended Eton and graduated from Oxford University. He also spent part of his childhood in California as his father, Raghavan Iyer, a Rhodes Scholar and expert on Mahatma Gandhi, taught at the University of California. Iyer describes himself as a citizen of the world, "a global village on two legs," and has developed a globe-trotting career as a reporter, essayist, and novelist. Iyer works as a freelance journalist and has contributed to publications, such as Time *magazine,* Harper's Magazine, Condé Nast Traveler, *and the* New York Review of Books. *Iyer established his reputation as a talented travel writer because of his gift for sympathetic observation. His best-known works include* Video Night in Kathmandu: And Other Reports from the Not-So-Far East *(1989),* Falling off the Map: Some Lonely Places of the World *(1994), and* Cuba and the Night *(1996). He has also written* Imagining Canada: An Outsider's Hope for a Global Future *(2001).*

This essay, which evaluates the significance of punctuation, first appeared in Time *magazine in 1988. Like Atwood's essay, "In Praise of the Humble Comma" is also a eulogy though not on the occasion of a death, nor in praise of a person. Iyer opens with an astonishing analogy, a partial comparison between the ability of the gods and the "humble comma." This pattern, an analogy followed by examples, is typical of Iyer's style in this essay.*

1   The gods, they say, give breath, and they take it away. But the same could be said—could it not?—of the humble comma. Add it to the present clause, and, of a sudden, the mind is, quite literally, given pause to think; take it out if you wish or forget it and the mind is deprived of a resting place. Yet still the comma gets no respect. It seems just a slip of a thing, a pedant's° tick, a blip on the edge of our consciousness, a kind of printer's smudge almost. Small, we claim, is beautiful (especially in the age of the microchip). Yet what is so often used and so rarely recalled, as the comma—unless it be breath itself?

2   Punctuation, one is taught, has a point: to keep up law and order. Punctuation marks are the road signs placed along the highway of our communication—to control speeds, provide directions and prevent head-on collisions. A period has the unblinking finality of a red light; the comma is a flashing yellow light that asks us only to slow down; and the semicolon is a stop sign that tells us to ease gradually to a halt, before gradually starting up again. By establishing the relations between words, punctuation establishes the relations between the people using words. That may be one reason why schoolteachers exalt° it and lovers defy it ("We love each other and belong to each other let's don't ever hurt each other Nicole let's don't ever hurt each other," wrote Gary Gilmore* to his girlfriend). A comma, he must have known, "separates inseparables," in the clinching° words of H. W. Fowler, King of English Usage.

3   Punctuation, then, is a civic prop, a pillar that holds society upright. (A run-on sentence, its phrases piling up without division, is as unsightly as a sink piled high with dirty dishes.) Small wonder, then, that punctuation was one of the first proprieties° of the Victorian age, the age of the corset, that the modernists threw off: the sexual revolution might be said to have begun when Joyce's Molly Bloom* spilled out all her private thoughts in 36 pages of unbridled°, almost unperioded and officially composed press; and another rebellion was surely marked when e.e. cummings first felt free to commit "God" to the lower case.

4   Punctuation thus becomes the signature of cultures. The hot-blooded Spaniard seems to be revealed in the passion and urgency of his doubled exclamation points and question marks ("¡Caramba! ¿Quien sabe?"), while the impassive Chinese traditionally added to his so-called inscrutability° by omitting directions from his ideograms°. The anarchy° and commotion of the '60s were given voice in the exploding exclamation marks, riotous capital letters and Day-Glo italics of Tom Wolfe's* spray-paint prose; and in Communist societies, where the State is absolute, the dignity—and divinity—of capital letters is reserved for Ministries, Sub-Committees and Secretariats.

5   Yet punctuation is something more than a culture's birthmark; it scores the music in our minds, gets our thoughts moving to the rhythm of our hearts. Punctuation is the notation in the sheet music of our words, telling us when to rest, or when to raise our voices; it acknowledges that the meaning of our discourse, as of any symphonic composition, lies not in the units but in the pauses, the pacing and the phrasing. Punctuation is the way one bats one's eyes, lowers one's voice or blushes demurely°. Punctuation adjusts the tone and color and volume till the feeling comes into perfect focus: not disgust exactly, but distaste; not lust, or like, but love.

6   Punctuation, in short, gives us the human voice, and all the meanings that lie between the words. "You aren't young, are you?" loses its innocence when it loses the question mark. Every child knows the menace° of a dropped apostrophe (the parent's "Don't do that" shifting into the more slowly enunciated "Do not do that"), and every believer, the ignominy° of having his faith reduced to "faith." Add an exclamation point to "To be or not to be . . . " and the gloomy Dane* has all the resolve he needs; add a comma, and the noble sobriety of "God save the Queen" becomes a cry of desperation bordering on double sacrilege°.

7　　Sometimes, of course, our markings may be simply a matter of aesthetics°. Popping in a comma can be like slipping on the necklace that gives an outfit quiet elegance, or like catching the sound of running water that complements, as it completes, the silence of a Japanese landscape. When V. S. Naipaul, in his latest novel, writes, "He was a middle-aged man, with glasses," the first comma can seem a little precious. Yet it gives the description a spin, as well as a subtlety°, that it otherwise lacks, and it shows that the glasses are not part of the middle-agedness, but something else.

8　　Thus all these tiny scratches give us breadth and heft° and depth. A world that has only periods is a world without inflections. It is a world without shade. It has a music without sharps and flats. It is a martial music. It has a jackboot rhythm. Words cannot bend and curve. A comma, by comparison, catches the gentle drift of the mind in thought, turning in on itself and back on itself, reversing, redoubling and returning along the course of its own sweet river music; while the semicolon brings clauses and thoughts together with all the silent discretion° of a hostess arranging guests around her dinner table.

9　　Punctuation, then, is a matter of care. Care for words, yes, but also, and more important, for what the words imply. Only a lover notices the small things: the way the afternoon light catches the nape of a neck, or how a strand of hair slips out from behind an ear, or the way a finger curls around a cup. And no one scans a letter so closely as a lover, searching for its small print, straining to hear its nuances°, its gasps, its sighs and hesitations, poring over the secret messages that lie in every cadence°. The difference between "Jane (whom I adore)" and "Jane, whom I adore," and the difference between them both and "Jane—whom I adore—" marks all the distance between ecstasy and heartache. "No iron can pierce the heart with such force as a period put at just the right place," in Isaac Babel's lovely words; the comma can let us hear a voice break, or a heart. Punctuation, in fact, is a labor of love. Which bring us back, in a way, to gods.

Notes

2 Gary Gilmore (1940–1977): convicted American murderer, the subject of *The Executioner's Song* by Norman Mailer

3 Molly Bloom: character in *Ulysses* (1922) by James Joyce, who is famous for unpunctuated stream-of-consciousness

3 e.e. cummings (1894–1962): American poet, known for unconventional punctuation and uncapitalized words

4 Tom Wolfe (1931–): American writer, who also uses unconventional punctuation

6 "gloomy Dane": Hamlet

Vocabulary

1 pedant (n): a person who is unnecessarily concerned with exact detail or literal meaning

2 exalt (v): praise highly

2 clinch (v): confirm a deal or settle an argument conclusively

3 proprieties (n): correctness of behaviour

3 unbridled (adj): without constraint, uninhibited

4 inscrutability (n): mysteriousness, impenetrability

4 ideograms (n): symbols used to represent a thing or an idea

4 anarchy (n): without government; social and political disorder

5 demurely (adv): modestly, shyly

6 menace (n): threat, danger

6 ignominy (n): shame, humiliation

6 sacrilege (n): a violation of what is sacred or holy; irreverence

7 aesthetics (n): philosophy of beauty, especially in art

7 subtlety (n): sensitivity, delicacy

8 heft (n): weight

8 discretion (n): carefulness, good judgment

9 nuances (n): subtle shades of meaning, fine distinctions

9 cadence (n): rhythm, intonation, modulation

 RESPONDING TO THE READING

- If the thesis is stated, identify it; if it is implied, write it in your own words.
- What do you think is the purpose of this essay? Give reasons for your opinion.
- Who do you think is the intended audience of this essay? Give reasons for your opinion.

Comprehension

1. What power does Iyer claim in his first two sentences that the comma has?
2. "Add it to the present clause, and, of a sudden, the mind is, quite literally, given pause to think; take it out if you wish or forget it and the mind is deprived of a resting place." How does Iyer provide an example of the comma at work in this sentence?
3. What analogy does Iyer introduce as an example in Paragraph 2?
4. Paraphrase this sentence: "By establishing the relations between words, punctuation establishes the relations between the people using words."
5. What is the key idea of Paragraph 3? How many examples does Iyer use to support it?
6. What sorts of examples does Iyer provide to support his claim that the comma is "the signature of cultures"?
7. Where could the comma go in "God save the Queen"? Explain what happens if you add the comma.

8. What is the effect of the series of repetitions in Paragraph 8?
9. What is the final example of the comma at work that Iyer includes?

Analysis

1. Explain what Iyer means by comparing the comma to each of the following: *a slip of a thing, a pedant's tick, a blip on the edge of our consciousness, a kind of printer's smudge.* How is each comparison ironic in the context of the first paragraph?
2. Why does Iyer say the comma is humble? How does he show that he regards humility as a virtue?
3. What is the purpose of Iyer's traffic sign analogy?
4. Iyer makes allusions to only 20th-century writers and characters. Why might that be?
5. Based on your experience, do you think that different cultures punctuate differently?
6. Do you agree with Iyer's claim that punctuation marks affect not only the meaning and cadence of a writer's words, but also our emotional response to them?
7. After each analogy, Iyer provides examples to show how the analogy works; often the very syntax he uses also acts as an example. Examine a paragraph in which this is the case.

Discussion/Writing Suggestions

1. Why would an English teacher love this essay?
2. What is your response to Iyer's essay? Provide examples from the essay to support your point of view.

   - Kurt Vonnegut (p. 72) and Russell Baker (p. 316) also wrote essays directly related to this subject.
   - Iyer's essay is about more than punctuation; it is also about human relationships. Other essays dealing with this subject are by Joseph Epstein (p. 36), Bertrand Russell (p. 64), Wayson Choy (p. 169), Timothy Findley (p. 92), Nicola Bleasby (p. 109), Stephen L. Carter (p. 132), Judith Viorst (p. 142), Charlie Angus (p. 180), Michael Dorris (p. 208), and Pat Capponi (p. 158).

Essay of Process Analysis

In depicting a process, sequence and chronology are vital components of the organization of the analysis. There are two types of process analysis. The first explains how something can be done step by step and is sometimes referred to as directional process analysis. The second explains how something happened or how something occurs and is sometimes referred to as informational process analysis. By reading the first type, readers can follow the process and achieve the same result (e.g., conducting a lab experiment or preparing a recipe), whereas the second type informs readers about a process or a past event (e.g., how snow falls or how World War II began) without expecting the process to be repeated.

Directional Process Analysis

All *how-to* process analyses have the same purpose: to enable readers to follow a procedure or a series of steps to achieve a desired result. You are familiar with a variety of *how-to* process analyses, such as recipes, manuals, and lab experiments. You may also have read articles in magazines or seen programs on television on such subjects as *how to* practise safe sex, *how to* make pasta primavera, or *how to* redecorate your room. You've already read essays that present these types of process analysis: Bill Bryson offers an amusing "how-to" process in his essay "Your New Computer" (p. 14); and Kurt Vonnegut gives guidelines on "How to Write with Style" (p. 72).

Writing Strategy

Here is a list of steps on how to compose a *how-to* process analysis. These numbered steps can be applied to writing all kinds of directional analyses, ranging from detailed instructions on how to use lab equipment to simple directions for finding something. Once you've read this list, apply it to the essay "How to Use Less Communication" (p. 103) to determine how closely the writer followed the ten steps.

1. Define your purpose and the desired result.
2. Start with a list and outline clearly the materials needed for the process.
3. Ask yourself: Is the list complete? Do some steps or materials need to be dropped for the sake of clarity?
4. Order your steps chronologically (strictly in time order). For things that happen at the same time, be especially clear in instructions. Remember: *Clarity* is rule number one in a directional process analysis.
5. Ask yourself again: What must my readers know to repeat these steps? Are any background details or definitions of terms needed?
6. Compose a thesis statement that names the process and states your purpose and desired result.
7. Write a clear introduction providing any necessary background details.
8. Write up the process after taking into consideration questions like "Should the directions be presented in three main stages, or are more body paragraphs needed?" and "How can my instructions be simple and clear?"
9. Write a conclusion that restates your purpose, summarizes the procedure, and reviews the desired result.
10. Revise your process analysis. Check for unity, coherence, and clarity. Be generous with transitions (e.g., *while, at the same time, before, after, first, then, at the end*) to show the exact sequential order.

Informational Process Analysis

As with the *how-to* process analysis, in preparing to write the informational process, you must begin with a list of the steps involved and determine where the process starts and where it ends.

In Leslie C. Smith's essay (p. 105), the start of the process was 1853 when blue jeans were born from canvas tents. Since Smith is interested in a historical subject, readers are aware that this process is descriptive in nature and that its purpose is to help readers understand a series of significant events that began in the past and still have influence today. In reading a process analysis, it is essential to note how a writer arranges ideas in separate units or steps and that these units are usually arranged in a time sequence, or a chronology.

Careful use of transitions (e.g., *then, only recently, until*) clarifies the chronology for the reader. Examples and reasons are also essential to this type of process analysis as they show readers *how* and *why* events occurred. The pattern of organization in such a process analysis should be clear so that readers easily find the thesis, note transitions, and identify separate steps in the procedure.

When writing this type of process analysis, you must first ask yourself if anything—background information—needs to be explained before you start to describe the process. For example, if you were to explain how a car engine works, would you have to define the main components of the engine before you began? Would readers need to know a brief history of combustion as a preface to the process? What does Leslie C. Smith do? She provides a brief description of the use of canvas in the California Gold Rush before leading the reader to the first step in the process analysis, which recounts how Levi Strauss "had a tailor cut the canvas up into tough workpants."

The *thesis statement* must state clearly the focused subject and identify where the process begins. Smith states her thesis in the opening paragraph by answering the question she wrote in her brief introduction. She then states in her second paragraph that jeans weren't intended to reshape the way people dress. This leads to her first step in the historical process.

The *body paragraphs* of an informational process essay are made up of the chronologically arranged events. Examples, anecdotes, and definitions may be included to sustain reader interest and to clarify how and why an event occurred.

Events in a process must develop logically. When writing the body, do not present each step separately. Group steps into *stages*, each stage making up a separate paragraph. Smith arranges her steps into three major stages. She begins with details illustrating the birth of jeans in the Gold Rush. Her second stage traces the evolution of jeans as popular clothing due to the influence of Hollywood movie stars, and her final stage discusses jeans in their maturity, as essential clothing for people from all walks of contemporary life.

To ensure unity and coherence, each stage should be defined sequentially. Smith uses dates in her essay to define her stages, but transition words and phrases also help to clarify stages for readers. To clarify her chronology, Smith effectively uses words like *yet, after,* and *recently* with her dates.

SAMPLE STUDENT ESSAY

The title of this essay, "How to Use Less Communication," tells you it is a *how-to* process essay and you expect it to provide instructions you can follow. As you read the following essay, don't read it at face value; otherwise, you would be puzzled by its tone and confused about its purpose. Why would the author instruct the reader on how to write badly, insult readers, and be illogical? You will quickly realize, however, the essay is ironic; that is, it says one thing while meaning the opposite. This essay is complex because of its ironic tone; otherwise, like most *how-to* process analyses, it is direct and straightforward.

How to Use Less Communication

Stuart Johns

1   First-year composition courses serve no useful purpose. Being able to think and express oneself clearly on paper will never be an asset. Despite the fact that employers list good communication skills as their #1 job requirement, learning to write clearly and correctly is redundant. Keep all of these ideas in mind as we tackle an essay of process analysis. Follow the steps given you and you will never master this means of communication: disregard the logical order of your content; refuse to think about the mechanics of your composition, and above all, show no consideration for your reader.

2   When you start to write a process analysis, remember that this rhetorical mode is really a procedure with a beginning, middle and end. Don't you hate the obvious! Keep your reader in suspense; whatever you do, don't organize steps into a coherent sequence. After all, if a step is missed it really doesn't matter that much. For example, why bother with an introduction? Just leap straight in. If the reader is unsure about the precise subject, and so isn't interested enough to read on, that's not your problem. The order of any process isn't carved in stone anyway, so why bother being organized? When you present the steps, assume the results are obvious and don't need to be described or explained in any way. Elaboration is boring. You can achieve confusion in your reader by jumping from one unconnected point to another. In addition, don't warn your reader of any upcoming step or resulting problem; clear signals are not the writer's concern. The reader will know better the next time! "Learn from your mistakes" is a great motto to live by.

3   While the reader will learn from mistakes, you have no responsibility for the mechanics of your composition. By that, I mean you shouldn't worry about grammar at all. Just go with the flow! Checking spelling is a waste of time; who cares about using a dictionary anyway? If these errors add to your reader's frustration, don't worry. It doesn't reflect on you at all. In keeping with the disregard for organization of steps, supply no transition words. Smooth style is for teachers of English, not real people. In fact, even the use of paragraphs is entirely optional and you could write the whole process in one long surging paragraph. However you decide to present the process, make sure it has no names, no margins, no double spacing, no pagination. Let the reader figure all that out.

4   Letting the reader figure it out has been the key to this essay so far. Although I've discussed organization and mechanics, our discussion has always related to the reader. With this in mind, the final step in producing a totally useless piece of communication demands a lack of concern for your reader. Don't tell your reader any essential background details and omit any stages that are preliminary to the successful completion of the process you are discussing. Assume your reader knows the meaning of any special terms you might use. Explaining something you know to someone who doesn't already possess that knowledge is time-consuming and requires effort. Finally, an air of superiority will convince the reader you really know what you're talking about.

5   Following these suggestions will ensure that your reader has no necessary background information and makes no allowances for possible variations in the process. Being unaware of your reader's needs will alienate the reader completely if the confusion of the process and the sloppiness of the mechanics haven't already succeeded in this accomplishment. Above all, don't relate your process to any other similar process. This might add relevance to your analysis and that is a waste of your time. Follow the steps given you and you will achieve a complete failure in communication. You will prove that being able to think and express yourself clearly is not an asset you possess. You will have demonstrated that, for you, a first-year composition course serves no useful purpose.

Comprehension

1. What is the thesis statement in this essay? Identify the focused subject and its key ideas.
2. How does the thesis inform the reader that this is a *how-to* process analysis?
3. How is this thesis linked to the opening ideas in the essay?
4. What attention-getting devices are used in the introduction?
5. Because this is a process analysis, each key idea in the thesis is actually a stage or sequence in the process. Each stage is composed of a series of related steps. List the separate steps in each stage.
6. The opening sentence of each body paragraph states a key idea/stage. It also gives readers a link with the previous paragraph. What is each link and how does this transition work effectively?
7. What is the link or transition between the conclusion and the rest of the essay?
8. How does the conclusion relate to the thesis and to the steps in the essay?
9. How does the title relate to the content of the essay?
10. What is the effect of repeating in the concluding line the idea from the opening line of the essay?
11. Based on your reading of this essay, what would you say are the correct steps to communicating effectively?

Analysis

1. A **pun** is a play on words. It is a word that says two things at once. Explain the pun in the title.
2. Why must writers be aware of readers? The essay talks about frustration, confusion, and an "air of superiority." Why are these negative things? Why should they be avoided by good writers?
3. An essay can be written in a humorous, serious, sarcastic, or ironic tone. How does the ironic tone of this essay create humour?
4. Do you think Stuart Johns is successful in supporting his thesis? Why or why not?
5. What is your opinion of this essay? Be prepared to support your response.

READINGS: ESSAYS OF PROCESS ANALYSIS

Of the four essays in this unit, the first essay, "Blue Jeans: Born to Last" by Leslie C. Smith, is clearly an informational process analysis; it gives a historical account of blue jeans and describes "how it happened." "How Can You Mend a Broken Heart?" by Nicola Bleasby contains personal advice; it offers suggestions you could actually follow, so it is a straightforward *how-to* essay. "A Contract Painkiller" by Maureen Littlejohn cleverly presents two processes: the efficacy of aspirin and the history of aspirin. "Ten Steps to the Creation of a Modern Media Icon" by Mark Kingwell is more sophisticated as it purports to offer "10 steps," yet none of us could undertake the process it describes, though, strangely, we do participate in it whenever we read about a celebrity. Kingwell's essay is a thoughtful and systematic analysis of a popular social phenomenon; its process analysis lies in depicting "how it happens."

Blue Jeans: Born to Last

Leslie C. Smith

> *Leslie C. Smith is a Toronto-based freelance writer. Smith specializes in humorous opinion pieces with a focus on fashion, lifestyle, and popular social trends. She has published articles in most major Canadian newspapers and has appeared on TV to discuss fashion and popular culture.*

> *The following article, which first appeared in the* Globe and Mail *in 1992, uses informal language. In spite of its slang expressions and light-hearted tone, the article, a brief history of blue jeans, is very organized in its structure. The first paragraph presents a clear thesis statement preceded by an attention-getting question: "What do an 1850s California gold miner, Marlon Brando and you have in common?" Once readers have moved on to the second paragraph, Smith's purpose and her pattern of organization become apparent: she is presenting a process analysis that traces, step by step, the development of blue jeans. Notice how Smith uses dates to define the stages of blue jeans' development from the canvas tent to the designer pant. You will notice how*

brief many of the paragraphs are; because the essay is a newspaper article, it is written in a series of "takes."

1   Question: What do an 1850s California gold miner, Marlon Brando* and you have in common? The answer is jeans—those ubiquitous° blue pants that have become, within the short span of a baby boomer's° lifetime, the very keystone of our casual wear wardrobes.

2   Jeans weren't intended to reshape the way we wear clothes. In fact, they didn't start out as pants at all. In 1853, they were a mere wagon load of brown canvas cloth, carted over the Sierras by a young, enterprising Bavarian immigrant by the name of Levi Strauss*.

stage 1 step

3   Strauss had it in mind to turn the canvas into miners' tents, and so make his fortune. But when he reached the California gold fields, an old prospector shook his head and said, "You should have brought pants." It seems regular trousers couldn't quite cut the mustard° in the rough-and-tumble world of gold mining.

4   Being a clever businessman, Strauss immediately revised his plans and had a tailor cut the canvas up into tough workpants. From then on, it was a race to keep his supply in line with the enormous demand. The button-flied, brown canvas trousers were alternately dubbed "Levi's" because of their designer's name, or simply "501s," which was the material's lot number for reordering.

5   At the close of the 1850s, a sturdy French cotton, *serge de Nîmes* (hence "denim"), replaced the canvas cloth. By this time, however, many people had started calling Levi Strauss's pants "jeans," a corruption of *Genes,* the French name for Genoa—a rather oblique° reference to the cotton-twill trousers worn by Italian sailors.

step (stage) 2

6   Jeans did not become blue until the year 1873. After much experimentation, Strauss decided that indigo was the best dye for his workpants, as that colour remained entirely consistent throughout the dyeing process. Around this time, too, he added brass rivets to the pants' pockets for better reinforcement.

(stage) 3 step

7   Less precisely documented is the moment when Strauss first chose to add the decorative wing-shaped stitching to the back pockets of his 501s. This was a tribute to his new land of opportunity—America, whose intrepid spirit is symbolized by the bald eagle.

8   Jeans, in their own right, began to symbolize the rugged endurance of the American West. The favoured garb° of cowboys, by the 1930s they were an established icon—one that Easterners, fresh from their vacations on popular dude ranches°, were happy to appropriate.

9   Yet it took until the 1950s before jeans really took off. In that decade, their rough individuality made them the uniform of nonconformists, as typified by film stars James Dean* in *Rebel Without a Cause* and Marlon Brando in *The Wild One.*

10 Anti-establishment chic° carried jeans through the turbulent 1960s; and by the 1970s, they had become so much a part of our lives that they moved, along with flower children°, into the mainstream. Like their wearers, they, too, were caught up in the excesses of the Me Decade: wherein designers, catering to Yuppie desires, raised jeans (and their own bank accounts) to ever more outrageous heights.

11 Only recently have we seen the wisdom in returning to the original, no-frills, five-pocket jeans. They speak to us of true value—not just of price, but of the tradition they represent.

12   Jeans are functional and down-to-earth, apolitical and unisexual. They are also fundamental: They provide a plain blue backdrop for a wealth of wardrobe options. Such versatility° makes them acceptable whether worn well-pressed and dressed-up with a blazer and tie, or faded and torn with a T-shirt and sneakers. And because they tend to conform to our bodies over time, we know that they are ultimately as individual as ourselves.

13   Perhaps the main reason for jeans' enduring° popularity is the difficulty of pigeon-holing° them. There are no set dress regulations governing the wearing of jeans, no denim dos and don'ts to bone up on. Jeans can go wherever and howsoever one wishes. Jeans are, through every fibre of their being, true wardrobe rebels.

Notes

1 Marlon Brando (1924–2004): American actor best known for his work in movies such as *The Godfather, A Streetcar Named Desire,* and *On the Waterfront*

2 Levi Strauss (1829–1902): German-born American clothing manufacturer and the creator of blue jeans

9 James Dean (1931–1955): American movie actor, now a cultural icon for his roles in *Rebel Without a Cause* and *East of Eden*

Vocabulary

1 ubiquitous (adj): existing everywhere

1 baby boomer (n): someone born between 1945 and 1960

3 cut the mustard (idiom): to reach the desired standard

5 oblique (adj): slanted, indirect, at an angle

8 garb (n): clothing

8 dude ranches (n): vacation resorts offering the experience of living like a cowboy

10 chic (n): style, elegance

10 flower children (n): young person in late 1960s and early 1970s who believed in universal peace and love as a solution to the world's problems

12 versatility (n): adaptability, flexibility

13 enduring (adj): lasting

13 pigeon-holing (v): classifying, stereotyping

RESPONDING TO THE READING

- If the thesis is stated, identify it; if it is implied, write it in your own words.
- What do you think is the purpose of this essay? Give reasons for your opinion.
- Who do you think is the intended audience of this essay? Give reasons for your opinion.

Comprehension

1. How does Smith begin to lead her readers through the process she describes?
2. How many separate steps are mentioned in the development of blue jeans? Number them.
3. Using skimming and scanning, answer the following True or False questions.
   a. Everybody owns a pair of blue jeans. _____
   b. Levi Strauss was the inventor of blue jeans. _____
   c. The first jeans were made from tent canvas. _____
   d. The name "jeans" was introduced in 1850. _____
   e. The word "denim" came from Genoa. _____
   f. Indigo was used to reinforce jeans in 1873. _____
   g. Blue jeans became more popular in the 1950s because they represented rebellion. _____
   h. Today, blue jeans are regarded as a basic item of clothing. _____

Analysis

1. How does the title of this article relate to its content? And to its structure?
2. What do you think of the reasons that Smith presents for their popularity? Are they valid reasons?
3. Do you think blue jeans really are ubiquitous?
4. Why do you think a national newspaper would print an article like this one?
5. Could the story of blue jeans have been as effective if Smith had reversed the order of her steps, by starting with the popularity of blue jeans today and going back into history, to the California Gold Rush? Why or why not?
6. What devices does Smith use to keep readers interested in her subject? Does she use anecdotes? Does she ask questions? Does she use examples effectively?

Discussion/Writing Suggestions

1. Do you wear blue jeans? Describe where, when, and why.
2. How would you explain the popularity of blue jeans in an essay?

   • Other essays that focus on popular culture are by Robertson Davies (p. 150), Mark Kingwell (p. 114), Sandra Stewart (p. 121), and Charlie Angus (p. 180).
   • Essays that contain historical accounts are by Ralph Nader (p. 28), Jay Ingram (p. 40), Robertson Davies (p. 150), Wayson Choy (p. 169), Charlie Angus (p. 180), Pier Giorgio Di Cicco (p. 196), Rosie DiManno (p. 211), Maya Angelou (p. 218), and Amartya Sen (p. 252).

How Can You Mend a Broken Heart?

Nicola Bleasby

Nicola Bleasby lived in Ottawa when she wrote this essay. It first appeared in the "Facts and Arguments" section of the Globe and Mail *on Valentine's Day, February 14, 1996.*

Nicola Bleasby's title makes the type of process analysis clear; she answers her question in the essay. This essay is notable for its vocabulary—you will need your dictionary!

1   Who says that a few bad clichés and an expanded vocabulary can't mend a broken heart? After the cookie has crumbled and the fat lady has sung, the last thing a bruised ego needs is to be at a loss for words when they're needed most. There may be plenty more fish in the sea, but words aren't as disposable. A good word is hard to find—the perfect word is worth its weight in gold.

2   When the flame in a relationship has been extinguished by someone other than yourself (when you have been dumped), the immediate future looks bleak. The most productive course of action to alleviate the agony is not to drown your sorrows in either liquor or nostalgia but to buy a new dictionary. Yes, a dictionary. A big one. The bigger the heartbreak, the bigger the dictionary required.

3   Within the confines of the alphabet it is possible in one month to conquer the most crushing heartbreak while simultaneously expanding your vocabulary. Greeting each day with a new letter inscribes into your consciousness (1) measured progress through emotional trauma; and (2) a vocabulary that puts you in touch with your emotions.

4   Have you got your dictionary handy? Are you sitting comfortably? Who says this can't be as easy as ABC?

5   The initial period post-*affair de l'amour* is the time for emotional primordiality, not composure. The first week begins with anger, bellicosity, perhaps contrition, perhaps contempt—another day, another diatribe. Suppress nothing. Draw strength from your dictionary. Delve into the depths of your psyche and come to terms with feelings of abandonment, betrayal, and disaffection. Many scathing expressions can be created using this week's material that can't be used in civil, everyday life. Execrate the—well, take your pick of any number of profane epithets befitting the individual responsible for your diminution.

6   This is also a time of contradictions. Your emotional behaviour will run the gamut between abnegation and the urge to gormandize; between ataraxy and garrulity.

7   On the eighth day, it is necessary to contend with reality. You can't hide from the truth no matter how painful it is. Love hurts. The halcyon days *de l'amour* with your *inamorato* are not coming back. He never loved you anyway. You deserve better.

8   If dealing with the H's seems simple, watch out—this could be the harbinger of an early rebound. Jumping from the frying pan into the fire will solve nothing. Be diligent in your reading for the next few days. If you have any "urges," it is

probably best to stay inside and read each letter's section—twice. If libidinal impulses persist, all you really have to do is suppress them until R: On rebound day, at least there is an excuse.

9   Even for the most dedicated philologist, L will be the most difficult day to deal with. Too many L words can bring back memories that might subvert all that has been accomplished in the preceding 11 days. Easy solution: Skip the section of the dictionary that falls between louse and low—there's no need to rub salt into a wound. Instead of sentimental thoughts, you'll be left with reasonably negative words that do not pertain to you.

10   It's clear sailing from M to Z. The valediction on Day 22 will be a piece of cake—with this I offer no hand-holding. I have only reached "I"—dealing with the iniquity of isolation, but I have outlined the intended course of my lexical progression. Tomorrow, I will jettison my filiopietistic tendencies (which I discovered a couple of days ago, but which then seemed unimportant). Then, I'm going to discard all the kitschy memories and synthesize the mantra of my autonomy.

11   When I reach Z, I will be ready to join the Zeitgeist with a potentiated vocabulary. It will be a personal triumph, an act of serendipity. After all, when life gives you lemons you've got to make lemonade.

Vocabulary

Check the definitions of all those new words.

RESPONDING TO THE READING

- If the thesis is stated, identify it; if it is implied, write it in your own words.
- What do you think is the purpose of this essay? Give reasons for your opinion.
- Who do you think is the intended audience of this essay? Give reasons for your opinion.

Comprehension

1. Which type of process analysis is this essay?
2. How many distinct steps does Nicola Bleasby give to readers to mend their broken hearts?
3. The steps are presented as two parallel processes. One is chronological. What is the organizing principle of the other?
4. Using your dictionary, define the word *cliché*. Then skim the article to find ten clichés and paraphrase them using more formal language.

5. Scan to find ten words that are not part of your everyday vocabulary. Define each by writing a sentence containing the word.
6. Why is the *L* section of a dictionary the most difficult to deal with according to Bleasby?
7. Does this essay conclude on a positive or a negative note? How does the content of the concluding sentence relate to that of the rest of the essay?

Analysis

1. Do you know people who use clichés constantly? Why do you think they do this?
2. Certain public figures use many clichés in their speech—sportscasters and politicians in particular. Why do you think they speak in that manner?
3. What is meant by the phrase "Get in touch with your inner philologist"? Don't just define the meaning of philologist.
4. Is Bleasby's advice serious? Is it really helpful or even realistic?
5. How is the date of publication of this essay appropriate for its content?

Discussion/Writing Suggestions

1. How would you advise someone to get over a broken heart? Be specific.
2. Have you ever felt your heart was breaking? What was the experience like and how did you recover?

    • Other essays that reflect on personal relationships are by Joseph Epstein (p. 36), Bertrand Russell (p. 64), Margaret Atwood (p. 85), Pico Iyer (p. 96), Timothy Findley (p. 92), Judith Viorst (p. 142), Sean Twist (p. 147), Judy Brady (p. 155), Charlie Angus (p. 180), Michael Dorris (p. 208), and Rosie DiManno (p. 211).

You Are a Contract Painkiller

Maureen Littlejohn

Maureen Littlejohn is an award-winning travel journalist and freelance writer. She has worked as a daily newspaper reporter and a lifestyle feature writer, TV music critic, editor, and managing editor of numerous consumer and trade magazines. Currently she is a freelance writer on pop culture. Maureen Littlejohn's articles have appeared in a variety of publications in Canada and the United States. They include the Smithsonian's Museum of the North American Indian, Convene *(the magazine of the Professional Convention Management Association),* Flare, *the* Financial Post, Canadian Musician, *and* Travel.

In this essay. Littlejohn makes extensive use of **personification,** *a literary technique in which an inanimate object or abstract quality is presented as human. This essay originally appeared in* Equinox *in 1997.*

1   You are a contract painkiller code name ASA, also known to your clients as aspirin. Pain is your gain—Canadians swallow almost one billion of your agents each year. You have achieved renown° by destroying headaches but you are equally effective in countering° sprains, burns, or blows. You stop swelling and reduce fever and research suggests you may even help prevent heart attack and stroke.

2   On your latest mission, your client has just had a fight with her boss, and her head is pounding. Involuntary° muscle contractions on her scalp and at the back of her neck, triggered° by the argument, are now causing swelling and throbbing. In reaction her body has produced an enzyme° called prostaglandin, which is sensitizing the nerve endings in her scalp, especially around her temples and sending a message of pain to her brain.

3   Taken with a modest stream of water or ginger ale, your chalky, round self begins the mission by moving through the host's esophagus°, into the stomach, then the upper small intestine, where you are dissolved and passed into the bloodstream. There, you slop into a molecular chain of events and disable the enzyme that converts the acid in cell membranes into prostaglandins. The nerve endings are now desensitized, that pain message to the brain is stopped, and your host is smiling again.

4   You reduce fever in a similar way. If your host were suffering from the flu, her white blood cells would be fighting the virus by producing prostaglandins that, in turn, cause the body's temperature to rise. You head off the prostaglandins and bring the fever down.

5   You are not the only pain relieving agent at work. Ibuprofen and other aspirin-like drugs known as nonsteroidal anti-inflammatory drugs (NSAIDs) do much the same thing. You all share possible side effects—in 2 to 6 percent of your clients, you cause stomach irritation and possibly bleeding and in extreme cases, kidney failure. Prostaglandins help maintain the integrity of the stomach lining, and in their absence, the acidic NSAIDs give the host a queasy° feeling.

6   As a tonic for hire, you have been around for a century, but your family tree goes back much further. In ancient Greece, Hippocrates noted that chewing on willow leaves reduced fever. In the 1800s, two Italian chemists confirmed that willow bark contains one of your main ingredients, the antipyretic (fever-reducing) salicin. A Swiss pharmacist then found that meadowsweet, a shrub in the spirea family, has even more of the magic substance than willow bark. And while experimenting with salicin, a German chemist created salicylic acid (the SA of ASA). He called it *Spirsäure* after spirea, hence the "spirin" part of your name. The "a" was added for "acetyl," the substances—including a salt—that made the SA easier on the stomach. In 1893, Felix Hoffmann at the Bayer AG Chemical Works in Germany purified and stabilized you, and that's when you first claimed celebrity status as one of the world's most popular, inexpensive pain relievers. Today you are synthesized from coal tar or petroleum instead of plants.

7   Beyond garden-variety° aches and pains, you are prescribed as a remedy° for arthritis because of your genius for blocking prostaglandins that trigger the pain and swelling of joints. Your most recent prostaglandin-fighting potential is to prevent heart attack and stroke. There is even talk that you may help ward off cancer and senility. Mission impossible? We'll see.

Vocabulary

1 renown(n): widespread fame and honour

1 countering (n): contradicting, arguing against

2 involuntary (adj): spontaneous, automatic

2 trigger (v): make something happen

2 enzyme (n): complex protein that acts as a catalyst

3 esophagus (n): passage down which food moves from throat to stomach

5 queasy (adj): nauseated, feeling like vomiting

7 garden-variety (adj, informal): common, ordinary

7 remedy (n): treatment for disease or its symptoms, cure

 # RESPONDING TO THE READING

- If the thesis is stated, identify it; if it is implied, write it in your own words.
- What do you think is the purpose of this essay? Give reasons for your opinion.
- Who do you think is the intended audience of this essay? Give reasons for your opinion.

Comprehension

1. To what is ASA compared in the opening paragraph?
2. What is it that ASA "kills"?
3. What type of process analysis is presented in Paragraphs 3 and 4?
4. What is ASA compared to in Paragraph 5 and why?
5. What type of process analysis is given in Paragraph 6?
6. What does ASA stand for?
7. When was ASA invented? By whom?
8. What was ASA made from originally? And what is it made from today?
9. Why has ASA become so popular over time?

Analysis

1. Do you think aspirin will continue to be popular? Why or why not?
2. What is Littlejohn's attitude to her subject and how can you tell?
3. Maureen Littlejohn uses technical words in this essay, for example, prostaglandins, nonsteroidal anti-inflammatory, antipyretic. Did you need to look up their meanings? Why or why not?
4. Do you think the use of personification is successful? Why or why not?
5. How does "Mission Impossible," in the conclusion, reflect the theme and development of the essay itself?

Discussion/Writing Suggestions

1. Do you prefer medications available from pharmacies or more natural remedies? Why?
2. Explain the allusion in the final question and consider the effectiveness of this allusion in shaping this essay.

   • Other essays on scientific or technical subjects are by Bill Bryson (p. 14), David Ginsburg (p. 33), Jay Ingram (p. 40), Rachel Carson (p. 123), James C. Rettie (p. 221), and Susan Jacoby (p. 176). Jay Ingram, James C. Rettie, and Maureen Littlejohn employ extensive use of analogy as do Wayson Choy (p. 169) and J. Anthony Lukas (p. 191).

Ten Steps to the Creation of a Modern Media Icon

Mark Kingwell

Mark Kingwell (1963–) is a Canadian writer and academic. He studied at the University of Toronto, Edinburgh University, and Yale University, graduating with a Ph.D. in 1991. He is a professor of philosophy at the University of Toronto and a Senior Fellow of Massey College, specializing in theories of politics and culture. A contributing editor to the Globe and Mail *Books Section, he was a former columnist for the* National Post *and a former contributing editor of* Saturday Night *magazine. He frequently appears on television and radio, often on the CBC, and is the author of many books, including* Practical Judgments *(2002) and* Catch and Release *(2003). His writing on culture and politics has appeared in more than 40 publications, including* Harper's Magazine, *where he is a contributing editor,* Utne Reader, *the* New York Times Magazine, Forbes, *and* Maclean's.

This essay is taken from his book Marginalia: A Cultural Reader *(1999).*

1   "Icon" is from the Greek *eikon,* which means "image," which is everything: The name of a camera. The word for all those little point-and-click pictures on your computer screen. Greek and Roman Orthodox religious objects. Little oil paintings of saints with elaborate gold panel coverings. Anybody who represents something to someone somewhere. The image that gives a debased Platonic° suggestion of reality without ever being it. So create an image—one the cameras, and therefore we, will love.

2   The image must be drastically beautiful or else compellingly ugly. It must, for women, show a smooth face of impenetrable maquillage° and impeccably "tasteful" clothing (Chanel*, Balenciaga*, Rykiel*; not Versace*, not Moschino*, definitely not Gauthier*), a flat surface of emotional projection, the real-world equivalent of a keyboard emoticon. Icon smiling at the cheering crowds: :-). Icon frowning bravely at diseased child or crippled former soldier in hospital bed: :-(. Icon winking slyly at the crush of press photographers as she steps into the waiting limousine: ;-).

There should be only one name, for preference a chummy° or faux-intimate diminutive°: Jackie*, Di*, Barbra*. Sunglasses are mandatory whenever the ambient° light rises above building-code-normal 250-foot candles. These can be removed or peered over to offer an image of blinking vulnerability°. Or else the image should be, in men, so overwhelmingly tawdry and collapsed, preferably from some high-cheekbone peak of youthful beauty, that it acquires a can't-look-away magnetism, the sick pull of the human car wreck. (The only exceptions: (1) Athletes—Tiger*, Michael*—whose downy° smoothness and transcendental physical abilities offer a male counterpoint that is almost female in appeal; they are the contraltos° of the icon chorus. And (2) actors, whose malleable° faces are so empty of particular meaning as to be innocent of intelligence). Folds of leathery skin, evidence of drug use and chain-smoking, the runes of dissipation etched on the pitted skin of hard living—they all have them. Johnny Cash*, Mick Jagger*, Leonard Cohen*, Kurt Cobain*, Chet Baker*, late Elvis*: the musician in ruins, the iconic face as crumbling stone monument. Basic black attire is effective but must be Armani, never Gap. This suggests wisdom and sexual power, deep and bitter knowledge of the world—but with dough°. The face need never change, its very stasis a sign of rich inner troubles. Sunglasses are superfluous. They smack° of effort.

3   There must be a narrative structure that bathes the icon in the pure light of the fairy tale or morality play. Beautiful princess beset by ugly siblings or nasty stepmother. Lovely rich girl mistakes the charisma of power for true character. Overweening° ambition turns simple boy into gun-toting, pill-popping maniac. Feisty° rebel takes on the establishment of (circle one) Hollywood/big business/ government/rock music/professional sports. Prodigy singled out for great things at an early age by psycho father. Indispensable words in the story: "trapped," "betray," "tragic," "love," "promise" (as both verb and noun), "happiness" (always without irony), "fame" (always with venom), and "money" (never spoken). The details of the story may change, but the overarching structure cannot: you can improvise° and elaborate, but never deviate°. Sometimes a new story (thrill-happy slut consorts with swarthy and disreputable jet-setter) will be temporarily substituted for an old one that no longer applies (virginal bride is unloved by philandering° husband). We can't be sure which story will win out until . . .

4   Death. Already, at step four? Yes, absolutely, for iconography is very much a post mortem affair. The death ends the life but does not quite complete it: that is the business of story-tellers and their audience, the cameras and their lights. Death is just the beginning. It should be, if possible, violent, messy and a bit mysterious. Unwise confrontations with fast-moving industrial machines—sports cars, airplanes, cargo trucks, high-speed trains, bullets. Accidents are good, having as they do an aura of adventitious innocence, followed closely in order of preference by murder, assassination, execution and suicide. If suicide it must be either a gun or an overdose of illicit drugs, usually in colorful and nasty combination: alcohol and barbiturates, crack and benzedrine, heroin and anything. In all cases, the death is "shocking" and "tragic," though in neither instance literally.

5   Now, an outbreak of hysterical mourning, baseless and all the more intense for being so. (Nobody feels so strongly about someone they actually know). Extended retrospectives on television. Numerous panel discussions and attempts to "make

sense," to "assess the life," to "provide context." Long broadcasts of the funeral or memorial service complete with lingering, loving shots of weeping crowds. Greedy close-ups of the well-known people in attendance, the bizarre° fraternity of celebrity which dictates that those famous for being born in a certain family has everything in common with those famous for singing pop tunes or throwing a ball in a designated manner. News agencies and networks must spend a great deal of money sending a lot of people somewhere distant to cover the death. They must then justify that expense with hours and hours of coverage. We must see images of the iconic face, beautiful or ruined, over and over and over. "Ordinary" people must be shown, on the media, insisting that the media have nothing to do with their deep feelings of loss. They must say that they "felt they knew him (her)," that "she (he) was like a member of the family." This keeps them happy and ensures that no larger form of public participation—say, protesting a tax hike or program cut, resisting a corporate takeover—will ever cross their minds as possible, let alone desirable.

6   A small backlash must gather strength, a token gesture of cultural protest that, in pointing out the real faults and shortcomings of the dead icon, unwittingly reinforces the growing "larger-than-life" status of the image. This is the culture's way of injecting itself with a homeopathic inoculation°, introducing a few strains of mild virus that actually beef up the dominant media antibodies. Those who have the temerity to suggest that the dead icon was not all he (she) is thought to be will be publicly scorned, accused of cynicism, insulted at dinner parties, but secretly welcomed. The final storyline of the icon-life will now begin to set, rejecting the foreign elements as dead-ends or narrative spurs, or else accepting them as evidence that the icon was "after all" human—a suggestion that, in its very making, implies the opposite. The media coverage will fall into line in telling this story because individual producers and anchors will be unable to imagine doing otherwise. Tag-lines and feature-story titles will help set the narrative epoxy for good, providing catchy mini-stories for us to hang our thoughts on to. Quickie books with the same titles will begin to appear—things like *Icon X: Tragic Ambition* or *Icon Y: Little Girl in Trouble.* The producers and anchors must then claim that they are not creating this tale, simply "giving the people what they want." Most people will accept this because to do otherwise would hurt their brains.

7   The image will now be so widely reproduced, so ubiquitously mediated on television, at the supermarket, in the bookstore, that it seems a permanent feature of the mediascape, naturalized and indispensable. It will now begin its final divorce from the person depicted. Any actual achievements—touchdowns thrown, elections won, causes championed—fall away like the irrelevancies they are. The face (or rather, The Face) looms outward from glossy paper, T-shirts, fridge magnets, posters, Halloween masks and coffee mugs. Kitschification° of the image is to be welcomed, not feared. It proves that the icon is here to stay. The basic unit of fame-measurement is of course, as critic Cullen Murphy once argued, the warhol*, a period of celebrity equal to fifteen minutes. Kitsch versions of the image augers° well: we're talking at least a megawarhol icon or better (that's 15 million minutes of fame, which is just over 10,400 days, or about 28.5 years—enough to get you to those standard silver-anniversary retrospectives). No kitsch, no staying power: a 100 kilowarhols or less, a minicon.

8　　There follow academic studies, well-meaning but doomed counter-assessments, sightings, and cameo appearances of the icon on a *Star Trek* spin-off series or
as an answer on *Jeopardy*. People begin to claim they can commune with the spirit
of the dead icon across vast distances of psychic space. Conspiracy theories refuse
to be settled by overwhelming evidence of a boringly predictable chain of events
involving a drunk driver, too much speed, and unused seatbelts. Or whatever.

9　　Television retrospectives every decade, with a mid-decade special at 25 years.
The final triumph of the image: entirely cut off now from its original body, it is free-
floating and richly polysemous°. Always more surface than depth, more depiction
than reality, the icon now becomes pure zero-degree image, a depicted lifestyle
without a life, a face without a person, a spiritual moment without context or
meaning. In other words, the pure pervasive triumph of cultural exposure, a sign
lacking both sense and referent. In still other words, the everything (and nothing)
we sought all along: communion without community.

10　　Now, for a religious experience, just point. And click.

Notes

2 Chanel, Balenciaga, Rykiel, Versace,
Moschino, Gauthier: names of famous
clothing designers

2 Jackie, Di, Barbra: Jacqueline
Kennedy/Onassis, Princess Diana, and
Barbra Streisand

2 Tiger, Michael: Tiger Woods the golfer,
Michael Jordan the basketball player

2 Johnny Cash, Mick Jagger, Leonard
Cohen, Kurt Cobain, Chet Baker, Elvis:
famous male musicians and singers

7 warhol (n, slang): moment of fame,
taken from Andy Warhol, a 20th-century
American artist who stated that each
person would have 15 minutes of fame
in a lifetime

Vocabulary

1 Platonic (adj): relating to Plato or his
philosophy

2 maquillage (n): makeup or the art of
applying makeup

2 chummy (adj, informal): friendly,
sociable

2 faux-intimate diminutive (n): a smaller
version of something (such as a name)
Using the shortened version of the
celebrity's name creates the false (faux)
illusion that you know them personally

2 ambient (adj): in the immediately sur-
rounding area, creating an atmosphere

2 vulnerability (n): open to emotional
harm, easily persuaded

2 downy (adj): soft, youthful

2 contraltos (n): lowest vocal range for a
woman

2 malleable (adj): able to be shaped,
easily influenced by others

2 dough (n, slang): money

2 smack (v): strongly suggest

3 overweening (adj): arrogant, excessive

3 feisty (adj): spirited, aggressive

3 improvise (v): to make up something
on the spot

3 deviate (v): to be different, to turn
away from a particular course

3 philandering (adj): having an affair,
flirtatious

5 bizarre (adj): strange

6 homeopathic inoculation: homeopathy is a form of medicine in which a patient is given minute doses of natural drugs that in larger doses would produce the symptoms of the disease itself in an attempt to create natural immunity

7 kitschification (n): process of creating kitsch; kitsch (n): artistic vulgarity, lack of artistic taste
7 auger (v): predict
9 polysemous (adj): having multiple meanings

RESPONDING TO THE READING

- If the thesis is stated, identify it; if it is implied, write it in your own words.
- What do you think is the purpose of this essay? Give reasons for your opinion.
- Who do you think is the intended audience of this essay? Give reasons for your opinion.

Comprehension

1. Step 1 is "So create an image—one the cameras, and therefore we, will love." Why does Mark Kingwell define icon before giving this step?
2. Step 2 is "The image must be drastically beautiful or else compellingly ugly." How does Kingwell support this step?
3. Step 3 is "There must be a narrative structure that bathes the icon in the pure light of the fairy tale or morality play." Explain what Kingwell means in this step.
4. Step 4 is "Yes, absolutely, for iconography is very much a post mortem affair." How does Kingwell show that death is an important step?
5. Step 5 is "Now, an outbreak of hysterical mourning, baseless and all the more intense for being so." Explain what Kingwell means by this step.
6. Step 6 is "A small backlash must gather strength, a token gesture of cultural protest that, in pointing out the real faults and shortcomings of the dead icon, unwittingly reinforces the growing 'larger-than-life' status of the image." What are the signs of this step?
7. Step 7 is "The image will now be . . . widely reproduced." How is the icon made ubiquitous according to Kingwell?
8. Step 8 is "There follow academic studies, well-meaning but doomed counter-assessments, sightings, and cameo appearances of the icon." What examples does Kingwell give for this step?
9. Step 9 is "Television retrospectives every decade." How does this step relate to the previous steps?
10. Step 10 is "Now, for a religious experience, just point. And click." Is this a suitable conclusion? Why or why not?

Analysis

1. How clearly has Kingwell outlined the creation of a celebrity in our culture? Does this process seem logical to you?
2. How can we, the general public, create a public icon? Are we responsible for the popularity of people like Paris Hilton, Princess Diana, Madonna, and Marilyn Monroe?
3. How many of the "icons" named in this essay did you recognize? How do you account for that?
4. How effective is Kingwell's examination of social behaviour in this instance? Support your response.
5. How would you describe Kingwell's tone in this essay? Support your answer.

Discussion/Writing Suggestions

1. Do you read celebrity gossip in magazines or watch entertainment gossip programs on TV? Why or why not?
2. Is a celebrity a hero in your opinion? Why or why not?

   - Other essays that focus on popular culture are by Ralph Nader (p. 28), David Ginsburg (p. 33), Jay Ingram (p. 40), Robertson Davies (p. 150), Sandra Stewart (p. 121), Leslie C. Smith (p. 105), Charlie Angus (p. 180), and Pier Giorgio Di Cicco (p. 196).

Essay of Comparison and Contrast

The essay of comparison and contrast presents two subjects side by side. Comparison shows how the two subjects are alike or similar; contrast demonstrates the differences between the two subjects. When both similarities and differences are examined, we are *comparing and contrasting*. However, the term *comparison* has generally become accepted to mean all three activities. Any act of comparison and contrast leads to a value judgment. How do you decide which shirt to wear? If you have a lot of clothes, you make a series of judgments about colours, pattern, sleeve length, and coordination. For some, the choice may lie between clean and dirty; nevertheless, a decision has to be made based on comparison and contrast. To draw a conclusion or make a value judgment is usually the purpose of writing an essay of comparison and contrast. The conclusion may even be to see things in a new way because they have been set side by side.

Writing Strategy

When composing this sort of essay, you must consider why you are comparing or contrasting the two subjects of your choice. What is your purpose in showing how the two subjects are alike or different? Do you want to demonstrate, for example, that a Big Mac is better than a cheeseburger from Burger King? Do you want to persuade your reader to adopt marketing strategy A rather than marketing strategy B? Do you want to shed new light on Johnny Depp by comparing him to, or contrasting him with, Brad Pitt?

In the introduction to any essay of comparison and contrast you must clearly identify your two subjects and your purpose for considering them together. Then you must establish your approach. There are two methods of organizing your materials for an essay of comparison/contrast: the block method and the point method.

- **Block Method:** With this method you concentrate on your first subject; you present all your key ideas and supporting details related to that subject. When you finish subject 1, you turn to subject 2 and follow the same procedure. For example, a comparison or contrast between apples and oranges in block format can be presented as:

  subject 1—apples   subject 2—oranges
  Introduction + thesis statement on the two types of fruit
  Block 1—Apples
  —taste
  —cost
  —storage
  Block 2—Oranges
  —taste
  —cost
  —storage
  Conclusion + thesis on apples and oranges restated

This method is more suitable for short-essay answers in an exam. It is also used strategically for essays in which the bias is absolutely clear, or those in which a "one-sided argument" is desirable.

- **Point Method:** With this method you discuss the two subjects alternately (subject A first and subject B second) in relation to taste, the first of your key ideas. Then you discuss the two subjects with regard to cost, your second key idea, before turning to compare or contrast storage methods. Using the "point method," your comparison/contrast can be organized as follows:

  subject 1—apples   subject 2—oranges
  Introduction + thesis statement on the two subjects in three aspects
  Aspect 1—taste   —apples vs. oranges
  Aspect 2—cost   —apples vs. oranges
  Aspect 3—storage   —apples vs. oranges
  Conclusion + thesis on apples and oranges restated

As you can see, this method is perfect for a formula five-paragraph essay. Although it requires better organizational skills, you can usually explain or argue more clearly and more convincingly in this format.

SAMPLE STUDENT ESSAY OF COMPARISON AND CONTRAST

✓ # Aladdin or Beauty and the Beast

Sandra Stewart

1   There seems to be a trend in movies recently: more interest in the human element, less in hi-tech spectacle. Ironically, two of the best movies I've seen in the last couple of years that explore the area of human relationships are cartoons. Both are Disney productions exemplifying the highest standards of artwork, complex musical scores, and a strong storyline. *Beauty and the Beast* and *Aladdin* are alike in these ways, but *Beauty and the Beast,* unlike *Aladdin,* is a movie with a message.

2   Both movies open with a narrative voice-over, setting the scene. In each the artwork is wonderful. The story *Aladdin* begins with the terrifying Tiger—God set against a deep, dark sky sparkling with stars. Even though it's all drawings, you feel the emptiness of the open spaces, and you know that the villain, Jafar, is really evil. *Beauty and the Beast* opens by moving the viewer through a forest. You really feel as if you are part of the scenery. Even though it's all a cartoon, the camera leads the eyes of the audience deeper through the tangled growth of forest bushes. What amazes me is how the cartoonists managed to give depth and perspective to that forest. In *Aladdin* the artwork is at its most brilliant in the wild carpet-rides, first through the cave of treasures and then in the romantic flight over the countryside that Aladdin and Jasmine take. In the case of *Aladdin,* the star is undoubtedly the Genie. The changes in his shape and size are so fast. This is amazing, especially when fluid movement is not sacrificed to that rapid pace. *Beauty and the Beast* excels in the flowing movements of all its characters, but especially Belle. She moves like a real ballerina with none of the jerkiness you'd expect from watching Saturday morning cartoons. In addition, Belle's face is so expressive. Her acting is better than some Hollywood movie stars. Moods are shown and she has this unruly lock of hair that is always falling across her face and which she brushes aside gracefully. It is this attention to "real" detail that makes this movie so brilliant technically.

3   The quality of the music in each movie is another example of attention to detail. Part of the energy in *Aladdin* comes from its musical score. The songs, with the exception of the beautiful and romantic "New World," are really lively and enter-taining. My particular favourites are the ones my little brother likes best, "Prince Ali" and "A Friend Like Me." The talents of Robin Williams, who gives voice to the Genie, are really outstanding. Just as *Aladdin* allows real actors a chance to shine, so does *Beauty and the Beast.* The spectacular "Be Our Guest" would be a showstopper on stage. Jerry Orbach sings his heart out as Lumière in this particular song. The romantic ballad "Beauty and the Beast" is so melodic that my little brother, who was only three and a half at the time, came out of the movie theatre singing it.

4   Both of the movies are based on really well-loved fairy stories. They have strong plots which everyone knows and the Disney writers have adapted to suit

today's society. In *Aladdin,* Princess Jasmine isn't only a "girl" expecting to be married off. She has her own strong personality and demands the right to choose whom she'll marry. She also helps Aladdin overcome the evil Jafar, so that they can "live happily ever after." However, it is in *Beauty and the Beast* that the most powerful changes to the fairy tale have been made. Belle is definitely the star of this movie, and again she's not a weak little girl. In the movie, Belle is a more fully developed character than in the fairy story. She's an active, intelligent modern woman who respects education more than good looks. She really despises the "macho" Gaston. Gaston is an addition to the original fairy story and this character really modernizes the plot. Through Gaston, the movie is able to make us think about "jock" behaviour, mob violence, and propaganda. It's critical of all of these things. *Beauty and the Beast* has a moral that *Aladdin* doesn't. It's more than a story. This is the real difference between the two movies. *Beauty and the Beast* shows how powerful and fragile love is. Even my little brother knew that this movie showed us that real love is for what a person is and not what a person looks like. He could see that the Beast became a handsome Prince only because he and Belle loved each other.

description imagery

5   Well, I hope I've convinced you to see these movies. They're both available on DVD. Believe me you'll enjoy both of them not only because they are spectacular and entertaining, but also because they teach you something about human relationships in a very realistic way. If you're embarrassed renting them, borrow a kid to accompany you to the local video store. You'll be glad you did.

Comprehension

1. In her introductory paragraph, Sandra Stewart identifies her two subjects. How does she do that?
2. Identify Stewart's thesis and the key ideas she uses to compare and contrast her two subjects.
3. What does Stewart say is her purpose in making this comparison/contrast?
4. Based on your identification of the key ideas in the essay's introduction, find the topic sentence in each paragraph.
5. If Stewart had chosen the block method of development, she would have concentrated first on *Aladdin* and then on *Beauty and the Beast*. Using Stewart's key ideas and her supporting details, write an outline for this essay using the block method.

Analysis

1. Do you think Sandra Stewart is successful in supporting her thesis? Why or why not?
2. Have you seen either of these two movies? If yes, what do you think of them? If no, has Stewart convinced you to see them?
3. What qualities do you look for in a good movie?
4. Which movie would you recommend to someone? Support your response.

READINGS: ESSAYS OF COMPARISON AND CONTRAST

These four essays compare and contrast very different subjects. Rachel Carson in "A Fable for Tomorrow" is concerned with the environment, and her essay is both a personal response and an impassioned plea from a scientist. She uses the *block* method. Anne McIlroy compares and contrasts what amuses men and women; her essay is a newspaper report on university research. Her organization uses the *point* method. "English, French: Why Not Both?" by Peggy Lampotang compares and contrasts her two languages and decides she enjoys her bilingualism. Stephen L. Carter contrasts honesty with integrity in his thoughtful essay, "The Insufficiency of Honesty." He seems to be using the point method; however, he focuses on honesty as a means of distinguishing between the two virtues.

A Fable for Tomorrow

Rachel Carson

"The more clearly we can focus our attention on the wonders and realities of the universe around us, the less taste we shall have for destruction."—Rachel Carson

Rachel Carson (1907–1964) was born in Pittsburgh, Pennsylvania. A zoologist and marine biologist, she is often credited with having launched the global environmental movement with her landmark book, Silent Spring. Silent Spring *initially appeared as a serialization in three parts in the June 16, June 23, and June 30 issues of* The New Yorker *magazine in 1962 and had an immense effect on the United States, where it spurred a reversal in national pesticide policy, and later around the world. She graduated from the Pennsylvania College for Women in 1929 after switching her major from English and creative writing to marine biology. She continued her studies in zoology and genetics at Johns Hopkins University, earning a master's degree in 1932. Rachel Carson's talent for writing led to a number of popular books on environmental issues. Apart from* Silent Spring, *her books include* Under the Sea Wind *(1941),* The Sea Around Us *(1951),* The Edge of the Sea *(1955), and* The Sense of Wonder *(1965).*

In this essay, taken from Silent Spring, *Rachel Carson draws comparisons and contrasts using the block method.*

1   There was once a town in the heart of America where all life seemed to live in harmony with its surroundings. The town lay in the midst of a checkerboard of prosperous farms, with fields of grain and hillsides of orchards where, in spring, white clouds of bloom drifted above the green fields. In autumn, oak and maple and birch set up a blaze of color that flamed and flickered across a backdrop of pines. The foxes barked in the hills and deer silently crossed the fields, half hidden in the mists of the fall mornings.

2   Along the roads, laurel, viburnum and alder, great ferns and wildflowers delighted the traveler's eye through much of the year. Even in winter the roadsides

were places of beauty, where countless birds came to feed on the berries and on the seed heads of the dried weeds rising above the snow. The countryside was, in fact, famous for the abundance° and variety of its bird life, and when the flood of migrants was pouring through in spring and fall people traveled from great distances to observe them. Others came to fish the streams, which flowed clear and cold out of the hills and contained shady pools where trout lay. So it had been from the days many years ago when the first settlers raised their houses, sank their wells, and built their barns.

3   Then a strange blight° crept over the area and everything began to change. Some evil spell had settled on the community: mysterious maladies° swept the flocks of chickens; the cattle and sheep sickened and died. Everywhere was a shadow of death. The farmers spoke of much illness among their families. In the town the doctors had become more and more puzzled by new kinds of sickness appearing among their patients. There had been several sudden and unexplained deaths not only among adults but even among children, who would be stricken° suddenly while at play and die within a few hours.

4   There was a strange stillness. The birds, for example—where had they gone? Many people spoke of them, puzzled and disturbed. The feeding stations in the backyards were deserted. The few birds seen anywhere were moribund°; they trembled violently and could not fly. It was a spring without voices. On the mornings that had once throbbed with the dawn chorus of robins, catbirds, doves, jays, wrens, and scores of other bird voices there was no sound; only silence lay over the fields and woods and marsh.

5   On the farms the hens brooded, but no chicks hatched. The farmers complained that they were unable to raise any pigs—the litters were small and the young survived only a few days. The apple trees were coming into bloom but no bees droned° among the blossoms, so there was no pollination and there would be no fruit.

6   The roadsides, once so attractive, were now lined with browned and withered vegetation as though swept by fire. These, too, were silent, deserted by all living things. Even the streams were now lifeless. Anglers no longer visited them, for all the fish had died.

7   In the gutters° under the eaves° and between the shingles° of the roofs, a white granular powder still showed a few patches; some weeks before it had fallen like snow upon the roofs and the lawns, the fields and streams. No witchcraft, no enemy action had silenced the rebirth of new life in this stricken world. The people had done it themselves.

8   This town does not actually exist, but it might easily have a thousand counterparts in America or elsewhere in the world. I know of no community that has experienced all the misfortunes I describe. Yet every one of these disasters has actually happened somewhere, and many real communities have already suffered a substantial number of them. A grim° specter° has crept upon us almost unnoticed, and this imagined tragedy may easily become a stark reality we all shall know.

Vocabulary

2 abundance (n): large amount

3 blight (n): generic plant disease caused by fungi, bacteria, or viruses

3 maladies (n): illnesses

3 stricken (v): badly affected as by illness

4 moribund (adj): dying, nearly dead

5 drone (v): make a low humming noise (a male worker bee is called a drone)

7 gutters (n): rain water channel

7 eaves (n): part of the roof that projects over its supporting wall

7 shingles (n): roof tiles

8 grim (adj): depressing, gloomy, forbidding

8 specter (n): unpleasant ghost

RESPONDING TO THE READING

- If the thesis is stated, identify it; if it is implied, write it in your own words.
- What do you think is the purpose of this essay? Give reasons for your opinion.
- Who do you think is the intended audience of this essay? Give reasons for your opinion.

Comprehension

1. What are the two subjects Rachel Carson compares and contrasts?
2. Because Carson develops the essay in block method, she concentrates on subject 1 first before turning to subject 2. Which paragraphs discuss subject 2?
3. Identify Carson's key ideas in each block.
4. Explain this image from Paragraph 1: "a checkerboard of prosperous farms."
5. Does Carson mention each season in Paragraph 1? Find her examples for each season.
6. Why does Carson devote so much of her supporting detail to bird life in Paragraphs 2, 4, and 5?
7. What is the effect of Carson's repetition of "strange" in the opening of Paragraphs 3 and 4?
8. What types of stillness does Carson present in Paragraphs 4, 5, and 6?

Analysis

1. What is Carson's purpose in discussing the "town in the heart of America"?
2. The discussion of her second subject is substantially longer than her discussion of the first. What details does she add?
3. Her final two paragraphs provide an explanation, a cause for the changes discussed in the essay. What effect does Carson produce by placing this information at the end of her essay?

4. Do you think this essay could have the same impact if it had been written using the point method? Explain your response.
5. What is a fable? What fable does Carson relate? Why is it called a fable?
6. Carson's language often suggests the supernatural. How many references to the supernatural can you find? In an essay that deals with the natural world, do you think the supernatural element is appropriate? Why or why not?

Discussion/Writing Suggestions

1. This essay was written in 1962. Is it still relevant? Support your response.
2. Rachel Carson's essay is frequently reprinted around the world. How would you explain its popularity?

- Other essays that discuss our natural environment are by James C. Rettie (p. 221), Sean Twist (p. 147), Catherine George (p. 194), Margaret Laurence (p. 202), and Sang Il Lee (p. 233). The following essays also tell stories: Charles Dickens (p. 10), Malcolm X (p. 19), David Ginsburg (p. 33), Margaret Atwood (p. 85), Timothy Findley (p. 92), Pat Capponi (p. 158), Michael Dorris (p. 208), Rosie DiManno (p. 211), Maya Angelou (p. 218), and Almas Zakiuddin (p. 240).

What's Funny to Him Is Funnier to Her

Anne McIlroy

Anne McIlroy is a science reporter for the Globe and Mail.

This essay, which appeared in the Globe and Mail *on November 8, 2005, compares and contrasts the different ways men and women respond to humour. Because it is a newspaper article, it is written in "takes," not full paragraphs.*

1 It is snowing in the cartoon, and two birds are perched on a branch looking at a kid directly below them who is trying to catch one of the big white flakes on his tongue. His mouth is open so wide his tonsils are a bulls-eye in the centre of his face. "Hey," one bird says to the other, "are you thinking what I'm thinking?"

2 When women process cartoons like this one they use more parts of their brain than men, a new study has found. But if reading the comics page is more work for women, it also may be more fun.

3 The experiment found that the reward centre of the brain—the part that is activated when people, for instance, win at gambling or snort crack cocaine—is more active in women than men when they get the joke that a cartoon delivers.

4 "Women appeared to have less expectation of a reward, which in this case was the punchline° of the cartoon," says Allan Reiss, a professor of Psychiatry and Behavioural Science at Stanford University in California. (The birds are planning to plop their own sticky white stuff into the boy's mouth.)

5 The experiment is the first to use brain-imaging to compare how women and men understand humour. It builds on earlier work that found important differences in what makes men and women laugh.

6   In general, men prefer jokes or slapstick° comedy, while women like funny stories or anecdotes, says Rod Martin, a psychology professor at the University of Western Ontario.

7   There are also important differences in why men and women use humour when dealing with others. Men are far more likely to slag° each other, and to use "hostile" humour to establish dominance, says Dr. Martin, who has spent 25 years studying humour.

8   "It reminds me a little of wrestling. You try to pin the other guy, then he tries to pin you."

9   Women, on the other hand, are more likely to be funny in order to build and maintain relationships and make others more comfortable.

10   Those gender differences emerge early. Daniela O'Neill, a researcher at the University of Waterloo who studies how children learn and use language, has noticed that even as toddlers, boys are more likely than girls to initiate conversations using knock-knock jokes.

11   Knock-knock jokes aside, there are also many similarities between males and females when it comes to humour, Dr. Martin says. Men and women are equally creative when they try to be funny. Both can laugh at themselves. Both enjoy sexual humour.

12   Dr. Martin is now investigating how couples use humour, and how that relates to how satisfied they are with their relationships. He videotaped 50 couples who discussed a problem. After a few minutes, they seemed to forget the camera was there, he says.

13   He is still analyzing the content of those conversations, but says both men and women used humour to get their points across. Sometimes it was positive, and used to deflect conflict or display a sense of commitment. But sometimes it got nasty and involved aggressive putdowns. He said he wondered why some of the couples stayed together.

14   The brain-imaging research is based on the idea that men and women have relatively similar funny bones°, says Eiman Azim, a graduate student who assisted with the experiment at Stanford.

15   There was no difference in the number of cartoons the 10 men and 10 women in the study found funny, how humorous they found them, or how long it took them to react with a laugh or a smile, says Mr. Azim, who is now studying at Harvard.

16   Both used the part of the brain responsible for processing language, when looking at cartoons, and the temporal lobe°, which is involved in semantics° and decoding°.

17   But the women had more activity in their prefrontal cortex°, which is involved in working memory, which allows someone to remember something for a short time, but not permanently. The limbic system, which processes emotion, was also more active, Mr. Azim says.

18   The study is published in today's *Proceedings of the National Academy of Sciences* journal in the United States.

Vocabulary

4 punchline (n): the last part of a joke that delivers the meaning and the humour

6 slapstick comedy (n): comedy with the emphasis on fast physical action and obvious visual jokes

7 slag (v, slang): to criticize or make abusive comments

14 funny bones (n, informal): the things that make one laugh

16 temporal lobe (n): part of the brain responsible for hearing

16 semantics (n): study of meaning in language

16 decode (v): decipher or interpret a message

17 prefrontal cortex (n): at the very front of the brain

RESPONDING TO THE READING

- If the thesis is stated, identify it; if it is implied, write it in your own words.
- What do you think is the purpose of this essay? Give reasons for your opinion.
- Who do you think is the intended audience of this essay? Give reasons for your opinion.

Comprehension

1. Is this an essay of comparison or contrast, or both? And how has Anne McIlroy organized her content, by point or block method?
2. The essay opens with a description of a cartoon. Explain its punchline.
3. Why is reading a joke more work for a woman than a man, according to Anne McIlroy's essay?
4. Explain the reason for the allusion to drugs in Paragraph 3.
5. Who is Allan Reiss and what is the experiment he is conducting?
6. What is the crucial difference between men and women when it comes to humour, according to the Stanford experiment?
7. Summarize Dr. Martin's experiment.
8. What is the point of the allusion to "knock-knock" jokes?
9. According to this article, what types of humour do men enjoy? And what types do women find funny?
10. Explain in your own words the similarities in how men and women respond to humour presented by graduate student Eiman Azim.
11. What differences in how men and women respond to humour does Eiman Azim present?

Analysis

1. How does Anne McIlroy introduce "Canadian content" into her essay? Why do you think she does that?
2. Are you surprised that "men and women have relatively similar funny bones"? Why or why not?
3. Why do you think researchers are interested in examining differences between men and women?
4. Based on the types of humour each gender finds funny, the researchers draw certain conclusions. What are they and what do you think of those conclusions?

Discussion/Writing Suggestions

1. Before you read this essay, did you think men and women found the same things funny? Support your response.
2. What sort of humour makes you laugh? Support your response.

    *   Other essays that offer a perspective on humour are by Bill Bryson (p. 14), Pico Iyer (p. 96), Robertson Davies (p. 150), Nicola Bleasby (p. 109), Mark Kingwell (p. 114), Maureen Littlejohn (p. 111), Sean Twist (p. 147), Judy Brady (p. 155), Michael Dorris (p. 208), and Russell Baker (p. 316).

English, French: Why Not Both?

Peggy Lampotang

Peggy Lampotang is a Toronto writer, artist, and photographer who has recently begun to write short stories.

She wrote this article for the "Facts and Arguments" section of the Globe and Mail. *It was published on August 12, 2005.*

1   When I came to Canada at the age of 20, I was very excited to be part of a bilingual country. I was born in Mauritius, a predominantly French-speaking island whose dialect is Creole and official language, English.

2   Creole is colourful but was considered a crude form of French and teachers forbade its use at school. French was the language of choice and I loved the way it flowed in my blood; I danced in it, flirted with it. When I spoke it, I felt alive.

3   I studied in a British system of education, and enjoyed writing in English, but speaking it was a different matter. The shock upon arriving in Toronto and discovering that French was limited to the Harbourfront Francophone Centre and the Alliance Française prompted me to take trips to Montreal.

4   I was fascinated by the lifestyle differences of the expressive Québécois and the reserved Torontonians. But I stayed in Toronto. I liked its industrious quality. I wanted to feel at home in English. My accent, source of much hilarity°, and sometimes, romantic speculations, was frustrating, but did open doors for me.

5   The first lesson I learned from a boyfriend was to curl my tongue, put its tip under the upper teeth, and blow gently the feathery sound "th" so that when I said

three, people knew it was number three and not tree, the wonder of nature that sprouts from the soil and grows into trunk, branches and leaves.

6   Soon I learned to respect the nuances° in each language, pronouncing words, delivering them in ways that sharpened my awareness of fundamental cultural differences between English and French.

7   Ever notice how French translations are much longer than English ones?

8   While reading a cereal box, I realized it wasn't a problem with the translator. This concise and brief statement instills° the down-to-earth, good sense of English: "It can be an important part of your family's nutritious breakfast." The French translation, however, with its lengthy enticing words, gives a frisson° about how pleasurable and extreme the cereal experience: "*Ces céréales irrésistibles occuperont sûrement une place de choix à votre table lors du petit déjeuner familial.*" (These irresistible cereals will surely occupy a place of choice on your table during the family breakfast).

9   During a French conversation, I can elaborate at leisure my descriptions; the more words, the better. However, in English, I use clear exact words, with the least repetition possible.

10   An Anglophone finds it hard to say certain French words such as *"cracher"* (to spit) because there's a tendency to roll the "r" with the tongue and utter the word with a half-open mouth. As an Anglophone, if one is willing to open one's mouth wide and throw the sound from the back of the throat, one will sense the openness of French. However, as a Francophone, the challenge of speaking English is to restrain the elasticity of one's lips. One has to roll words out on one's curled tongue while decreasing the opening of one's mouth to feel the smooth fluidity of English. How else would one make Toronto sound as if it has only two syllables?

11   Anglophones struggle with the letter u as in *"écureuil"* (squirrel) because they can't keep the tongue down and form the lips into a tiny oval shape to emit the sound as if it's easing into a kiss. On the other hand, Francophones could alleviate their difficulty with silent h as in, '"Ow 'is 'e?" if they are willing to make the h sound come out as a short breathy exhalation.

12   The economy of movement in delivering words in English, whether it's from the mouth or the rest of the body, gives a feeling of preciseness but also of control. The French language, however, with its constant shifting of the mouth opening, from the jaw-breaking "Ah" to the pouting "Oh," while the hands point, close, open, spread, or jiggle in all directions, expresses unbound passion. An Anglophone could see this openness as too dramatic, vulnerable and exposed, but a Francophone could interpret the lack of movement of the Anglophone as rigid and cold.

13   I have lived in Toronto for almost three decades. I even dream in English.

14   There were times when my craving for French made me feel part of me was missing. When I enrolled my children in French Immersion, I discovered with pleasant surprise a new community of bilingual parents.

15   The opportunity to speak French regularly has brought a new balance in my life. I feel lucky to be among Canadians who can speak both languages.

16   My personality changes when I switch from one language to the other.

17   I feel in charge, efficient, and love the flow of English sounds rolling and swishing from my mouth.

18   When I speak French, I feel sensual, demonstrative, perhaps a bit excitable, but I relish° its intensity.

19   Fluency in English and French brings familiarity to the quirkiness of their inherent° differences and makes it easier for me to tolerate and accept both.

20   My experience with these two languages makes me see the depth of Pierre Trudeau's vision for this country when he implemented official bilingualism.

21   *Allez-y, Canada.* Let's get along. Why not both, hey?

Vocabulary

4 hilarity (n): amusement, merry laughter

6 nuances (n): subtle differences

8 instill (v): impart ideas gradually

8 frisson (n, French): shiver of excitement, thrill

18 relish (v): enjoy

19 inherent (adj): inborn, innate, characteristic

RESPONDING TO THE READING

- If the thesis is stated, identify it; if it is implied, write it in your own words.
- What do you think is the purpose of this essay? Give reasons for your opinion.
- Who do you think is the intended audience of this essay? Give reasons for your opinion.

Comprehension

1.   What exactly is Peggy Lampotang comparing? How has she organized her comparison/contrast: by block or point method?

2.   What are Lampotang's main points of comparison?

3.   How many languages does Peggy Lampotang say she speaks? What accounts for this?

4.   Why did Lampotang love speaking French when she lived in Mauritius?

5.   What examples does Lampotang provide of the inherent difficulties in pronouncing French?

6.   What reasons does Lampotang give for her different appreciation of each language?

7.   Summarize how Lampotang says she feels when she speaks English as opposed to when she speaks French.

8.   How does Lampotang characterize the differences in the movement of the mouth each language requires?

9.   What pleasure did Lampotang discover when she enrolled her children in a French immersion school?

10. How does Peggy Lampotang describe the differences in her personality when speaking English as opposed to when she speaks French?

Analysis

1.   What is the point of the allusion to Pierre Trudeau in Paragraph 20?
2.   Are Lampotang's final three sentences effective? Why or why not?
3.   In your experience, do people move differently when they speak another language? Explain.
4.   Do you think language affects people's personalities as Peggy Lampotang claims in Paragraphs 16 to 18? Why or why not?
5.   Do you think Peggy Lampotang stereotypes Anglophones or Francophones? Why or why not?

Discussion/Writing Suggestions

1.   If you speak another language, how would you compare your abilities in and feelings about both languages?
2.   Peggy Lampotang says the use of language expresses fundamental cultural differences. Do you agree with her? Why or why not?

   •   Other essays that deal with cultural issues, and Canada in particular, include those by Hugh MacLennan (p. 5), Margaret Atwood (p. 85), Timothy Findley (p. 92), Mark Kingwell (p. 114), Wayson Choy (p. 169), Pier Giorgio Di Cicco (p. 196), Rosie DiManno (p. 211), and Almas Zakiuddin (p. 240).

The Insufficiency of Honesty

Stephen L. Carter

Stephen L. Carter (1954–) is an American law professor, legal and social policy writer, columnist, and novelist. He is the William Nelson Cromwell Professor of Law at Yale University, where he has taught since 1982. He earned a B.A. at Stanford University in 1976 and a J.D. from Yale University in 1979. After graduation, Carter clerked for U.S. Supreme Court JusticeThurgood Marshall. He is a prolific writer whose non-fiction works include Reflections of an Affirmative Action Baby *(1991),* The Culture of Disbelief *(1994),* Integrity *(1997),* The Dissent of the Governed: A Meditation on Law, Religion, and Loyalty *(1999),* Civility *(1999),* God's Name in Vain: The Wrongs and Rights of Religion in Politics *(2001). His first novel is* The Emperor of Ocean Park *(2002). He was selected by* Time *magazine as one of 50 leaders for the new millennium. Stephen L. Carter's writings have won praise from across the political spectrum.*

This essay first appeared in the February 1996 issue of The Atlantic Monthly.

1   A couple of years ago I began a university commencement° address by telling the audience that I was going to talk about integrity. The crowd broke into applause. Applause! Just because they had heard the word "integrity": that's how starved for it they were. They had no idea how I was using the word, or what I was going to

say about integrity, or, indeed, whether I was for it or against it. But they knew they liked the idea of talking about it.

2   Very well, let us consider this word "integrity." Integrity is like the weather: everybody talks about it but nobody knows what to do about it. Integrity is that stuff that we always want more of. Some say that we need to return to the good old days when we had a lot more of it. Others say that we as a nation have never really had enough of it. Hardly anybody stops to explain exactly what we mean by it, or how we know it is a good thing, or why everybody needs to have the same amount of it. Indeed the only trouble with integrity is that everybody who uses the word seems to mean something slightly different.

3   For instance, when I refer to integrity, do I mean simply "honesty"? The answer is no; although honesty is a virtue of importance, it is a different virtue from integrity. Let us, for simplicity, think of honesty as not lying; and let us further accept Sissela Bok's definition of a lie: "any intentionally deceptive message which is *stated.*" Plainly, one cannot have integrity without being honest (although, as we shall see, the matter gets complicated), but one can certainly be honest and yet have little integrity.

4   When I refer to integrity, I have something very specific in mind. Integrity, as I will use the term, requires three steps: discerning° what is right and what is wrong; acting on what you have discerned, even at personal cost; and saying openly that you are acting on your understanding of right and wrong. The first criterion° captures the idea that integrity requires a degree of moral reflectiveness. The second brings in the ideal of a person of integrity as steadfast°, a quality that includes keeping one's commitments. The third reminds us that a person of integrity can be trusted.

5   The first point to understand about the difference between honesty and integrity is that a person may be entirely honest without ever engaging in the hard work of discernment that integrity requires: she may tell us quite truthfully what she believes without ever taking the time to figure out whether what she believes is good and right and true. The problem may be as simple as someone's foolishly saying something that hurts a friend's feelings; a few moments of thought would have revealed the likelihood of the hurt and the lack of necessity for the comment. Or the problem may be more complex, as when a man who was raised from birth in a society that preaches racism states his belief in one race's inferiority as a fact, without ever really considering that perhaps this deeply held view is wrong. Certainly the racist is being honest—he is telling us what he actually thinks—but his honesty does not add up to integrity.

Telling Everything You Know

6 A wonderful epigram sometimes attributed to the filmmaker Sam Goldwyn goes like this: "The most important thing in acting is honesty; once you learn to fake that, you're in." The point is that honesty can be something one *seems* to have. Without integrity, what passes for honesty often is nothing of the kind; it is fake honesty—or it is honest but irrelevant and perhaps even immoral.

7   Consider an example. A man who has been married for fifty years confesses to his wife on his deathbed that he was unfaithful thirty-five years earlier. The

dishonesty was killing his spirit, he says. Now he has cleared his conscience and is able to die in peace.

8   The husband has been honest—sort of. He has certainty unburdened himself. And he has probably made his wife (soon to be his widow) quite miserable in the process, because even if she forgives him, she will not be able to remember him with quite the vivid image of love and loyalty that she had hoped for. Arranging his own emotional affairs to ease his transition to death, he has shifted to his wife the burden of confusion and pain, perhaps for the rest of her life. Moreover, he has attempted his honesty at the one time in his life when it carries no risk; acting in accordance with what you think is right and risking no loss in the process is a rather thin and unadmirable form of honesty.

9   Besides, even though the husband has been honest in a sense, he has now twice been unfaithful to his wife: once thirty-five years ago, when he had his affair, and again when, nearing death, he decided that his own peace of mind was more impor- tant than hers. In trying to be honest he has violated his marriage vow by acting toward his wife not with love but with naked and perhaps even cruel self-interest.

10   As my mother used to say, you don't have to tell people everything you know. Lying and nondisclosure, as the law often recognizes, are not the same thing. Sometimes it is actually illegal to tell what you know, as, for example, in the disclosure of certain financial information by market insiders. Or it may be uneth- ical, as when a lawyer reveals a confidence entrusted to her by a client. It may be simple bad manners, as in the case of a gratuitous° comment to a colleague on his or her attire. And it may be subject to religious punishment, as when a Roman Catholic priest breaks the seal of the confessional—an offense that carries automatic excommunication.

11   In all the cases just mentioned, the problem with telling everything you know is that somebody else is harmed. Harm may not be the intention, but it is certainly the effect. Honesty is most laudable° when we risk harm to ourselves; it becomes a good deal less so if we instead risk harm to others when there is no gain to anyone other than ourselves. Integrity may counsel keeping our secrets in order to spare the feelings of others. Sometimes, as in the example of the wayward hus- band, the reason we want to tell what we know is precisely to shift our pain onto somebody else—a course of action dictated less by integrity than by self-interest. Fortunately, integrity and self-interest often coincide, as when a politician of integrity is rewarded with our votes. But often they do not, and it is at those moments that our integrity is truly tested.

Error

12   Another reason that honesty alone is no substitute for integrity is that if forthright- ness is not preceded by discernment, it may result in the expression of an incorrect moral judgment. In other words, I may be honest about what I believe, but if I have never tested my beliefs, I may be wrong. And here I mean "wrong" in a particular sense: the proposition in question is wrong if I would change my mind about it after hard moral reflection.

13   Consider this example. Having been taught all his life that women are not as smart as men, a manager gives the women on his staff less-challenging assignments than

he gives the men. He does this, he believes, for their own benefit: he does not want them to fail, and he believes that they will if he gives them tougher assignments. Moreover, when one of the women on his staff does poor work, he does not berate° her as harshly as he would a man, because he expects nothing more. And he claims to be acting with integrity because he is acting according to his own deepest beliefs.

14   The manager fails the most basic test of integrity. The question is not whether his actions are consistent with what he most deeply believes, but whether he has done the hard work of discerning whether what he most deeply believes is right. The manager has not taken this harder step.

15   Moreover, even within the universe that the manager has constructed for himself, he is not acting with integrity. Although he is obviously wrong to think that the women on his staff are not as good as the men, even were he right, that would not justify applying different standards to their work. By so doing he betrays both his obligation to the institution that employs him and his duty as a manager to evaluate his employees.

16   The problem that the manager faces is an enormous one in our practical politics, where having the dialogue that makes democracy work can seem impossible because of our tendency to cling to our views even when we have not examined them. As Jean Bethke Elshtain has said, borrowing from John Courtney Murray, our politics are so fractured and contentious° that we often cannot even reach *disagreement.* Our refusal to look closely at our own most cherished principles is surely a large part of the reason. Socrates thought the unexamined life not worth living. But the unhappy truth is that few of us actually have the time for constant reflection on our views—on public or private morality. Examine them we must, however, or we will never know whether we might be wrong.

17   None of this should be taken to mean that integrity as I have described it presupposes a single correct truth. If, for example, your integrity-guided search tells you that affirmative action is wrong, and my integrity-guided search tells me that affirmative action is right, we need not conclude that one of us lacks integrity. As it happens, I believe—both as a Christian and as a secular citizen who struggles toward moral understanding—that we *can* find true and sound answers to our moral questions. But I do not pretend to have found very many of them, nor is an exposition of them my purpose here.

18   It is the case not that there aren't any right answers but that, given human fallibility°, we need to be careful in assuming that we have found them. However, today's political talk about how it is wrong for the government to impose one person's morality on somebody else is just mindless chatter. *Every* law imposes one person's morality on somebody else, because law has only two functions: to tell people to do what they would rather not or to forbid them to do what they would.

19   And if the surveys can be believed, there is far more moral agreement in America than we sometimes allow ourselves to think. One of the reasons that character education for young people makes so much sense to so many people is precisely that there seems to be a core set of moral understandings—we might call them the American Core—that most of us accept. Some of the virtues in this American Core are, one hopes, relatively noncontroversial. About 500 American

communities have signed on to Michael Josephson's program to emphasize the "six pillars" of good character: trustworthiness, respect, responsibility, caring, fairness, and citizenship. These virtues might lead to a similarly noncontroversial set of political values: having an honest regard for ourselves and others, protecting freedom of thought and religious belief and refusing to steal or murder.

Honesty and Competing Responsibilities

20   A further problem with too great an exaltation° of honesty is that it may allow us to escape responsibilities that morality bids us bear. If honesty is substituted for integrity, one might think that if I say I am not planning to fulfill a duty, I need not fulfill it. But it would be a peculiar morality indeed that granted us the right to avoid our moral responsibilities simply by stating our intention to ignore them. Integrity does not permit such an easy escape.

21   Consider an example. Before engaging in sex with a woman, her lover tells her that if she gets pregnant, it is her problem, not his. She says that she understands. In due course she does wind up pregnant. If we believe, as I hope we do, that the man would ordinarily have a moral responsibility toward both the child he will have helped to bring into the world and the child's mother, then his honest statement of what he intends does not spare him that responsibility.

22   This vision of responsibility assumes that not all moral obligations stem from consent or from a stated intention. The linking of obligations to promises is a rather modern and perhaps uniquely Western way of looking at life, and perhaps a luxury that only the well-to-do can afford. As Fred and Shulamit Korn (a philosopher and an anthropologist) have pointed out, "If one looks at ethnographic accounts of other societies, one finds that, while obligations everywhere play a crucial role in social life, promising is not preeminent among the sources of obligation and is not even mentioned by most anthropologists." The Korns have made a study of Tonga, where promises are virtually unknown but the social order is remarkably stable. If life without any promises seems extreme, we Americans sometimes go too far the other way, parsing° not only our contracts but even our marriage vows in order to discover the absolute minimum obligation that we have to others as a result of our promises.

23   That some societies in the world have worked out evidently functional structures of obligation without the need for promise or consent does not tell us what we should do. But it serves as a reminder of the basic proposition that our existence in civil society creates a set of mutual responsibilities that philosophers used to capture in the fiction of the social contract. Nowadays, here in America, people seem to spend their time thinking of even cleverer ways to avoid their obligations, instead of doing what integrity commands and fulfilling them. And all too often honesty is their excuse.

Vocabulary

1 commencement (n): graduation ceremony

4 discerning (adj): selective, showing good judgment or good taste

4 criterion (n): standard for making critical judgment; notice this is the singular form—criteria is the plural

4 steadfast (adj): firm in purpose, loyal

10 gratuitous (adj): unnecessary and unjustifiable

11 laudable (adj): praiseworthy

13 berate (v): scold vigorously, rebuke at length

16 contentious (adj): creating disagreement

18 fallibility (n): capable of being wrong or misleading

20 exaltation (n): feeling of great happiness, praising something highly

22 parsing (v): analyzing the grammar

RESPONDING TO THE READING

- If the thesis is stated, identify it; if it is implied, write it in your own words.
- What do you think is the purpose of this essay? Give reasons for your opinion.
- Who do you think is the intended audience of this essay? Give reasons for your opinion.

Comprehension

1. Is this an essay of comparison or contrast, or both? And how has Stephen L. Carter organized his content, by point or block method?
2. With what technique does Carter introduce his essay in Paragraph 1?
3. What is the point Carter makes in Paragraphs 2 and 3?
4. In your own words, what are the three steps Carter says integrity requires?
5. What key differences between honesty and integrity does Carter discuss in Paragraph 5?
6. What does Carter say about racists?
7. Paragraph 6 begins with an **epigram**. What is an epigram? Reword the meaning of this one.
8. What conclusions does Carter draw from his hypothetical anecdote of the dying husband's confession in Paragraphs 7 to 11?
9. According to Carter, when is honesty the right course of action?
10. Carter begins to consider the second key difference between honesty and integrity in Paragraph 12. What is that difference?
11. In Paragraphs 13 to 16, Carter presents another hypothetical analogy. What is it?
12. Why does Carter claim the manager lacks integrity even though he is honest?
13. What point does Carter make about affirmative action?
14. What do you understand Carter to mean by the "American Core"?
15. In Paragraph 20, Carter begins to focus on the third key difference between honesty and integrity. What does he say it is?

16. What support does he offer for this difference?
17. What point does Carter make with his allusion to Tonga?
18. Explain the conclusion of Stephen Carter's essay.

Analysis

1. Look again at the end of Paragraph 5, from which the reader can infer that racists may be honest, but they lack integrity. How can Carter validate this claim?
2. What did you think of each of the three extended anecdotes Carter includes? What are the responsibilities of a husband, a boss, or a lover who has integrity?
3. Why does Carter include Paragraphs 17 and 18? What do they add to his discussion?
4. According to Carter, when does a society function best? Do you agree with him?
5. How useful are the subheadings for you in this essay? Explain.

Discussion/Writing Suggestions

1. Carter never explicitly defines the word integrity; instead, the examples he uses throughout the essay suggest and clarify the word's meaning. Do you think Carter is successful in differentiating between these two terms? Why or why not?
2. Do you agree with the distinction Carter makes between honesty and integrity? How would you define these two words? Give examples to support your definition. Is there a time in your life when you've behaved with honesty but not with integrity?

   • Other essays that consider social mores are by Charles Dickens (p. 10), Joseph Epstein (p. 36), Pico Iyer (p. 96), Robertson Davies (p. 150), Mark Kingwell (p. 114), Judith Viorst (p. 142), Amartya Sen (p. 252), Charlie Angus (p. 180), and Pier Giorgio Di Cicco (p. 196).

Essay of Classification

Classification is a process in which information about people, places, things, and ideas is arranged into categories sharing common traits. A strong organizing principle determines the kind and number of traits used and classifies objects into categories, kinds, or types. There are two ways to approach classification. In the first, a variety of subjects sharing common traits is brought together and sorted into classes on the basis of what they have in common; in the second, a subject is divided into categories that share common traits in order to understand the subject better. The second method is sometimes referred to as *division*. In a classification essay, the thesis statement alerts the reader to the *number* of types to be discussed as well as the *principle* upon which the types have been chosen.

Writing Strategy

You classify all the time, often without knowing it. Look around at your fellow students. How would you put them into categories? By gender, clothing style, major program? Consider the world of business and government. Employees are classified according to the work they do and the pay they receive. What do you think the "pay equity" initiative is based on? That's right—job classification!

In order to write an effective classification essay, you need to begin your process by asking these three specific questions:

1. Can my subject be narrowed down and further focused?
2. Can my subject be broken down into distinct categories?
3. Can my categories relate to one another based on an organizing principle?

To demonstrate how you could classify a subject into valid categories based on an organizing principle, let us take "students" as our subject.
Subject: students

1. Can this subject be further focused?
   - Which group of students: high school, college, university?
2. Can one of these focused subjects be organized into groups?
   - College students can be classified as full-time students, part-time students, new high school graduates, mature students, students who use English as a second language, students in different programs and with various interests, etc.
3. Can you sort students based on a principle of organization?
   - You could classify students according to their behaviour and attitudes as the class clown, the teacher's pet, the workaholic, the nerd, the party animal, the rebel, the whiner, the norm, and so on.

All groupings must have an organizing principle upon which to define traits and to limit the scope of the type. When you write out your focused subject and your types or groups, be sure to find an organizing principle that will lend unity and coherence to your essay.

Organizing Principle

An organizing principle defines the common trait of a group. To determine your organizing principle, ask yourself these questions:

1. What are the activities or qualities of the group?
2. What motivates the action or thought of the group?
3. What background or potential is shared by the group?

Then it is time to write your thesis statement. A thesis statement for a classification essay must

1. State the focused subject
2. Outline the groups to be discussed
3. State the organizing principle

If you were to write an essay on the types of students in the classroom based on behaviour, your thesis statement might read:

> College students behave in different ways both in and out of the classroom.
> Three common types are the norm, the workaholic, and the party animal.

It is essential to discuss each group separately in your body paragraphs. As in essays using other organizational patterns, each paragraph must have a topic sentence that states the focal point to be discussed. All supporting details must relate to the organizing principle stated in the thesis. For example, if you were to discuss the workaholics, you should cite common traits shared by the group, such as staying up late, studying for many hours a day, and never taking time off just to relax. If, however, you talked about what workaholics *feel* about work or what their religious beliefs are, you would be off topic and violate the principle of unity. In addition, don't forget the principle of coherence, so you need to *glue* your sentences and paragraphs *together* as much as you can.

Your conclusion could restate your thesis, or you could comment on the possible reasons behind the variety of student behaviour in the college classroom. You might conclude by pointing out that all behaviour is motivated by needs—for some it is a need for recognition, for others a need to release tension and anxiety. The choice is yours as long as you bring your essay to a strong and stimulating close.

SAMPLE STUDENT ESSAY OF CLASSIFICATION

The Canadian Dream

Julie-Ann Yoshikuni

1   "So, do you speak Oriental?" Not long ago, I was actually asked this disturbing question. I refer to this as "Continental Genericism," a term used to conveniently group all members of like Continents into a single, homogeneous unit. The essence of my Canadian Dream is simple; the mechanics of it, complex. My wish is to be recognized foremost as a Canadian, a difficult task given my unmistakable Asian features. Being classified as an "Oriental" is not always easy to take. For example, everyone expects me to be an academic genius, most people simply assume I am of Chinese descent, and the general public fears I am a hazard on the road.

2   Many people believe that Orientals are inherently superior in intelligence. I find this somewhat bothersome, but I will not complain. I have worked very hard to perpetuate this popular myth and, consequently, it has driven me to crank out some of my best work. How would I feel knowing that I was not prepared for a test, when three habitual cheaters were counting on me? The pressure to excel in mathematics and computer science is often overwhelming. English is my only haven because everyone "knows" we are incapable of spelling. Despite the fact that academic performance is usually a function of the amount of time spent studying, many people will continue to believe Orientals have a "special" capacity for numbers.

3   Most people assume that all Orientals are Chinese. This is not surprising since the Chinese population in Toronto is very large. However, as a third generation Canadian of Japanese descent, I have certainly had my share of frustrating experiences. For example, I get tired of explaining to people that I really don't know whether 1991 is the year of the pig, snake or rabbit. I have reached the conclusion that people are simply attempting to make polite small talk when saying things such as "We knew a Chinese guy once, maybe you know him?" or "We really do like chicken balls and egg rolls."

4   In my own little way, I have learned to deal with these situations, but I have yet to conquer the reckless driver presumption. "They can cook, they can count, but watch out, because they sure can't drive." If you are a Canadian, and you have the slightest difficulty figuring out which ethnic group this statement pertains to, then you must be living in a vacuum. I am the first to admit that there are poor drivers who are, indeed, Oriental. However, not all Orientals are incapable of operating a motorized vehicle. Contrary to popular belief, our ability to drive is not hampered by a lack of peripheral vision. This vehicular hostility directed at Orientals has led me to deduce that perhaps this animosity stems from the fact that we make better cars. Unfortunately, as long as there are Oriental drivers, there will always be a good joke.

5   My Canadian Dream come true is simply to be recognized and treated as a Canadian. However, due to circumstances beyond my control, I am left to deal with the stigma attached to being Oriental: that is, being smart, Chinese and careless on the road. All I can say is, it looks like I'm 0 for 3!

Comprehension

1. Julie-Ann Yoshikuni coins the term "continental genericism." What does she mean by it? Can you think of some examples to explain it?
2. Define in your words Yoshikuni's "Canadian dream."
3. Paraphrase Yoshikuni's thesis statement.
4. What aspects of stereotyping does Yoshikuni face because of her appearance?
5. The author suggests advantages and disadvantages in being identified as "an academic genius." What examples can you find of each?
6. How do the examples you found for Question 5 reflect stereotyping?
7. What examples of frustrating experiences does Yoshikuni provide?

Analysis

1. Yoshikuni attacks two "popular beliefs" about the Chinese people. How does she attack them and how effective are the attacks?
2. What examples of the author's use of irony and sense of humour can you find?
3. Do you agree with Yoshikuni when she says the mechanics of achieving her dream are complex?

4. How well do you think the author handles being stereotyped?

5. Will this essay by a fellow student affect your attitude when you hear a racist joke?

READINGS: ESSAYS OF CLASSIFICATION

In her essay about friends, Judith Viorst introduces a number of elements to classify her groups. First, she uses numbers and titles to define each group. She also bases her data on personal experience. In reading through Viorst's essay, note that she divides and categorizes the people she knows into types. Sean Twist's essay is also a personal piece as he reflects on the types of birds in his backyard and what they have come to mean to him. Robertson Davies classifies the various manifestations of superstition and their origins. Judy Brady ironically exploits classifications in her famous essay, "I Want a Wife." Finally, Pat Capponi directly addresses the impact of stereotyping in her essay "Dispatches from the Poverty Line."

Friends, Good Friends—And Such Good Friends

Judith Viorst

Judith Viorst (1931–) is an American author and the recipient of various awards for her journalism and psychological writings. A graduate of the Washington Psychoanalytic Institute, Viorst is the author of eight collections of poetry and five books of prose, including the bestsellers Necessary Losses *and* Imperfect Control *and a comic novel,* Murdering Mr. Monti. *However, Judith Viorst is perhaps best known for her children's literature. Her 12 children's books include* The Tenth Good Thing About Barney *(about the death of a pet) and the Alexander series of short books, which include among them the classic* Alexander and the Terrible, Horrible, No Good, Very Bad Day.

In this essay, Viorst is articulate about how much her friends mean to her and how different friends belong to certain groups. Her focused subject is complicated, yet she is able to simplify her groupings and make them accessible to her readers. In particular, she divides her groups very clearly, making sure there is no overlapping. She defines for each group a unifying principle or central trait and then adds other traits and examples to fill out her analysis. Notice she does not use generalizations as supporting details. That is, Viorst avoids making vague statements about her types of friends. Each type is portrayed with specific and individual details. This article appeared in Redbook *in 1977.*

1   Women are friends, I once would have said, when they totally love and support and trust each other, and bare to each other the secrets of their souls, and run—no questions asked—to help each other, and tell harsh truths to each other (no, you can't wear that dress unless you lose ten pounds first) when harsh truths must be told.

2   Women are friends, I once would have said, when they share the same affection for Ingmar Bergman*, plus train rides, cats, warm rain, charades, Camus*, and hate with equal ardor° Newark and Brussels sprouts and Lawrence Welk* and camping.

3 In other words, I once would have said that a friend is a friend all the way, but now I believe that's a narrow point of view. For the friendships I have and the friendships I see are conducted at many levels of intensity, serve many different functions, meet different needs and range from those as all-the-way as the friendship of the soul sisters mentioned above to that of the most nonchalant° and casual playmates.

4 Consider these varieties of friendship:

1. Convenience friends

These are the women with whom, if our paths weren't crossing all the time, we'd have no particular reason to be friends: a next-door neighbor, a woman in our car pool, the mother of one of our children's closest friends or maybe some mommy with whom we serve juice and cookies each week at the Glenwood Co-op Nursery.

5 Convenience friends are convenient indeed. They'll lend us their cups and silverware for a party. They'll drive our kids to soccer when we're sick. They'll take us to pick up our car when we need a lift to the garage. They'll even take our cats when we go on vacation. As we will for them. But we don't, with convenience friends, ever come too close or tell too much; we maintain our public face and emotional distance. "Which means," says Elaine, "that I'll talk about being overweight but not about being depressed. Which means I'll admit being mad but not blind with rage. Which means I might say that we're pinched this month but never that I'm worried sick over money." But which doesn't mean that there isn't sufficient value to be found in these friendships of mutual aid, in convenience friends.

2. Special-interest friends

6 These friendships aren't intimate, and they needn't involve kids or silverware or cats. Their value lies in some interest jointly shared. And so we may have an office friend or a yoga friend or a tennis friend or a friend from the Women's Democratic Club.

7 "I've got one woman friend," says Joyce, "who likes, as I do, to take psychology courses. Which makes it nice for me—and nice for her. It's fun to go with someone you know and it's fun to discuss what you've learned, driving back from the classes." And for the most part, she says, that's all they discuss.

8 "I'd say that what we're doing is *doing* together, not being together," Suzanne says of her Tuesday-doubles friends. "It's mainly a tennis relationship, but we play together well. And I guess we all need to have a couple of playmates."

9 I agree.

10 *My* playmate is a shopping friend, a woman of marvelous taste, a woman who knows exactly *where* to buy *what,* and furthermore is a woman who always knows beyond a doubt what one ought to be buying. I don't have the time to keep up with what's new in eyeshadow, hemlines and shoes and whether the smock look is in or finished already. But since (oh, shame!) I care a lot about eyeshadow, hemlines and shoes, and since I don't *want* to wear smocks if the smock look is finished, I'm very glad to have a shopping friend.

3. Historical friends

11 We all have a friend who knew us when . . . maybe way back in Miss Meltzer's second grade, when our family lived in that three-room flat in Brooklyn, when our

dad was out of work for seven months, when our brother Allie got in that fight where they had to call the police, when our sister married the endodontist° from Yonkers and when, the morning after we lost our virginity, she was the first, the only, friend we told.

12   The years have gone by and we've gone separate ways and we've little in common now, but we're still an intimate part of each other's past. And so whenever we go to Detroit we always go to visit this friend of our girlhood. Who knows how we looked before our teeth were straightened. Who knows how we talked before our voice got unBrooklyned. Who knows what we ate before we learned about artichokes. And who, by her presence, puts us in touch with an earlier part of ourself, a part of ourself it's important never to lose.

13   "What this friend means to me and what I mean to her," says Grace, "is having a sister without sibling rivalry°. We know the texture of each other's lives. She remembers my grandmother's cabbage soup. I remember the way her uncle played the piano. There's simply no other friend who remembers those things."

4. Crossroads friends

14   Like historical friends, our crossroads friends are important for *what was*—for the friendship we shared at a crucial, now past, time of life. A time, perhaps, when we roomed in college together; or worked as eager young singles in the Big City together; or went together, as my friend Elizabeth and I did through pregnancy, birth and that scary first year of new motherhood.

15   Crossroad friends forge powerful links, links strong enough to endure with not much more contact than once-a-year letters at Christmas. And out of respect for those crossroads years, for those dramas and dreams we once shared, we will always be friends.

5. Cross-generational friends

16   Historical friends and crossroads friends seem to maintain a special kind of intimacy—dormant° but always ready to be revived—and though we may rarely meet, whenever we do connect, it's personal and intense. Another kind of intimacy exists in the friendships that form across generations in what one woman calls her daughter–mother and her mother–daughter relationships.

17   Evelyn's friend is her mother's age—"but I share so much more than I ever could with my mother"—a woman she talks to of music, of books and of life. "What I get from her is the benefit of her experience. What she gets—and enjoys—from me is a youthful perspective. It's a pleasure for both of us."

18   I have in my own life a precious friend, a woman of 65 who has lived very hard, who is wise, who listens well; who has been where I am and can help me understand it; and who represents not only an ultimate ideal mother to me but also the person I'd like to be when I grow up.

19   In our daughter role we tend to do more than our share of self-revelation; in our mother role we tend to receive what's revealed. It's another kind of pleasure—playing wise mother to a questing° younger person. It's another very lovely kind of relationship.

6. Part-of-a-couple friends

20 Some of the women we call our friends we never see alone—we see them as part of a couple at couples' parties. And though we share interests in many things and respect each other's views, we aren't moved to deepen the relationship. Whatever the reason, a lack of time or—and this is more likely—a lack of chemistry, our friendship remains in the context of a group. But the fact that our feeling on seeing each other is always, "I'm *so* glad she's here" and the fact that we spend half the evening talking together says that this too, in its own way, counts as a friendship.

21 (Other part-of-a-couple friends are the friends that came with the marriage, and some of these are friends we could live without. But sometimes, alas, she married our husband's best friend; and sometimes, alas, she *is* our husband's best friend. And so we find ourself dealing with her, somewhat against our will, in a spirit of what I'll call *reluctant*° friendship.)

7. Men who are friends

22 I wanted to write just of women friends, but the women I've talked to won't let me—they say I must mention man–woman friendships too. For these friendships can be just as close and as dear as those that we form with women. Listen to Lucy's description of one such friendship:

23 "We've found we have things to talk about that are different from what he talks about with my husband and different from what I talk about with his wife. So sometimes we call on the phone or meet for lunch. There are similar intellectual interests—we always pass on to each other the books that we love—but there's also something tender and caring too." In a couple of crises, Lucy says, "He offered himself, for talking and for helping. And when someone died in his family he wanted me there. The sexual, flirty part of our friendship is very small, but *some*—just enough to make it fun and different." She thinks—and I agree—that the sexual part, though small, is always there when a man and a woman are friends. It's only in the past few years that I've made friends with men, in the sense of a friendship that's *mine,* not just part of two couples. And achieving with them the ease and the trust I've found with women friends has value indeed. Under the dryer at home last week, putting on mascara and rouge, I comfortably sat and talked with a fellow named Peter. Peter, I finally decided, could handle the shock of me minus mascara under the dryer. Because we care for each other. Because we're friends.

24 There are medium friends, and pretty good friends, and very good friends indeed, and these friendships are defined by their level of intimacy. And what we'll reveal at each of these levels of intimacy is calibrated° with care. We might tell a medium friend, for example, that yesterday we had a fight with our husband. And we might tell a pretty good friend that this fight with our husband made us so mad that we slept on the couch. And we might tell a very good friend that the reason we got so mad in that fight that we slept on the couch had something to do with that girl who works in his office. But it's only to our very best friends that we're willing to tell all, to tell what's going on with that girl in his office.

25 The best of friends, I still believe, totally love and support and trust each other, and bare to each other the secrets of their souls, and run—no questions asked—to help each other, and tell harsh truths to each other when they must be told.

26   But we needn't agree about everything (only 12-year-old girl friends agree about *everything*) to tolerate each other's point of view. To accept without judgment. To give and to take without ever keeping score. And to *be* there, as I am for them and as they are for me, to comfort our sorrows, to celebrate our joys.

Notes

2 Ingmar Bergman (1918–): Swedish movie director

2 Camus (Albert) (1913–1960): French author

2 Lawrence Welk (1903–1992): American band leader

Vocabulary

3 nonchalant (adj): unconcerned and casual

11 endodontist (n): dentist specializing in tooth decay and gum diseases

13 sibling rivalry (n): competition between brothers and sisters

16 dormant (adj): inactive, sleeping

19 questing (v, adj): searching

21 reluctant (adj): unwilling, unenthusiastic

24 calibrate (v): measurements taken to establish or test the accuracy of the measuring instrument

RESPONDING TO THE READING

- If the thesis is stated, identify it; if it is implied, write it in your own words.
- What do you think is the purpose of this essay? Give reasons for your opinion.
- Who do you think is the intended audience of this essay? Give reasons for your opinion.

Comprehension

1. How does Judith Viorst limit her subject in the first three paragraphs?
2. "I once would have said." Why does Viorst repeat this statement in her first three paragraphs?
3. Paraphrase Viorst's definition of friendship as stated in her introduction.
4. Are the headings Viorst introduces in the body of her essay useful?
5. What sort of support does Viorst typically use to describe each type of friend?
6. Could one compare "convenience friends" with "special-interest friends"? On what grounds? Take your details from Viorst's examples.
7. How does Viorst further categorize friends in Paragraph 11 to 13? And how is this categorization different from the rest of the essay?

8. What points of similarity exist between "historical friends" and "crossroads friends"?
9. What problem in friendships between men and women is identified by the author?
10. In what way are Paragraphs 24 to 26 different from the rest of the essay?
11. According to Viorst, what defines a best friend?

Analysis

1. Explain Viorst's meaning in Paragraph 3 and how it influences the development of her essay.
2. Find examples of Viorst's use of *loaded* (emotive) words. What is their effect?
3. On what principles would you classify your friends? Is this an appropriate way of thinking about your friends?
4. What do you think of Viorst's treatment of men?
5. Which of Viorst's categories are most meaningful to you? Why?
6. The author uses a conversational style; why do you think she chooses to write in this fashion?

Discussion/Writing Suggestions

1. Classification can lead to stereotyping. Do you think Judith Viorst manages to avoid this danger?
2. Define friendship and explain what it means to you.

   • Other essays dealing with relationships are by Joseph Epstein (p. 36), Bertrand Russell (p. 64), Margaret Atwood (p. 85), Pico Iyer (p. 96), Timothy Findley (p. 92), Nicola Bleasby (p. 109), Judy Brady (p. 155), Charlie Angus (p. 180), Michael Dorris (p. 208), and Rosie DiManno (p. 211).

Bird-Feeder Enlightenment

Sean Twist

Sean Twist (1965–) is a Canadian author, freelance newspaper columnist, and broadcaster who lives in London, Ontario. He writes a regular column for the London Free Press. *His work has also appeared in the* Globe and Mail. *He is the co-author of a book entitled* Conspiracy Theories *and is currently working on a series of fantasy novels.*

This essay first appeared in the "Facts and Arguments" section of the Globe and Mail *in 2006.*

1   It had been a bad day. Work had succeeded in reaching new levels of sadistic° soul grinding, leaving me feeling both angry and empty. Then, to add the cherry to this particular toxic sundae, my back tooth had broken, necessitating emergency dental surgery.

2   As I said, a bad day.

3   So after being ground down on both the physical and spiritual levels, I headed for home, feeling about as cheerful as a Smiths* song. Grabbing the bills from the mailbox, I grumpily let myself into my home, dropped my satchel° on the kitchen table, and glanced out my patio doors. Then I smiled, despite the dental freezing. There, near my feeder, a duck was sitting in a birdbath. For the first time that day, I burst into laughter. Because as everyone knows, nothing is funnier than a duck in a birdbath.

4   Once again the avian° community that hangs around my birdfeeder had delivered a boon° when I needed it most. Until recently, I paid scant° attention to the constant feathered goings-on around the feeder. I had installed it in a fit of post-Thoreau*, pre-Kyoto* environmental guilt. While I am unable to stop global warming or the whale hunt, I could at least make sure the local birds went to sleep with full stomachs. So I bought a shepherd's hook, hung a cheap wooden feeder from it, and felt slightly better about myself.

5   Yet filling it just became another chore, something I did as part of the daily routine. I would glance occasionally at the swarms of sparrows hopping around the fallen seed, but that was it. There was e-mail to answer, dinner to prepare, fretting to be done. Maybe it's because I turned 40 recently, combined with the attendant realization that so much that I thought was important (see above) simply isn't. Or perhaps it's something deeper, a need that I don't have a library of self-help books to recognize. But for whatever reason, I've taken to watching my birds, and the glances are turning into minutes of complete fascination. To the bird-feeding community, my feeder is definitely low-rent. I don't ascribe [I think he means subscribe!]to the bird-feeding snobbery° I've seen in others—there are no VIP feeders here (please, nuthatches only!) and not a squirrel baffle in sight. As a result, a small mob gathers each day, feathers and fur munching side by side.

6   I've made a few observations, sipping juice at my patio door. Sparrows are a constant, like AM radio. They seem to be the blue-collars of the bird community, and could probably take over the world if properly organized. I'm fond of them— once I stopped seeing them as a grey multiform mass, I could discern the various idiosyncrasies° each sparrow had. Sure, they're all idiots, but there are degrees of idiocy. For instance, there are the "close-talker" sparrows—the ones who chirp frantically at their compatriots° as though they are trying to explain this really cool dream they had, but don't notice the hawk circling overhead.

7   Compare them to the Panic Wings: the apparently over-caffeinated head-cases who freak out and scream for the trees if so much as an air molecule stirs beside them. Idiots all—and I adore them for it.

8   Another common bird (or "garbage bird" as I've heard snooty bird-people call them) are grackles. Being a science fiction fan, I adore their gurgling, almost alien call. This almost makes me forgive them for being sadistic bastards, since I've had to run out a few times, trying to stop them from randomly attacking—and then decapitating—my beloved loopy sparrows.

9   On the science-fiction side again, cardinals often make the best laser-pistol sounds. Their call is so sharp and piercing, I almost expect to see the feeder go up in flames from direct hit. The squirrels—the bane of most feeders—to me are the furry equivalent of The Three Stooges*, taking small-mammal comedy to new heights each day.

10   Then there are the unexpected visitors. The pale, ghost-like sparrow that was a few hundred miles out of range. The lonely baby crow that sat beside the fountain and then died. There was a budgie one day, hanging with the sparrow crew. (I even attempted to rescue it, doing my middle-aged ninja best to sneak up behind it towel in hand. The look of pure budgie disdain° persuaded me I should leave my stealth moves to the double agent Splinter Cell.)

11   And of course, the ducks. They do recon each day around dusk, roughly around the same time the cardinals drop by. Each day the drake (See? Bird lingo°! I'm learning!) stands sentinel while his mate eats.

12   And every day, just as he starts to tuck in, she flies away. You can almost see him sigh as he takes wing after her.

13   Maybe that's why he was in the fountain alone that day. The poor guy, like me, just needed a break.

Notes

3 Smiths: 1980s musical group famous for songs of misery

4 Thoreau (1817–1862): American writer, naturalist, and philosopher

4 Kyoto: 1997 international agreement on the environment and climate change;

named for Japanese city in which the agreement was signed

9 The Three Stooges: American comedy act who made movies in 1940s and 1950s

Vocabulary

1 sadistic (adj): gaining pleasure from causing physical or emotional pain to another

3 satchel (n): book bag

4 avian (adj): relating to birds

4 boon (n): benefit, gift

4 scant (adj): inadequate

5 snobbery (n): behaviour of one who considers others inferior

6 idiosyncrasies (n): way of behaving or thinking that is peculiar to an individual, quirk

6 compatriots (n): those from the same country, fellow worker

10 disdain (n): scorn, contempt

11 lingo (n, slang): language

RESPONDING TO THE READING

- If the thesis is stated, identify it; if it is implied, write it in your own words.
- What do you think is the purpose of this essay? Give reasons for your opinion.
- Who do you think is the intended audience of this essay? Give reasons for your opinion.

Comprehension

1. Sean Twist uses narration in his first two paragraphs. What is the main point of his narrative?
2. What reasons does Twist give for having set up his bird-feeder?
3. In Paragraph 5, Twist outlines a process. What is it and what does he say initiates it?
4. To what does Twist compare sparrows?
5. Twist describes a variety of birds; how does he classify them?
6. Twist tells anecdotes of three particular types of birds. What are they?
7. Sean Twist begins and ends his essay with the drake. How is that appropriate?

Analysis

1. Find examples of Twist's humour in this essay.
2. Other than humorous, how would you describe Twist's tone? Use examples from the essay to support your response.
3. What is Twist's attitude to the birds he watches? Support your response with examples from the essay.
4. Twist's essay is humorous and seemingly light-hearted; however, there is a seriousness to it too. Find evidence of that serious attitude and explain it.

Discussion/Writing Suggestions

1. Sean Twist has not become an ornithologist, but he does enjoy the birds in his backyard. Clearly he is interested in them, and watching them is a means of relaxation for him. Do you find solace in nature or have concerns about the environment? Why or why not?
2. What do you do to unwind after a stressful day? Do you have a routine like the one Twist has? Explain the benefits of your hobby.

   • Other essays that discuss the natural world are by Rachel Carson (p. 123), James C. Rettie (p. 221), Catherine George (p. 194), Margaret Laurence (p. 202), and Sang Il Lee (p. 233).

A Few Kind Words for Superstition

Robertson Davies

Robertson Davies (1913–1995) was one of Canada's best-known and most popular authors. He was born in Thamesville, Ontario, and educated at Upper Canada College, Queen's University, and Oxford University in England. As a celebrated novelist, playwright, critic, satirist, and journalist, Davies was one of Canada's most distinguished "men of letters," though ironically this was a term of which he disapproved. His novels, which brought him most fame, include Tempest-Tost *(1951),* Leaven of Malice *(1954),* A Mixture of Frailties

(1958), Fifth Business *(1970),* The Manticore *(1972),* World of Wonders *(1976),* What's Bred in the Bone *(1985), and* The Lyre of Orpheus *(1989). Robertson Davies was a professor of English at the University of Toronto and the founding master of Massey College, a graduate college at the University of Toronto. He served as governor of the Stratford Shakespearean Festival. He was a fellow of the Royal Society of Canada, a recipient of the Stephen Leacock Medal for Humour, and a member of the Order of Canada. He was the first Canadian to become an honorary member of the American Academy and Institute of Arts and Letters.*

In this essay, first published in 1978, Robertson Davies defines superstition. In doing so, he provides examples and anecdotes, as well as classifying types of superstition and superstitious behaviour.

1   In grave discussions of "the renaissance° of the irrational" in our time, superstition does not figure largely as a serious challenge to reason or science. Parapsychology°, UFO's, miracle cures, transcendental meditation and all the paths to instant enlightenment are condemned, but superstition is merely deplored. Is it because it has an unacknowledged hold on so many of us?

2   Few people will admit to being superstitious; it implies naïveté° or ignorance. But I live in the middle of a large university, and I see superstition in its four manifestations°, alive and flourishing° among people who are indisputably° rational and learned.

3   You did not know that superstition takes four forms? Theologians° assure us that it does. First is what they call Vain Observances, such as not walking under a ladder, and that kind of thing. Yet I saw a deeply learned professor of anthropology, who had spilled some salt, throwing a pinch of it over his left shoulder; when I asked him why, he replied, with a wink, that it was "to hit the Devil in the eye." I did not question him further about his belief in the Devil: but I noticed that he did not smile until I asked him what he was doing.

4   The second form is Divination, or consulting oracles°. Another learned professor I know, who would scorn to settle a problem by tossing a coin (which is a humble appeal to Fate to declare itself), told me quite seriously that he had resolved a matter related to university affairs by consulting the I Ching°. And why not? There are thousands of people on this continent who appeal to the I Ching, and their general level of education seems to absolve them of superstition. Almost, but not quite. The I Ching, to the embarrassment of rationalists, often gives excellent advice.

5   The third form is Idolatry, and universities can show plenty of that. If you have ever supervised a large examination room, you know how many jujus°, lucky coins and other bringers of luck are placed on the desks of the candidates. Modest idolatry, but what else can you call it?

6   The fourth form is Improper Worship of the True God. A while ago, I learned that every day, for several days, a $2 bill (in Canada we have $2 bills, regarded by some people as unlucky) had been tucked under a candlestick on the altar of a college chapel. Investigation revealed that an engineering student, worried about a girl, thought that bribery of the Deity might help. When I talked with him, he did not

think he was pricing God cheap, because he could afford no more. A reasonable argument, but perhaps God was proud that week, for the scientific oracle went against him.

7   Superstition seems to run, a submerged° river of crude religion, below the surface of human consciousness. It has done so for as long as we have any chronicle of human behavior, and although I cannot prove it, I doubt if it is more prevalent today than it has always been. Superstition, the theologians tell us, comes from the Latin *supersisto,* meaning to stand in terror of the Deity. Most people keep their terror within bounds, but they cannot root it out, nor do they seem to want to do so.

8   The more the teaching of formal religion declines°, or takes a sociological form, the less God appears to great numbers of people as a God of Love, resuming his older form of a watchful, minatory° power, to be placated° and cajoled°. Superstition makes its appearance, apparently unbidden, very early in life, when children fear that stepping on cracks in the sidewalk will bring ill fortune. It may persist even among the greatly learned and devout, as in the case of Dr. Samuel Johnson, who felt it necessary to touch posts that he passed in the street. The psychoanalysts have their explanation, but calling a superstition a compulsion neurosis does not banish it.

9   Many superstitions are so widespread and so old that they must have risen from a depth of the human mind that is indifferent to race or creed. Orthodox Jews place a charm on their door-posts; so do (or did) the Chinese. Some peoples of Middle Europe believe that when a man sneezes, his soul, for that moment, is absent from his body, and they hasten to bless him, lest the soul be seized by the Devil. How did the Melanesians come by the same idea? Superstition seems to have a link with some body of belief that far antedates the religions we know— religions which have no place for such comforting little ceremonies and charities.

10   People who like disagreeable historical comparisons recall that when Rome was in decline, superstition proliferated° wildly, and that something of the same sort is happening in our Western world today. They point to the popularity of astrology, and it is true that sober newspapers that would scorn to deal in love philters carry astrology columns and the fashion magazines count them among their most popular features. But when has astrology not been popular? No use saying science discredits it. When has the heart of man given a damn for science?

11   Superstition in general is linked to man's yearning° to know his fate, and to have some hand in deciding it. When my mother was a child, she innocently joined her Roman Catholic friends in killing spiders on July 11, until she learned that this was done to ensure heavy rain the day following, the anniversary of the Battle of Boyne, when the Orangemen would hold their parade. I knew an Italian, a good scientist, who watched every morning before leaving his house, so that the first person he met would not be a priest or a nun, as this would certainly bring bad luck.

12   I am not one to stand aloof° from the rest of humanity in this matter, for when I was a university student, a gypsy woman with a child in her arms used to appear every year at examination time, and ask a shilling of anyone who touched the Lucky Baby; that swarthy° infant cost me four shillings altogether, and I never failed an examination. Of course, I did it merely for the joke—or so I thought then. Now, I am humbler.

Vocabulary

1 renaissance (n): revival of art and literature

1 parapsychology (n): the study of psychic phenomena, outside the sphere of normal psychology

2 naïveté (n, French): innocence, foolishly credulous

2 manifestation (n): clear appearance, obvious indication

2 flourish (v): grow vigorously, thrive

2 indisputably (adv): in a way that cannot be denied or argued against

3 theologian (n): expert in the study of religion and religious doctrine

4 oracle (n): source of prediction, divine advice

4 I Ching (n): Chinese system of fortune-telling

5 jujus (n): an object of good luck, lucky charm

7 submerge (v): place underwater, be obscured

8 decline (v): become gradually less strong, effective or good

8 minatory (adj): threatening, menacing

8 placate (v): soothe, appease by concessions

8 cajole (v): persuade with flattery, coax

10 proliferate (v): increase in number, reproduce

11 yearning (n): desire, need

12 aloof (adj): unsympathetic, at an emotional distance

12 swarthy (adj): of a dark complexion

RESPONDING TO THE READING

- If the thesis is stated, identify it; if it is implied, write it in your own words.
- What do you think is the purpose of this essay? Give reasons for your opinion.
- Who do you think is the intended audience of this essay? Give reasons for your opinion.

Comprehension

1. How does Robertson Davies introduce the subject of superstition?
2. What definition of superstition does Davies offer to begin this essay?
3. In your own words, explain the four categories of superstition Davies defines.
4. What sorts of examples of superstition does Davies give in Paragraphs 7 to 11?
5. "Superstition seems to run, a submerged river of crude religion, below the surface of human consciousness." Explain what Davies means in this quotation.
6. In Paragraph 8, what reasons does Davies give for the continuing existence of superstition?
7. How would you categorize the examples Davies provides in Paragraph 9?
8. Which popular form of superstition does Davies give in Paragraph 10?

9. In Paragraph 11, Davies begins to make his examples personal. How does he do that?
10. How do the last two sentences relate to the title?

Analysis

1. To what does the phrase "the renaissance of the irrational" in the first sentence refer? What examples does Davies use? What examples can you add to the list?
2. What is Davies's answer to the last question in the first paragraph? Why do you think Davies places a question here rather than a statement?
3. Do you think Davies is right to claim that the four types of superstition are prevalent in our culture?
4. According to Davies, what is the relationship between superstition and religion, between superstition and science, and between superstition and history?
5. In Paragraph 11, Davies states that "superstition in general is linked to man's yearning to know his fate, and to have some hand in deciding it." Do you think he is right? Why or why not?
6. In the last paragraph, Davies admits that what he did jokingly as a college student to ensure passing his examinations was actually done in earnest. How has he realized this?
7. What is Davies's definition of superstition?

Discussion/Writing Suggestions

1. Do you believe in any of the superstitions that Davies describes? Do you know of people who do?
2. Why do you think people continue to believe in superstitions?

- Other essays that focus on aspects of popular culture are Bill Bryson (p. 14), Joseph Epstein (p. 36), David Ginsburg (p. 33), David Suzuki (p. 88), Leslie C Smith (p. 126), Mark Kingwell (p. 114), Sandra Stewart (p. 121), Anne McIlroy (p. 126), Stephen L. Carter (p. 132), Judy Brady (p. 155), Dan Zollman (p. 166), Susan Jacoby (p. 176), Charlie Angus (p. 180), Pier Giorgio Di Cicco (p. 196), and Almas Zakiuddin (p. 240).

Stereotype

When we classify people (e.g., co-workers as keeners, shirkers, or workaholics), we have to keep in mind that each category is composed of individuals who will vary from the typical traits we have established for it. A **stereotype** is a particular kind of classification based on fixed ideas or images that are not true in reality: a stereotype is fixed as an accepted image and it represents all the people, ideas, or things that belong to that category. In its oversimplification and falsification, a stereotype is therefore an invalid form of classification.

Julie-Ann Yoshikuni's essay (p. 140) is an examination of stereotype. Stereotypes are most often based on gender, race, or religion. Examples are "the dumb blonde" or "the uptight WASP." When a person is denied individuality because of stereotyping, bigotry and prejudice result. Jokes based on stereotypes, while they seem harmless, are nonetheless pernicious because they dehumanize the persons involved. Many writers, with their strong social conscience and sharp critical insight, have examined the issue head on, or else enjoy pushing the boundaries of stereotype while exploring its harmful impact.

I Want a Wife

Judy Brady

Judy (Syfers) Brady (1937–) was born in San Francisco. She graduated from the University of Iowa with a B.F.A. in painting, but has become well-known as a freelance writer and a social activist. Brady focuses on women's issues, environmental concerns, and cancer research and treatment.

Judy Brady's essay "I Want a Wife" originally appeared in Ms *magazine in 1971 under the name Judy Syfers—a pun on the word "cipher." The essay has been reprinted and anthologized numerous times since then. In her essay, Brady examines the serious subject of stereotypical gender roles, treating her subject with wit and humour.*

1   I belong to that classification of people known as wives. I am A Wife. And, not altogether incidentally, I am a mother.

2   Not too long ago a male friend of mine appeared on the scene fresh from a recent divorce. He had one child, who is, of course, with his ex-wife. He is obviously looking for another wife. As I thought about him while I was ironing one evening, it suddenly occurred to me that I, too, would like to have a wife. Why do I want a wife?

3   I would like to go back to school so that I can become economically independent, support myself, and, if need be, support those dependent upon me. I want a wife who will work and send me to school. And while I am going to school I want a wife to keep track of the children's doctor and dentist appointments. And to keep track of mine, too. I want a wife to make sure my children eat properly and are kept clean. I want a wife who will wash the children's clothes and keep them mended. I want a wife who is a good nurturant° attendant to my children, who arranges for their schooling, makes sure that they have an adequate social life with their peers, takes them to the park, the zoo, etc. I want a wife who takes care of the children when they are sick, a wife who arranges to be around when the children need special care, because, of course, I cannot miss classes at school. My wife must arrange to lose time at work and not lose the job. It may mean a small cut in my wife's income from time to time, but I guess I can tolerate that. Needless to say, my wife will arrange and pay for the care of the children while my wife is working.

4   I want a wife who will take care of *my* physical needs. I want a wife who will keep my house clean. A wife who will pick up after me. I want a wife who will keep my clothes cleaned, ironed, mended, replaced when need be, and who will see to

it that my personal things are kept in their proper place so that I can find what I need the minute I need it. I want a wife who cooks the meals, a wife who is a *good* cook. I want a wife who will plan the menus, do the necessary grocery shopping, prepare the meals, serve them pleasantly, and then do the cleaning up while I do my studying. I want a wife who will care for me when I am sick and sympathize with my pain and loss of time from school. I want a wife to go along when our family takes a vacation so that someone can continue to care for me and my children when I need a rest and a change of scene.

5   I want a wife who will not bother me with rambling complaints about a wife's duties. But I want a wife who will listen to me when I feel the need to explain a rather difficult point I have come across in my course of studies. And I want a wife who will type my papers for me when I have written them.

6   I want a wife who will take care of the details of my social life. When my wife and I are invited out by my friends, I want a wife who will take care of the babysitting arrangements. When I meet people at school that I like and want to entertain, I want a wife who will have the house clean, will prepare a special meal, serve it to me and my friends, and not interrupt when I talk about the things that interest me and my friends. I want a wife who will have arranged that the children are fed and ready for bed before my guests arrive so that the children do not bother us. I want a wife who takes care of the needs of my guests so that they feel comfortable, who makes sure that they have an ashtray, that they are passed the hors d'oeuvres°, that they are offered a second helping of the food, that their wine glasses are replenished° when necessary, that their coffee is served to them as they like it.

7   And I want a wife who knows that sometimes I need a night out by myself.

8   I want a wife who is sensitive to my sexual needs, a wife who makes love passionately and eagerly when I feel like it, a wife who makes sure that I am satisfied. And, of course, I want a wife who will not demand sexual attention when I am not in the mood for it. I want a wife who assumes the complete responsibility for birth control, because I do not want more children. I want a wife who will remain sexually faithful to me so that I do not have to clutter up my intellectual life with jealousies. And I want a wife who understands that *my* sexual needs may entail more than strict adherence° to monogamy°. I must, after all, be able to relate to people as fully as possible.

9   If, by chance, I find another person more suitable as a wife than the wife I already have, I want the liberty to replace my present wife with another one. Naturally, I will expect a fresh, new life; my wife will take the children and be solely responsible for them so that I am left free.

10   When I am through with school and have a job, I want my wife to quit working and remain at home so that my wife can more fully and completely take care of a wife's duties.

11   My God, who wouldn't want a wife?

Vocabulary

3 nurturant (adj): providing care, food and training

6 hors d'oeuvres (n, French): appetizer

6 replenish (v): refill

8 adherence (n): sticking to, following rules

8 monogamy (n): practice of marrying or having sexual relationship with only one partner at a particular time

RESPONDING TO THE READING

- If the thesis is stated, identify it; if it is implied, write it in your own words.
- What do you think is the purpose of this essay? Give reasons for your opinion.
- Who do you think is the intended audience of this essay? Give reasons for your opinion.

Comprehension

1. Judy Brady begins with a statement of classification. What does she say or suggest a typical wife does?
2. What motivated Brady to want a wife?
3. What five major areas of personal life does Brady suggest a wife should manage?
4. Brady's definition of a wife depends on the job classification, not on gender. How do you know this?
5. Brady's supporting details are essentially lists of duties. What is the effect of those lists?
6. Is Brady accurate and fair in her assessment of a wife's duties?
7. Do you think Brady has stereotyped the role of a wife? Why or why not?
8. Has Brady stereotyped men? Why or why not?

Analysis

1. "I want" is repeated throughout this essay. What effect does this repetition have on you?
2. Brady repeats the word "wife" and never uses the pronouns "she" or "her." What effect does this create and why does she do this?
3. Does Brady succeed in being ironic? Give examples to support your view.
4. What is the point of the rhetorical question at the end of this essay?
5. How does Brady show that stereotyping limits individual ability and achievement?

Discussion/Writing Suggestions

1. Do you agree with any of Brady's argument? Argue against Brady's position by claiming that you want a husband.
2. This essay was written in 1971. Is it still relevant to modern marriage? Why or why not?

   - Other essays that discuss personal relationships are by Bertrand Russell (p. 64), Wayson Choy (p. 169), Timothy Findley (p. 92), Nicola Bleasby (p. 109), Stephen L. Carter (p. 132), Judith Viorst (p. 142), Charlie Angus (p. 180), Michael Dorris (p. 208), and Rosie DiManno (p. 211).

Dispatches from the Poverty Line

Pat Capponi

Pat Capponi (1949–) is an author, journalist, public speaker, community worker, and social activist. She has served on many agencies and hospital boards; she developed a leadership facilitation program for the psychiatric survivor community and is a founding member of the Gerstein Centre in Toronto. She has been awarded the Order of Ontario and the C. M. Hincks Award from the Canadian Mental Health Association. As a survivor of psychiatric illness, psychiatric wards, and long periods of unemployment and also as a social activist, Pat Capponi is doubly familiar with the world of the sick and the poor. She has written extensively on mental health, addictions, and poverty issues. Her books include Upstairs in the Crazy House: The Life of a Psychiatric Survivor *(1992),* Dispatches from the Poverty Line *(1997),* The War at Home: An Intimate Portrait of Canada's Poor *(1999),* Bound by Duty: Walking the Beat with Canada's Cops *(2000), and* Beyond the Crazy House: Changing the Future of Madness *(2003), and she is a regular contributor to* NOW *magazine.*

This essay is taken from Dispatches from the Poverty Line *(1997).*

1   We live in a time when manipulation of public opinion has been elevated to a science, when stereotypes are accepted as true representatives of their segment of the population. And, as always, stereotypes cause a great deal of pain to those tarred with the same brush. . . .

2   I am not innocent as far as taking refuge in stereotypes goes. As much as I try to catch myself at it, on occasion I'm forced to admit to myself, and sometimes to others, that I've fallen prey to its comforting lure.

3   I've served on many committees, task forces, working groups and boards in my seventeen years of mental health advocacy°. Before consumer involvement became more widely accepted, I was often the only ex-patient at the table, trying to deal with hospital administrators, bureaucrats, psychiatrists, nurses and family groups. I didn't think any board could scare me again, or silence me through intimidation.

4   I was, however, being forced to admit that one hospital board in particular was giving me a great deal of angst°. It left me feeling as though I'd been flung back through time. . . . I used to tell audiences of consumers and mental health staff that one of our biggest problems was that there was no consensus in the system concerning the value of involving clients in the management and delivery of services. One day I'd be working with an agency that possessed the equivalent of New York sophistication around the issues, and the next I'd feel as though I were in Alabama before the civil rights movement got under way. It wasn't unusual for these opposites to be within a few city blocks of each other.

5   That was part of my problem with this board, that it was Alabama-like while believing itself to be cutting edge. But there was more. There were deep and obvious class distinctions, and even though I was, at the time, gainfully employed, a published author, someone who possessed the respect of my community, I felt intimidated, looked down on, stereotyped and all the rest. It got so that I had to force myself to attend.

6   The board was a status board, composed of high-powered bankers, lawyers, publishers and consultants, as well as hospital executives. I was the only one in jeans, in a hat. I was the only one from my particular class and background. I was the only voice expressing criticism of the liberal establishment we were running. . . . Meetings were corporate; when I would leave for a cigarette I felt I should be bowing and backing up to the door. Nobody laughed, it seemed, ever. Nobody talked out of turn.

7   Then, one afternoon when I had screwed up my courage to attend, I bumped into the "fat cat" lawyer in the hallway. He made a joke, and I made one back before I had time to think about it. We both laughed and . . . we both stared at each other, surprised at the unlikely evidence of a sense of humour beneath the stereotype. Ice got broken. Then the banker who had offered me lifts home before, which I'd declined—what would I have to talk to him about in the car?—offered again, and I accepted. I even teased him about his brand new BMW and the pervasive smell of leather from the seats. He demonstrated how his car phone responded to voice orders to dial numbers, and I confess I got a kick out of the gimmickry. . . .

8   I remember another kind of breakthrough event at that board. I was trying once again to explain why I needed more people like me (from my class and experience) around the table. How easy it was to get intimidated in the setting we were in if you didn't find the corporate air invigorating. How easy it was to dismiss the views I was putting forward because it was only me they were hearing them from. How our class differences, our life experiences, created gulfs between us.

9   My banker friend took umbrage°. He was sure, he said, that he was quite capable of relating to me as a person, as another human being. He felt we were operating on a level playing field, and that I wasn't giving them enough credit.

10   My lawyer friend then made a remarkable statement.

11   "That's not true," he said. "Pat didn't start out on a level playing field with me. I took one look at her and summed her up. It wasn't until later that I started to see her differently."

12   "And I," I said, "did the same thing, summed up you guys at a glance, and what I felt was your attitude towards me. It got easier to walk around with a chip on my shoulder than to try and relate to you."

13   Even the publisher chimed in:

14   "I understand what you mean about intimidation. I never saw myself as intimidating, I like to think I'm an easygoing, friendly guy. But some of my staff have been pointing out to me that people who work for me don't have that same picture, because I have power over them. It's not easy or comfortable to realize that you may scare people, but a lot of times it's true."

15   Only the banker held out for the level playing field precept, but of course the conversation was ruled out of order and we were on to the next item on the agenda.

16   A month or two later, I decided to transfer my bank account to a branch nearer my residence. To get an account in the first place had been a challenge. I don't have credit cards, or a driver's licence: therefore, I don't have a system-recognized identity. This is a very common dilemma for those who make up the underclass, and it accounts for the prevalence° and huge success of Money Mart cheque-cashing services in poor areas. As long as I've been an advocate, various groups of workers have tried to break through the banking system, to work out generally acceptable ways of identifying clients to tellers through letters of introduction, or special cards, with no real success. . . .

17   In order for me to get an account in the first place, my publisher, Cynthia Good, had to take me into her branch, where we met with her "personal banking representative," and on the basis of Cynthia's knowledge of me, I got an account in time to deposit the cheque I'd received for the movie rights to my book.

18   I confess I felt quite mainstream for a while, with my PIN number and cheques and accounts book, as though I'd arrived. It was enough to make me overconfident. I decided it was silly to travel forty minutes to that branch when there was one a few blocks from me. I still had a balance of a little over $5,000, so I didn't anticipate any problems. I walked into my local branch and was soon seated across from yet another "personal banking representative."

19   "What I can do for you today?" she asked, pleasantly.

20   "I'd like to transfer my account to here, please," I responded, handing over my account book and bank card.

21   "I see, um, would you have some identification?"

22   I was puzzled.

23   "Nothing you guys seem to accept. But I only want to transfer, not open, an account."

24   She persists: "A major credit card? A driver's licence?"

25   I have a birth certificate. I remember trying to rent a video using it, and the owner of the store turning the card over and saying, "Your signature's not on it."

26   I shake my head. I give her the card of the other personal banking representative, the one in whose presence I had been validated°. She phones. She shakes her head. That person is on vacation. She purses her lips, not liking to create difficulties for me, but there are rules.

27   "I'm sorry, we really do need identification."

28   I'm getting angry, and I suspect she feels it, which accounts for her visible nervousness. It won't help to get snippy with her. I could just pack it in and leave—it wouldn't be the end of the world, after all. But the battle for reason is under way. It would feel too much like defeat to withdraw now.

29   I try for a reasoned, measured tone.

30   "I don't want to withdraw anything. I have $5,000 in my account. You have my card, my cheques, my account book."

31   I hear steps behind me, I'm sure the security guard is getting ready to pounce.

32   "It's a different branch of the same bank. C'mon, be reasonable."

33   "Don't you even have your Indian Status Card?"

34   "I'm not Indian!"

35   Ordinarily, I would take it as a compliment, being mistaken for one of the First People, but in this context, I know there's some heavy stereotyping, and quite possibly some heavy attitude, going on.

36   I get a flash. I'm terrible about names, remembering names. I can recall the most minute details of conversations, mannerisms, backgrounds and clothing but not names. But I do remember the division my BMW banker is president of. And I do remember it's this same corporation.

37   I ask her to look up the name of the guy in charge of——.

38   "Why?" she asks, immediately suspicious.

39   "I know him, he can tell you I exist."

40   Perhaps to humour me, she flips open a book and recites some names.

41   "That's him," I cry, vindicated°. "Give him a call, will you?"

42   I suppose it's like telling a private to ring up a general at the request of a possible lunatic, an aboriginal impersonator: it's not done.

43   She excuses herself to consult with a superior. Long minutes pass. I feel myself being examined from the glassed-in cubicles where the decision-makers sit. I feel the breath of the security officer. I feel renewed determination.

44   She's back.

45   "I'm sorry for the delay. His secretary had some difficulty reaching him, he's in a meeting. But he is available now."

46   My understanding smile is as false and strained as her apology.

47   She picks up the phone and annoyingly turns her chair away from me while she speaks in low tones into the receiver. A few heartbeats, then she passes the phone to me.

48   Not waiting for his voice, I say:

49   "I told you there's no level playing field."

50   He laughs, loudly and honestly.

51   In under ten minutes, I have my new account, my new card, cheques and a small degree of satisfaction.

52   Chalk up one for the good guys.

53   I take refuge in a nearby park, liking and needing the sun and a place to enjoy it. I've checked out the four or five in my neighbourhood, and on days when I need to walk, I go up to the one opposite the Dufferin Mall. I love the solitude, the birds, the green—a perfect setting for reading and tanning. Picking an empty bench, away from small clumps of people dotting the large park, I open my paperback and disappear into it.

54   It doesn't seem very long (my watch died a few months ago) before an old fellow, tottering on his cane, shuffles towards me. I look up at his approach, smile briefly and dive back into P. D. James. I am dismayed when he chooses to perch on

the other end of my bench, and I try to ignore his presence while my conscience starts bothering me. Now, I only smiled at him because I am aware that some folks think I look a bit tough, and I didn't want him worrying, but he might have mistaken the gesture for a come-chat-with-me invitation. He's probably lonely, isolated, this is probably his big daily outing. Would it kill me to spend a couple of minutes talking to him? Damn.

55   I close my book, look over at him looking over at me expectantly.

56   "Beautiful day, isn't it?"

57   I can barely make out his reply, cloaked in a thick accent, but his head bobbing up and down is pretty clear. I'm stuck for the next sentence, but he keeps going enthusiastically. I make out his name, repeating it triumphantly: "Victor! Hi, I'm Pat."

58   One arthritic hand grasps mine briefly, then goes back to rest on his cane with the other one.

59   "I'm retired." He's getting better at speaking clearly, maybe it was just a lack of opportunity that made him rusty. "I was an engineer."

60   "You live around here?"

61   He turns painfully, pointing vaguely over his shoulder.

62   "Right over there, a beautiful place. Very beautiful place."

63   "Good for you."

64   I offer him a cigarette, which he accepts, and we sit in companionable silence in the sun. I'm thinking after the smoke I will move on, find another park, maybe nearer my home.

65   He's talking again, and when I realize what he's saying my jaw drops open.

66   "If you come see my place, I will give you twenty dollars."

67   "Jesus Christ! Are you crazy?" I'm so annoyed, and shocked, and thrown off balance by his offer, that I'm blustering°. I want to whack him, except he'd probably fall over, like the dirty-old-man character on *Laugh-In*.

68   "Listen to me," I lecture, as I shake my finger in his face. "First off, you're committing a crime. Secondly, it's stupid and dangerous for you. You can't go around offering money to people you don't know for things I don't want to think about. You've insulted me. I could have you arrested! Do you understand?"

69   Now I'm pretty sure what his daily tour of the park is about, and I worry about the school-age girls that hang out at lunch time.

70   "If I see you doing this to anyone else, I will report you, do you get that? I'll be watching you!"

71   He's stuttering out an apology, which I don't believe, and refrain from kicking his cane, though I really want to.

72   On my way home, in between feeling outraged and feeling dirtied, I start to laugh at my own stereotyping of a lonely old man in need of conversation in juxtaposition° with his own stereotyping of me.

73   People ought to wear summing-up signs sometimes, just so you'd know what to expect.

Vocabulary

3 advocacy (n): work done on behalf of others, giving others a voice

4 angst (n): anxiety

9 umbrage (n): offence, objection

16 prevalence (n): widespread occurrence

26 validate (v): confirm the truthfulness of

41 vindicate (v): justify, clear someone of suspicion

67 bluster (v): speak loudly and arrogantly

72 in juxtaposition (prepositional phrase): side by side

 # RESPONDING TO THE READING

- If the thesis is stated, identify it; if it is implied, write it in your own words.
- What do you think is the purpose of this essay? Give reasons for your opinion.
- Who do you think is the intended reader of this essay? Give reasons for your opinion.

Comprehension

1. What point about stereotyping does Pat Capponi make in Paragraphs 1 and 2?
2. Capponi's essay is arranged in three sections: Paragraphs 1 to 15, 16 to 52, and 53 to 73. How would you categorize each section?
3. What reasons does Capponi provide for being intimidated by this hospital board?
4. How does Capponi stereotype three members of this hospital board?
5. How does Capponi overcome her bias and what are the immediate effects of this?
6. What is the point of the discussion of the "level playing field" in Paragraphs 9 to 15?
7. How does Capponi directly link this discussion of the "level playing field" to her experiences in the bank?
8. What reasons does Capponi give for her difficulties in using a bank?
9. Why was Capponi successful in opening her first bank account?
10. In what ways does the "personal banking representative" in her local branch stereotype Capponi?
11. How does Capponi manage to succeed in transferring her account?
12. In the second anecdote, why doesn't Capponi want to talk to the old man in the park, but why does she speak to him anyway?
13. What stereotypes does Capponi have of the old man before they talk and after they talk?
14. What does the old man say to offend Capponi?
15. Why is Capponi's conclusion an effective response to the two incidents?

Analysis

1. Based on information about her throughout the essay, how would you describe Capponi's appearance and attitude?
2. Explain the allusion to Alabama and civil rights in Paragraphs 4 and 5. How is it appropriate in the context of this essay?
3. The publisher discusses the effect each of us has on others in Paragraph 14. How aware do you think you are of your effect on others?
4. Capponi writes most of this essay in dialogue. What is the effect of that? Why do you think she does it?
5. Why do you think Capponi chose to show instances in which she is stereotyped as well as times when she stereotypes others?
6. Has this essay affected how you will see street people? Why or why not?

Discussion/Writing Suggestions

1. Have you been stereotyped? What happened and how did you handle it?
2. Capponi has overcome tremendous adversity to become the accomplished and influential woman she is today. How have the challenges in your life shaped the person you now are? Explain.

   - Other essays that focus on social issues are those by Hugh MacLennan (p. 5), Charles Dickens (p. 10), David Suzuki (p. 88), Stephen L. Carter (p. 132), Judy Brady (p. 155), Wayson Choy (p. 169), Derek Cohen (p. 173), Charlie Angus (p. 180), and Rosie DiManno (p. 211).

Essay of Cause and Effect

Essays of cause and effect are in essence **causal analyses** that link conditions and consequences by explaining *how* and *why* they are connected. An essay using a cause-and-effect organizational pattern could look ahead for *effect(s)* (to predict what results follow) or look back for *cause(s)* (to analyze why things happened). Occasionally, some writers also choose to conduct a comprehensive causal analysis by looking both ways.

Writing Strategy

When you write a cause-and-effect essay, state from the beginning what your subject is and how it deserves an explanation of connections between causes and effects. Writing cause-and-effect essays requires a number of careful approaches:

1. Make sure the cause-and-effect relationship between two or more things is valid, and not just based on coincidence.

For example, a causal analysis would be invalid if it were based on this statement: "For years it was rumoured that cigarette smoking caused cancer." Clearly, no logical conclusion can be drawn from any rumour or mere coincidence. Only ample scientific data can prove the convincing link between the cigarette and lung cancer. In contrast, Dan Zollmann presents a solid causal analysis by grounding his examination of the effects of illiteracy in *his own* experience as a functional illiterate.

2. Be sure to gather adequate data and examples to support your analysis. Sufficient evidence to prove your point is essential in cause-and-effect writing. As you will see, Susan Jacoby presents extensive anecdotal evidence and research data to support her analysis of the causes and effects of "math anxiety." Her findings are essential to her conclusion. Similarly, without the ample causes presented earlier, no reader would feel the petrifying effect of illiteracy on Dan Zollmann when he claims, "I became paralyzed with fear when faced with the most trivial of daily tasks" in Paragraph 4 of his essay.

3. Do not create a connection between causes and effects if none exists. It is tempting to assume proof or to depend on bias, but evidence must be shown before a cause-and-effect relationship can be considered valid. Also, do not ever assume that because one event follows another, the first *causes* the second. You must keep in mind sequence is not the same thing as a causal relationship. Pat Capponi's eye-opening anecdotes in "Dispatches from the Poverty Line" (p. 159) show clearly how assuming a cause from an effect can be misleading.

4. Be aware that there are two types of causes:
   a. **immediate causes**—causes that at first glance are obviously related to effects;
   b. **ultimate causes**—causes that stand out above all others as main motivations.

   Example: If a child is crying, the immediate cause could be a skinned knee. If a child skins a knee frequently and cries, the ultimate cause might be a poor sense of balance or a low pain threshold.

   In Dan Zollmann's essay, all the examples of his type of illiteracy form the immediate causes of his inability to communicate effectively; the ultimate cause of his alienation from society, however, lies in his inability to communicate with others in a meaningful manner. A convincing causal analysis should always go beyond the immediate causes and search for the ultimate causes.

When you read Dan Zollmann's essay, try to separate the reasons he gives for feeling illiterate from their effects and see how his analysis proceeds.

SAMPLE STUDENT ESSAY OF CAUSE AND EFFECT

Illiterate Like Me

Dan Zollmann

[margin note: general statement to shocking]

1   Most Canadians believe that something should be done to help the illiterate. Yet other social issues often take precedence when it comes to distributing tax dollars. If illiteracy were simply an inconvenience suffered by a handful of Canadians, then the low priority we accord to dealing with it would be justified because time and money are finite, and we must allocate these scarce resources on the basis of importance. However, illiteracy is not merely an inconvenience, nor does it afflict only a few Canadians. Instead, illiteracy is nothing less than political, economic, and social alienation of a large number of individuals from their society. As such, it is as urgent as any other social problem we face.

[margin note: no topic]

2   What is it really like to be illiterate? I do not know, nor will I ever be capable of knowing, any more than I could know what it would be like to be blind, or to be a paraplegic. Four years ago, however, I moved to Quebec City to study French at Laval University, an experience that provided me with some insight into the reality of illiteracy. As someone who had learned to speak French by ear, I knew the alphabet, could recognize a few words, but had almost no practical experience reading and writing French. In other words, at age twenty I joined the ranks of the illiterate.

[margin note: no topic]

3   How does an illiterate survive in a situation requiring a higher level of literacy than most jobs in Canada require, namely, as a university student? With great difficulty. Although in high school I had participated a great deal in class discussion, in university I stopped offering my opinions because I had no confidence in my understanding of the texts under discussion. Always a good writer in high school, I now found myself incapable of finishing an essay exam question within the time limit, never mind producing logical, concise answers. Even the basics of dealing with the university's administration became a struggle: calendars, course changes, registration forms, regulations, all were a complete mystery to me. Sometimes the results were disastrous: for example, I accidentally signed a form that forced me to spend hours the following year trying to get re-admitted to the university. Moreover, I had no idea how services such as guidance, tutoring, or the ombudsman could help me deal with these problems since I was incapable of fully comprehending my student handbook.

[margin note: no topic]

4   Not only was attending university difficult, but many problems that literate people daily overcome suddenly became insurmountable. I opened a bank account without even attempting to understand the form I had to sign. My furnace broke down several times in the winter, yet I had no idea to whom I should complain. Moreover, I was incapable of writing a letter of complaint even if I had known where to send it. Although I had some idea of the basics of written French, using it every day was extraordinarily difficult because I knew that when I wrote in French I made mistakes in grammar that most people stopped making after Grade Three.

This embarrassed me to the point that I was afraid to put up an advertisement on the bulletin board to sell last term's textbooks, or to fill out a job application, or to leave a note for someone on my apartment door, or even to write down a phone message for a roommate. I became paralyzed with fear when faced with the most trivial of daily tasks.

5   My inability to read or write also had a profound effect on the way I related to my community. I constantly saw things around me that aroused my anger, yet I was powerless to change them. For example, I wanted to write a letter of complaint to the owners of the pulp mill that filled my lungs with sulphur dioxide gas every time I passed by on the way to the university, yet I knew that any letter I wrote would first be laughed at, and then ignored. Since we tend to judge a person's intelligence by his or her ability to write, how could I expect the owners of the pulp mill, or the editors of a newspaper, to take seriously the complaint of someone who appeared to be too ignorant to write beyond the primary school level?

6   Gradually, I became divorced from the world in which I lived. I voted in the provincial elections, but I did not understand the brochures delivered to my apartment by the candidates. I occasionally bought *Le Devoir* with the intention of reading it cover to cover, yet found myself incapable of following any article longer than a few paragraphs. Unable to read newspapers, I had to accept the second-hand reports of literate people around me. Unable to understand political debate, I judged on the basis of appearance, rather than issues. Incapable of communicating with my own community, I renounced all personal responsibility, hoping that others would write letters, circulate the petitions, and lobby local officials. In short, I gave up, resigning myself to the frustrated yet passive existence of the alienated.

7   The comparison between my experiences in Quebec City and those of someone who is truly illiterate, however, can go only so far. After all, I was already literate in one language and was in Quebec by choice, not necessity. In contrast, the millions of Canadians who can neither read nor write either official language cannot simply pack their bags and return to their home province when they grow tired of their alienation. Moreover, it is quite possible that most of these people are not even aware of the extent to which they are isolated from society because they know no other existence, no other way of living. This, in turn, highlights the ultimate tragedy of illiteracy, namely that those who suffer from it are powerless to exert the political pressure necessary to change their situation.

8   Illiteracy is, therefore, more than merely a minor inconvenience. In Canada, and in all other Western societies, an inability to read and write means alienation from one's community and from one's country. At a political level, illiteracy makes a mockery of the democratic process by creating an oligarchy composed of an educated elite. At a personal level, illiteracy means subjection to an economic and political marginalization; in short, the exploitation of one of the most vulnerable groups in society.

Comprehension

1. What are the three key ideas around which Dan Zollmann develops his essay?
2. What does Zollmann do to catch readers' interest in his subject? Why does he believe illiteracy should receive more attention and literacy movements be better funded than they currently are?
3. What is the effect of beginning Paragraphs 2 and 3 with a question?
4. What problems are presented as examples of how difficult it is to be illiterate?
5. In Paragraph 4, Zollmann develops his topic sentence by using two distinct techniques: examples and cause and effect. Identify the two and explain how they illustrate the key idea in the topic sentence.
6. Explain the effects Zollmann presents to prove how powerless he became as a functional illiterate in Quebec.
7. What does Zollmann mean by "the ultimate tragedy of illiteracy"?
8. How does the concluding paragraph relate to the thesis statement and the essay as a whole?
9. Using context clues, define the word "oligarchy," which appears in Paragraph 8.

Analysis

1. Why does Zollmann give his essay the title "Illiterate Like Me"? After all, Zollmann is not illiterate. What is the impact of this title?
2. In what ways do you believe an illiterate could be like a paraplegic?
3. Writers often use **hyperbole.** That is, they overstate an idea or a case to achieve a dramatic effect. Does Zollmann indulge in hyperbole when he says "I became paralyzed with fear when faced with the most trivial of daily tasks"? What evidence in other paragraphs suggests that similar statements are fact and not hyperbole?
4. Is it true that as a society "we tend to judge a person's intelligence by his or her ability to write"?
5. What parallels with Dan Zollmann's examples can you see in your own experiences?

Discussion/Writing Suggestions

1. Is there an issue about which you have felt strongly and that moved you to act or complain in public? What were the results of your actions?
2. Zollmann empathizes with the illiterate. Is there a group of people for whom you feel great empathy? Explain why you empathize—be careful to distinguish between empathy and sympathy.

READINGS: ESSAYS OF CAUSE AND EFFECT

In his essay "I'm a Banana and Proud of It," Wayson Choy examines the causes and effects of Chinese immigration to Canada; he examines these causes through a series of historical data, personal reminiscences, and historical details that end with this powerful conclusion: "We are all Chinese." In his essay based on his memories of South Africa, Derek Cohen describes the many social effects that stem from the ultimate cause: apartheid. Susan Jacoby examines what causes girls in high school to drop math courses and the personal and social effects of their decisions. Finally, Charlie Angus analyzes two sets of causes and effects: first, why we are fascinated by violence in movies and its effect on us; second, how serial killers exploit that fascination and we, in turn, treat murders as entertainment. The result, Angus claims, is social alienation.

I'm a Banana and Proud of It

Wayson Choy

Wayson Choy (1939–) is a celebrated Canadian writer. Choy was born in Vancouver and attended the University of British Columbia before moving to Toronto in 1962. He taught at Humber College and the Humber School for Writers from 1967 to 2004. Choy was president of Cahoots Theatre Company of Toronto from 1999 to 2002. His novel The Jade Peony *(1995) won the Trillium Book Award and the City of Vancouver Book Award. Choy also wrote the memoir* Paper Shadows: A Chinatown Childhood *(1999), which won the Edna Staebler Creative Non-Fiction Award and was nominated for the Governor General's Award. His latest novel,* All That Matters, *was published in 2004. In 2005, he was named a member of the Order of Canada.*

Through his writing, Wayson Choy explores the challenges of growing up with his Chinese heritage often in conflict with the influence of the North American culture. Much of Choy's writing focuses on his experiences in Vancouver's Chinatown. He describes his childhood as being "like a Chinese box that opens in a variety of different ways, revealing different levels, each sliding compartment a secret." In this essay, which appeared in the Globe and Mail on July 18, 1997, Choy proudly defines himself as a "banana," a nickname for Canadian children of Chinese parents.

1   Because both my parents came from China, I look Chinese. But I cannot read or write Chinese and barely speak it. I love my North American citizenship. I don't mind being called a "banana," yellow on the outside and white inside. I'm proud I'm a banana.

2   After all, in Canada and the United States, native Indians are "apples" (red outside, white inside); blacks are "Oreo cookies" (black and white); and Chinese are "bananas." These metaphors assume, both rightly and wrongly, that the culture here has been primarily anglo-white. Cultural history made me a banana.

3   History: My father and mother arrived separately to the B.C. coast in the early part of the century. They came as unwanted "aliens." Better to be an alien here than to be dead of starvation in China. But after the Chinese Exclusion laws* were passed in North America (late 1800s, early 1900s), no Chinese immigrants were granted citizenship in either Canada or the United States.

4   Like those Old China village men from Toi San who, in the 1850s, laid down cliff-edge train tracks through the Rockies and the Sierras, or like those first women who came as mail-order wives or concubines and who as bond-slaves were turned into cheaper labourers or even prostitutes—like many of those men and women, my father and mother survived ugly, unjust times. In 1917, two hours after he got off the boat from Hong Kong, my father was called "chink" and told to go back to China. "Chink" is a hateful racist term, stereotyping the shape of Asian eyes: "a chink in the armour," an undesirable slit. For the Elders, the past was humiliating. Eventually, the Second World War changed hostile attitudes toward the Chinese.

5   During the war, Chinese men volunteered and lost their lives as members of the American and Canadian military. When hostilities ended, many more were proudly in uniform waiting to go overseas. Record Chinatown dollars were raised to buy War Bonds. After 1945, challenged by such money and ultimate sacrifices, the Exclusion laws in both Canada and the United States were revoked°. Chinatown residents claimed their citizenship and sent for their families.

6   By 1949, after the Communists took over China, those of us who arrived here as young children, or were born here, stayed. No longer "aliens," we became legal citizens of North America. Many of us also became "bananas."

7   Historically, "banana" is not a racist term. Although it clumsily stereotypes many of the children and grandchildren of the Old Chinatowns, the term actually follows the old Chinese tendency to assign endearing nicknames to replace formal names, semicomic names to keep one humble. Thus, "banana" describes the generations who assimilated so well into North American life.

8   In fact, our families encouraged members of my generation in the 1950s and sixties to "get ahead," to get an English education, to get a job with good pay and prestige. "Don't work like me," Chinatown parents said. "Work in an office!" The *lao wah-kiu* (the Chinatown old-timers) also warned, "Never forget—you still be Chinese!"

9   None of us ever forgot. The mirror never lied.

10   Many Chinatown teen-agers felt we didn't quite belong in any one world. We looked Chinese, but thought and behaved North American. Impatient Chinatown parents wanted the best of both worlds for us, but they bluntly labelled their children and grandchildren *"juk-sing"* or even *"mo no."* Not that we were totally "shallow bamboo butt-ends" or entirely "no brain," but we had less and less understanding of Old China traditions, and less and less interest in their village histories. Father used to say we lacked Taoist° ritual, Taoist manners. We were, he said, *"mo li."*

11   This was true. Chinatown's younger brains, like everyone else's of whatever race, were being colonized by "white bread" U.S. family television programs. We began to feel Chinese home life was inferior. We co-operated with English-language magazines that showed us how to act and what to buy. Seductive Hollywood movies made some of us secretly weep that we did not have movie-star faces. American music made Chinese music sound like noise.

12   By the 1970s and eighties, many of us had consciously or unconsciously distanced ourselves from our Chinatown histories. We became bananas.

13   Finally, for me, in my 40s or 50s, with the death first of my mother, then my father, I realized I did not belong anywhere unless I could understand the past. I needed to find the foundation of my Chinese-ness. I needed roots.

14   I spent my college holidays researching the past. I read Chinatown oral histories, located documents, searched out early articles. Those early citizens came back to life for me. Their long toil and blood sacrifices, the proud record of their patient, legal challenges, gave us all our present rights as citizens. Canadian and American Chinatowns set aside their family tongue differences and encouraged each other to fight injustice. There were no borders. "After all," they affirmed, *"Daaih ga tohng yahn . . .* We are all Chinese!"

15   In my book, *The Jade Peony,* I tried to recreate this past, to explore the beginnings of the conflicts trapped within myself, the struggle between being Chinese and being North American. I discovered a truth: these "between world" struggles are universal.

16   In every human being, there is "the Other"—something that makes each of us feel how different we are to everyone else, even to family members. Yet, ironically, we are all the same, wanting the same security and happiness. I know this now.

17   I think the early Chinese pioneers actually started "going bananas"° from the moment they first settled upon the West Coast. They had no choice. They adapted. They initiated assimilation. If they had not, they and their family would have starved to death. I might even suggest that all surviving Chinatown citizens eventually became bananas. Only some, of course, were more ripe than others.

18   That's why I'm proudly a banana: I accept the paradox° of being both Chinese and not Chinese.

19   Now at last, whenever I look in the mirror or hear ghost voices shouting, "You still Chinese!", I smile.

20   I know another truth: In immigrant North America, we are all Chinese.

Note

3 Chinese Exclusion Laws: In 1885, Canada imposed a head tax on Chinese seeking to enter the country; it started at $50 and rose to a maximum of $500 in 1903. In 1892, Canada enacted the Immigration Act, commonly known as the Chinese Exclusion Act, making the Chinese the only people Canada has ever excluded explicitly on the basis of race.

Vocabulary

5 revoke (v): withdraw, cancel

10 Taoist (adj): from Chinese, Dao (right way) a philosophy of humility and harmony

17 going bananas (slang): going crazy, acting foolishly

18 paradox (n): apparent contradiction

RESPONDING TO THE READING

- If the thesis is stated, identify it; if it is implied, write it in your own words.
- What do you think is the purpose of this essay? Give reasons for your opinion.
- Who do you think is the intended audience of this essay? Give reasons for your opinion.

Comprehension

1. Wayson Choy offers two definitions of "banana" in his first paragraph. What does the term "banana" mean according to Choy?
2. What voice does Choy use in this essay? Find examples to support your claim.
3. Find an example of Choy's humour.
4. Choy presents a historical account of the Chinese in Canada as well as a personal history. What does Choy say about his parents' experiences in coming to Canada?
5. Paragraphs 7 and 12 return to the term "banana." How does Choy define it here and how do these definitions compare with the one in Paragraph 1?
6. In Paragraph 10, Choy introduces a new point of view. What is the change? Find examples of it.
7. What motivated Choy to research the past?
8. What sort of research did Choy do, and what did he actually discover?
9. What sort of understanding does Choy claim he now has, and what examples does he give as support?

Analysis

1. How is the use of the term "banana" different from "apple" and "Oreo cookie" as Choy uses them?
2. What does Choy mean by "rightly and wrongly" in the following quotation from Paragraph 2: "These metaphors assume, both rightly and wrongly, that the culture here has been primarily anglo-white."
3. Choy differentiates between nicknames and racist terms. Is his distinction appropriate?
4. In Paragraph 8, Choy discusses ambition; how do you react to his examples?
5. How do the many Chinese terms Choy includes in this essay add to his self-definition?
6. Is Choy right when he claims, "In every human being, there is 'the Other'"?
7. How does the conclusion of this essay relate to its title?

Discussion/Writing Suggestions

1. Nicknames are an important concept in this essay. What role do nicknames play in our lives? Who assigns nicknames? Who uses them? Do you have a nickname? Does it appropriately reflect who you are?
2. How would you define yourself?

   • Essays by these writers deal with racism, stereotyping, or national identity: Hugh MacLennan (p. 5), Ralph Nader (p. 28), Peggy Lampotang (p. 129), Julie-Ann Yoshikuni (p. 140), Derek Cohen (p. 173), Pier Giorgio Di Cicco (p. 196), Rosie DiManno (p. 211), Pat Capponi (p. 158), and Amartya Sen (p. 252).

The New Apartheid

Derek Cohen

Derek Cohen (1943–) was born in Pretoria, South Africa, and was educated in that country at Rhodes University and in the United States at New York University. He is a professor of English at York University, Toronto. He has published numerous articles on Renaissance and 18th-century English drama and several books, including The Politics of Shakespeare *(Macmillan, 1993),* Shakespearean Motives *(1988), and* Shakespeare's Culture of Violence *(Macmillan 1992). He has co-edited (with Deborah Heller)* Jewish Presences in English Literature *(McGill/Queen's, 1991). His most recent book is* Searching Shakespeare: Studies in Culture and Authority *(2004). He has also written widely on South African literature and the South African experience. He recently published "How I Nearly Became a Terrorist" in* Dissent *magazine (2005); that article recounts the dangers he encountered as an anti-racist activist under the regime of apartheid in South Africa.*

In this essay, "The New Apartheid," which was published in 1992 in Canadian Forum, *Cohen poignantly describes the human effects of the apartheid policy in his homeland.*

1   My first and most lasting impression of South Africa, and my oldest memory of the country, is of black people walking. Wherever you are in South Africa, in the most crowded parts of the largest cities or on the remotest country roads, you see black people walking. In the cities or on the busy highways, as whites go whizzing° by in their cars, there are always black men, women and children walking in both directions. They are going home or they are going to work, but they are always there. In the country you can be a hundred miles from the nearest town, and out there on the dry veld° roads, you will come upon small clusters° of black people walking to and from. Women with bundles on their heads and babies tied to their backs, children in unaccountable° and anomalous° school uniforms and bare feet, working men, old men and women, usually in small numbers or alone, going ever towards some place that you usually can't see. There are, as everyone knows, villages scattered

throughout the hills and flats. But you also realize that great distances have to be covered by foot for these people to reach them.

2   This is the secret South Africa, this slow-moving horde° of pedestrians whose lives are silently lived in remote places. These resigned foot travellers whose true labour is the simple but hard job of getting from one place to another. They are always there; they are always remote from white life, from sophisticated life. They trudge° the streets and roads of the land in a procession of daily life, ubiquitous° and silent. The rest of the nation glides by them in their cars, so used to them as to be almost unaware of them. These people are part of the South African landscape, blending almost picturesquely° into the background. The visitor who sees a black woman walking a country road, with a large bundle of clothes, food, furniture or even a small hutch of poultry° on her head, is immediately moved to wonder at the co-ordination she must possess to manage the load. She is an artist of balance and a paragon° of female strength with her oversized bundle on her head. Her poverty is less wonderful than her virtuosity°.

3   These walking hordes are a comfort to most white South Africans. They are a visible reminder of the gap that still exists between themselves and significant change. Poverty sustains° the difference. And while white South Africa likes to point with pride to the occasional black with a large car and a large income, he is still enough of an exception and oddity° to be merely curious. Most white South Africans (like most Americans or Canadians, I would guess) would cheerfully endure the prospect of one black dentist living on their street. Such an event would ensure them of the end of apartheid and world isolation, and also demonstrate their own tolerance of other races.

4   Growing up "liberal" in South Africa, and being known to oppose racism, I was constantly asked, from very early in my life, how I would like my sister to marry a black, sometimes in less polite terms than that. I used to dismiss the question as racist and would not take it very seriously, replying facetiously° that it would suit me fine as long as he was Jewish. Now I know that my interrogators° were right; that this really *is* the essential question. That if you cannot say, I wouldn't care; race makes no difference to me in judging another human being as my brother-in-law, or son-in-law, or greengrocer, or neurosurgeon, then you are guilty of accepting racial ideology in some measure. By this same—to me, essential—criterion, the overwhelming majority of white people in the West are racists. Of course, not liking black people—or Jews or Kurds—is not the same thing as beating or killing them, and racism like most things comes in different degrees. But in South Africa it has so long been official policy, legislated° into the brains of oppressors and oppressed alike, that it takes on a peculiarly virulent° form. Racism and race are national obsessions in that country. There is no area of life in which it is not the chief matter. Go to the beach and you will notice or be shown that either there are blacks swimming in a formerly segregated° place or, alternatively, that there are no blacks swimming there. In other words, no experience in South Africa can be innocent of race. It is in small matters like this that South Africa is different from the rest of the white world, where innocence is still possible. In South Africa, from infancy, the ideology of race permeates° every corner of experience.

Vocabulary

1 whizz (v): speeding

1 veld (n): grassland in South Africa

1 clusters (n): groups, bunches

1 unaccountable (adj): unidentifiable, strange

1 anomalous (adj): abnormal

2 horde (n): crowd, throng

2 trudge (v): to walk, step

2 ubiquitous (adj): pervasive, present everywhere

2 picturesquely (adv): strikingly, vividly

2 hutch of poultry (n): pen or coop of chickens

2 paragon (n): model, ideal

2 virtuosity (n): perfectionism, mastery

3 sustain (v): to maintain, keep, preserve

3 oddity (n): peculiarity

4 facetiously (adv): amusingly, jokingly

4 interrogators (n): people who ask questions in an aggressive or threatening manner

4 legislate (v): to enact, pass into law

4 virulent (adj): fatal, deadly

4 segregate (v): isolate, keep apart

4 permeate (v): pervade, fill, penetrate

 RESPONDING TO THE READING

- If the thesis is stated, identify it; if it is implied, write it in your own words.
- What do you think is the purpose of this essay? Give reasons for your opinion.
- Who do you think is the intended audience of this essay? Give reasons for your opinion.

Comprehension

1. In Paragraphs 1 and 2, Derek Cohen describes his "first and most lasting impression of South Africa." What is that impression? Is it a cause or an effect?

2. In Paragraph 1, how many examples does Cohen give of black people walking? How many times does he repeat the word "walking"? Where are the people walking to?

3. Despite the many examples of blacks walking, Cohen's only mention of white people in Paragraph 1 is that they "go whizzing by in their cars." What do you understand from this contrast?

4. In Paragraph 2, what does Cohen mean by "the secret South Africa"?

5. How does Cohen support his idea of a secret South Africa?

6. In your own words, explain why Cohen says "these walking hordes are a comfort to most white South Africans"?

7. Cohen says "poverty sustains the difference." How has Cohen established poverty as an immediate cause of this difference between black and white South Africans?

8. Explain how, as an anti-racist, Cohen was taunted by racists.

9. How does Cohen support his claim that in South Africa race and racism are national obsessions?

10. The ultimate cause in this essay is apartheid, racism legislated as official policy. Why does Cohen wait until the end of his essay to reveal that?

Analysis

1. What is the author's attitude toward black South Africans? How can you tell?

2. What is the effect of Cohen's evocative descriptions of black people, given that he says most white South Africans don't notice them?

3. How does Cohen demonstrate that one of the effects of apartheid is that most white South Africans did not regard black South Africans as people?

4. What is Cohen's essential criterion for determining if someone is racist? Do you agree with him? Why or why not?

5. What does Cohen mean by "innocent" in this essay? Are there other words whose meanings he tests in a similar manner?

Discussion/Writing Suggestions

1. The example of "one black dentist" given by Cohen is an example of "tokenism"; that is, the presence of an "outside" person in a dominant group that seems to prove there is no discrimination. What other examples of tokenism are there besides those based on race? What are the possible reasons for tokenism?

2. Cohen says that "racism like most things comes in different degrees." Before apartheid was banished, Canada was among the countries to impose economic and political sanctions on South Africa to force its government to put an end to the policy of apartheid. What is your opinion of the use of international sanctions against governments that violate human rights?

   • Other essays that discuss human rights issues include those by Hugh MacLennan (p. 5), Malcolm X (p. 19), Ralph Nader (p. 28), David Suzuki (p. 88), Wayson Choy (p. 169), Stephen L. Carter (p. 132), Pat Capponi (p. 158), and Amartya Sen (p. 252).

When Bright Girls Decide That Math Is "A Waste of Time"

Susan Jacoby

Susan Jacoby (1945–) is a graduate of Michigan State University. The recipient of many awards, she began her journalistic career as an education reporter for the Washington Post *in 1963. Jacoby has written extensively on women's issues, Russian culture, health and medicine, religion, and civil liberties. Her articles and reviews have appeared in the* New York Times, *the* Washington Post, Newsday, The Nation, Harper's, Vogue, *and the* AARP Magazine, *among other publications. Jacoby is the author of six books, including* The Possible She, *a collection of essays on women originally published in the* New York Times; Half-Jew: A Daughter's Search for Her Family's Buried Past, Moscow Conversations; *and* Wild Justice: The Evolution of Revenge, *which was a Pulitzer Prize finalist in nonfiction. Jacoby is currently director of the metropolitan New York branch of the Center for Inquiry, a secular humanist research and advocacy organization.*

The following article was published in 1983, and, as the title suggests, it examines the consequences of girls' dropping math in high school. Jacoby also searches for the possible causes for this behaviour.

1   Susannah, a 16-year-old who has always been an A student in every subject from algebra to English, recently informed her parents that she intended to drop physics and calculus in her senior year of high school and replace them with a drama seminar and a work-study program. She expects a major in art or history in college, she explained, and "any more science or math will just be a waste of my time."

2   Her parents were neither concerned by nor opposed to her decision. "Fine, dear," they said. Their daughter is, after all, an outstanding student. What does it matter if, at age 16, she has taken a step that may limit her understanding of both machines and the natural world for the rest of her life?

3   This kind of decision, in which girls turn away from studies that would give them a sure footing in the world of science and technology, is a self-inflicted female disability that is, regrettably, almost as common today as it was when I was in high school. If Susannah had announced that she had decided to stop taking English in her senior year, her mother and father would have been horrified. I also think they would have been a good deal less sanguine° about her decision if she were a boy.

4   In saying that scientific and mathematical ignorance is a self-inflicted female wound, I do not, obviously, mean that cultural expectations play no role in the process. But the world does not conspire° to deprive° modern women of access to science as it did in the 1930s, when Rosalyn S. Yallow, the Nobel Prize-winning physicist, graduated from Hunter College and was advised to go to work as a secretary because no graduate school would admit her to its physics department. The current generation of adolescent girls—and their parents, bred on old expectations about women's interests—are active conspirators in limiting their own intellectual development.

5   It is true that the proportion of young women in science-related graduate and professional schools, most notably medical schools, has increased significantly in the past decade. It is also true that so few women were studying advanced science and mathematics before the early 1970s that the percentage increase in female enrollment does not yet translate into large numbers of women actually working in science.

6   The real problem is that so many girls eliminate° themselves from any serious possibility of studying science as a result of decisions made during the vulnerable period of mid-adolescence, when they are most likely to be influenced—on both

conscious and subconscious levels—by the traditional belief that math and science are "masculine" subjects.

7   During the teen-age years the well-documented phenomenon of "math anxiety" strikes girls who never had any problem handling numbers during earlier schooling. Some men, too, experience this syndrome°—a form of panic, akin to a phobia°, at any task involving numbers—but women constitute the overwhelming majority of sufferers. The onset of acute math anxiety during the teen-age years is, as Stalin was fond of saying, "not by accident."

8   In adolescence girls begin to fear that they will be unattractive to boys if they are typed as "brains." Science and math epitomize° unfeminine braininess in a way that, say, foreign languages do not. High-school girls who pursue an advanced interest in science and math (unless they are students at special institutions like the Bronx High School of Science where everyone is a brain) usually find that they are greatly outnumbered by boys in their classes. They are, therefore, intruding on male turf at a time when their sexual confidence, as well as that of the boys, is most fragile.

9   A 1981 assessment of female achievement in mathematics, based on research conducted under a National Institute for Education grant, found significant differences in the mathematical achievements of 9th and 12th graders. At age 13 girls were equal to or slightly better than boys in tests involving algebra, problem solving and spatial ability°; four years later the boys had outstripped the girls.

10   It is not mysterious that some very bright high-school girls suddenly decide that math is "too hard" and "a waste of time." In my experience, self-sabotage of mathematical and scientific ability is often a conscious process. I remember deliberately pretending to be puzzled by geometry problems in my sophomore° year in high school. A male teacher called me in after class and said, in a baffled tone, "I don't see how you can be having so much trouble when you got straight A's last year in my algebra class."

11   The decision to avoid advanced biology, chemistry, physics and calculus in high school automatically restricts academic and professional choices that ought to be wide open to anyone beginning college. At all coeducational universities women are overwhelmingly concentrated in the fine arts, social sciences and traditionally female departments like education. Courses leading to degrees in science- and technology-related fields are filled mainly by men.

12   In my generation, the practical consequences of mathematical and scientific illiteracy are visible in the large number of special programs to help professional women overcome the anxiety they feel when they are promoted into jobs that require them to handle statistics.

13   The consequences of this syndrome should not, however, be viewed in narrowly professional terms. Competence in science and math does not mean one is going to become a scientist or mathematician any more than competence in writing English means one is going to become a professional writer. Scientific and mathematical illiteracy—which has been cited in several recent critiques by panels studying American education from kindergarten through college—produces an incalculably impoverished vision of human experience.

14   Scientific illiteracy is not, of course, the exclusive province of women. In certain intellectual circles it has become fashionable to proclaim° a willed, aggressive ignorance

about science and technology. Some female writers specialize in ominous°, uninformed diatribes° against genetic research as a plot to remove control of childbearing from women, while some well-known men of letters proudly announce that they understand absolutely nothing about computers, or, for that matter, about electricity. This lack of understanding is nothing in which women or men ought to take pride.

15   Failure to comprehend either computers or chromosomes leads to a terrible sense of helplessness, because the profound impact of science on everyday life is evident even to those who insist they don't, won't, can't understand why the changes are taking place. At this stage of history women are more prone to such feelings of helplessness than men because the culture judges their ignorance less harshly and because women themselves acquiesce° in that indulgence.

16   Since there is ample evidence of such feelings in adolescence, it is up to parents to see that their daughters do not accede° to the old stereotypes about "masculine" and "feminine" knowledge. Unless we want our daughters to share our intellectual handicaps, we had better tell them no, they can't stop taking mathematics and sciences at the ripe old age of 16.

Vocabulary

3 sanguine (adj): cheerfully optimistic, confident

4 conspire (v): work together to cause a result usually harmful or inconvenient

4 deprive (v): not to allow to have, take away

6 eliminate (v): take somebody or something away, remove from competition

7 syndrome (n): group of identifying signs and symptoms of a disease or disorder

7 phobia (n): morbid fear

8 epitomize (v): exemplify, be highly representative

9 spatial ability (phrase): understanding of concepts relating to space and area

10 sophomore (n): student in the second year of high school, college or university

14 proclaim (v): declare publicly

14 ominous (adj): threatening, menacing

14 diatribes (n): verbal or written attacks

15 acquiesce (v): agree, say yes

16 accede (v): assent, agree to

RESPONDING TO THE READING

- If the thesis is stated, identify it; if it is implied, write it in your own words.
- What do you think is the purpose of this essay? Give reasons for your opinion.
- Who do you think is the intended audience of this essay? Give reasons for your opinion.

Comprehension

1. What is the point of the anecdote about Susannah in Paragraphs 1 and 2?
2. What does Susan Jacoby mean by "self-inflicted female disability" in Paragraph 3?
3. What does she say about English and high school boys in Paragraph 3?

4. Explain the allusion to Rosalind Yallow in Paragraph 4.
5. List the effects Jacoby presents in Paragraphs 4 to 7. What is their cause?
6. Restate Jacoby's definition of "math anxiety" in your own words.
7. What does Jacoby mean by "male turf" in Paragraph 8?
8. What reasons does Jacoby give to explain the prevalence of math anxiety among high school girls?
9. In Paragraph 12, Jacoby examines the consequences of mathematic and scientific illiteracy. What are they?
10. What advice does Jacoby offer parents in her conclusion?

Analysis

1. How does Jacoby dismiss the possibility that girls are genetically incapable of success in math?
2. Do you think the social reasons Jacoby gives to explain why girls lose ability in math are valid? Why or why not?
3. Do you agree that inability in math does lead to "an incalculably impoverished vision of human experience"? Why or why not?
4. What do you think the social costs of "math anxiety" are?

Discussion/Writing Suggestions

1. How would you rate your ability and interest in math? Explain the causes for your attitude.
2. This essay was written in 1983. Is it out of date? Why or why not?

   • Other essays that focus on education include those by Charles Dickens (p. 10), Malcolm X (p. 19), Margaret Atwood (p. 85), Peggy Lampotang (p. 129), Dan Zollmann (p. 166), and Northrop Frye (p. 244).

Deliberate Strangers

Charlie Angus

Charlie Angus, who was born in Timmins, Ontario, in 1962, is a progressive, social justice-oriented member of the Roman Catholic Church and supporter of the Catholic Worker Movement. Angus began his career as community activist in Toronto, where he ran a homeless shelter. After a successful career as a Canadian writer, broadcaster, and musician, Angus was elected as a New Democratic Party (NDP) candidate in the Ontario riding of Timmins-James Bay. He has been the NDP parliamentary critic for Canadian Heritage since 2004.

This essay was published in Compass. *In "Deliberate Strangers," Charlie Angus dissects our society and discusses how we have become estranged from one another and the effects of that estrangement.*

1 It's Saturday night and the kids want a movie. At the local video store, row after row of neatly packaged carnage° assails° the eyes. *The Toolbox Murders, Sorority*

House Massacre, and *Three on a Meathook* compete with such old-time classics as *Texas Chainsaw Massacre.* There are video covers featuring victims being hunted with knives, chainsaws, hooks, and drills.

2   As you search in vain for an old Disney classic, the kids are crying out to see Jason. Jason? Who is Jason? They hand you a video called *Friday the 13th,* a film that has spawned° four sequels and countless imitations. The basic story is rarely changed, movie to movie: a psychopath named Jason dons a mask and mutilates° local teenagers.

3   "He's sort of a cult hero," the guy behind the counter explains.

4   Okay, so vampires, werewolves, and things that go bump in the night have always been part of our folklore. People love a good ghost story and always have. Bram Stoker's Dracula, the most famous figure in horror history, has been frightening people for generations.

5   It can be said that horror provides a way of synthesizing unexplainable evil. Tales like *Dracula* provide a safe way of confronting the darker side of human relationships. The reader is able to step over the line of the great unknown, comforted by the fact that the beast is always defeated in the end. The reign of darkness is broken by dawn, and Nosferatu* is foiled in his evil plans.

6   Hollywood accepted this basic premise° of horror for years. The heroine was always rescued from the fate of the undead, and Bela Lugosi always died before the credits rolled. But then, in 1960, Alfred Hitchcock released the film *Psycho,* and nothing has been the same since. For the first time, the monster in a horror film was another human being—a psychopath. Hitchcock tapped a growing fear that strangers could be monsters. Howling at the full moon was replaced with the brutal depiction of Janet Leigh being slashed in the shower. A generation of film-goers would never feel the same again about closing the shower curtain. In this one scene, Hitchcock changed forever the way viewers perceive fear.

7   A trip to the video store is enough to realize how far-reaching the effects of *Psycho* have been. Supernatural monsters have been replaced by Jason and the genre of psycho killers. The techniques of presenting horror have also continued to change. In the 1970's, Brian DePalma released *Dressed to Kill,* which used the camera as if it were the eyes of the killer. The audience was allowed to share in the excitement of the hunt, the gore of the kill. Our focus has been shifted from the thrill of stopping the villain to the thrill of hunting down the victim. The modern horror movie has taught us to be wary of seemingly tranquil country roads. Who knows where someone might be waiting with a chainsaw or an axe?

8   Horror has made a clear shift from identifying with victims as subjects to regarding them merely as objects. Is this shift a harmless flight into fantasy, or have the borders of our culture, the substance of our collective soul, been altered? Welcome to the age of Jason, an age when the serial killer has become a culture hero.

9   Meet Ted Bundy, all-American boy. He was popular and good-looking, and it was said that he had an almost Kennedy-like charisma°. A former employer described Ted Bundy as a man who believed in the system. In particular, Ted believed in success. At one time he studied law. In 1972, he completed his degree in psychology and worked at a crisis clinic in Seattle.

10   Over the next four years, he raped and killed as many as 50 women. When finally apprehended after murdering two women and assaulting a third in a Florida sorority house, Ted Bundy became an instant celebrity. His trial was a classic event of the 1980s. Two hundred and fifty reporters, representing readers on five continents, applied for press credentials to the first televised murder trial in history. *ABC News* set up a special satellite hookup to bring the trial to 40 million American living rooms—a television horror drama.

11   The man of the hour did not let his public down. Bundy presented a persona that was charming and witty. When interest seemed to wane°, he resorted to out-rageous stunts for the cameras. The case moved further into the realm of absurdity when Bundy announced to the court that he had married a woman who fell in love with him during the trial. Those who missed such highlights the first time round could relive the experience when *The Deliberate Stranger,* a made-for-TV dramati-zation, was shown on prime time. Even radio claimed a piece of the pie with the songs *The Battle of Ted Bundy* and *Just Say It Ted.* Ted Bundy found the success he had craved.

12   The hype° of the trial and Bundy's celebrity status served to underline America's fascination with serial killers. Bundy was a star in the quickly growing field of *lustmord°:* killing for the thrill of it. Historically, there have been occasional instances of serial killers, but such cases were rare. According to Elliot Leyton in *Hunting Humans,* in the period between 1920 and 1950, the United States did not average more than two serial killers a decade. In the 1960s, this number rose to five (for an average of one new serial killer every twenty months). In the 1970s, the number of known serial killers rose to seventeen (for an average of one every seven months). Between 1980 and 1984, the figure jumped to 25 known serial killers, signifying a new serial killer every 1.8 months.

13   The rise of serial killers is disproportionate to population growth and to the increase in the murder rate in general. Newspapers are full of information on the latest killers, their particular "styles," their kill ratios in relation to existing "records." The Son of Sam, the Hillside Strangler, John Wayne Gacy, Henry Lee Lucas, Charles Ng, the Green River Killer, Clifford Olson—countless books, movies, and articles chronicle the exploits of these killers with a fascination that borders on adulation°.

14   Ted Bundy became something of a spokesperson for this new breed of killer. He showed the world that psychopaths are not deranged°. Most serial killers have passed previous psychological testing. They are well liked and never socially suspect. Psychopaths, however, relate to other human beings as objects. They lack the ability to empathize. Psychopathy is the extreme form of self-centredness.

15   The testimony at the trial underlined how easily such a disordered personality could fit in with social convention. At the time of Bundy's arrest, his friends were unable to reconcile the man they thought they knew with the brutal murderer described in the press. "He was one of us," one friend explained. Although it was overshadowed by the revelations of murder and mayhem, this detail is a key to unlocking the world of Ted Bundy. As a young Republican, as a yuppie, and as a brutal killer, he was one of us. His killings, like everything in his life, were a mirror image of the world around him.

16   After his conviction, Ted Bundy spent many hours being interviewed by his biographers, Hugh Aynsworth and Stephen Michaud. Calmly and dispassionately, he articulated the roots of his murderous inclinations: "If we took this individual from birth and raised him, say, in the Soviet Union or Afghanistan, or in eighteenth-century America, in all likelihood he would lead a normal life. We're talking about the peculiar circumstances of society and of the twentieth century in America." Ted Bundy knew he was a psychopath. Perhaps we all have some of the psychopath in us.

17   This is an age of impersonal violence. Television has brought saturation bombing in Vietnam, genocide in Cambodia, sniping in Beirut, and street wars in Los Angeles into our homes. Every night around suppertime, the living room is filled with footage of strangers killing strangers. Our response to tragedy has become shallow. Horrified for a minute, interested for an hour, we soon turn our attention from the dead and dying on our screen. The victims have become merely objects eliciting° prurient° interest instead of subjects eliciting heartfelt empathy. We no longer relate to them as human beings. Neither did Ted Bundy. "What's one less person on the face of the earth anyway?" he asked his interrogators.

18   Ironically, while becoming numb in the face of death, we are still aroused by violence. We have witnessed the deaths of thousands, both real and imagined. We have been spectators in an endless parade of shootings, stabbings, bombings, burnings, and stranglings. In the realm of fiction, Jason is just the latest in a long line of cultural figures who testify to the power of violence in solving problems, settling scores, and putting zest into one's day. What makes fictionalized killing palatable° is that the audience doesn't have to relate to those killed. Bad guys are dispatched with style and the audience is spared the messy details about grieving families and friends.

19   Ted Bundy did not kill to solve problems or expiate° childhood trauma. He killed to possess status goods. His victims were all socially desirable women. "What really fascinated him," Bundy said, "was the thrill of the hunt, the adventure of searching out his victims. And to a degree, possessing them as one would a potted plant, a painting, or a Porsche. Owning, as it were, this individual."

20   In his world view, sex and violence were simply two faces of the same coin. "This condition," he told his interrogators, "...manifests° itself in an interest concerning sexual behaviour, sexual images.... But this interest, for some unknown reason, becomes geared toward matters of a sexual nature that include violence." The stimulation we receive from media violence and sex rests on our ability to see others as objects. They become commodities to be consumed. "Once the individual had her [the victim]," Bundy explained, "where he had, you know, security over her, there would be minimum of conversation...to avoid developing some kind of relationship."

21   This is indeed an era of peculiar circumstances. The days when one's neighbours were like family are long gone. We do not know our neighbours; perhaps we are not even interested in knowing them. This rift has been the price paid in the pursuit of commodity culture. In advanced capitalist societies, everything has a price, and every obligation is judged by its ability to advance individual interests. The ties of community, family, and even marriage have been weighed in the balance and found wanting. The modern ethic chooses pleasure over obligation,

career over community, the self over the other. We have become a culture of deliberate strangers.

22   Serial killers are nurtured in this breakdown of community. In the absence of strong social interrelationships, the alienated mind begins to perceive others as objects for personal gratification°, whether financial, sexual, or violent. On a spiritual level, *lustmord* is the logical extreme of our cultural sickness. Murder has become the ultimate act of self-worship. Gone are the crimes of passion, the relationships gone wrong, the fated love affairs. The killings reflect a cold brutality, the sterile control of subject over object.

23   Ted Bundy went to his death on January 24, 1989. His execution served as a gruesome conduit of hate and media sorcery. Two hundred reporters, camped out near the grounds of the prison, detailed every aspect of Bundy's date with the electric chair as if it were a major sports event. Cheering crowds gathered outside the prison gates. Street vendors reported a brisk trade in "I like my Ted Bundy well-done" T-shirts.

24   In the eyes of the public, it was not a fellow human being who was dying, but an object, a thing fit for ridicule and murder. His public revelled in the gruesome details, spurred on by reports of his fear and remorse. In the end, it was as mechanical and empty as his own crimes, again the sterile control of subject over helpless object. Ted Bundy died reaffirming America's belief in murder. No wounds were healed, no victims' families made whole once again. The beast is not dead but remains lurking in the gulf between neighbours. The electric chair and the cheering crowds serve only as reminders that Ted Bundy was one of us.

25   Ted Bundy was not a monster. He was a human being, and his path toward the ultimate in evil is a path that is well trodden in our culture. He made the choices that commodity consciousness dictates: pleasure, self-worship, and alienation from true relationships. His obsessions with violence and death were extreme, but the path that led there is a path we have all walked in our viewing and in our minds. If Ted Bundy's life and death are to have any meaning, we have to realize that the pursuit of self-interest is not a harmless choice. It fundamentally affects the fabric of human relationships. It is time to repair the bonds of community and stop being deliberate strangers.

Note

5 Nosferatu: a vampire in the 1922 classic movie

Vocabulary

1 carnage (n): widespread slaughter, massacre

1 assail (v): attack

2 spawn (v): produce, give rise to

2 mutilate (v): remove or damage body parts, damage seriously

6 premise (n): statement given as evidence for a conclusion, basis of argument

9 charisma (n): magnetic personality

11 wane (v): become smaller or less

12 hype (n): exaggerated publicity

12 *lustmord* (n, German): sexual murder

13 adulation (n): excessive admiration

14 deranged (adj): completely unreasonable

17 elicit (v): draw out something hidden

17 prurient (adj): having unwholesome sexual interest

18 palatable (adj): acceptable

19 expiate (v): atone for wrongdoing, make amends

20 manifest (v): show clearly

22 gratification (n): pleasure, satisfaction

RESPONDING TO THE READING

- If the thesis is stated, identify it; if it is implied, write it in your own words.
- What do you think is the purpose of this essay? Give reasons for your opinion.
- Who do you think is the intended audience of this essay? Give your reasons for your opinion.

Comprehension

1. What effects does Charlie Angus present in Paragraphs 1 to 4?
2. Explain what is meant by a "cult hero."
3. What does Angus outline in Paragraph 5?
4. What is the "basic premise of horror" that has been accepted by Hollywood for years?
5. According to Angus, in what way has Alfred Hitchcock's *Psycho* affected how we perceive fear?
6. What "far-reaching effects" does Angus present in Paragraph 7?
7. What change in attitude does Angus observe in his discussion of DePalma's movie *Dressed to Kill?*
8. What relationship is drawn between Hitchcock's *Psycho* and DePalma's *Dressed to Kill?*
9. The essay apparently changes its focus in Paragraph 9. In what ways has the writer already prepared readers for Ted Bundy? What techniques of unity and coherence are used to organize this essay?
10. Explain where Charlie Angus finds his title. Why is it appropriate?
11. How many examples of other serial killers are presented?
12. Scan for examples of impersonal violence that have numbed us. Define *psychopath* in your own words.
13. What reasons are given for why Ted Bundy killed?
14. What reasons does Angus provide to show how serial killers "are nurtured in this breakdown of community"?

Analysis

1. Angus uses informal language in the first four paragraphs of "Deliberate Strangers." Why do you think he begins his essay in this manner?
2. Do you believe we need "a safe way of confronting the darker side of human relationships"? Why or why not?
3. In Paragraph 7, Angus says that the victims in movies have become objects to the audience. What does he mean and what is he implying?
4. Is the question Angus asks in Paragraph 8 rhetorical? And how does he deal with it?
5. Explain how Angus shows that Ted Bundy has become entertainment. What is the effect of this according to Angus?
6. Ted Bundy refers to himself in the third person and claims America created him. Why do you think Angus includes these details?
7. Do you agree with what Angus says about our society in Paragraph 17? Why or why not?
8. Paraphrase "In the eyes of the public, it was not a fellow human being who was dying, but an object, a thing fit for ridicule and murder." What was your reaction when you read this sentence and then realized later in the same paragraph (24) that Angus was comparing the average person to Ted Bundy?
9. Do you believe that Angus's conclusion follows logically from the examples given throughout the essay? Why or why not?

Discussion/Writing Suggestions

1. How many of the movies referred to in the essay have you ever seen or heard of? Do you think there is a link between the images we see in Hollywood movies and on TV and how we regard violence in our life?
2. In Paragraph 21, Angus states, "The modern ethic chooses pleasure over obligation, career over community, the self over the other. We have become a culture of deliberate strangers." What is your response to this statement?

   - Other essays that consider social dynamics are by Joseph Epstein (p. 36), David Suzuki (p. 88), Mark Kingwell (p. 114), Stephen L. Carter (p. 132), Amartya Sen (p. 252), Pier Giorgio Di Cicco (p. 196), and Pat Capponi (p. 158).

Writing That Affects the Reader

Description, Narration, Argumentation/Persuasion

> *"All art, therefore, appeals primarily to the senses, and the artistic aim when expressing itself in written words must also make its appeal through the senses, if its high desire is to reach the secret spring of responsive emotions."* (*Joseph Conrad [1857–1924]*)

The following rhetorical modes—description, narration, and argumentation/ persuasion—are used not only to explain, but also to create a designed effect upon readers' feelings, ideas, and actions.

Essay of Description

Description is a means of conveying information vividly by appealing to a reader's senses. It attempts to reproduce through words the physical qualities of a previous experience, to enable the reader to see what you have seen, to hear what you have heard, and to experience what you have experienced. A careful reading of the following passage from Margaret Laurence's descriptive essay "The Shack" should help to show how **sensory details** (those perceived through the senses of sight, sound, smell, taste, and touch) are essential to recreating memories and past experience:

> . . . we used to slither with an exhilarating sense of peril down the steep homemade branch and dirt shelf-steps, through the stands of thin tall spruce and birch trees slender and graceful as girls, passing moss-hairy fallen logs and the white promise of wild strawberry blossoms, until we reached the sand and the hard bright pebbles of the beach at the edge of the cold spring-fed lake where at nights the loons still cried eerily, before too much humanshriek made them move away north. (p. 203)

Description helps the writer to sway the reader's feelings, and so it is most often a technique employed to enhance the style of a piece of writing. Whether it be a process analysis, an essay of example, comparison and contrast, or argumentation/

persuasion, writers may use description to get their ideas effectively across. Compared with the other rhetorical modes, description requires the writer to have an enhanced vocabulary and to be particularly skillful in reproducing images using adjectives, adverbs, similes, metaphors, and other literary devices. Read the following passages taken from Pico Iyer's essay "In Praise of the Humble Comma" (p. 96) and see how a cleverly used simile and metaphor can activate familiar images in the reader's mind and enliven the otherwise dry, and potentially boring, topic of punctuation.

> A run-on sentence, its phrases piling up without division, is as unsightly as a sink piled high with dirty dishes (p. 97).

Can you spot the simile? Do you think this sentence would be as effective without it?

> . . . the semicolon brings clauses and thoughts together with all the silent discretion of a hostess arranging guests around her dinner table. (p. 98)

Can you spot the metaphor? Imagine what the sentence would be like without it.

To appreciate how concrete images help the reader to connect what is new and unfamiliar with what is familiar, look at how Pier Giorgio Di Cicco describes his first impression of London:

> The tower of London, next to gherkin-shaped skyscrapers, the cluster of theatre districts, the mix of ghettos, the regal palaces. It looks a little like the epochal theme park that is Las Vegas. . . . (p. 197)

Here the imagery works to scale down the massive size and history of London into a manageable idea with a reference to the "theme-park"; this image also ironically captures an attitude toward London that many North Americans have when confronted by its long history so evident in its architecture. The use of specific nouns and adjectives also greatly adds to this description: *gherkin-shaped skyscrapers, cluster of . . ., mix of . . ., regal palaces,* and *epochal theme park.*

Description is most effective and appealing when carefully selected details are portrayed in specific and precise words. Consider Charles Dickens's description of Bitzer in "Murdering the Innocents" and examine how, with distinct details described in well-chosen words, Dickens succeeds in swaying readers' response to the boy with nothing but a close-up of his *pale* face:

> . . . the boy was so light-eyed and light-haired that the selfsame rays appeared to draw out of him what little colour his eyes possessed. His cold eyes would hardly have been eyes but for the short ends of lashes which, by bringing them into immediate contrast with something paler than themselves, expressed their form. His short-cropped hair might have been a mere continuation of the sandy freckles on his forehead and face. His skin was so unwholesomely deficient in the natural tinge, that he looked as though, if he were cut, he would bleed white. (p. 12)

Description can also be used to heighten emotion; this example from Michael Dorris demonstrates the effectiveness of appropriate allusions in adding to the nostalgia he creates. He alludes to typical Christmas cards and to the classic Christmas movie *It's a Wonderful Life* in this quotation from "The Minnie Mouse Kitchen":

> A gentle snow had begun to fall, and here and there as I drove along the road toward town, colored Christmas lights twinkled through the windows of houses with smoking chimneys. New England in winter can, at such moments, seem like one giant Hollywood set, a Currier and Ives scene ready for a heart-warming story to happen. In this version, my part would have been played by Jimmy Stewart: awkward, stalwart, the honest gallumph who carried the American dream like a red, white, and blue banner. He was out to do a deed, to accomplish one of those minor miracles that make life wonderful and annually bring a smile to Donna Reed's eyes. (p. 209)

To help you realize the importance of sensory details and specific words in descriptive writing, compare the two passages below. The first is by James Rettie, and the second is a paraphrased version of his passage written with little attention paid to sensory details and use of specifically descriptive words.

1. Rains will pour down on the land and promptly go booming down to the seas. There will be no clear streams anywhere except where the rains fall upon hard rock. Everywhere on the steeper ground the stream channels will be filled with boulders hurled down by rushing waters. Raging torrents and dry stream beds will keep alternating in quick succession. High mountains will seem to melt like so much butter in the sun. (p. 223)
2. Rains will hit the ground before going down to the seas. With no streams of water other than the rains around, you can only see rocks coming down with waters. You see a lot of water at one moment, and then everything is dry at the next. Big mountains will disappear in no time.

Undoubtedly, with sensory details taken out of the passage together with specific words like pour, promptly, booming, clear, hard, steeper, filled with, boulders, hurled down, rushing, raging torrents, dry stream beds, alternating in quick succession, high, and melt like so much butter in the sun, Version 2, unlike Version 1, fails to make the reader visualize, hear, touch, and feel.

Writing Strategy

The thesis statement: In an essay of description, the thesis presents the predominant impression you want to convey to the reader of the event, object, or person you have chosen to describe. Thus the thesis determines the focus for your description, but it should also provide the purpose of the essay.

- Here is the thesis of "Pinball" by J. Anthony Lukas:
  Pinball is a metaphor for life, pitting man's skill, nerve, persistence, and luck against the perverse machinery of human existence. (p. 192)
  Lukas's subject is clearly pinball, but he also states the predominant impression he will convey and why he is describing pinball.

Supporting Details

- To describe effectively, you must first of all observe closely. Descriptive writing hinges on sensory details, details filled with colours, smells, sounds, shapes, feel, and taste to appeal to the readers' senses as well as their imagination. Those details must be depicted in evocative words—words that conjure images, memories, and associations. Remember: you don't have to rack your brains for fancy, polysyllabic words for your description to be impressive. As you may have noticed in the passages quoted so far in this introduction to description, simple and precise words are just as effective, if not more so, when they are crafted into impressive imagery.
- Consider how Catherine George uses **personification** (endowing something inanimate or nonhuman with human characteristics) to introduce "Nature" as a dazzling Las Vegas showgirl and to convey the colour of autumn she has experienced:

She'll blaze across the hills and down the valleys in a flamboyant cloak of many colors, oranges, crimsons, purples, and a crown of gold, in a season finale that's sure to get rave reviews from even the most jaded of critics. (p. 194)

Unity and Coherence

- Just as when you write an essay using other rhetorical modes and organizational patterns, unity and coherence are vital qualities in an essay of description. Description must rely on the selection and organization of details that will be most useful for creating the main effect—its purpose.
- Unity is ensured only if you remain focused on your purpose whether you are re-creating a scene in its physical dimension or describing a moment in time and the feelings you experienced. An essay describing your grandmother's home as a place that provoked and sustained your earliest memories must stay on track. While it is tempting perhaps to describe your grandmother's loving qualities or lapses in memory, you do so *only* when these details serve to support your thesis: the predominant impression of grandmother's home.

Include sensory details only when these details support your thesis statement. Ask yourself, what *main effect* do I want to create for the reader; what is the purpose of this description? Notice how details and words are selected in Di Cicco's descriptive passage. Could you identify the author's focus by using the *italicized* words in the passage as clues?

. . . it's amazing that Toronto *bristles with artistic life* fuelled by the *resources of artists* who manage their *enthusiasm* into *public delight. Queen Street, Kensington Market, theatre companies, galleries, poetry readings, street art, mixed-media events, festivals*; there is a *"grass roots" vitality* here that will not be repressed; and it is *"home-grown,"* not strategized. (p. 198)

Pier Giorgio Di Cicco is intent upon demonstrating that, despite typical Canadian reserve, Toronto does indeed have the "buzz" he is seeking.

To describe effectively, you need to follow the principle of coherence very closely too. As in composing exposition, a writer must not only decide on a specific point of view, but a clear order should also be chosen to arrange the carefully selected descriptive details. In description, more than in any other types of writing, spatial order is often adopted to portray a picture caught at a specific moment of time. Just as a photographer who uses a video camera to pan, say, an exhibition hall, needs to move his camera in a certain direction, such as from the entrance to the exit, from the ceiling to the floor, and from the east wall to the west wall, the writer of description must follow a logical or spatial order. Otherwise, the reader or viewer is bound to feel confused.

Read the following passage taken from Maya Angelou's essay "The Fight" and notice how the descriptive details are presented in a spatial order, so the reader can feel how those in the piece were squeezed into the room:

> The last inch of space was filled, yet people continued to wedge themselves along the walls of the Store. Uncle Willie had turned the radio up to its last notch so that youngsters on the porch wouldn't miss a word. Women sat on kitchen chairs, dining-room chairs, stools and upturned wooden boxes. Small children and babies perched on every lap available and men leaned on the shelves or on each other. (p. 218)

Notice, too, how words like *yet, so that,* and *and* are used to make the description more coherent.

In short, in spite of its special features, an essay of description, like all the other types of essays, also expects the writer to follow the common rules that govern effective writing in general.

READINGS: ESSAYS OF DESCRIPTION

The four essays in this section represent very different sorts of description for very different reasons: Anthony Lukas presents a description of a game of pinball; however, his essay is in effect an extended analogy, which makes his essay a *de facto* description of his philosophy of life. Catherine George tries to seduce the reader into getting out and experiencing the glory of autumn. Pier Giorgio Di Cicco paints a panoramic backdrop of four European cities against which he proudly draws a silhouette of his own city, Toronto. In the last piece of the selection, Margaret Laurence reflects with an exquisite serenity on the sustaining power of the natural world.

Pinball

J. Anthony Lukas

J. Anthony Lukas (1933–1997) was an American journalist and writer. He worked for both the Baltimore Sun *and the* New York Times. *The winner of two Pulitzer Prizes, the National Book Award, and the National Book Critics Circle Award, Lukas wrote about America's social and political landscape in brilliant books, such as* Big Trouble. *Lukas is best known, though, for his widely praised book about desegregation in Boston,* Common Ground: A Turbulent Decade in the Lives of Three American Families *(1985), which won the National Book award.*

In the following brief essay, Lukas compares life to pinball. This essay first appeared in The Atlantic Monthly *in 1979.*

1 Pinball is a metaphor for life, pitting° man's skill, nerve, persistence, and luck against the perverse° machinery of human existence. The playfield is rich with rewards: targets that bring huge scores, bright lights, chiming bells, free balls, and extra games. But it is replete° with perils, too: culs-de-sac°, traps, gutters, and gobble holes down which the ball may disappear forever.

2 Each pull of the plunger launches the ball into a miniature universe of incalculable possibilities. As the steel sphere hurtles into the eclipse at the top of the playfield, it hangs for a moment in exquisite tension between triumph and disaster. Down one lane lies a hole worth thousands, down another a sickening lurch to oblivion. The ball trembles on the lip, seeming to lean first one way, then the other.

how do you define success?

3 A player is not powerless to control the ball's wild flight, any more than man is powerless to control his own life. He may nudge the machine with hands, arms, or hips, jogging it just enough to change the angle of the ball's descent. And he is armed with "flippers" which can propel the ball back up the playfield, aiming at the targets with the richest payoffs. But, just as man's boldest strokes and bravest ventures often boomerang°, so an ill-timed flip can ricochet° the ball straight down "death alley," and a too vigorous nudge will send the machine into "tilt." Winning pinball, like a rewarding life, requires delicate touch, fine calibrations, careful discrimination between boldness and folly.

Vocabulary

1 pit (v): set up in opposition

1 perverse (adj): purposefully unreasonable, deviating from what is good and proper

1 replete (adj): fully equipped, completely supplied

1 culs-de-sac (n, French): streets closed at one end, dead-end

3 boomerang (v): cause harm to the initiator of the action, to backfire

3 ricochet (v): hit a surface and bounce, travelling away in a different direction

RESPONDING TO THE READING

- If the thesis is stated, identify it; if it is implied, write it in your own words.
- What do you think is the purpose of this essay? Give reasons for your opinion.
- Who do you think is the intended audience of this essay? Give reasons for your opinion.

Comprehension

1. How effectively has J. Anthony Lukas selected his details? List the similarities between the game of pinball and "the game of life" as Lukas sees them.
2. Organization of details is crucial in description. How does Lukas organize his essay?
3. Do you think Lukas could have strengthened his essay by explicitly pointing out the comparisons and contrasts between pinball and life throughout the essay? What would be the effect on the reader if he had?
4. What words does Lukas use to convey the colours, sounds, and shapes—the experience—of playing pinball? List them.
5. "Winning pinball, like a rewarding life, requires delicate touch, fine calibrations, careful discrimination between boldness and folly." This is the conclusion of the essay. Does it sum up the essay appropriately or not? Explain your response.

Analysis

1. "The playfield is rich with rewards: targets that bring huge scores, bright lights, chiming bells, free balls, and extra games." What does Lukas imply about life in the list of rewards when playing pinball?
2. "But it is replete with perils, too: culs-de-sac, traps, gutters, and gobble holes down which the ball may disappear forever." What does Lukas imply are the "perils" in life in his list of pinball disasters?
3. What is the sense that Lukas appeals to primarily? Identify some sensory details presented in the essay to support your response.
4. After his first sentence, Lukas doesn't mention life (the "real" subject) directly again until the final sentence. He lets his discussion of pinball represent what he wants to say about life. Do you agree or disagree with his point of view? Support your response.
5. "Pinball is a metaphor for life," says Lukas. What analogy would you choose to discuss the meaning of life? Why?

Discussion/Writing Suggestions

1. Does Lukas's analogy suggest life is fatalistic or filled with choices? Explain. What is your view of life?
2. Does the use of analogy make a philosophical essay easier to read or not? Explain your response.

   - Other essays that question the significance of life include those by Malcolm X (p. 19), Joseph Epstein (p. 36), David Ginsburg (p. 33), Bertrand Russell (p. 64), Pico Iyer (p. 96), Stephen L. Carter (p. 132), Charlie Angus (p. 180), and Margaret Laurence (p. 202).

Curtain Up

Catherine George

Catherine George is a Toronto-based freelance travel writer. Her work appears in many Canadian newspapers and magazines.

This essay was first published in the Travel section of the Globe and Mail *in September 1991.*

1   Sit back, relax and enjoy. It's showtime in Ontario. And you're in for an eye-popping treat. In the next few weeks, right here on our country stage, the curtain will rise on a color spectacle to rival the flashiest of show-biz extravaganzas°.

2   Watch Mother Nature, the star of the show, in her role as leading lady. Like a classy Vegas showgirl, she'll do a quick change right before your eyes. She'll coyly shed her subdued° summer wardrobe and, with a flourish, transform into a brightly-painted vixen°, boldly strutting her stuff centre stage.

3   She'll blaze across the hills and down the valleys in a flamboyant cloak of many colors, oranges, crimsons, purples, and a crown of gold, in a season finale that's sure to get rave reviews from even the most jaded° of critics. Best of all, everyone gets a free front-row seat.

4   Though the travelling show isn't officially due to open in southern Ontario for a couple of weeks, you can catch a sneak preview in the hardwood forests farther north where the elevations are higher and the climate change occurs a little earlier.

5   And, contrary to what some of us have been told, Jack Frost doesn't have a thing to do with changing the color of the leaves. In fact, he is often the spoiler if he arrives too soon, causing them to shrivel and drop before they get a chance to flaunt their fiery hues. What it takes is sufficient rainfall, cool (not frosty) nights and bright sunny days that cause the sugars in the leaves to produce those red, orange and yellow pigments.

6   With the exception of a few remote areas in Asia, no place on earth puts on an autumn display to rival the one you'll see in Ontario, Quebec, the Maritimes, and over the border in New England and northern New York state. Though no one can predict for certain, late September through Thanksgiving weekend should be the best time for leaf peepers to plan a jaunt into the countryside.

7   If you watch the ads you'll find a number of bus tour operators offering foliage° tours in Ontario, Quebec and across the border. Cruise boats operate regularly on the Muskoka, Kawartha and Haliburton lakes, a pleasant day's outing for the family. It's probably too late this year but for next autumn you might think about renting a house-boat and taking the family for a color cruise on the Trent–Severn waterways system.

8   Algoma Central runs a train trip from Sault Ste. Marie into the spectacular Agawa canyon until mid-October. Some of the conservation areas such as the Kortright Centre near Kleinburg sponsor autumn color walks. So there are plenty of ways you can put a touch of color in your life.

9   But the best bet for catching the scenery is in the family car. All you need is a tank of gas, a picnic basket and your camera. When the mood strikes or a particular setting appeals you can stop for lunch under a cathedral of color, buy a pumpkin at a roadside stand or pick up a fresh apple pie at a country bakery.

You might try to plan your jaunt° to coincide with one of the agricultural fairs or harvest festivals taking place in the small communities all across Ontario from now until Thanksgiving.

Vocabulary

1 extravaganzas (n): lavish and spectacular entertainment

2 subdued (adj): not bright or harsh, quiet or softened

2 vixen (n): female fox

3 jaded (adj): bored, no longer interested in something because of over-exposure to it

7 foliage (n): leaves

10 jaunt (n): excursion, trip for pleasure

 # RESPONDING TO THE READING

- If the thesis is stated, identify it; if it is implied, write it in your own words.
- What do you think is the purpose of this essay? Give reasons for your opinion.
- Who do you think is the intended audience of this essay? Give reasons for your opinion.

Comprehension

1. What sorts of specific details does Catherine George provide to support her thesis?
2. What is the analogy that is established in the thesis and operating throughout this essay?
3. Paragraphs 2 and 5 contain examples of personification. What are they?
4. What comparison is made between Mother Nature and Jack Frost?
5. Find five examples of George's use of vivid language. What specific words does she use to describe a colour spectacle? How many colours does she present in the first five paragraphs?
6. Does she make use of simile and metaphor? Find examples of each.
7. In the last five paragraphs, George presents a process analysis as she makes a number of suggestions to her readers about how to get a "front-row seat." What are they?

Analysis

1. George sets up an analogy: between the brilliant natural world of the woods and the flamboyant artificial Las Vegas floor show. Identify the "real" subject, and explain how the analogy works. Is it effective?
2. How would you describe the sort of language George uses and what is its effect on you?

3. What is the sense that George appeals to primarily? Identify some sensory details presented in the essay.

4. Is George's use of language appropriate to her subject? Why or why not? Give examples that show the level of language and vocabulary.

5. Given George wants to persuade you that autumn is beautiful and to convince you to get out and enjoy it, how successful is she?

Discussion/Writing Suggestions

1. Do you enjoy looking at nature? Why or why not?
2. What is your favourite season? Describe what you love about it.

- Other essays that focus on appreciation of the natural world include those by James D. Rettie (p. 221), Rachel Carson (p. 123), Sean Twist (p. 147), Margaret Laurence (p. 202), and Sang Il Lee (p. 233).

Chasing Buzz

Pier Giorgio Di Cicco

Pier Giorgio Di Cicco (1949–) was born in Arezzo, Italy, and came to Canada in 1952. He was educated at the University of Toronto (B.A. 1973, B.Ed. 1976, M.Div. 1990). In 1984, Di Cicco entered an Augustinian monastery, and in 1990 he was ordained as a priest in the Archdiocese of Toronto. A seminal figure in Canadian multiculturalism, Di Cicco edited the first anthology of Italian-Canadian writers, Roman Candles, *in 1978,* which *received the Governor General's Award. Di Cicco is a respected and prolific poet of 18 collections of poetry, including* Living in Paradise *(2001) and* The Dark Time of Angels *(2004), which was nominated for the Trillium Award. In 2004, Pier Giorgio Di Cicco was appointed by the City of Toronto as its second poet laureate. That same year he was the Emilio Goggio Visiting Professor in Italian Studies at the University of Toronto. In 2005, he became the curator for the City of Toronto's Humanitas museum project.*

This essay, published in the Toronto Star on August 14, 2005, describes a trip that Di Cicco took as part of a delegation of city officials to Europe. This one-week mission was to investigate what makes cities attractive to tourists and investors. The article presents his impressions of four cities. It also reflects his interest in the urban aesthetic, the relationship between culture and a livable and sustainable city.

1   Everyone's looking for a "buzz." Cities too. In the fever to compete with global economies, in the panic to counter the Chinese with some kind of "software" to match their "hardware" of productivity, the craze has hit Western cities in the last ten years— the craze to be a "creative city." Municipal governments want to lever the principles of "creativity" into the marketplace, to kick-start industries bogged down by "steam-engine" notions of capitalism into a sense of cutting-edge thinking, where invention

and innovation are fuelled by something deeper than ledger-ambitions, or short-term vision. And we've been besieged° by short-term visions, in development, in urban planning. Look at our cities . . . hodge-podges° of skyline, smothered in bad air, zoning laws bungled° by infrastructures we can't afford. "Sustainability" has become the new catchword of city thinking; how to render° cities livable and profitable. Somewhere, the quality of life has crept back into the discussion; how to compete, without making ourselves unhappy in the means of competing.

2   Enter the word "buzz," that thing that makes cities attractive and makes people want to move to a city. Lots of cities offer opportunities, but a city that offers excitement, livability, culture, will always have a better drawing card. Industries are becoming aware that the showcase of the town they thrive in is the best insurance of continued profits. And they're aware that cutting-edge thinkers and really creative people will offer their skills only to a city that looks and feels creative.

3   Such is the thinking of Richard Florida, American economist and city guru°, whose notion of the "bohemian° index" measures the factors contributing to a creative city, factors such as ethnic diversity and bohemian presence. Cities, says Florida, must dispense with stale theories of economic development and spend more on cultural amenities. They must become trendy, happening places to become economic powerhouses. The glamour of Florida's ideas has become gospel to city thinkers. And the same wildfire has spread across Europe through exponents such as Charles Landry. Major cities are in a race to draw tourist dollars and creative citizens.

4   So we are on the move; The Ontario Government and The City of Toronto have spearheaded an initiative (together with London, England) to see how Toronto and London stack up to major cities. We are a delegation° of some fifteen planners, movers and dreamers, flying to Barcelona, London and Berlin to compare "buzz," to find out how "creative" these cities are, to learn if and how their industries speak to the "creative," the soul of a city. For that's the measure and resource of a city—its soul—the product of a way of life, without which a city produces nothing. We know New York and Paris have a soul (history helps). We are sure that Barcelona and London and Berlin will have a soul. We're not too sure if Toronto has a soul (we have "Torontonian" doubts). We are eager to find out. And on board we have a poet laureate reputedly expert at sniffing out the productions or absenteeisms of "culture."

5   We arrive in London; London regales° us with a showcasing of regional skills and "creative hub" communities, ingenious urban strategies and serious funding for the arts. They're trying to break down the separate silos of the industrial and the creative. They are listening closely to what their immigrants offer, and plan intelligently. They see their communities as creative resources. It works. History and tourism don't hurt either. Buzz? How can London not have it? The tower of London, next to gherkin-shaped skyscrapers, the cluster of theatre districts, the mix of ghettos, the regal palaces. It looks a little like the epochal° theme park that is Las Vegas; coherence is something the global city doesn't have. But it has "buzz," or at least the excitement that camouflages what tears at the seams of any global city—the awesome diversity and the ideological factioning that must lead to such tragedies as the recent bombings. London meets these global challenges with resolve°.

6   We move on to Berlin, bold and bankrupt; its citizens recovering from the dim of a communist nightmare. It has built wildly, freshly; but a weird exodus° has left the

buildings as the cheapest real-estate that a street-artist could hope to afford. It has strategies and bohemia, banks and tourists, world-class designers, and an awful grief for its twentieth century. Buzz is not what is happening, so much as hope. Berlin is on hold. And its multicultural problems are unmanaged and their top-notch architects are aloof° from the local arts and crafts shops and the cabarets. The cultural strands don't mesh°. Special interests visit Berlin, and can't get together.

7   Barcelona, confidant and opulent°; the "Gaudi°" gem by the Mediterranean, with avenues that are corridors of cafes, and wide-eyed tourists and officials that are big on "high art," with CEO's savvy on the continental trends of information technology, with curators and cultural sheiks who boast great museums and design institutes. Barcelona plays it up: history, and the confidence of being Spanish (or Catalonian). Finally, we see something Toronto can use. Confidence exudes° from the streets, the manner of walking, the ritual of coffee, the way a building goes up. Barcelona has statement without self-consciousness; it has fiscal° ambition with a flair for the good things of life; more importantly, it takes "pleasure" in the good things of life. Still, Barcelona is not a creative city. It lacks the restlessness of the North American. It lacks that sense of the "newly arrived," that sense that people have of building a world freshly. It lacks that sense of danger that doesn't take refuge in historical narrative. History disempowers the cutting edge. It intimidates the recklessness that creativity thrives° on.

8   We are beleaguered°. Three cities in one week; flow-charts, briefings on cultural "levers," "strategies," "infrastructure," terrible heat-waves, late nights hunting the "bohemian index"; endless notes on what makes these cities "buzz." How does Toronto measure up?

9   What doesn't measure up is what we see as we drive back from the airport—those box-like testimonies to the quick dollar called out-lying industries and house farms. It's as if a little imagination were too high a price to pay for mixing business with a cheerful way to live—a sad introduction to a metropolis with a skyline that is the signature of prosperity. We ignore the travesty° of a lovely lake hidden from its citizens by the hammer of condo high-rises. The Gardiner looks more like a drawbridge over a concrete moat. Leave architecture alone; it's just the expression of the space "between" people; the way they live, love, or don't love—the way they encounter, and dream; and Toronto's dreams are just vexed by the nightmares of any global city; ruthless business ethics, de-humanizing cyber-technology and the sheer confusion of diversity in every form.

10   As we settle into Toronto, it stuns us to realize that Toronto lacks for nothing in the pageant° of the global; except perhaps for the scarcity of dollars directed to cultural enterprises. With that in mind, it's amazing that Toronto bristles with artistic life fuelled by the resources of artists who manage their enthusiasm into public delight. Queen Street, Kensington Market, theatre companies, galleries, poetry readings, street art, mixed-media events, festivals; there is a "grass roots" vitality here that will not be repressed; and it is "home-grown," not strategized. Our industries have the knack of making useful whatever catches the popular imagination, and our street commerce quickly absorbs the unique, the fanciful. Inventiveness dialogues rapidly with business, and the "creative class" is everywhere becoming the middle class. The risk of being "gentrified°" is at every corner checked by the antics of

creative and young minds, impatient with the comforts of globalization, and eager to "not" conform. Where the random of "punk" and "alternative" become tiresome, the easy neighborhoods of conviviality° cut in; the Annex, Cabbagetown, the Little Italies, Little Portugals. The ethnic ghettos are not ghettos but places to wander in if one has a mind to treat multiculturalism as exotic. And yes, even the protocol° that annoys Toronto in its presbyterianness makes the traffic of curiosity run smoother.

11   Buzz? If you can make out an excitement from the civic grace with which Toronto visits itself, you have something more than "buzz," or "sustainability." You have a texture of life that Torontonians have failed to see as glamorous, as they waste their time ogling° the myths of London, New York or Paris. The final word on "buzz" might belong to a couple of eminent London planners who secretly told me they were thinking of moving to Toronto. And why? All "creative" cities being equal (in terms of assets) there is one thing Toronto does in the multicultural forum that dumbfounds° other cities. Toronto sidesteps the matter of "culture" in the business of daily life. This is the best kept secret in Toronto; that the people get along with each other because they have jumped to the "universals," with the understanding that cultures will just snag° them down. And this has nothing to do with becoming Canadian, or learning about other cultures (who has the time to do more than "visit" another culture?).

12   What the citizens of diversity do here is understand that a code of common humanity is all that will keep them from tearing each other apart. The alphabet of this humanity has nothing to do with social strategy, policy or the branding of cheap notions of "tolerance." The alphabet is made up by the native sense of the universal heart—an instinct that says we are "all in this together," and that the only way to survive in a globalized environment is by identifying with "another"; not by claiming your identity, but by identifying with the next person. No one knows by what weird alchemy° this takes place in Toronto, but it is becoming a matter of fact among other cities—that Toronto has this odd elixir° that might keep global multiculturalism from the "explosive." Wishful thinking? This might all change with a subway bomb. But if the chances are good that we as Torontonians have discovered universals as a means of living together, we might do well to glamorize it, and even call it something like "soul."

13   Finally, that's what we fail at in Toronto. We fail to glamorize the production of soul. Guru Richard Florida lists Toronto as one of the top four "creative cities" in North America. How much more creative could we be if we relaxed into a confidence about it? "Passion" might be useful. Passion might be the style of our creativity if we turned our mealy-mouthed criticisms into endorsements of self-love. We're getting closer to passion judging by the upswell of disdain° over the recent branding of Toronto as "Toronto Unlimited." Torontonians seem to be clear on what they are not. Now it's just a matter of being clear on who we are. We are a world class city, like it or not, with a defiance° that must change into casual grace, with no need to define ourselves against Americans, with no need of the entrenched myths of Continental cities, with no need to rally ourselves with the virtues of inclusivity, diversity and reform. We do things very well. And it may be time to put that fact behind us and simply turn to our enthusiasms, and lose that self-consciousness we call "Toronto." For the city has outgrown our questions about ourselves, and it may be time to inhabit it.

Vocabulary

1 besiege (v): surround by opponents, harass

1 hodge-podges (n, slang): messy assortment, jumble

1 bungle (v): spoil by carelessness

1 render (v): give help to make

3 guru (n, Indian, slang): influential leader, revered teacher

3 bohemian (n): somebody with an unconventional lifestyle, artist

4 delegation (n): group representing others

5 regale (v): entertain by telling stories

5 epochal (adj): characteristic of a period of history

5 resolve (n): determination

6 exodus (n): departure involving a large number of people

6 aloof (adj): remote in manner

6 mesh (v): fit together

7 opulent (adj): lavish, characterized by wealth

7 Gaudi (n): famous Spanish architect, especially in Barcelona

7 exude (v): display something in abundance

7 fiscal (adj): related to finance

7 thrive (v): be successful, grow vigorously

8 beleaguer (v): besiege, hem in

9 travesty (n): distorted version, grotesque imitation

10 pageant (n): elaborate and colourful procession, spectacular show

10 gentrified (adj): renovated, made to appear prosperous

10 conviviality (n): friendliness, sociability

10 protocol (n): code of conduct

11 ogle (v): stare in a desirous manner

11 dumbfound (v): make speechless with surprise

11 snag (v): obstruct, tangle, create problem

12 alchemy (n): power of transformation

12 elixir (n): magical substance, cure-all

13 disdain (n): intense scorn or contempt

13 defiance (n): hostile refusal, disobedience

RESPONDING TO THE READING

- If the thesis is stated, identify it; if it is implied, write it in your own words.
- What do you think is the purpose of this essay? Give reasons for your opinion.
- Who do you think is the intended audience of this essay? Give reasons for your opinion.

Comprehension

1. Pier Giorgio Di Cicco has organized this essay into three major sections: what are they?
2. What reasons does Di Cicco give for being among the delegates from Toronto to Europe?
3. What is the purpose of Di Cicco's trip to Europe?
4. In what ways does Di Cicco define "buzz"?
5. In what ways does Di Cicco define "soul"?

6. In your own words briefly sum up Di Cicco's impression of each of the three cities he visits: London (Paragraph 5), Berlin (Paragraph 6), and Barcelona (Paragraph 7).
7. What happens during a typical day on Di Cicco's trip?
8. How does Di Cicco describe his response to this trip?
9. Is Di Cicco impressed by Toronto immediately on his return? Find examples to support your response.
10. Of what aspects of Toronto is Di Cicco critical? Find examples to support your response.
11. What does Di Cicco appreciate about Toronto? Find examples to support your response.
12. Does he decide Toronto has "buzz"? Find examples to support your response.

Analysis

1. Di Cicco's vocabulary allows him to compress meaning. Explain the meaning of the following quotation; now reword the italicized phrases:

    > Municipal governments want *to lever the principles of "creativity"* into the marketplace, to kick-start industries bogged down by *"steam-engine" notions of capitalism* into a sense of cutting-edge thinking, where invention and innovation are fuelled by something deeper than *ledger-ambitions*, or short-term vision.

2. What are the senses that Di Cicco appeals to? Identify some sensory details presented in the essay.
3. "For that's the measure and resource of a city—its soul—the product of a way of life, without which a city produces nothing." Does what Di Cicco says about a city and creativity apply to people too? Why or why not?
4. What sort of "buzz" does London, Berlin, or Barcelona have, according to Di Cicco? Which of these cities sounds most interesting to you and why?
5. Di Cicco says that London has "the excitement that camouflages what tears at the seams of any city." What images do his words suggest? What does he then say could tear a city apart?
6. Di Cicco describes Berlin as having "an awful grief for its twentieth century." To what is he alluding?
7. Di Cicco says Barcelona "takes 'pleasure' in the good things of life." What device does he use here? What does he say Toronto can learn from Barcelona?
8. In Paragraph 9, how does Di Cicco define architecture and what is the implication of his definition?
9. What does Di Cicco say is the "best kept secret" in Toronto? How does this secret affect the daily lives of its inhabitants?
10. What is your response to Di Cicco's closing lines? Explain.
11. Di Cicco uses a lot of slang, jargon, and **neologisms** (the creation of new words or expressions). Find examples that show the types of language he employs. Is Di Cicco's use of language appropriate to his subject? Why or why not?

Discussion/Writing Suggestions

1. Di Cicco tells us that city planners are concerned with "sustainability," which includes economic viability, but also quality of life. What does quality of life mean to you? How important is it?

2. Di Cicco says, "We are sure that Barcelona and London and Berlin will have a soul. We're not too sure if Toronto has a soul (we have 'Torontonian' doubts)." Do you think those doubts can be considered "Canadian"? How do we see ourselves as a nation? How do we define ourselves?

   • Other essays that consider self-identity and creativity include those by Hugh MacLennan (p. 5), Joseph Epstein (p. 36), Bertrand Russell (p. 64), Pico Iyer (p. 96), Wayson Choy (p. 169), Timothy Findlay (p. 92), Stephen L. Carter (p. 132), J. Anthony Lukas (p. 191), Margaret Laurence (p. 202), and Rosie DiManno (p. 211).

The Shack

Margaret Laurence

Margaret Laurence (1926–1987), born in Neepawa, Manitoba, was a Canadian novelist and short story writer. In 1944, Laurence attended Winnipeg's United College on a scholarship, graduating in 1947 with a degree in English. Soon afterwards, she was hired as a reporter for the Winnipeg Citizen, *where she wrote book reviews and a daily radio column and covered labour issues. Her husband, John Fergus Laurence, was an engineer whose work took them to England (1949), the then-British protectorate of Somaliland (1950–1952) and Ghana (1952–1957), and Laurence's great admiration for Africa and the African peoples can be seen in her writing. In the seventies, now divorced, Laurence settled in Lakefield, Ontario. She also bought a cabin on the Otonabee River near Peterborough, where she wrote* The Diviners *(1974) during the summers from 1971 to 1973. Laurence served as chancellor of Trent University in Peterborough from 1981 to 1983.*

Margaret Laurence had a keen eye. She saw shadows, colours, and shapes, and she drew comparisons. She knew the names of objects and animals, as well as the ways to talk about what they did and why they existed. Her descriptions are full of details that express her strong love of the Canadian outdoors. This essay appeared in Heart of a Stranger *(1976).*

1 The most loved place, for me, in this country has in fact been many places. It has changed throughout the years, as I and my circumstances have changed. I haven't really lost any of the best places from the past, though. I may no longer inhabit them, but they inhabit me, portions of memory, presences in the mind. One such place was my family's summer cottage at Clear Lake in Riding Mountain National

Park, Manitoba. It was known to us simply as The Lake. Before the government piers and the sturdy log staircases down to the shore were put in, we used to slither° with an exhilarating° sense of peril down the steep homemade branch and dirt shelf-steps, through the stands of thin tall spruce and birch trees slender and graceful as girls, passing moss-hairy fallen logs and the white promise of wild strawberry blossoms, until we reached the sand and the hard bright pebbles of the beach at the edge of the cold spring-fed lake where at nights the loons still cried eerily, before too much humanshriek made them move away north.

2   My best place at the moment is very different, although I guess it has some of the attributes of that long-ago place. It is a small cedar cabin on the Otonabee River in southern Ontario. I've lived three summers there, writing, birdwatching, river-watching. I sometimes feel sorry for the people in speedboats who spend their weekends zinging up and down the river at about a million miles an hour. For all they're able to see, the riverbanks might just as well be green concrete and the river itself flowing with molten plastic.

3   Before sunup, I'm wakened by birdvoices and, I may say, birdfeet clattering and thumping on the cabin roof. Cursing only slightly, I get up *temporarily,* for the pre-dawn ritual of lighting a small fire in the old black woodstove (mornings are chilly here, even in summer) and looking out at the early river. The waters have a lovely spooky quality at this hour, entirely mist-covered, a secret meeting of river and sky.

4   By the time I get up to stay, the mist has vanished and the river is a clear ale-brown, shining with sun. I drink my coffee and sit looking out to the opposite shore, where the giant maples are splendidly green now and will be trees of flame in the fall of the year. Oak and ash stand among the maples, and the grey skeletons of the dead elms, gauntly° beautiful even in death. At the very edge of the river, the willows are everywhere, water-related trees, magic trees, pale green in early summer, silvergreen in late summer, greengold in autumn.

5   I begin work, and every time I lift my eyes from the page and glance outside, it is to see some marvel or other. The joyous dance-like flight of the swallows. The orange-black flash of the orioles who nest across the river. The amazing takeoff of a red-winged blackbird, revealing like a swiftly unfolded fan the hidden scarlet in those dark wings. The flittering of the goldfinches, who always travel in domestic pairs, he gorgeous in black-patterned yellow feathers, she (alas) drabber° in greenish grey-yellow.

6   A pair of great blue herons have their huge unwieldy° nest about half a mile upriver, and although they are very shy, occasionally through the open door I hear a sudden approaching rush of air (yes, you can *hear* it) and look up quickly to see the magnificent unhurried sweep of those powerful wings. The only other birds which can move me so much are the Canada geese in their autumn migration flight, their far-off wilderness voices the harbinger° of winter.

7   Many boats ply° these waterways, and all of them are given mental gradings of merit or lack of it, by me. Standing low in the estimation of all of us along this stretch of the river are some of the big yachts, whose ego-tripping skippers don't have the courtesy to slow down in cottage areas and whose violent wakes scour

out our shorelines. Ranking highest in my good books are the silent unpolluting canoes and rowboats, and next to them, the small outboard motorboats put-putting along and carrying patient fishermen, and the homemade houseboats, unspeedy and somehow cosy-looking, decorated lovingly with painted birds or flowers or gaudy° abstract splodges°.

8   In the quiet of afternoon, if no boats are around, I look out and see the half-moon leap of a fish, carp or muskie, so instantaneous that one has the impression of having seen not a fish but an arc of light.

9   The day moves on, and about four o'clock Linda and Susan from the nearby farm arrive. I call them the Girls of the Pony Express. Accompanied by dogs and laughter, they ride their horses into my yard, kindly bringing my mail from the rural route postbox up the road. For several summers it was Old Jack who used to drive his battered Volkswagen up to fetch the mail. He was one of the best neighbours and most remarkable men I've ever known. As a boy of eighteen, he had home-steaded a hundred miles north of Regina. Later, he'd been a skilled toolmaker with Ford. He'd travelled to South America and done many amazing things. He was a man whose life had taught him a lot of wisdom. After his much-loved wife died, he moved out here to the river, spending as short a winter as possible in Peterborough, and getting back into his cottage the first of anyone in the spring, when the river was still in flood and he could only get in and out, hazardously°, by boat. I used to go out in his boat with him, late afternoons, and we would dawdle° along the river, looking at the forest stretches and the open rolling farmlands and vast old barns, and at the smaller things close by, the heavy luxuriance of ferns at the water's rim, the dozens of snapping turtles with unblinking eyes, all sizes and generations of the turtle tribe, sunning themselves on the fallen logs in the river. One summer, Old Jack's eighty-fourth, he spent some time planting maple saplings on his property. A year later, when I saw him dying, it seemed to me he'd meant those trees as a kind of legacy°, a declaration of faith. Those of us along the river, here, won't forget him, nor what he stood for.

10   After work, I go out walking and weed-inspecting. Weeds and wildflowers impress me as much as any cultivated plant. I've heard that in a year when the milk-weed is plentiful, the Monarch butterflies will also be plentiful. This year the light pinkish milkweed flowers stand thick and tall, and sure enough, here are the dozens of Monarch butterflies, fluttering like dusky orange-gold angels all over the place. I can't identify as many plants as I'd like, but I'm learning. Chickweed, the ragged-leafed lambs' quarters, the purple-and-white wild phlox with its expensive-smelling perfume, the pink and mauve wild asters, the two-toned yellow of the tiny butter-and-eggs flowers, the burnt orange of devil's paintbrush, the staunch° nobility of the huge purple thistles, and, almost best of all, that long stalk covered with clusters of miniature creamy blossoms which I finally tracked down in my wild-flower book—this incomparable plant bears the armorial name of the Great Mullein of the Figwort Family. It may not be the absolute prettiest of our wildflowers, but it certainly has the most stunning pedigree°.

11   It is night now, and there are no lights except those of our few cottages. At sunset, an hour or so ago, I watched the sun's last flickers touching the rippling river, making it look as though some underwater world had lighted all its candles

down there. Now it is dark. Dinner over, I turn out the electric lights in the cabin so I can see the stars. The black skydome (or perhaps skydom, like kingdom) is alive and alight.

12   Tomorrow the weekend will begin, and friends will arrive. We'll talk all day and probably half the night, and that will be good. But for now, I'm content to be alone, because loneliness is something that doesn't exist here.

Vocabulary

1 slither (v): slide

1 exhilarating (adj): feeling happy and lively

4 gauntly (adv): thinly, starkly

5 drabber (adj): not bright or colourful, of pale greyish brown colour

6 unwieldy (adj): not easy to handle, awkward

6 harbinger (n): someone or something that announces something

7 ply (v): work hard at

7 gaudy (adj): showy, overdecorated

7 splodges (n): large irregular spots

9 hazardously (adv): dangerously

9 dawdle (v): move slowly or idly

9 legacy (n): something handed down from the past

10 staunch (adj): loyal, dependable

10 pedigree (n): line of ancestors, family background

 ## RESPONDING TO THE READING

- If the thesis is stated, identify it; if it is implied, write it in your own words.
- What do you think is the purpose of this essay? Give reasons for your opinion.
- Who do you think is the intended audience of this essay? Give reasons for your opinion.

Comprehension

1. The first two paragraphs act as Margaret Laurence's introduction based on her opening line, "The most loved place . . ." What is this place and how do you know?
2. The last sentence of Paragraph 1 offers an evocative description of the first place Laurence loved most. Identify the adjectives, adverbs, similes, metaphors, and personification in this sentence.
3. What is the controlling pattern of organization Laurence uses from Paragraph 3 to the end? How does she organize her supporting details within this pattern?
4. Explain her "pre-dawn ritual" and paraphrase her last sentence in this paragraph: "The waters have a lovely spooky quality at this hour, entirely mist-covered, a secret meeting of river and sky."

5. Paragraph 4 focuses on the trees around Laurence's cabin. Find examples of simile and metaphor at work here.
6. The bird is often used as a symbol of our imagination. Find examples of Laurence's descriptions of the birds and explain the implied analogy in Paragraph 5.
7. In Paragraph 7, what sorts of classifications of boats does Laurence present?
8. In Paragraph 9 Laurence pauses in her description of her day to tell an anecdote about Old Jack. Is this an effective break? Why or why not?
9. In Paragraph 10 Laurence employs cause and effect. Find other examples of this pattern of organization.
10. Do you think Laurence's final sentence could stand as her thesis statement? Why or why not?

Analysis

1. Do you think there is a distinction between being lonely and being alone? How does Laurence's essay support your point of view?
2. What are the senses that Laurence appeals to? Identify some sensory details presented in the essay.
3. Laurence succeeds in condensing the details of Old Jack's life into a single paragraph. How is it that we feel we know him and "what he stood for"?
4. Compare Laurence's attitude to nature to that of Catherine George. You might wish to consider their word choice and techniques. What is the major difference?
5. "The black skydome (or perhaps skydom, like kingdom) is alive and alight." The play on words—skydome/skydom—is a pun. What does Laurence achieve by the use of this pun?
6. Laurence presents a typical day at her cabin. The simple events she relates, through their repetition—both in action and words—take on a greater significance for Laurence; that is, they become a *ritual*, a form of celebration or praise, often having spiritual overtones. To what extent is Laurence's account of her day a ritual?

Discussion/Writing Suggestions

1. Describe in detail a favourite place where you have recently spent time. Choose words to convey to readers what this place looks and feels like; be sure to say why it is significant to you.
2. Thinking of Laurence's celebration of each day at her cottage, what rituals are important to you? What do they celebrate?

   • Other essays that focus on appreciation of the natural world include those by James C. Rettie (p. 221), Rachel Carson (p. 123), Sean Twist (p. 147), Catherine George (p. 194), and Sang Il Lee (p. 233); these essays celebrate "place": Hugh MacLennan (p. 5), Timothy Findlay (p. 92), and Pier Giorgio Di Cicco (p. 196).

Essay of Narration

Narration is essentially storytelling. A narrative can be as brief as an anecdote, as casual as a joke, and as interesting as gossip about the weekend. Short stories and novels are narratives, but they are **fictional** accounts mainly based on imaginary events. An essay of narration is non-fictional writing; it is written based on facts and actual happenings. Good narrative skills are necessary for your success both at university or college today and on your job tomorrow. As you can imagine, there will be many occasions that require you to recount in writing what happened, the sequence of events, the beginning, middle, and end of an occurrence.

Writing Strategy

Like all the other types of essays, an effective narrative essay should follow some common principles and general guidelines. Here is a list of suggestions or reminders for you to consider when writing your narrative essay:

1. Choose a focal point (a thesis) for your essay.

As with any essay, an essay in narrative form must have a central point, its thesis. Telling a joke without a punchline would be similar to writing a narrative without making a point. If you wish to tell a story, say, about a friend who won a lottery, the point of your story could be to show luck does play a part in our life, or how sudden wealth could bring both happiness and despair.

Once the essay has a thesis, all you need is to construct your narrative around it. For example, to arrive at his final question: "We have just arrived upon this earth. How long will we stay?" James Rettie decides to narrate the key moments in the history of geological development in his fable.

2. Select supporting details according to the principle of unity.

Draft an outline to figure out what to include and what to exclude for the sake of unity. *Only* those details that support your thesis should be included in your essay; otherwise, leave it out.

3. Arrange the details coherently and narrate the events chronologically.

Normally the clearest way to tell or retell a story is to place events in a chronological order, the order in which events occur in time. You can find a good example in Michael Dorris's essay below, which tells the story of one particular Christmas with the series of events arranged in time order, from the afternoon of December 24 to the early morning of December 25. Although sometimes a narrative is interrupted by a **flashback** or an elaborate description of a scene (as Maya Angelou does in her essay), readers expect to see the events in the story develop climactically to some kind of end or resolution.

Narratives of everyday life have already happened before they are told on paper. Thus, the use of the *past tense* is common in writing a narrative. Also narrative often requires some background information. For example, readers may need to know details about the people in a story before the actual events are described. Remember: an essay of narration is no different from expository or descriptive essays; it also requires effective use of transitions, implied as well as stated, to glue sentences and paragraphs together into an *organic whole*.

READINGS: ESSAYS OF NARRATION

In "The Minnie Mouse Kitchen," Michael Dorris tells the story of a particular Christmas. The gift his daughters want from Santa provides both a challenge and a lesson for him and his wife. Rosie DiManno tells the story of her childhood experience of trying to be "Canadian" in "Growing up on Grace." Her title refers directly to the name of her street in Toronto, but DiManno's narrative contains many anecdotes of grace or gratitude. In "The Fight," Maya Angelou appears to be telling a simple story about a group of people listening to a boxing match on the radio. Actually, Angelou tells a number of stories at the same time—each one relating directly to the boxing match and its effect on the people in the room. In the last essay, "'But a Watch in the Night': A Scientific Fable," James C. Rettie expresses an environmental concern in the form of a fable, one of the oldest forms of narration. In fact, "'But a Watch in the Night'" is an example of an extended analogy. By using analogy, Rettie achieves two things: he makes a powerful distinction between geological and historical time; he is also able to demonstrate how colossal the impact on the earth of human beings has been.

The Minnie Mouse Kitchen

Michael Dorris

Michael Dorris (1945–1997) was a well-known Native American novelist and scholar. In 1989 Dorris won the National Book Critics award for his non-fiction The Broken Cord. *In this book, Dorris recounted the struggles the family experienced with his adopted son who suffered from Fetal Alcohol Syndrome (FAS). This account led to legislation warning of the dangers of drinking alcohol during pregnancy and encouraged research into FAS. He was married to Louise Erdrich, a native American novelist and poet.*

In this narrative essay, Michael Dorris describes his and his wife's attempts to raise their daughters in a gender-neutral environment. While Dorris's struggle with stereotyping is serious, the essay is written in a humorous and self-deprecating style. This essay appeared in Parents *magazine in December 1990.*

1   My wife, Louise, and I, well-intentioned parents of two young daughters, are ever vigilant° lest our girls limit their horizons because of sexist stereotyping. Each, we believe, should aim for whatever her talents and inclinations dictate—be it president or Nobel Prize physicist, Supreme Court justice or space-shuttle pilot.

2   So, what did we do last year when, for their special Christmas present, five-year-old Persia and four-year-old Pallas' collective wish was for the complete Minnie Mouse kitchen?

3   Despair. Despite all of our gender-neutral picture books, they had clearly already been molded by the subtle messages of media and popular culture. White aprons, not lab coats, loomed in their future.

4   How about a chess set? we suggested. A magic kit? An ant farm?

5   No. Persia was firm, Pallas obdurate°: It was Minnie Mouse or nothing. Tucked under the pillow of their imaginations was the page torn from a wish book in which two future mommies happily baked miniature angel foods, washed tiny plastic dishes, and planned the week's menu by perusing° their stock of brand-name products.

6   Early December became the time for an unstated battle of wills, a contest of aspiration° over who knew best what two of us wanted. Louise and I made the issue a symbol that spanned from suffrage° to the Equal Rights Amendment. Our daughters, however, remained steadfast in their inclination° toward home ec., though ultimately they seemed to resign themselves to the inequities° of power. Their complaints would be saved, no doubt, for some future psychoanalyst.

7   Then on Christmas Eve, as I was preparing my grandmother's special sweet-potato balls (whipped, flavored with brandy, formed around a marshmallow, and dredged in cornflake crumbs) and Louise was making a family favorite, wild rice stuffing for the turkey, a string of startling insights simultaneously occurred to us: *We* loved to cook. *We* spent lots of time doing it. *We* were Minnie Mouse.

8   Yikes! It was almost 4:00 p.m., and the stores would soon close.

9   A gentle snow had begun to fall, and here and there as I drove along the road toward town, colored Christmas lights twinkled through the windows of houses with smoking chimneys. New England in winter can, at such moments, seem like one giant Hollywood set, a Currier and Ives scene ready for a heart-warming story to happen. In this version, my part would have been played by Jimmy Stewart: awkward, stalwart°, the honest galumph° who carried the American dream like a red, white, and blue banner. He was out to do a deed, to accomplish one of those minor miracles that make life wonderful and annually bring a smile to Donna Reed's eyes.

10   The problem was, every store within a hundred miles was sold out of the Minnie Mouse kitchen.

11   "The last one went ten minutes ago," the salesman noted, driving a stake through my heart as I finally stood at the head of a long line of shoppers.

12   I was a poor excuse for a father. I looked from right to left in search of any idea, and there it was, suspended by wires from the ceiling: every one of Minnie's treasures—stove, sink, and "frigerator," its doors invitingly ajar.

13   "How about that one?" I pleaded.

14   "Oh, no," the man said. "That's the display model."

15   "It's not for me," I argued, perhaps unnecessarily. "It's for my little girls. They're only four and five." I paused dramatically, then fired my best shot: "It's Christmas Eve."

16   The man hesitated as Minnie teetered° between us: rules, or little girls' dreams come true?

17   "Sell it to him," the grandmother behind me snarled° menacingly. "What are you, Mr. Scrooge?"

18   "Call the manager," protested a man waiting to buy a snow shovel.

19   "Climb up there and take it down," demanded a very pregnant woman with an ominously quiet voice. "Or I will."

20   There were holes in the plywood facades° of Minnie's major appliances where hooks had been, but no matter. They fit into the backseat, jauntily red and white. Jimmy Stewart drove home singing carols with the radio.

21   After our daughters were in bed, Louise and I arranged the kitchen beneath the tree, amid the puzzles and books and telescopes. Then we rose early to witness the girls' reaction. Right on cue° they ran into the room, stopped still, and stared. What would each do first? Cook? Scour a pot? Clean out the freezer? Anything was possible.

22   Persia and Pallas held hands for what seemed a long time. Then, as one, they turned to where we sat and ran to squeeze between us.

23   "We knew you would," Persia said.

24   And Pallas nodded in agreement. "We knew it all the time."

Vocabulary

1 vigilant (adj): watchful, on guard

5 obdurate (adj): stubborn, not easily persuaded

5 peruse (v): read the entire thing in either a leisurely or careful manner

6 aspiration (n): ambition, hope

6 suffrage (n): right to vote

6 inclination (n): feeling towards, tendency

6 inequities (n): injustices, unfairness

9 stalwart (adj): dependable, loyal

9 galumph (n, slang): a person who behaves in a boisterous or clumsy manner

16 teeter (v): be in a precarious position, move back and forth

17 snarl (v): speak in an angry manner, growl

20 facades (n): surfaces

21 cue (n): signal, prompt

 RESPONDING TO THE READING

- If the thesis is stated, identify it; if it is implied, write it in your own words.
- What do you think is the purpose of this essay? Give reasons for your opinion.
- Who do you think is the intended audience of this essay? Give reasons for your opinion.

Comprehension

1. In the opening sentence of the essay, Michael Dorris talks about "sexist stereotyping." What does he fear?
2. Explain the meaning of the sentence, "White aprons, not lab coats, loomed in their future."
3. How does Dorris stereotype "mommies"?
4. Paraphrase "a contest of aspiration," "a symbol that spanned from suffrage to the Equal Rights Amendment," and "the inequities of power."

5. Why does Dorris use italics (for the word "we") three times at the end of Paragraph 7?
6. What happens to Dorris to make him exclaim "Yikes!" at the beginning of Paragraph 8? What do you assume will happen next given the details of Paragraph 8?
7. Paragraph 9 exploits a number of stereotypical Christmas scenes. How many can you identify?
8. The three customers in line behind Dorris work *against* stereotype. Explain how.
9. Why does Dorris in Paragraph 20 refer to himself as Jimmy Stewart?
10. What final image of Dorris's family does he leave readers with?

Analysis

1. What evidence can you find that Dorris is presenting himself as the stereotypically well-intentioned parent? How does he overcome the stereotype?
2. The ambitions he has for his daughters are expressed ironically. How? Why?
3. The sentence with which Paragraph 21 ends, "Anything was possible," appears to have greater implications than the list of tasks (cook, scour, and clean) that precedes it. What does this suggest to you? (Hint: reread Paragraph 1.)

Discussion/Writing Suggestions

1. What expectations should parents have for their children? What expectations did your parents have for you and do you think you've met their expectations?
2. How important is family to you? Do you participate in family celebrations regularly? If you are far away from your family, how do you stay in touch?

   • Other essays that discuss personal relationships are by Bertrand Russell (p. 64), Wayson Choy (p. 169), Timothy Findlay (p. 92), Nicola Bleasby (p. 109), Stephen L. Carter (p. 132), Judith Viorst (p. 142), Judy Brady (p. 155), Charlie Angus (p. 180), and Rosie DiManno (p. 211).

Growing up on Grace

Rosie DiManno

Rosie DiManno is a columnist and sports writer for the Toronto Star.

This article appeared in the Toronto Star *on June 28, 1997.*

1   I was about 6 years old when I discovered that I was a Canadian.

2   This came as a rude shock.

3   Insofar as I had a vague image of a huge world with a bunch of different countries in it, I thought I was an American.

4   My parents are Italian immigrants and I was born in Toronto, grew up on Grace St. downtown, but didn't learn English until I started school. In my household,

whenever the adults spoke of leaving their old country for this new one, it was always put in these terms: We came to *America.* They made no distinction between the United States and Canada, or maybe I just didn't grasp it.

5   *America.* Sometimes it was said with regret and sadness, other times in terms of a bold adventure, but never with a sense of belonging. It was always this alien place in which they found themselves, and to which they were grateful for whatever comforts they had acquired. But their suspicions and their sense of isolation lingered°. It's why they—and every other ethnic group that ventures to this city—clustered in self-contained, unilingual neighbourhoods, both to shun and to defend themselves from shunning. They weren't cultural ghettos; they were outposts of the familiar, like pioneer forts in a hostile land. The land of the *Inglese.*

6   It was the early '60s. I watched American TV beamed from Buffalo: *Captain Kangaroo* and *Commander Tom.* Sitcoms like *Petticoat Junction* and *The Honeymooners*—which had no similarities to our own existence on Grace St., but which I misunderstood as that larger American reality, from which I was excluded only because of my parentage, not by geographic boundaries. And certainly not because these were phony, idealized domestic situations that only existed within a television tube.

7   This, I thought—flipping between *Leave It to Beaver* and *I Love Lucy*—is how people *really* live, except on my street: The privileged people, not the interlopers° (like us), the imposters (like us); the ones who have proprietary° first dibs on the country, the ones who drink milk at the dinner table, who have cereal for breakfast, who make sandwiches from pre-sliced white bread, who wear high heels in the house.

8   There was no Canadian flag, remember, as the most visible national icon. At Clinton Public School, they flew the Union Jack, but I thought that was just a weird variation on the Stars and Stripes. There was a photograph of the Queen at the head of the class, and this got me to thinking about the relationship between the Queen and the president, who was also familiar to me from American TV news. We sang "God Save the Queen" in school, but at night, when the TV stations signed off, it was the American national anthem that accompanied the fade to black. There was no "O Canada."

9   Perhaps my main problem is that I never watched the CBC.

10   It dawned on me, somewhere around Grade 1, that I was not American at all, although this growing suspicion was something I kept to myself for awhile. It's not the kind of thing you ask an adult about, lest you appear colossally stupid, and I was not in the habit of asking my parents anything. They were probably more alien to me than the Ricardos.

11   When I was forced to accept this reality, it was with a sense of loss. Here I had been trying to visualize myself growing up and fitting into this bustling American lifestyle, this energetic and self-confident and purposeful country. But I was stuck with dreary old/young Canada. Second-rate by ancestry, third-rate by an accident of birth.

12   This dismay wore off, of course. Certainly, it was shed abruptly when I met my bosom friend Barbara Zloty, in Grade 5. She really was an American but had moved to Toronto with her mother to stay with relatives because her father was fighting in Vietnam. I could not imagine having a father fighting a war in a distant country,

maybe getting killed, maimed. Eventually, Barbara's father was wounded, and they returned to El Paso.

13   Barbara made me my first grilled-cheese sandwich, which seemed terribly decadent° and decidedly *Inglese.* My mother, who did not believe that we should ever enter the homes of anyone outside the extended family—and rarely were any of us invited—had forbidden me to have lunch at Barbara's. I went anyway. When I got home from school that afternoon, my mother met me halfway up the street and hit me with her shoe.

14   This is supposed to be a narrative about My Canada, yet I'm not sure what that means. I can tell you only small stories about growing up in a small piece of the country, as insular as any tumbleweed-tossed Prairie town or desolate Maritime hamlet.

15   I grew up not in a country but on a street. My territory stretched from Bloor to Harbord, with traffic lights at either end, Christie Pits to the north, Bickford Park directly across from the house, Montrose Park to the south. Bickford Park, where I climbed every tree, had no amenities: no playground, no pool, no soccer pitch. Just a weary little softball diamond, one drinking fountain, and a huge sewer grate that was cool against your face when you lay across it on hot summer days.

16   And yet the park fascinated us, we over-protected young children who were never allowed to roam beyond the busy thoroughfares° at either end of Grace. Once I saw a man running through the park with his mangled left arm hanging by just a few strands of sinew. Once I found a gold signature pin that said: Rosalba. That is my real name, abbreviated and Anglicized once I started school, in a desperate attempt to be less Italian, more English. It fills me with wonder, still, that I should have found such a pin, with that odd name, in the grass at Bickford Park.

17   There were many Italians on that street, some relatives, some merely *paisans,* some with no ancestral connection but part of the cultural fraternity that kept Us separate from Them. There were several Jewish families, too, and I remember feeling a kinship with them, because they were also aliens. (Later on, in my teens, we would move to a predominantly Jewish neighbourhood in Downsview. This resulted in one curious anomaly°: My mother now speaks English with a Yiddish accent and is as likely to make a brisket for dinner as lasagna.)

18   I was mortified°, in those days, by our Italian-ness. I begged my mother to shave her legs, to which she finally acquiesced, although she never did understand the fuss. I hated the tomatoes and tangle of vegetables in our backyard and longed for the banality of a grass carpet. I hated the pepper and onions that my mother would string like braids on the front porch.

19   In late spring, my father—a farmer and shepherd before emigrating—would dump a load of manure on the front lawn because this is the world's best fertilizer. On those occasions, returning from school, I would walk right past my house lest any classmates realize that I lived in such a Munsters-like place.

20   My father—and I respect him for this only in retrospect—never attempted to ingratiate° himself with the *Inglese* by being less Italian or by altering the rhythms of his life, although he was impeccably° hospitable and generous.

21   He hunted, not for sport, but for food, and I can see him now, skinning jackrabbits over the cellar sink. In the fall, he would slaughter a pig; at Easter, a lamb.

22   My parents made sausages and strung them to dry inside a makeshift smoke-house. Prosciutto would be salted and hung for a year in the wine cellar. My mother would spend weeks slicing fresh tomatoes and bottling them for sauce, sterilizing the bottles in a steel drum of boiling water in the backyard, stoking the fire underneath. She'd pickle cucumbers and artichokes, cauliflower and olives.

23   I loved all these foods, so common now in Italian restaurants and grocery stores, but I was ashamed of them then. I would throw away my lunch at school and starve rather than expose these peculiar items to my *Inglese* friends. I pined° for peanut-butter sandwiches.

24   Sometimes, I would go grocery shopping with my mother just so I could persuade her to buy all this ostensibly° tasty English stuff that I saw advertised on TV: jelly rolls, Cap'n Crunch cereal, Pop Tarts, Wonderbread, SpaghettiOs, Campbell's soup, Kraft macaroni and cheese, marshmallows. It all tasted foul, it made me gag. But if this is what it took to be *Inglese,* I would suffer for my pride.

25   In autumn, after weeks of consultation and innumerable taste-testing expeditions, the crates of grapes would be delivered to the house: hundreds of them, stacked on the lawn. California grapes for homemade wine. Families would help each other out in the complicated wine-making process, churning and pressing and sifting and decanting. It was, I suppose, a different version of the barn-building efforts in other cultures, a community event.

26   Invariably, I would step on a nail.

27   Menstruating women were not allowed near the mulch, lest they spoil the wine. I, still a child, was humiliated on behalf of these women, who would be sent upstairs to make themselves otherwise useful. I only realized later that they considered it a blessing to be so ostracized° from such backbreaking work, and the constant curses of the men.

28   I rebelled against all of it. The religious processions that were the highlight of the calendar year; refusing to parade along the street in my bride-like Communion gown; refusing to attend the Catholic school in which I had been enrolled (hiding out in the sewer pipes at Christie Pits) until my mother threw up her hands in defeat; refusing to kiss the aunts and the uncles (all of whom had chin whiskers); refusing to eat anything that had a hint of tomato in it; refusing to speak Italian.

29   Education was not valued highly in our family, which possibly made us, our sub-group of Italian immigrants, different from other ethnic groups washing ashore in Canada. Education was feared by these Italians—a fear nurtured and encouraged by the Catholic church. Education would take children away from their parents, the priests said, would make them question authority, would draw them into the outside world, which was a forbidden place.

30   Yet every week, from the time I was very small, my mother would take me, in a clandestine° venture, to the St. George main library, a good 20-block hike from our house. She could barely read Italian but she wanted me to learn something from the ridiculed pleasure of books.

31   An education, particularly a post-secondary education, was considered a waste on a girl. If I were to have any profession at all, it was decided on my behalf, I would become a teacher: a feminine profession, respectable, akin to mothering. I played along and planned my escape.

32   So there came a time when the street, and the neighbourhood, became too small and too cramped an existence for me. Symbolically, it was enough for my parents. They finally felt safe and entrenched. They knew nothing about the rest of the country and did not care. They didn't know the difference between a city and a province.

33   They were clueless about the vastness of Canada, although they had come to Toronto from Halifax by train. They never ventured outside the city, rarely strayed from the neighbourhood. The most ambitious foray I can recall is one winter when we took the streetcar to the College St. Eaton's store—the most WASPish of establishments—to buy me a typewriter. I'd never seen an escalator before.

34   My parents never took a vacation—in 45 years, my father has yet to return to Italy for a visit—never mingled with another ethnic group (save for an Indian friend who was my dad's hunting companion, and the Jewish family in whose coin laundry my mother had once worked), never had any curiosity about politics or social issues or even the most innocent of *Inglese* pleasures. My father has never been to a movie, never gone to a hockey game, never attended a parent night at school.

35   When I'm being generous, I convince myself that he was merely shy, that he felt ignorant in this English culture. But I'm more included to believe that he lived completely within himself, and even his family was an intrusion.

36   Perhaps I have inherited his discomfort, his diffidence, because I don't feel particularly connected to this country, either, although I have a genuine fondness for it.

37   Too long an outsider, faking it, beseeching° entry. Relentlessly *Inglese* in attitude and tastes, irredeemably Italian in my genes. But not hyphenated, never hyphenated. A clumsy hybrid, maybe.

38   I used to fret so much, in my younger days, about how I could ever reconcile these two cultures, how I could be Rosalba and Rosie and still stay intact. The struggle doesn't seem very important any more.

39   But I am constantly astonished by third-generation Italian Canadians who seem more proud of their ancestral homeland than the country of their birth, who chatter in Italian on St. Clair Ave., who seem more Italian to me now than my parents did 30 years ago. Cultural pride is one thing, but so much of this overt° Italian sensibility seems to me to be a betrayal—of Canada, and to those of us who broke all the rules so that we didn't have to stay insularly Italian, imprisoned by culture, in this country.

40   I don't wave flags and I find the notion of Canada Day contrived, if sweet. But I have felt moments of intense patriotism. Little moments, like spotting a Maple Leaf on a teenager's backpack in Europe. Grand moments, like when a Canadian wins a gold medal at the Olympics. Aching moments, like when I visit the Canadian war cemetery in Cassino, just down the mountain from my parents' village. (As children, they survived the battle of Monte Cassino.) And historical moments, like covering the referendum in Montreal in 1995, and feeling a sudden swell of anxiety, as if we were letting something very precious slip away, through carelessness and self-absorption.

41   As an adult, when I visit my ancestral village in Italy—which lost half its population to Toronto after the war—they always ask about life in *America*. I have given

up trying to make the distinction. It just doesn't seem significant, from the perspective of a mountain top south of Naples.

42 It's funny, though. From the first time I set foot on Italian soil, I felt as if I belonged. I looked like everyone else, my name didn't sound foreign. I felt a thousand years of history rushing through my blood. But I couldn't live there.

43 And every time I come through Canada Customs, travel back across the border, I breathe a sigh of relief. Home.

44 My parents are Canadian citizens now. Grace St. is long ago and far away. They are living the good, Canadian life: a suburban home, a cottage, two cars, a truck, money in the bank. They take occasional trips, mostly church-organized, and are finally seeing a little more of the country. They vote. And they try very hard to pretend that we are not a fractured, dysfunctional family.

45 They do not read English. They will not read this story. They have never read a word I have written.

Vocabulary

5 linger (v): persist, stay around

7 interlopers (n): intruders

7 proprietary (adj): assuming ownership

13 decadent (adj): immoral

16 thoroughfares (n): main streets

17 anomaly (n): irregularity, peculiarity

18 mortified (adj): extremely embarrassed

20 ingratiate (v): seek to please

20 impeccably (adv): perfectly

23 pine (v): yearn, long for

24 ostensibly (adv): seeming true but open to doubt

27 ostracize (v): exclude

30 clandestine (adj): secret, furtive

37 beseech (v): plead, beg

39 overt (adj): unconcealed

 ## RESPONDING TO THE READING

- If the thesis is stated, identify it; if it is implied, write it in your own words.
- What do you think is the purpose of this essay? Give reasons for your opinion.
- Who do you think is the intended audience of this essay? Give reasons for your opinion.

Comprehension

1. What reasons does Rosie DiManno give for the "rude shock" when she realized she was Canadian and not American?
2. How does DiManno demonstrate the pervasive influence of American culture in daily Canadian life?

3. Explain the various allusions to popular TV shows that DiManno mentions.
4. What comparisons does DiManno draw between Canada and the United States?
5. Who is Barbara Zloty and why is she important to DiManno?
6. What does the gold pin with "Rosalba" on it represent to DiManno?
7. How would you characterize DiManno's attitude to her parents when she was a child?
8. How does DiManno account for her attitude toward her parents?
9. In what ways did DiManno's parents preserve the culture of Italy in their daily life?
10. Why did DiManno's mother take her daughter to the library each week, and why was this a surprising thing?
11. What does DiManno believe she has inherited from her father and why?
12. In her conclusion, DiManno indicates the ways in which her parents have changed and adapted to life in Canada. What are they?

Analysis

1. What does DiManno mean when she says, "They weren't cultural ghettos; they were outposts of the familiar, like pioneer forts in a hostile land. The land of the *Inglese*"?
2. DiManno acknowledges that the TV shows she watched as a child were "phony, idealized domestic situations." How does this reflect on her attitudes to her family and to Canada as she was growing up?
3. Why did DiManno want to reject her Italian heritage and become part of the establishment? Does she still feel that way?
4. What were DiManno's feelings on visiting Italy? What is the reason for her ambivalence?
5. DiManno refers to herself as "not hyphenated" and a "clumsy hybrid maybe." What does she mean?
6. What is the effect of DiManno's final three sentences?

Discussion/Writing Suggestions

1. What is your experience of life in Canada? Are you or your parents immigrants? What do you think are the challenges of being Canadian?
2. Is your cultural heritage part of your self-identity? What would you want your children to know and retain as part of their Canadian backgrounds?

   - Other essays that discuss aspects of Canadian culture are those by Hugh MacLennan (p. 5), Margaret Atwood (p. 85), Timothy Findlay (p. 92), Wayson Choy (p. 169), Pier Giorgio Di Cicco (p. 196), Margaret Laurence (p. 202), and Almas Zakiuddin (p. 240).

The Fight

Maya Angelou

Maya Angelou (1928–) was born Marguerite Ann Johnson in St. Louis, Missouri. She is a well-respected writer, poet, singer, actress, educator, and civil rights activist. While her autobiographical writings have gained her most fame, her poetry collection Just Give Me a Cool Drink of Water 'Fore I Die *(1971) was nominated for a Pulitzer Prize. At the request of Bill Clinton, Angelou read her poem "On the Pulse of the Morning" at his presidential inauguration in 1993. A gifted linguist, Angelou is also fluent in French, Spanish, Italian, Arabic, and Ghanian Fante. She has received numerous academic honours, including fellowships with Yale University and the Rockefeller Foundation. Angelou has taught at universities in Italy and Ghana; she holds a lifetime chair at the University of Kansas and is the Z. Smith Reynolds Professor of American Studies at Wake Forest University. She has been nominated for the Woman of the Year Award and the Tony Awards. In 2005, Angelou was honoured by Oprah Winfrey at her Legends Ball with 25 other African-American women.*

This narrative is taken from her best-selling autobiography, I Know Why the Caged Bird Sings *(1969).*

1   The last inch of space was filled, yet people continued to wedge themselves along the walls of the Store. Uncle Willie had turned the radio up to its last notch so that youngsters on the porch wouldn't miss a word. Women sat on kitchen chairs, dining-room chairs, stools and upturned wooden boxes. Small children and babies perched on every lap available and men leaned on the shelves or on each other.

2   The apprehensive mood was shot through with shafts of gaiety, as a black sky is streaked with lightning.

3   "I ain't worried 'bout this fight. Joe's gonna whip that cracker° like it's open season."

4   "He gone whip him till that white boy call him Momma."

5   At last the talking was finished and the sing-along songs about razor blades were over and the fight began.

6   "A quick jab to the head." In the Store the crowd grunted. "A left to the head and a right and another left." One of the listeners cackled like a hen and was quieted.

7   "They're in a clench, Louis is trying to fight his way out."

8   Some bitter comedian on the porch said, "That white man don't mind hugging that niggah now, I betcha."

9   "The referee is moving in to break them up, but Louis finally pushed the contender away and it's an uppercut to the chin. The contender is hanging on, now he's backing away. Louis catches him with a short left to the jaw."

10   A tide of murmuring assent poured out the doors and into the yard.

11   "Another left and another left. Louis is saving that mighty right . . ." The mutter in the Store had grown into a baby roar and it was pierced by the clang of a bell and the announcer's "That's the bell for round three, ladies and gentlemen."

12   As I pushed my way into the Store I wondered if the announcer gave any thought to the fact that he was addressing as "ladies and gentlemen" all the Negroes around the world who sat sweating and praying, glued to their "master's voice."

13   There were only a few calls for R.C. Colas, Dr. Peppers, and Hire's root beer. The real festivities would begin after the fight. Then even the old Christian ladies who taught their children and tried themselves to practice turning the other cheek would buy soft drinks, and if the Brown Bomber's victory was a particularly bloody one they would order peanut patties and Baby Ruths also.

14   Bailey and I lay the coins on top of the cash register. Uncle Willie didn't allow us to ring up sales during a fight. It was too noisy and might shake up the atmosphere. When the gong rang for the next round we pushed through the near-sacred quiet to the herd of children outside.

15   "He's got Louis against the ropes and now it's a left to the body and a right to the ribs. Another right to the body, it looks like it was low . . . Yes, ladies and gentlemen, the referee is signalling but the contender keeps raining the blows on Louis. It's another to the body, and it looks like Louis is going down."

16   My race groaned. It was our people falling. It was another lynching, yet another Black man hanging on a tree. One more woman ambushed and raped. A Black boy whipped and maimed. It was hounds on the trail of a man running through slimy swamps. It was a white woman slapping her maid for being forgetful.

17   The men in the Store stood away from the walls and at attention. Women greedily clutched the babes on their laps while on the porch the shufflings and smiles, flirtings and pinching of a few minutes before were gone. This might be the end of the world. If Joe lost we were back in slavery and beyond help. It would all be true, the accusations that we were lower types of human beings. Only a little higher than the apes. True that we were stupid and ugly and lazy and dirty and, unlucky and worst of all, that God Himself hated us and ordained° us to be hewers° of wood and drawers of water, forever and ever, world without end.

18   We didn't breathe. We didn't hope. We waited.

19   "He's off the ropes, ladies and gentlemen. He's moving towards the center of the ring." There was no time to be relieved. The worst might still happen.

20   "And now it looks like Joe is mad. He's caught Carnera with a left hook to the head and a right to the head. It's a left jab to the body and another left to the head. There's a left cross and a right to the head. The contender's right eye is bleeding and he can't seem to keep his block up. Louis is penetrating every block. The referee is moving in, but Louis sends a left to the body and it's the uppercut to the chin and the contender is dropping. He's on the canvas, ladies and gentlemen."

21   Babies slid to the floor as women stood up and men leaned toward the radio.

22   "Here's the referee. He's counting. One, two, three, four, five, six, seven . . . Is the contender trying to get up again?"

23   All the men in the Store shouted, "NO."

24   "—eight, nine, ten." There were a few sounds from the audience, but they seemed to be holding themselves in against tremendous pressure.

25   "The fight is all over, ladies and gentlemen. Let's get the microphone over to the referee . . . Here he is. He's got the Brown Bomber's hand, he's holding it up . . . Here he is . . ."

26   Then the voice, husky and familiar, came to wash over us—"The winnah, and still heavyweight champeen of the world . . . Joe Louis."

27   Champion of the world. A Black boy. Some Black mother's son. He was the strongest man in the world. People drank Coca-Colas like ambrosia° and ate candy bars like Christmas. Some of the men went behind the Store and poured white lightning in their soft-drink bottles, and a few of the bigger boys followed them. Those who were not chased away came back blowing their breath in front of themselves like proud smokers.

28   It would take an hour or more before the people would leave the Store and head for home. Those who lived too far had made arrangements to stay in town. It wouldn't do for a Black man and his family to be caught on a lonely country road on a night when Joe Louis had proved that we were the strongest people in the world.

Vocabulary

3 cracker (n, slang): white man from southern United States

17 ordain (v): order or establish by authority

17 hewers (n): those who cut wood or chop down trees

27 ambrosia (n): food of the gods, a treat

RESPONDING TO THE READING

- If the thesis is stated, identify it; if it is implied, write it in your own words.
- What do you think is the purpose of this essay? Give reasons for your opinion.
- Who do you think is the intended audience of this essay? Give reasons for your opinion.

Comprehension

1. How does Maya Angelou set the scene to let readers know this is an important event?
2. The events of the story are interspersed with dialogue. What is the effect of the dialogue on the telling of the story?
3. Explain the reference to "their 'master's voice.'"
4. What is the dramatic effect Angelou creates by describing the people's reactions to the radio commentary on the Joe Louis fight?
5. How many stories are actually told here? Identify each one.
6. "The real festivities . . . Baby Ruths also." Explain the irony in this passage.
7. In the paragraph beginning "My race groaned," Angelou uses parallel structure: "It was. . . ." What is the effect of this?

8. What are the implications of the phrase "hewers of wood and drawers of water, forever and ever, world without end"? What does the phrase allude to?
9. A lot of brand names of products are included in the story. What do these tell you about the young narrator?
10. What is the reaction of the crowd in the store to the Brown Bomber's victory?

Analysis

1. Joe Louis became a symbol for his people. What passages or single details demonstrate this in the story?
2. What are the people in the store really like? What is their social standing? What are their fears and dreams? What is their daily life like? Base your answer on the details Angelou provides.
3. What does the store represent to the people in the story?
4. Angelou presents this narrative based on her own childhood memories. She shapes those memories for a definite purpose. What is it and how successful is she?
5. Discuss the irony in the final paragraph.

Discussion/Writing Suggestions

1. Write a simple narrative about a series of events that had several meanings for you. For example, write about your high school graduation but point out how the actions in that story had broader implications in your life.
2. Discuss the importance of a "hero" or a role model in a person's life.

   • Other essays that focus on racial discrimination are those by Malcolm X (p. 19), Ralph Nader (p. 28), Wayson Choy (p. 169), and Derek Cohen (p. 173); and those that reflect on memories are by Timothy Findley (p. 92), Michael Dorris (p. 208), Wayson Choy (p. 169), and Rosie DiManno (p. 211).

"But a Watch in the Night": A Scientific Fable

James C. Rettie

James C. Rettie (1904–1969) was an American natural resources economist. He attended graduate school at Yale University and at the London School of Economics. His first major professional assignment was with the National Resources Planning Board in Portland, Oregon. He was then chief of the Alaska Office of NRPB from 1940 to 1943. His last position at the time of his death in 1969 was economic adviser to the Secretary of the Interior in Washington, D.C. He had held that post since the beginning of the Kennedy administration. While in the federal government service from 1935 to 1969, he wrote many papers and studies, only a few of which bore his name as author.

In 1948, while Rettie was working at the Forest Experiment Station in Upper Darby, he wrote and published this "little essay" for which he has become famous. This remarkable essay appeared in a book called The Land *and was the cover story of a popular magazine of the day under the title "The Greatest Movie Ever Made." It has been published over the years in collections of essays and notable writings and is often used in writing classes. Science fiction writing and movies often present an implicit criticism of our society by comparing it to an imagined alien culture. James C. Rettie sets his essay within that framework. The title is taken from the Bible, Psalm 90, and thus it is an allusion.*

1   Out beyond our solar system there is a planet called Copernicus*. It came into existence some four or five billion years before the birth of our Earth. In due course of time it became inhabited by a race of intelligent men.

2   About 750 million years ago the Copernicans had developed the motion picture machine to a point well in advance of the stage that we have reached. Most of the cameras that we now use in motion picture work are geared to take twenty-four pictures per second on a continuous strip of film. When such film is run through a projector, it throws a series of images on the screen and these change with a rapidity that gives the visual impression of normal movement. If a motion is too swift for the human eye to see it in detail, it can be captured and artificially slowed down by means of the slow-motion camera. This one is geared to take many more shots per second—ninety-six or even more than that. When the slow-motion film is projected at the normal speed of twenty-four pictures per second, we can see just how the jumping horse goes over a hurdle.

3   What about motion that is too slow to be seen by the human eye? That problem has been solved by the use of the time-lapse camera. In this one, the shutter is geared to take only one shot per second, or one per minute, or even one per hour—depending upon the kind of movement that is being photographed. When the time-lapse film is projected at the normal speed of twenty-four pictures per second, it is possible to see a bean sprout growing up out of the ground. Time-lapse films are useful in the study of many types of motion too slow to be observed by the unaided, human eye.

4   The Copernicans, it seems, had time-lapse cameras some 757 million years ago and they also had superpowered telescopes that gave them a clear view of what was happening upon this Earth. They decided to make a film record of the life history of Earth and to make it on the scale of one picture per year. The photography has been in progress during the last 757 million years.

5   In the near future, a Copernican interstellar° expedition will arrive upon our Earth and bring with it a copy of the time-lapse film. Arrangements will be made for showing the entire film in one continuous run. This will begin at midnight of New Year's Eve and continue day and night without a single stop until midnight of December 31. The rate of projection will be twenty-four pictures per second. Time on the screen will thus seem to move at the rate of twenty-four years per second; 1440 years per minute, 86,400 years per hour; approximately two million years per day; and sixty-two million years per month. The normal life-span of individual man will occupy about three seconds. The full period of earth history that will be unfolded on the screen (some 757 million years) will extend from what the geologists

call Pre-Cambrian times up to the present. This will, by no means, cover the full time-span of the earth's geological history but it will embrace the period since the advent of living organisms.

6   During the months of January, February, and March the picture will be desolate and dreary. The shape of the land masses and the oceans will bear little or no resemblance to those that we know. The violence of geological erosion° will be much in evidence. Rains will pour down on the land and promptly go booming down to the seas. There will be no clear streams anywhere except where the rains fall upon hard rock. Everywhere on the steeper ground the stream channels will be filled with boulders hurled down by rushing waters. Raging torrents° and dry stream beds will keep alternating in quick succession. High mountains will seem to melt like so much butter in the sun. The shifting of land into the seas, later to be thrust up as new mountains, will be going on at a grand scale.

7   Early in April there will be some indication of the presence of single-celled living organisms in some of the warmer and sheltered coastal waters. By the end of the month it will be noticed that some of these organisms have become multi-cellular. A few of them, including the Trilobites, will be encased in hard shells.

8   Toward the end of May, the first vertebrates° will appear, but they will still be aquatic creatures. In June about 60 per cent of the land area that we know as North America will be under water. One broad channel will occupy the space where the Rocky Mountains now stand. Great deposits of limestone will be forming under some of the shallower seas. Oil and gas deposits will be in the process of formation—also under shallow seas. On land there will still be no sign of vegetation. Erosion will be rampant°, tearing loose particles and chunks of rock and grinding them into sand and silt to be spewed out by the streams into bays and estuaries.

9   About the middle of July the first land plants will appear and take up the tremendous job of soil building. Slowly, very slowly, the mat of vegetation will spread, always battling for its life against the power of erosion. Almost foot by foot, the plant life will advance, lacing down with its root structures whatever pulverized° rock material it can find. Leaves and stems will be giving added protection against the loss of the soil foothold. The increasing vegetation will pave the way for the land animals that will live upon it.

10   Early in August the seas will be teeming° with fish. This will be what geologists call the Devonian period. Some of the races of these fish will be breathing by means of lung tissue instead of through gill tissues. Before the month is over, some of the lung fish will go ashore and take on a crude lizard-like appearance. Here are the first amphibians.

11   In early September the insects will put in their appearance. Some will look like huge dragonflies and will have a wing spread of 24 inches. Large portions of the land masses will now be covered with heavy vegetation that will include the primitive spore-propagating trees. Layer upon layer of this plant growth will build up, later to appear as the coal deposits. About the middle of this month, there will be evidence of the first seed-bearing plants and the first reptiles. Heretofore, the land animals will have been amphibians that could reproduce their kind only by depositing a soft egg mass in quiet waters. The reptiles will be shown to be freed from the aquatic bond because they can reproduce by means of a shelled egg in

which the embryo and its nurturing liquids are sealed and thus protected from destructive evaporation. Before September is over, the first dinosaurs will be seen—creatures destined to dominate the animal realm for about 140 million years and then to disappear.

12   In October there will be series of mountain uplifts along what is now the eastern coast of the United States. A creature with feathered limbs—half bird and half reptile in appearance—will take itself into the air. Some small and rather unpretentious animals will be seen to bring forth their young in a form that is a miniature replica of the parents and to feed these young on milk secreted by mammary glands in the female parent. The emergence of this mammalian form of animal life will be recognized as one of the great events in geologic time. October will also witness the high water mark of the dinosaurs—creatures ranging in size from that of the modern goat to monsters like Brontosaurus that weighed some 40 tons. Most of them will be placid vegetarians, but a few will be hideous°-looking carnivores, like Allosaurus and Tyrannosaurus. Some of the herbivorous dinosaurs will be clad in bony armor for protection against their flesh-eating comrades.

13   November will bring pictures of a sea extending from the Gulf of Mexico to the Arctic in space now occupied by the Rocky Mountains. A few of the reptiles will take to the air on bat-like wings. One of these, called Pteranodon, will have a wing-spread of 15 feet. There will be a rapid development of the modern flowering plants, modern trees, and modern insects. The dinosaurs will disappear. Toward the end of the month there will be a tremendous land disturbance in which the Rocky Mountains will rise out of the sea to assume a dominating place in the North American landscape.

14   As the picture runs on into December it will show the mammals in command of the animal life. Seed-bearing trees and grasses will have covered most of the land with a heavy mantle° of vegetation. Only the areas newly thrust up from the sea will be barren. Most of the streams will be crystal clear. The turmoil of geologic erosion will be confined to localized areas. About December 25 will begin the cutting of the Grand Canyon of the Colorado River. Grinding down through layer after layer of sedimentary strata, this stream will finally expose deposits laid down in Pre-Cambrian times. Thus in the walls of that canyon will appear geological formations dating from recent times to the period when the Earth had no living organisms upon it.

15   The picture will run on through the latter days of December and even up to its final day with still no sign of mankind. The spectators will become alarmed in the fear that man has somehow been left out. But not so; sometime about noon on December 31 (one million years ago) will appear a stooped, massive creature of man-like proportions. This will be Pithecanthropus, the Java ape man. For tools and weapons he will have nothing but crude stone and wooden clubs. His children will live a precarious° existence threatened on the one side by hostile animals and on the other by tremendous climatic changes. Ice sheets—in places 4000 feet deep—will form in the northern parts of North America and Eurasia. Four times this glacial ice will push southward to cover half the continents. With each advance the plant and animal life will be swept under or pushed southward. With each recession of the ice, life will struggle to re-establish itself in the wake of the retreating glaciers. The woolly mammoth, the musk ox, and the caribou all will fight to maintain

themselves near the ice line. Sometimes they will be caught and put into cold storage—skin, flesh, blood, bones and all.

16   The picture will run on through supper time with still very little evidence of man's presence on the Earth. It will be about 11 o'clock when Neanderthal man appears. Another half hour will go by before the appearance of Cro-Magnon man living in caves and painting crude animal pictures on the walls of his dwelling. Fifteen minutes more will bring Neolithic man, knowing how to chip stone and thus produce sharp cutting edges for spears and tools. In a few minutes more it will appear that man has domesticated the dog, the sheep and, possibly, other animals. He will then begin the use of milk. He will also learn the arts of basket weaving and the making of pottery and dugout canoes.

17   The dawn of civilization will not come until about five or six minutes before the end of the picture. The story of the Egyptians, the Babylonians, the Greeks, and the Romans will unroll during the fourth, the third, and the second minute before the end. At 58 minutes and 43 seconds past 11:00 PM (just 1 minute and 17 seconds before the end) will come the beginning of the Christian era. Columbus will discover the new world 20 seconds before the end. The Declaration of Independence will be signed just 7 seconds before the final curtain comes down.

18   In those few moments of geologic time will be the story of all that has happened since we became a nation. And what a story it will be! A human swarm will sweep across the face of the continent and take it away from the . . . red men. They will change it far more radically than it has ever been changed before in a comparable time. The great virgin forests will be seen going down before ax and fire. The soil, covered for eons by its protective mantle of trees and grasses, will be laid bare to the ravages of water and wind erosion. Streams that had been flowing clear will, once again, take up a load of silt and push it toward the seas. Humus° and mineral salts, both vital elements of productive soil, will be seen to vanish at a terrifying rate. The railroads and highways and cities that will spring up may divert attention, but they cannot cover up the blight of man's recent activities. In great sections of Asia, it will be seen that man must utilize cow dung and every scrap of available straw or grass for fuel to cook his food. The forests that once provided wood for this purpose will be gone without a trace. The use of these agricultural wastes for fuel, in place of returning them to the land, will be leading to increasing soil impoverishment°. Here and there will be seen a dust storm darkening the landscape over an area a thousand miles across. Man-creatures will be shown counting their wealth in terms of bits of printed paper representing other bits of a scarce but comparatively useless yellow metal that is kept buried in strong vaults°. Meanwhile, the soil, the only real wealth that can keep mankind alive on the face of this earth, is savagely being cut loose from its ancient moorings° and washed into the seven seas.

19   We have just arrived upon this earth. How long will we stay?

Note

1 Copernicus (1473–1543): Polish astronomer, famous for theory of a solar system; i.e., planet in orbit around the sun

Vocabulary

5 interstellar (adj): between stars

6 erosion (n): wearing away of rock by wind, water or ice

6 torrents (n): fast and powerful rush of water

8 vertebrates (n): creatures with segmented backbones and developed brains

8 rampant (adj): happening in a wild manner, usually a menace

9 pulverize (v): crush to powder

10 teem (v): be full of a large number of creatures

12 hideous (adj): horrible to see

14 mantle (n): covering that envelops

15 precarious (adj): unsafe, unstable

18 humus (n): organic component of soil

18 impoverishment (n): to make something or someone poor

18 vaults (n): strengthened room for valuables

18 moorings (n): place for securing boat or ship

RESPONDING TO THE READING

- If the thesis is stated, identify it; if it is implied, write it in your own words.
- What do you think is the purpose of this essay? Give reasons for your opinion.
- Who do you think is the intended audience of this essay? Give reasons for your opinion.

Comprehension

1. How many paragraphs does James Rettie use for his introduction? Why does he need so many?
2. What process is explained in Paragraphs 2 and 3?
3. How many years of earth time are compressed into the Copernican movie and how long does the movie actually last?
4. The body of this essay is a process analysis. What process is analyzed?
5. What happens in the movie from January to August?
6. In the movie, what is remarkable about October?
7. In this movie, what is significant about December 25?
8. On what date and at what time do humans first appear in this movie?
9. At what time does human civilization begin?
10. What is significant about 11:58:43 p.m. on December 31? How is this event ironic?
11. What is described in Paragraph 18?
12. "We have only just arrived upon this earth." How has Rettie supported this final statement in his essay?

Analysis

1. What analogy does Rettie exploit in this essay?
2. What does Rettie say is the only real wealth of the earth? Why does he make this claim?
3. What relationship does Rettie establish between geologic time and the final seven seconds?
4. Why does Rettie spend so much time describing the earth's evolution before turning to his "real" subject (civilization)?
5. Rettie's conclusion is contained in two short sentences. How do they relate to the implied thesis?
6. Is Rettie's last question a rhetorical question?
7. Explain the effectiveness of the allusion in "Copernicus," the name Rettie gives to the planet.
8. Rettie is an American writing for an American audience. How can you tell this from his essay?
9. Consider the source of the first part of Rettie's title. How does the title relate to his content?
10. What images are conjured up by the title?

Discussion/Writing Suggestions

1. How is this essay a fable? What lesson can readers learn from?
2. This essay was written in 1948. Does its date surprise you? Why or why not? The essay has never been out of print since then. Explain the popularity of this essay.

    *   Other essays that focus on environmental issues include the ones by David Suzuki (p. 88), Rachel Carson (p. 123), Sean Twist (p. 147), Catherine George (p. 194), and Margaret Laurence (p. 202).

Essay of Argument and Persuasion

Argument and persuasion is a distinct rhetorical mode: all writers of argument and persuasion pieces share the express purpose of influencing readers by effecting a change, not only in their opinions and beliefs, but also in their attitudes and actions.

An **argument** normally refers to a piece of writing that forms and states a reasoned position based on the author's supporting evidence. For examples of argument, read Ruth Grogan's essay, "Playing the Piano: Body, Embodiment, and Gender," and Almas Zakiuddin's piece called "Rediscovering Christmas." Both writers conclude their essays with a position that has been supported by personal experience and careful reasoning.

Persuasion is slightly different. It involves further efforts to convince the readers to join the authors in pursuing a proposed course of action. For this reason, writers in their persuasive mood tend to use sentences beginning with "we should . . ." or "we must . . ." to call on the reader to take action.

Many writers, however, choose to use both argument and persuasion together. When you read the pieces by Sang Il Lee, Northrop Frye, and Carol Shields, you will see that they both *argue* and *persuade*. Thus, argument and persuasion, like comparison and contrast, can be used separately or together.

The writer's purpose determines the nature of a piece of writing and marks the real difference between argument and persuasion and other types of essays. It is true that other kinds of writing, especially exposition, often include an element of argument and persuasion. Think about "A Fable for Tomorrow" by Rachel Carson (p. 123) and "Dispatches from the Poverty Line" by Pat Capponi (p. 158). However, for an essay to be truly *argumentative and persuasive*, the author's major purpose has to be to argue or persuade rather than to inform or entertain. For example, in "Smoking Is Good for My Business," David Ginsburg (p. 33) attempts to persuade readers against smoking through his anecdotal evidence, which argues smoking has harmful social and personal consequences. You can test all the essays collected in this chapter against that "touchstone" and see how their emphases are different from expository, descriptive, and narrative writings.

In order to achieve their purposes, writers use a variety of patterns of development. For example, one may begin an essay with narration, as Almas Zakiuddin does in "Rediscovering Christmas," or perhaps they switch to description in the middle paragraphs, as the essays by Ruth Grogan and Carol Shields demonstrate. Regardless of their topics, styles, and approaches, writers all present examples, sometimes get into the mood of process analysis, and freely make use of causal analysis (e.g., Sang Il Lee), comparison and contrast (e.g., Carol Shields), classification (e.g., Amartya Sen), and definition (e.g., Northrop Frye) to help them to deliver and argue their points.

Give Frye's essay a careful reading (p. 244) and then return to this page to follow this critical discussion about it.

Frye's argument is meticulously built on logical reasoning. After presenting the issue—high school students' confusion about the interrelationship between *language, reading and writing* and *thinking*—in the first three paragraphs, Frye points out in Paragraph 4 the different meanings of *thinking,* one of the three key phrases introduced in the beginning paragraphs. In Paragraph 5 he links *thinking* to *language,* another word crucial to his argument, by stating that "[t]here is no such thing as an inarticulate idea waiting to have the right words wrapped around it." Paragraphs 6 and 7 then proceed to provide a clear definition of *thinking* and a further connection between *thinking* and words (*language*).

Paragraph 8 places the issue in the context of Canadian society and its lack of interest in *literacy,* a word that encompasses *language, reading and writing,* and *thinking*. Further social observations are made in Paragraph 9 when Frye zeroes in on "strong currents at work against the development of articulateness" and young adolescents' antipathy toward "speaking articulately." Paragraphs 10 and 11 consist of a cogent causal analysis that paves the way for the essay's persuasive conclusion. In Frye's words, the two major causes behind the widespread lack of "verbal competency" are "the powerful anti-intellectual drive which is constantly present in our society" and the "various epidemics sweeping over society which use unintelligibility as a weapon to preserve the present power structure." By alluding to George

Orwell, he finally points out the close link between language and politics as he brings his argument to an insightful climax at the end of Paragraph 11: "The kernel of everything reactionary and tyrannical in society is the impoverishment of the means of verbal communication." By this point, the importance of "powers of articulateness" has been fully emphasized.

It might be hard for you to see the connection between *language, reading and writing,* and *thinking* and politics at first. However, if you follow Frye's reasoning closely, the logical links between these concepts display themselves step by step as every paragraph unfolds. That is the magic of clear logical reasoning.

By switching to a persuasive pitch, Frye brings the essay to a forceful close in the last two paragraphs. He first identifies his major targets as "prejudices and clichés" and "verbal formulas that have no thought behind them but are put up as pretense of thinking" in Paragraph 12. Then in the last paragraph he directly calls on teachers (who are obviously part of his intended audience) to "fight against illiteracy and for the maturation of the mental process," thus tying the final paragraph with the key word in his title—thinking. The predominant imagery in the ending paragraph is unmistakably militant—Frye keenly urges educators, especially teachers of humanities, to take up arms against the "pretense of thinking."

Now that we have clarified that boundaries between different rhetorical modes and organizational patterns are not there to confine writers to any type of writing, we need to point out that because of its special purpose, an effective essay of argument and persuasion requires the writer to pay special attention to certain rules besides the same principles that govern effective writing in general.

Writing Strategy

1. Choose a topic that is worth arguing for or against. Remember: you cannot argue about facts, only about opinions; that is, about how the facts should be interpreted. Try to avoid arguing about matters of personal taste or preference, but do make sure you care about the subject, or that you have some personal opinion to express about it.

2. Have in your mind a clear concept of who your intended readers are, how much they know about your topic, and what stand they likely take on the issue. These are the important factors that will help you choose your approach, level of language, and tone, all of which are essential to the success of your essay.

   Understanding who the readers are enables the writer to anticipate their responses to the proposed argument, and to decide on how to appeal to their *heads* as well as to their *hearts* by presenting the right kind of evidence at the right time and in the right order. In her essay "The Case for Curling Up with a Book," for example, Carol Shields argues for focused reading and persuades readers to renew their interest in literature and "print on the page" in general by appealing to both their intellect and their emotions. Examine the essay closely and find out how both your *head* and *heart* are called into action to respond to Shields's passionate argument and persuasion.

3. Select specific and convincing examples to support your thesis. Do some research on your topic if possible. Argument and persuasion writing often poses a daunting challenge to writers in training because this kind of writing demands that the writer arrange the well-selected supporting details in an almost seamless order so as to convince the reader of the position that is being advocated or argued for. Indeed, the key to successful argument and persuasion writing lies in how the author provides concrete, specific, precise, and convincing evidence to win over the reader.

For example, if you took away the abundance of concrete and convincing examples and factual data, Amartya Sen's argument against the theory on "clashing civilizations" would carry no weight in spite of his fame and the serious issue he deals with. Similarly, the essays by Frye and Shields would not make as big an impact on the reader, despite their status as big names in the literary world, if their arguments for literacy and literature were not properly supported. They both select and order valid and significant evidence to enhance the power of their arguments.

4. A clear thesis acts as the focal point that holds all parts of the essay together, and the principles of unity and coherence should be carefully practised. Write a clear thesis statement that reflects your major argument and, if possible, includes your supporting arguments.

5. Write an outline or the first draft to find out the most effective and logical way to present your argument.

6. Revise and edit your essay to ensure strong logical reasoning and avoid fallacies.

Unity and Coherence

As with the other rhetorical modes and patterns of development, unity and coherence form two essential components of a successful essay. In an essay of argument and persuasion, they are achieved by paying careful attention to logical reasoning, induction and deduction, and refutation.

Logical Reasoning: As you will notice in the following essays, writers organize their supporting details in whatever order they see fit for developing their arguments. For instance, Sang Il Lee, the student writer, decides to arrange the three supporting arguments in a climactic order, moving from the basic human expectations of nature to moral and ethical values associated with nature. Almas Zakiuddin, on the other hand, chooses chronological order to lead the reader through her personal search for the new meaning of Christmas. Nevertheless, most writers, like Ruth Grogan, Northrop Frye, Carol Shields, and Amartya Sen, opt to develop their argument and persuasion in logical order by showing the reader how one idea leads to another and finally to the author's point, the inevitable conclusion derived from clear logical reasoning.

Induction and Deduction: As two principal methods of reasoning, induction and deduction are used separately or in combination in argument and persuasion. Knowing how each works will help you read more analytically and write more effectively.

Inductive reasoning argues from the particular to the general, using specific examples to support a general proposition. This type of reasoning is often called the *scientific method* and is commonly used in lab experiments, mathematical problem solving, etc. To make sure your inductive reasoning is sound, you must provide solid and sufficient evidence, as induction depends on facts and reliable supporting information.

Deductive reasoning argues from the general to the particular. It begins with facts or generally accepted assumptions or principles and applies them to specific instances. For example, we all know that nonrenewable energy sources, such as oil and other forms of fossil fuels, will presumably be depleted someday and that the world's energy needs are increasing every day. Based on these facts, we come to the conclusion that it is extremely important for us to conserve our limited resources and develop alternative sources of energy. In many senses, deductive reasoning forms the basis for causal analysis, one of the most useful methods in logical reasoning.

Induction and deduction often work together in argument and persuasion. For example, you use induction to establish the general proposition of the harmful effects that smoking has on health. Then you implicitly turn to deduction, using that proposition as the basis for your conclusion: Smoking is harmful to health; therefore, smokers must quit smoking. David Ginsburg manipulates this pattern in his essay, "Smoking Is Good for My Business" (p. 33) so cleverly that he is able to leave it unsaid and allow the readers, including those who smoke, to arrive at the conclusion that smokers should stop smoking. Think about the many examples, anecdotes, and allusions used in, say, the essays by Sen and Frye, which work either inductively or deductively to support the two authors' reasoning. To figure out how the two methods are intermingled, you may want to read those two essays again.

Refutation: Sometimes a writer writes an essay of argument and persuasion primarily to refute or to rebut (to argue against) a statement or theory by proving that it is not true or fair. This type of argument is called refutation. It can take the form of a whole essay, a paragraph, or part of an essay. Refutations normally involve using either or both of these two strategies:

1.   Present opposite or contradictory evidence to show the theory is untrue, and
2.   Point out inadequate or illogical reasoning to prove the theory is faulty and invalid.

In general refutations give you the opportunity to hone your skills in logical reasoning through counterargument.

"A World Not Neatly Divided" by Amartya Sen serves as a typical example of refutation. Notice how Sen uses "heavy ammunition" in the first paragraph by accusing those who classify the world population according to "civilizational categories" of missing the central issue and basing their theory on inadequate, crude, and inconsistent factors. Then he proceeds to back up all his accusations or refutational arguments with specific examples and facts. Step by step, from Paragraph 2 to Paragraph 6, he thoroughly reveals the inadequacy and coarseness of civilizational categories, such as "Hindu civilization," "the Islam world," and "the Western world," and scathingly refutes the theory on "clashing civilizations." After all that, Sen pronounces his belief in "the plurality of our identities," *his* theory for a harmonious world, when the reader is ready.

Since logical reasoning is of prime importance to argument and persuasion writing, it is helpful if you know some basic concepts related to logic. However, if you find the following terms and explanations confusing, skip the following section. You can learn more about these concepts by searching on the Internet or consulting a traditional reference tool like a specialized dictionary or a writer's handbook.

Common Logical Fallacies

A **fallacy** is a false idea or an illogical way of reasoning. To know what a fallacy is and how it distorts or destroys logical reasoning is helpful in your writing and thinking. You will not only be aware of the possible pitfalls in composing your own argument and persuasion pieces, but you will also be able to spot loopholes in other people's writings, placing you in a stronger position for counterargument.

Here are a few common fallacies:

Ad hominem or **Attacking the person**: Making personal, even untrue, remarks about a person rather than presenting a reasoned argument.

Example: All politicians are self-serving and corrupt, so [insert your chosen politician's name] can't be trusted to do any good for the people of Canada.

Ad populum or **Bandwagon**: Appealing to popular prejudices, fears, or feelings irrelevant to the issue often by using vague and unexamined popular feelings about religion, patriotism, tradition, etc. The stereotypical or bandwagon approach claims mass appeal and associates it with virtue or correctness—if so many people are doing this or thinking this way, it must be good or true.

Example: Everyone knows that the Chinese are the worst drivers on the road.

Begging the question or **Circular reasoning**: Assuming the truth of a questionable opinion by restating it rather than providing reasonable evidence to support it.

Example: The rich should pay more taxes because taxes should be higher for people who are wealthy.

Hasty generalization: Jumping to a conclusion based on weak or inadequate evidence.

Example: Global warming is a reality because temperatures across North America last year exceeded the fifty-year average by two degrees.

Non sequitur or **Unclear reasoning**: *Non sequitur* is a Latin term meaning "it does not follow." The term could apply to any of the fallacies listed above or any conclusion that does not logically follow from the evidence presented.

Example: I've put a great deal of time and effort into this project; my grade should reflect that fact.

Now read the essay "Our Earthly Fate" by Sang Il Lee and see how he *argues* and *persuades* on a popular issue. Identify what makes his argument interesting and convincing.

SAMPLE STUDENT ESSAY

Our Earthly Fate

Sang Il Lee

1   Long gone are the days when human beings could pursue their hopes and dreams of collective advancement without any worry about what their goals might entail other than the power of imagination. With our unhindered and often careless march toward progress, we have finally hit upon a barrier. Although science has given us the potential to relieve much suffering and grief, human beings have transformed that potential to unfortunate environmental degradation, disease, and quite possibly, total annihilation of the world. Rachel Carson in her essay, "A Fable for Tomorrow" (1962), signalled the warning of a chemical devastation of our environment, the likes of which we have never seen. She lamented the general attitude of people who saw nature as something to be exploited and used without limit, an attitude that still persists today. Although thankfully the scenario that Rachel Carson depicted has been avoided, we might still be following that same doomed path, albeit in slow motion. Complacency may yet accelerate this process so the words of Rachel Carson resound strongly today. To avoid this seemingly inevitable movement toward environmental, and consequently, human destruction, we must change our attitude toward nature with respect to the resources it provides, the environment it creates, and the intangible values we attach to the earth.

2   Historically, human populations have been small enough and technology much too primitive to allow all the burning, extracting, and plowing of the land to reach a level to affect the earth as a whole. The material need of human beings could be more than satisfied by the abundant resources of the earth. However, as the human population increased and technology improved in an exponential fashion, the earth started to become much smaller. We now have the potential to alter drastically the chemical and physical landscape of the earth, and with this power comes the necessity to think in sustainable terms of our earthly resources. Rivers and lakes will no longer flow with clean water unless we all guard them against pollution. This means regulating, and punishing those that defile our water without considering the subsequent economic losses. The same goes for our soil and air. Sacrifice must be made by everyone with a clear realization that if our resources are lost to pollution, mismanagement, or whatever it may be, we will all lose in the end.

3   The promotion of a more sustainable future for the environment must also require a shift in our attitude about geography. Especially when dealing with the issue of global warming, it is necessary to think beyond personal or nationalistic interests and act in global terms. The saying that we are all in the same boat is true enough when it comes to the climate crisis we are now facing. A person living in a northern climate who welcomes the news of rising temperatures is in fact tacitly approving the possible and uncountable deaths caused by famine, flooding or

drought, and other adverse effects of global warming in other parts of the world. Instability in one region of the world, especially in the third-world countries where global warming will have the greatest effect, will mean instability elsewhere. Instead of simply focusing on seeking solutions to the climate changes in their own nations, the Western World must also realize that they have the responsibility to help the third-world countries fix the climate problem, the cause of which is largely theirs.

4   A fundamental shift in attitude toward the tangible parts of our earth may ultimately depend on whether we can draw a more intimate connection with earth. I believe the determination and persistence necessary to truly reverse the course toward environmental degradation can only come from a love and respect for what feeds and sustains us. A human connection with nature on the emotional level will guard against complacency and gather the strength necessary to launch an effective attack against the destruction of our environment. Of course, since this change of attitude is solely up to each individual, the fate of the earth may depend on the discovery of our true human nature.

5   Mother Nature, being the unfailing provider of resources and living environment necessary for our existence, deserves our love, care, and respect. History has proved that any shortsighted move that is made for the benefit of a limited number of people within a limited time and space can only result in irreversible damage to the earth. Take the atrocious deforestation across the world as an example. Trees that took thousands of years to grow were destroyed within a few minutes, ironically with the help of modern tools. For sure, short-term needs are satisfied and huge profits have been gained, but the human losses are immeasurable when the century-old ecosystems dwindle and disappear. We are fast approaching the time when we should make decisions on our own path forward. Hopefully we will make the right choice, for our earth and for ourselves.

Comprehension

1. What is the thesis statement in this essay? Identify the focused subject and its key ideas.
2. How is this thesis linked to the opening ideas in the essay?
3. In what order are the supporting arguments arranged?
4. How are the three body paragraphs linked?
5. What is the author's attitude toward the earth and nature? Provide evidence for your answer.
6. How does the conclusion relate to the thesis?
7. Is the title appropriate for the essay? Why or why not?
8. Does Lee try to persuade the reader to take action for the sake of earth? If yes, at what point of his essay and how?

Analysis

1. The author uses a number of examples in the essay to support his argument. Could you find at least five of them?
2. "With our unhindered and often careless march toward progress, we have finally hit upon a barrier." The word "barrier" is used metaphorically here. What is Lee referring to by it?
3. Do you think Sang Il Lee is successful in supporting his thesis? Why or why not?
4. What is your opinion of this essay as a piece of argument and persuasion? Be prepared to support your response.

READINGS: ESSAYS OF ARGUMENT AND PERSUASION

The following five essays represent the basic types of argument and persuasion essays. The essays by Ruth Grogan and Almas Zakiuddin are primarily argument pieces in which the writers are not particularly interested in persuading the reader to share their opinions or take any further action. Once their arguments are clearly presented, the authors feel their purposes are achieved. In contrast, Northrop Frye and Carol Shields both intend to persuade the reader to act on their belief as much as they intend to argue for those ideas. Theirs are essays more concerned with social issues than with personal experience and inner feelings. The essay by Amartya Sen, on the other hand, presents a good example of refutation, an effort to counterargue an existing theory by pointing out its inadequacy and loopholes. Each of these essays is well organized and skillfully written; together they will expose you to an array of styles, approaches, and tones in essays of argument and persuasion.

Playing the Piano: Body, Embodiment, and Gender

Ruth Grogan

Ruth Grogan (1939–) was a professor of English at York University with her main interests being in modern and contemporary poetry. As a dedicated teacher of literature, Grogan always tried to instill in her students a true love for literature because "a liberal arts education," she believes, "and the study of literature in particular, is about more than simply getting a job; it makes you open to life. . . . You become a person of great sensitivity to everything going on around you and inside you." Her service to York University includes time spent as associate dean in the Faculty of Arts, Chair of the Faculty of Arts Council, and Chair of the Senate. After teaching for 36 years, she retired in 2004. Since then, she says, she "has changed course and become dedicated to playing the piano."

She wrote the following essay in 2006 at the request of a friend, an editor of a women's studies publication. In this "personal and non-scholarly essay," Grogan reflects on her new life interest and presents an argument on its gender implications.

1   Two years ago, having retired from the York English Department, I returned to playing the piano. Five decades had gone past during which I did no more than occasionally run my hands nostalgically and inexpertly across piano keys. Much joy has ensued—and many surprises. One major surprise is the degree to which playing the piano engages one's whole being—emotions, intellect, and body. The emotional and intellectual aspects I must have experienced fifty years ago: as a child, I loved playing, I don't recall having to be coaxed° or scolded° into practising, and my old conservatory books have pencilled evidence of analysis of Bach inventions and fugues°. So, returning to the piano, I expected to recover and intensify the emotional and intellectual satisfactions I'd experienced long ago. What I didn't expect was the sheer physical engagement.

2   This sounds peculiar. Of course 50 years ago I "knew" that it was my body that sat on a piano bench and my fingers that made material contact with keys. But if anyone had asked me to say more about the body's role (and no one did) I think my teenage self might have said that the body is a sort of necessary but inconvenient bridge to the music, something you had to use and eventually transcend° (if you were a Glenn Gould*), even if it took years and years of intensive training. (I'm omitting the question of physical ears and the sensations of hearing, as another issue altogether.)

3   I am now conscious of how weightily and intrinsically° the body contributes to the Whole Piano-Playing Being. This realization comes, not through reading or thinking, but via a brilliant teacher's at-hand guidance. She demonstrates how the sound coming out of that big machine is characterised through and through by a body's different interactions with it. Eyes, for instance: playing with your eyes on the sheet music differs from playing blindfold, and playing with eyes on fingers and keyboard differs again. It is as if I must learn the same piece in three ways, using different parts of the brain. Fingers: the tone coming from the machine depends on how the cushion just behind the finger tip pulls on the key, or on how the finger tip springs up from the key, or even occasionally hits it a good bang. Hands: there are no muscles in the fingers, so it is muscles in the hands, forearms, shoulders, and back that determine the precise type of touch, and hence tone and volume. Posture: the body sits straight, head balanced on top, the position of pelvis°, back, and shoulders allowing for relaxation and power. If all goes well, I breathe and feel relaxed, and the energy flows into the key mechanisms with an audible° difference. It has been shown *to* me, and *through* me, that although hunching over the piano and flinging hair and arms about might be emotionally expressive, it is not musically expressive.

4   In addition to learning how to put kinetic°, muscular, and pressure sensations to musical work, there is the complication that verbal descriptions and prescriptions for the piano-playing body are often couched° in contradictory or paradoxical°

terms. Pressure on keys must be applied both gently and forcefully; muscles must feel loose and at the same energetically directed; whether the hand is still or moving, the wrist bones must always be in motion, like ball-bearings°; sometimes as an exercise I'm told to "fall into the piano," and yet not brace my hands for the falling, but rather simultaneously push the piano away from me and pull the keys towards myself! The end of a musical phrase may be a heard pause or it may be merely conceptual, significant in the performer's interpretation of a piece; either way the body must effect a renewed energy in the notes that follow. Each rendition° of a piece must feel and be heard as spontaneous° even though it is the result of long discipline and many repetitions. It seems impossible. And yet my body tries to do what my teacher says, and occasionally succeeds.

5   Feminists know that embodiment is engenderment, and especially perhaps for the sexual, child-bearing, athletic, diseased, adorned, embarrassed, pleasured bodies of women. I ask myself whether this is also true of the bodily practices of piano-playing—or of the female body practising. Music in its broad aspects is indeed connected with gender, and I can't begin to enumerate° the ways. Operatic stories depend on gendered, often stereotypical roles; the vocal production of men and women is different; until fairly recently composers and performers were almost always male. To focus on the piano specifically, it was the site in 19th and early 20th century middle-class households where young women demonstrated their accomplishments, and the wife and mother soothed and civilized her family. None of these facts seems relevant to the bodily experience I have just described. Other possible gender distinctions come to mind—do women piano players have the large muscular strength of most men? or do men have the fine motor and digital skills considered characteristically female?—but these distinctions are confounded by listening to distinguished contemporary pianists, male and female. Personally, as I practise, I feel enough muscular strength and stamina° to do the job, and I'm slowly developing the fine motor skills. What's difficult is to refine and channel what I have of both those micro-athletic capacities into music-making; and no doubt any man would feel the same.

6   I'm tempted on the basis of my own experience, and contrary to strong theories of gender that show it encoded° in almost any human activity, to say that the embodiment characteristic of piano-playing is not gendered. I might speculate further that the *Whole Piano-Playing Being,* emotional, intellectual, and embodied, is not gendered. Perhaps the luscious° liberation I feel in returning to the piano is at least partly a liberation from gender.

Note

2 Glenn Gould: accomplished Canadian pianist and composer (1932–1982)

Vocabulary

1 coax (v): to persuade someone to do something by talking in a kind and gentle way

1 scold (v): speak angrily, esp. to children when they do something wrong

1 fugue (n): a piece of music

2 transcend (v): go beyond the usual limits

3 intrinsically (adv): belonging to the real nature of something

3 pelvis (n): boney cavity formed by base of the spine and hips and connecting to legs

3 audible (adj): can be heard clearly

4 kinetic (adj): produced by movement

4 couch (v): say or write words in a particular style (sometimes used to imply that something is hidden or contained within something)

4 paradoxical (adj): containing two opposing ideas that make it seem impossible although it is probably true

4 ball-bearings (n): small metal balls used in a machine to enable the parts to turn smoothly

4 rendition (n): performance of a piece of music

4 spontaneous (adj): not planned but done because of sudden urge

5 enumerate (v): name or list things one by one

5 stamina (n): physical or mental strength that enables you to do something difficult for a long time

6 encode (v): program, embed

6 luscious (adj): having a rich pleasant taste

RESPONDING TO THE READING

- If the thesis is stated, identify it; if it is implied, write it in your own words.
- What do you think is the purpose of this essay? Give reasons for your opinion.
- Who do you think is the intended audience of this essay? Give reasons for your opinion.

Comprehension

1. What came as a total surprise to the author when she returned to piano playing after 50 years?
2. Which aspect of her engagement with the piano does Ruth Grogan focus on in the essay? Can you tell why after reading Paragraph 2?
3. Grogan describes how different parts of her body interact with the piano in Paragraph 3. In what order does she arrange her descriptive details?
4. In Paragraph 4, Grogan points out "the complication that verbal descriptions and prescriptions for the piano-playing body are often couched in contradictory or paradoxical terms." What examples does she use to support her observation? Identify them.
5. Is *engenderment* a word you could find in your dictionary? If not, guess its meaning.

6. Paragraph 5 marks the stage at which Grogan connects her bodily experience in piano playing with the gender issue—the real topic of her essay. How does she establish a logical connection?
7. Grogan agrees that "music in its broad aspects is indeed connected with gender" in Paragraph 5. What are the examples she uses to support that point?
8. How does she then argue for the opposite opinion that piano playing is free from engenderment?
9. What ideas does Grogan present in her concluding paragraph?

Analysis

1. Is the title appropriate for the essay? Why or why not?
2. What is the basis of Grogan's argument? Do you find her conclusion reasonable and convincing? Why or why not?
3. If you were to divide the essay into sections, how many sections would there be? Provide reasons for your decision.
4. Do you think Grogan's argument is presented in the most effective manner? Why or why not?
5. Does the author ever try to persuade the reader to act on her new discovery in the essay? If yes, at what point and how?
6. What level of language is used in the essay? Provide evidence for your answer.
7. Using three to five adjectives, describe the author's tone.

Discussion/Writing Suggestions

1. Ruth Grogan presents us with a typical example of personal essay in which the author explores the social implications of a personal experience. Write a personal essay modelled on Grogan's and present an opinion (argument) demonstrating how an experience has caused you to reflect on society or what you have unexpectedly learned from a particular experience.
2. Gender is a popular yet complicated issue in our society. Does it interest you? Write an essay to argue for or against the present-day discussion on a specific gender-related issue.

   • Other essays that relate personal experiences to social issues include those by Malcolm X (p. 19), David Ginsburg (p. 33), Timothy Findlay (p. 92), Sean Twist (p. 147), Judy Brady (p. 155), Pat Capponi (p. 158), Margaret Laurence (p. 202), Michael Dorris (p. 208), and Maya Angelou (p. 218).

Rediscovering Christmas

Almas Zakiuddin

Almas Zakiuddin (1949–) Almas Zakiuddin was born in Bangladesh in 1949 and moved to Canada in 1994. She spent her childhood in Dhaka, Bangladesh, and adolescence in Karachi, Pakistan. In the late 1970s, Almas moved with her husband and two sons to the United Arab Emirates where she worked for nearly two decades as a journalist and editor. As a CNN reporter, CBC Newsworld editor, and Gulf News *editor of Muslim background, she provides a unique perspective on the September 11 terrorist attacks on the World Trade Center. Almas teaches courses on Women and Media and Women and Islam at Simon Fraser University and Gender and Islam at UBC.*

This essay was originally published in the Globe and Mail *on December 23, 1999.*

1   It was my first winter in Toronto and so cold it froze the frown on my face. I frowned a lot in those days, before I rediscovered Christmas. Of course, I always knew about Christmas. I had read about it, even seen people celebrate Christmas. I was a typical convent-school-English-educated South Asian, brought up in a family that combined Muslim postcolonial nationalism with heady° tales of the good old British Raj°. Which meant that we used knives and forks at the table, but said our *isha* prayers before sitting down to dinner. I was (and still am) a Muslim.

2   Before I came to Canada, I was under the impression that I was not supposed to celebrate Christmas; it was not the done thing. I told no one, certainly not my parents, but once in a while I used to wonder: What if I had been born in a family that celebrated Christmas? Like the family of (let's call her) Jennifer McDonald.

3   I was 15 years old, a plump, pimply day student at a convent school for girls in Karachi, Pakistan. Jennifer McDonald was that kind of person known as an "anglo°," of mixed South Asian–British ancestry. She had golden-tan skin, light brown curly hair and hazel eyes. She wore lipstick (my mother said only "fast" girls wore lipstick), a skin-tight beige skirt, and an even tighter white blouse to school. I was made to wear a loose beige tunic, with baggy trousers called a *shalwar* and a white scarf.

4   Jennifer McDonald appeared at our end-of-term charity bazaar in the school gym in this incredible, short, fluffy, pink dress with frills that swished° when she moved. She flounced° to the centre of the room, tossed her curls, crossed her legs. "So what're yoa'll doin' fer Christmas, men?" she asked. ("Men" was a favourite term of endearment among anglos.) "I'm gonna have a bloody good time!" she laughed. ("Bloody" was another favourite anglo term.)

5   It was almost four decades later that I thought again about Jennifer McDonald. I was in a different country, almost a different civilization.

6   "And what are you doing for Christmas then?" asked the young woman at the corner store near my subway stop in Toronto. If I looked up in surprise it was because the young woman had not said a word to me in the six weeks I had been

patronizing her store. "Oh, Christmas . . . ? I don't know really. I'm . . . uh . . ." I mumbled, unsure of my plans. Someone wanted a jar of honey from the top shelf and the young woman disappeared. I wasn't sure why she had asked about my Christmas plans: It might have been because she wanted to be friendly.

7   It occurred to me, then, that people in Canada change during Christmas, becoming almost friendly. I mean, they talk to strangers, even smile at them, occasionally. All this in spite of the cold, the wind-chill factor (minus 24 that evening), and the reality that I was yet another addition to the swelling ranks of hyphenated, multicultural Canada.

8   In the next week or so, I found myself experiencing a different kind of Canada. There were new sounds, new sights, new smells, and new flavours, and they all connected, somehow, with Christmas. There were lights everywhere, there was mistletoe, decorations, tiny marzipan° angels, tinsel. There were stockings waiting to be filled and red bows for doorways, and a bright costume for the old man, Father Christmas, Santa Claus. There was an air of fun that had not existed before. Neighbours appeared where none had been noticeable before, inviting me into their homes, showing me their lights, their decorations, their preparations. I went and got my own lights and spent a weekend doing up my front window—my tiny apartment looked quite festive when they were on.

9   As the holiday season progressed, I watched the people around me, of all ages and backgrounds, people at the parties to which I was invited, people shopping, going to the cinema, ice skating, people at work. Everyone walked and talked with a little spring in their step. I turned on the radio, and the carols were beautiful, full of hope and joy. I quietly gave a few extra coins to an old man on the street, more conscious of the need to share the good things of life. Not a gloomy sign did I see anywhere in these otherwise dark and bitterly cold days in Canada. I stopped frowning all the time. There was something happening here, something that I had not seen before. People were participating in a festival that was universal—or could be, if we allowed ourselves to make it so.

10   And this is when I rediscovered Christmas. During my first winter in Canada, I realized that you don't have to be a Christian to celebrate Christmas. After all, Christmas hardly belongs exclusively to Christianity. By all accounts, the feast is originally pagan Roman, the tree of German innovation, the sleigh and reindeer Scandinavian. Santa himself is a mythical Nordic invention, the trimmings are now probably shipped from Bangladesh, and the carols recorded in Taiwan on digital equipment made in Hong Kong!

11   Christmas might trace some of its roots to an Anglo-Saxon heritage, but so do the days of the week, the English language, the pizza, and the ballpoint pen—all of which are pretty essential to my personal survival. It is as ludicrous° to expect me to forgo° any benefit from these things simply because their inventors were not of my race or religion as it is to expect the western world to stop counting because the modern world's numerals originally "belonged" to the Arabs.

12   Indeed, Christmas does not "belong" to anyone. At an office party later that week, I heard the many different languages, dialects, and accents. We were as multicultural a bunch of human beings as could exist on God's earth. There were Christians of various denominations°—Greek Orthodox to Catholic—and the

Jewish, Muslim, Hindu, and Parsi faiths, as well as people from virtually every continent.

13   This is when she came to mind, my classmate from a previous life, Jennifer McDonald, she of the pink, frilly, swishing dress who first made me want to celebrate Christmas—who first made me want to be different. I realized we were all, in one way or another, like Jennifer. Each of us has taken something—a ritual or a tradition or a tool, an item of food—from someone other than our "pure laine"° ancestors.

14   I realized that it was okay to be a little "anglo." Here in Canada, you can be a Muslim, as I am. You can be a Canadian, as I am. This is the only country in the world where you can be everything you are and want to be.

15   And I realized that here, in Canada, you can celebrate Christmas, if you want to. Or not, if you don't want to.

Vocabulary

1 heady (adj): having a strong effect on your senses, making you excited

1 Raj (n): refers to the period of British colonial rule

3 anglo (n): a colloquial term for white people or people of English descent

4 swish (v): move quickly in a way that makes a soft sound

4 flounce (v): move in a way that draws attention

8 marzipan (n): a sweet firm substance made from almonds, sugar, and eggs

11 ludicrous (adj): ridiculous and unreasonable

11 forgo (v): decide not to do something you would like to do

12 denomination (n): a sect of a particular religion

13 pure laine (n): literally 100% wool (French), but in Quebec used to refer to those of pure French ancestry

RESPONDING TO THE READING

- If the thesis is stated, identify it; if it is implied, write it in your own words.
- What do you think is the purpose of this essay? Give reasons for your opinion.
- Who do you think is the intended audience of this essay? Give reasons for your opinion.

Comprehension

1. What does the author mean by saying Christmas was not "the done thing" in Paragraph 2?
2. Who is Jennifer McDonald? Is this the real name of a girl Almas Zakiuddin used to know at school?

3. What incident marks the beginning of the author's search for a new understanding of Christmas?
4. What did Zakiuddin do to be part of the Christmas festivities?
5. What reason does Zakiuddin suggest caused everyone to walk "with a little spring in their step" (Paragraph 9)?
6. What arguments does Zakiuddin make in Paragraph 10?
7. What examples does she present in Paragraphs 10 and 11 to support her arguments?
8. What does Zakiuddin mean by saying in Paragraph 13 "we were all, in one way or another, like Jennifer"?
9. In the last eight lines of her essay, Zakiuddin uses a parallel structure to sum up her "rediscovery." Identify it and comment on its effect.

Analysis

1. Is the title appropriate for the essay? Why or why not?
2. What is the basis of Zakiuddin's argument? Do you find her conclusion reasonable and convincing? Why or why not?
3. Analyze how Zakiuddin uses Jennifer McDonald to link the past and present and to tie her essay together.
4. Zakiuddin takes the reader back to her first winter in Toronto and narrates her experience in a chronological order. Do you think her argument is presented in the most effective way? Why or why not?
5. Does the author ever try to persuade the reader to act on her "rediscovery" of Christmas? If yes, at what point and how?
6. What level of language is used in the essay? Provide evidence for your answer.
7. Using three to five adjectives, describe the author's tone.

Discussion/Writing Suggestions

1. Almas Zakiuddin states in her essay "This is the only country in the world where you can be everything you are and want to be." Do you agree with her? Write an essay to argue for or against Zakiuddin's statement.
2. Do you think Canada should practise multiculturalism? Consider the pros and/or cons of multiculturalism in Canada and support your position on this issue.

    • Other essays that examine Canadian society include those by Hugh MacLennan (p. 5), Margaret Atwood (p. 85), Peggy Lampotang (p. 129), Wayson Choy (p. 169), Pier Giorgio Di Cicco (p. 196), and Rosie DiManno (p. 211).

Don't You Think It's Time to Start Thinking?

Northrop Frye

Northrop Frye (1912–1991) is one of the most important literary critics of his generation. Born in Sherbrooke, Quebec, he earned his master's degree at Oxford University, England, after graduating from the University of Toronto with a B.A. in philosophy and English. He worked as a pastor for the United Church of Canada before turning to teaching in 1939. In 1967, he became a professor at the University of Toronto, where he remained teaching until his death in 1991. As an eminent English scholar and literary critic, Frye won many awards for his seminal and inspirational works, such as Anatomy of Criticism *(1957),* The Return of Eden *(1965),* A Study of English Romanticism *(1968), and* The Critical Path *(1971); he also received 36 honorary degrees from colleges and universities in Canada and the United States. Margaret Atwood praised Frye for making the field of literary criticism available to a nonprofessional audience. She said that Frye, as one of only a handful of critics that are read by the general public "did not lock literature into an ivory tower; instead he emphasized its centrality to the development of a civilized and humane society."*

This essay was originally published in the Toronto Star, *January 25, 1986. As one of the greatest thinkers and communicators in Canada, Northrop Frye eloquently argues for the intimate relation between language and thinking and calls for a fight against illiteracy and inarticulateness—the lack of the verbal skills to express oneself.*

1   A student often leaves high school today without any sense of language as a structure.

2   He may also have the idea that reading and writing are elementary skills that he mastered in childhood, never having grasped the fact that there are differences in levels of reading and writing as there are in mathematics between short division and integral calculus.

3   Yet, in spite of his limited verbal skills, he firmly believes that he can think, that he has ideas, and that if he is just given the opportunity to express them that he will be all right. Of course, when you look at what he's written you find it doesn't make any sense. When you tell him this he is devastated.

4   Part of his confusion here stems from the fact that we use the word "think" in so many bad, punning ways. Remember James Thurber's* Walter Mitty* who was always dreaming great dreams of glory. When his wife asked him what he was doing he would say, "Has it ever occurred to you that I might be thinking?"

5   But, of course, he wasn't thinking at all. Because we use it for everything our minds do, worrying, remembering, daydreaming, we imagine that thinking is something that can be achieved without any training. But again it's a matter of practice. How well we can think depends on how much of it we have already done.

Most students need to be taught, very carefully and patiently, that there is no such thing as an inarticulate idea waiting to have the right words wrapped around it.

6   They have to learn that ideas do not exist until they have been incorporated into words. Until that point you don't know whether you are pregnant or just have gas on the stomach.

7   The operation of thinking is the practice of articulating° ideas until they are in the right words. And we can't think at random either. We can only add one more idea to the body of something we have already thought about. Most of us spend very little time doing this, and that is why there are so few people whom we regard as having any power to articulate at all. When such a person appears in public life, like Mr. Trudeau*, we tend to regard him as possessing a gigantic intellect.

8   A society like ours doesn't have very much interest in literacy. It is compulsory to read and write because society must have docile and obedient citizens. We are taught to read so that we can obey the traffic signs and to cipher so that we can make out our income tax, but development of verbal competency is very much left to the individual.

9   And when we look at our day-to-day existence we can see that there are strong currents at work against the development of powers of articulateness. Young adolescents today often betray° a curious sense of shame about speaking articulately, of framing a sentence with a period at the end of it.

10   Part of the reason for this is the powerful anti-intellectual drive which is constantly present in our society. Articulate speech marks you out as an individual, and in some settings this can be rather dangerous because people are often suspicious and frightened of articulateness. So if you say as little as possible and use only stereotyped, ready-made phrases you can hide yourself in the mass.

11   Then there are various epidemics sweeping over society which use unintelligibility as a weapon to preserve the present power structure. By making things as unintelligible as possible, to as many people as possible, you can hold the present power structure together. Understanding and articulateness lead to its destruction. This is the kind of thing that George Orwell* was talking about, not just in *Nineteen Eighty-Four,* but in all his work on language. The kernel of everything reactionary and tyrannical in society is the impoverishment of the means of verbal communication.

12   The vast majority of things that we hear today are prejudices and clichés, simply verbal formulas that have no thought behind them but are put up as pretence of thinking. It is not until we realize these things conceal meaning, rather than reveal it, that we can begin to develop our own powers of articulateness.

13   The teaching of humanities is, therefore, a militant job. Teachers are faced not simply with a mass of misconceptions and unexamined assumptions. They must engage in a fight to help the student confront and reject the verbal formulas and stock responses, to convert passive acceptance into active, constructive power. It is a fight against illiteracy and for the maturation of the mental process, for the development of skills which once acquired will never become obsolete°.

Notes

4 James Thurber (1894–1961): American short story writer, humorist, and cartoonist whose best-known short story "The Secret Life of Walter Mitty" (1941) was turned into a movie in 1947

4 Walter Mitty: main character in Thurber's story, a daydreamer who lives in his dreams

7 Pierre Elliott Trudeau (1919–2000): prime minister of Canada (1968–1979, 1980–1984)

11 George Orwell (1903–1950): pen name of Eric Blair, a British writer and satirist who is best known for his political satires *Animal Farm* (1945) and *Nineteen Eighty-Four* (1949)

Vocabulary

7 articulate (v; adj): express thoughts and feelings clearly in words; good at explaining ideas clearly in words

9 betray (v): show

13 obsolete (adj): no longer used because something new has been invented

RESPONDING TO THE READING

- If the thesis is stated, identify it; if it is implied, write it in your own words.
- What do you think is the purpose of this essay? Give reasons for your opinion.
- Who do you think is the intended audience of this essay? Give reasons for your opinion.

Comprehension

1. Do you see a pun in how *think* and *thinking* are used in Northrop Frye's title? Explain your answer.
2. How does Frye explain in Paragraph 2 that there are differences in levels of reading and writing? What literary device does he use?
3. What does Frye mean when he says "we use the word 'think' in so many bad, punning ways" in Paragraph 4?
4. In what ways are words (language) important to the thinking procedure according to what Frye says in Paragraphs 5 to 7?
5. Paragraphs 8 to 11 contain a causal analysis of the literacy issue presented in the introductory paragraphs. Summarize these paragraphs by listing all the causes that Frye names in his analysis.
6. Frye points out in Paragraph 11 "The kernel of everything reactionary and tyrannical in society is the impoverishment of the means of verbal communication." Paraphrase this sentence to demonstrate your understanding of his argument here.

7. Frye uses a number of allusions to facilitate his argument. Locate them all and discuss their effect in their specific contexts.
8. What are the things that Frye calls "pretense of thinking"?
9. Use your dictionary to find the meaning(s) and parts of speech of the italicized words:

   inarticulate idea (5), power to *articulate* (7), power of *articulateness* (9), and *articulate* speech (10).
10. Frye uses quite a few words in his final paragraph which create military imagery. Identify them all.
11. In his final sentence Frye calls on his reader to fight for "the development of skills which once acquired will never become obsolete." What "skills" do you think Frye refers to?

Analysis

1. Is the title appropriate for the essay? Why or why not?
2. What is the basis of Frye's argument? Do you find his conclusion reasonable and convincing? Why or why not?
3. If you were to divide the essay into sections, how many sections would there be? Provide reasons for your decision.
4. Do you think Frye's argument is presented in the most effective manner? Why or why not?
5. Does Frye try to persuade the reader to act on his belief? If yes, at what point in the essay and how?
6. What level of language is used in the essay? Provide evidence for your answer.
7. Using three to five adjectives, describe Frye's tone.

Discussion/Writing Suggestions

1. In his essay Frye advocates strengthening the teaching of language skills at school and promoting literacy in Canadian society. His argument is based on the theory that little thinking is possible without language. This theory can be traced back to Thomas Carlyle (1795–1881), a Scottish political philosopher, who says in *Sartor Resartus* (1834), "Language is called the garment of thought: however, it should rather be, language is the flesh-garment, the body, of thought." Using the quotation from Carlyle as your attention grabber, write an essay to state your position on the importance of language skills.
2. Write an essay to refute (argue against) Frye's argument.

   • Other essays that examine the influence and power of language include those by Malcolm X (p. 19), Rosemary Afriye (p. 54), Richard Marius (p. 68), Kurt Vonnegut (p. 72), Margaret Atwood (p. 85), Timothy Findley (p. 92), Pico Iyer (p. 96), Nicola Bleasby (p. 109), Peggy Lampotang (p. 129), Stephen L. Carter (p. 132), Dan Zollmann (p. 166), Rosie DiManno (p. 211), and Carol Shields (p. 248).

The Case for Curling Up with a Book

Carol Shields

Carol Shields (1935–2003) was an award-winning novelist, playwright, poet, and short story writer. A graduate of Hanover College in the United States, she came to Canada after her marriage and received her M.A. degree from the University of Ottawa. After working briefly as an editorial assistant with Canadian Slavonic Papers, she formally began her writing career in 1974 when Intersect, *her first collection of poems, was published. She was a professor at the University of Manitoba beginning in 1980 and Chancellor of the University of Winnipeg from 1996 until 2000. Her best-known novels include* The Stone Diaries *(1994),* Larry's Party *(1998), and* Unless *(2002), which won her many prestigious awards, such as the Governor General's Award and the Pulitzer Prize for fiction. Shields's works have been translated into many languages, including Swedish, Italian, French, Chinese, Norwegian, German, Spanish, Danish, Korean, Japanese, and Polish. To quote from novelist Margaret Atwood, "The extraordinariness of ordinary people was Carol's forte."*

This essay was originally published in The Journal *in 1997. In it, Carol Shields, the avid book lover and accomplished book maker, makes the case for books and reading.*

1   Some years ago a Canadian politician, one of our more admirable figures, announced that he was cutting back on his public life because it interfered with his reading. *His reading*—notice the possessive pronoun, like saying his arm or his leg—and notice too, the assumption that human beings carry, like a kind of cerebral° brief case, this built-in commitment to time and energy[:] *their reading.*

2   I'm told that people no longer know how to curl up with a book. The body has forgotten how to curl. Either we snack on paperbacks while waiting for the bus or we hunch over our books with a yellow underliner in hand. Or, more and more, we sit before a screen and "interact."

3   Curling up with a book can be accomplished in a variety of ways: in bed for instance, with a towel on a sunlit beach, or from an armchair parked next to a good reading lamp. What it absolutely requires is a block of uninterrupted time, solitary time and our society sometimes looks with pity on the solitary, that woman alone at the movies, that poor man sitting by himself at his restaurant table. Our hearts go out to them, but reading, by definition, can only be done alone. I would like to make the case today for solitary time, for a life with space enough to curl up with a book.

4   Reading, at least since human beings learned to read silently (and what a cognitive° shift that was!) requires an extraordinary effort at paying attention, at remaining alert. The object of our attention matters less, in a sense, than the purity of our awareness. As the American writer Sven Birkerts says, it is better, better in terms of touching the self within us, that we move from a state of half-distraction to one of full attention. When we read with attention, our inner circuit of the brain

is satisfyingly completed. We feel our perceptions sharpen and acquire edge. Reading, as many of you have discovered, is one of the very few things you can do only by shining your full awareness on the task. We can make love, cook, listen to music, shop for groceries, add up columns of figures all with our brain, our self that is, divided and distracted. But print on the page demands all of us. It is so complex, its cognitive circuitry so demanding; the black strokes on the white page must be apprehended and translated into ideas, and ideas fitted into patterns, the patterns then shifted and analyzed. The eye travels backward for a moment; this in itself is a technical marvel, rereading a sentence or a paragraph, extracting the sense, the intention, the essence of what is offered.

5   And ironically, this singleness of focus delivers a doubleness of perception. You are invited into a moment sheathed° in nothing but itself. Reading a novel, *curled up* with a novel, you are simultaneously in your arm chair and in, for instance, the garden of Virginia Woolf* in the year 1927, or a shabby Manitoba farmhouse conjured by Margaret Laurence, . . . participating fully in another world while remaining conscious of the core of your self, that self that may be hardwired° into our bodies or else developed slowly, created over the long distance of our lives.

6   We are connected through our work, through our familial chain and, by way of the Internet, to virtually everyone in the world. So what of the private self which comes tantalizingly° alive under the circle of the reading lamp, that self that we only occasionally touch and then with trepidation°. We use the expression "being lost in a book," but we are really closer to a state of being found. Curled up with a novel about an East Indian family for instance, we are not so much escaping our own splintered and decentred world as we are enlarging our sense of self, our multiplying possibilities and expanded experience. People are, after all, tragically limited: we can live in only so many places, work at a small number of jobs or professions; we can love only a finite° number of people. Reading, and particularly the reading of fiction . . . lets us be other, to touch and taste the other, to sense the shock and satisfaction of otherness. A novel lets us be ourselves and yet enter another person's boundaried world, to share in a private gaze between reader and writer. *Your* reading, and here comes the possessive pronoun again, can be part of your life and there will be times when it may be the best part. . . .

7   [A] written text, as opposed to electronic information, has formal order, tone, voice, irony, persuasion. We can inhabit a book; we can possess it and be possessed by it. The critic and scholar Martha Nussbaum believes that attentive readers of serious fiction cannot help but be compassionate and ethical citizens. The rhythms of prose train the empathetic° imagination and the rational emotions. . . .

8   Almost all of [us are] plugged into the electronic world in one way or another, reliant on it for its millions of bytes of information. But a factoid°, a nugget of pure information, or even the ever-widening web of information, while enabling us to perform, does relatively little to nourish us. A computer connects facts but cannot reflect upon them. There is no depth, no embeddedness. It is, literally, software, plaintext, language prefabricated° and sorted into byte sizes. It does not, in short, aspire; it rarely sings. Enemies of the book want to see information freed from the

prison of the printed page, putting faith instead in free floating information and this would be fine if we weren't human beings, historical beings, thinking beings with a hunger for diversion, for narrative, for consolation°, for exhortation°.

9 We need literature on the page because it allows us to experience more fully, to imagine more deeply, enabling us to live more freely. Reading, [we] are in touch with [our best selves], and I think, too, that reading shortens the distance we must travel to discover that our most private perceptions are, in fact, universally felt. *Your* reading will intersect with the axis° of *my* reading and of his reading and of her reading. Reading, then, offers us the ultimate website, where attention, awareness, reflection, understanding, clarity, and civility come together in a transformative experience.

Note

5 Virginia Woolf (1882–1941): British novelist and literary critic whose novel *To the Lighthouse* (1927) is partially set in a garden

Vocabulary

1 cerebral (adj): relating to the brain

4 cognitive (adj): connected with mental processes of understanding

5 sheathe (v): put a knife or sword into a sheath (a cover that fits closely over the blade)

5 hardwired (adj): (of computer functions) built into the permanent system

6 tantalizingly (adv): in the manner of something that cannot be had

6 trepidation (n): great fear of something unpleasant that may happen

6 finite (adj): limited and fixed

7 empathetic (adj): showing the ability to understand another person's feelings

8 factoid (n): something that is believed to be true simply because it has appeared in print

8 prefabricate (v): make in sections that can be put together later

8 consolation (n): something that makes you feel better when you are unhappy or disappointed

8 exhortation (n): act of persuading someone to do something

9 axis (n): an imaginary line through the centre of an object

 # RESPONDING TO THE READING

- If the thesis is stated, identify it; if it is implied, write it in your own words.
- What do you think is the purpose of this essay? Give reasons for your opinion.
- Who do you think is the intended audience of this essay? Give reasons for your opinion.

Comprehension

1. Carol Shields begins her essay with an interesting attention grabber. Do you think it is effective? Why or why not?
2. In Paragraph 2 Shields observes: "[M]ore and more, we sit before a screen and 'interact'." What *screen* is she referring to?
3. What does Shields mean by "I would like to make the case for" in Paragraph 3? What situation does the expression remind you of?
4. Why do you think Shields quotes from another writer, Sven Birkerts, in Paragraph 4?
5. Summarize what Shields says about the "singleness of focus" and "doubleness of perception" in Paragraph 5 to demonstrate your understanding of her point.
6. In Paragraph 6 Shields describes articulately and vividly how reading enlightens and connects us. Explain in your own words what Shields means when she states, "Reading, and particularly the reading of fiction . . . lets us be other, to touch and taste the other, to sense the shock and satisfaction of otherness."
7. According to what Shields says in Paragraph 7, how does a written text differ from electronic information? How do *attentive* readers benefit from *serious* fiction?
8. In Paragraph 8, the *screen* referred to in Paragraph 2 and the *Internet* mentioned in Paragraph 6 are turned into open targets of Shields's criticism. What are her major objections to the Internet?
9. What ideas does Shields present in her concluding paragraph?

Analysis

1. Is the title appropriate for the essay? Why or why not?
2. What does Shields mean by "curling up with a book"? What kind of *book* does she have in mind when writing this essay?
3. What makes Shields think it is necessary to argue for reading "print on the page" that requires our "full awareness"?
4. Examine the development of Shields's argument from paragraph to paragraph. Would you describe it as inductive, deductive, logical, or a combination? Support your response with examples.
5. Does the author try in the essay to persuade the reader to curl up with a book? If yes, at what point and how?
6. What level of language is used in the essay? Provide specific evidence for your answer.
7. Using three to five adjectives, describe the author's tone.
8. In this essay Carol Shields demonstrates impressive mastery of the English language partly through her metaphorical use of words. Explain how the italicized words in the following sentences add to the interest of reading:
    a. . . . either we *snack* on paperbacks while waiting for the bus . . . (2)
    b. We feel our perceptions *sharpen* and *acquire edge*. (4)

c. You are invited into a moment *sheathed* in nothing but itself. (5)

d. A novel lets us be ourselves and yet *enter another person's boundaried world, to share in a private gaze between reader and writer.* (6)

e. Almost all of [us are] *plugged into* the electronic world. . . . (8)

f. Reading, then, offers us the ultimate *website.* . . . (9)

Discussion/Writing Suggestions

1. Write an essay of refutation to make the case for the Internet and counter Shields's argument for the book. Your refutation can be based on the points Shields presents in Paragraph 8 of the essay.

2. In her essay Shields shares her reading experience with the reader when she makes comments, such as "We use the expression 'being lost in a book,' but we are really closer to a state of being found" (6) and "We can inhabit a book; we can possess it and be possessed by it" (7). Have you had such experience with books? Write an essay to discuss your reading experience.

   • Other essays that discuss the power of the imagination and the necessity of art include those by Charles Dickens (p. 10), Malcolm X (p. 19), Rosemary Afriye (p. 54), Bertrand Russell (p. 64), Margaret Atwood (p. 85), Timothy Findley (p. 92), Pico Iyer (p. 96), Mark Kingwell (p. 114), Pier Giorgio Di Cicco (p. 196), Margaret Laurence (p. 202), and Northrop Frye (p. 244).

A World Not Neatly Divided

Amartya Sen

Born in Santinketan, India, Amartya Sen (1933–) was educated at the universities of Calcutta and Cambridge. He was awarded the Nobel Prize in Economics in 1988 for his work on welfare economics. An important academic, Dr. Sen was Master of Trinity College at Cambridge University from 1998 to 2004. He is currently the Lamont University Professor at Harvard University. He has also taught at Jadavpur University, the Delhi School of Economics, the London School of Economics, and Oxford University. Amartya Sen's works have been translated into more than 30 languages. His major works include Collective Choice and Social Welfare *(1970),* On Economic Inequality *(1973), and* Poverty and Famines: An Essay on Entitlement and Deprivation.

This essay appeared in the New York Times *on November 23, 2001.*

1   When people talk about clashing civilizations, as so many politicians and academics do now, they can sometimes miss the central issue. The inadequacy of this thesis begins well before we get to the question of whether civilizations must clash. The basic weakness of the theory lies in its program of categorizing people of the world according to a unique, allegedly commanding system of classification.

This is problematic because civilizational categories are crude and inconsistent and also because there are other ways of seeing people (linked to politics, language, literature, class, occupation or other affiliations).

2   The befuddling° influence of a singular classification also traps those who dispute the thesis of a clash: To talk about "the Islamic world" or "the Western world" is already to adopt an impoverished vision of humanity as unalterably divided. In fact, civilizations are hard to partition in this way, given the diversities within each society as well as the linkages among different countries and cultures. For example, describing India as a "Hindu civilization" misses the fact that India has more Muslims than any other country except Indonesia and possibly Pakistan. It is futile° to try to understand Indian art, literature, music, food or politics without seeing the extensive interactions across barriers of religious communities. These include Hindus and Muslims, Buddhists, Jains, Sikhs, Parsees, Christians (who have been in India since at least the fourth century, well before England's conversion to Christianity), Jews (present since the fall of Jerusalem), and even atheists° and agnostics°. Sanskrit has a larger atheistic literature than exists in any other classical language. Speaking of India as a Hindu civilization may be comforting to the Hindu fundamentalist, but it is an odd reading of India.

3   A similar coarseness can be seen in the other categories invoked, like "the Islamic world." Consider Akbar and Aurangzeb, two Muslim emperors of the Mogul dynasty in India. Aurangzeb tried hard to convert Hindus into Muslims and instituted various policies in that direction, of which taxing the non-Muslims was only one example. In contrast, Akbar reveled in his multiethnic court and pluralist laws, and issued official proclamations insisting that no one "should be interfered with on account of religion" and that "anyone is to be allowed to go over to a religion that pleases him."

4   If a homogeneous° view of Islam were to be taken, then only one of these emperors could count as a true Muslim. The Islamic fundamentalist would have no time for Akbar; Prime Minister Tony Blair, given his insistence that tolerance is a defining characteristic of Islam, would have to consider excommunicating° Aurangzeb. I expect both Akbar and Aurangzeb would protest, and so would I. A similar crudity is present in the characterization of what is called "Western civilization." Tolerance and individual freedom have certainly been present in European history. But there is no dearth of diversity here, either. When Akbar was making his pronouncements on religious tolerance in Agra, in the 1590's, the Inquisitions were still going on; in 1600, Giordano Bruno was burned at the stake, for heresy, in Campo dei Fiori in Rome.

5   Dividing the world into discrete° civilizations is not just crude. It propels us into the absurd belief that this partitioning is natural and necessary and must overwhelm all other ways of identifying people. That imperious° view goes not only against the sentiment that "we human beings are all much the same," but also against the more plausible understanding that we are diversely different. For example, Bangladesh's split from Pakistan was not connected with religion, but with language and politics.

6   Each of us has many features in our self-conception. Our religion, important as it may be, cannot be an all-engulfing identity. Even a shared poverty can be a source

of solidarity across the borders. The kind of division highlighted by, say, the so-called "antiglobalization" protesters—whose movement is, incidentally, one of the most globalized in the world—tries to unite the underdogs of the world economy and goes firmly against religious, national or "civilizational" lines of division.

7   The main hope of harmony lies not in any imagined uniformity, but in the plurality° of our identities, which cut across each other and work against sharp divisions into impenetrable civilizational camps. Political leaders who think and act in terms of sectioning off humanity into various "worlds" stand to make the world more flammable°—even when their intentions are very different. They also end up, in the case of civilizations defined by religion, lending authority to religious leaders seen as spokesmen for their "worlds." In the process, other voices are muffled and other concerns silenced. The robbing of our plural identities not only reduces us; it impoverishes the world.

Vocabulary

2 befuddling (v): confusing

2 futile (adj): useless

2 atheists (n): those who do not believe in the existence of God

2 agnostics (n): those who are skeptical that whether God does or does not exist can be known

4 homogeneous (adj): consisting of similar parts or elements

4 excommunicating (v): excluding from membership in a church; expelling

5 discrete (adj): composed of distinct parts

5 imperious (adj): arrogant

7 plurality (n): numerous and different, society having many different groups within it

7 flammable (adj): easily ignited

 RESPONDING TO THE READING

- If the thesis is stated, identify it; if it is implied, write it in your own words.
- What do you think is the purpose of this essay? Give reasons for our opinion.
- Who do you think is the intended audience of this essay? Give reasons for your opinion.

Comprehension

1. What is the theory that Amartya Sen refutes in his essay? Who believes and advocates the theory?

2. Sen points out in his introductory paragraph the *inadequacy* and *weakness* of the theory and calls its basis *crude* and *inconsistent*. Could you find one synonym for each of the italicized words?

3. What is the key point Sen makes in Paragraph 2? What examples does he use to support his point?
4. Who are Akbar and Aurangzeb? Why are they important to Sen's argument about "the Islamic world"?
5. What is Sen's opinion about the concept *Western civilization?* How does he argue against it?
6. What is the key point Sen makes in Paragraph 5? How does he argue for his point?
7. Paraphrase the following sentences: "Our religion, important as it may be, cannot be an all-engulfing identity. Even a shared poverty can be a source of solidarity across the borders." What point is Sen conveying here? How does he support it in Paragraph 6?
8. Explain in your own words what Sen thinks is the "main hope of harmony."
9. Who are the targets of Sen's refutation? How can you tell?
10. Paraphrase Sen's concluding sentence to show your understanding of his argument.

Analysis

1. Is the title appropriate for the essay? Why or why not?
2. Examine the development of Sen's argument from paragraph to paragraph. Do you think it is effectively presented? Why or why not?
3. What is the main strategy that Sen uses to refute the theory of clashing civilizations? Provide evidence to support your answer.
4. What is Sen's counterargument to "we human beings are all much the same"? Do you find it convincing? Why or why not?
5. What factors other than religion can influence individual identity in Sen's opinion?
6. What level of language is used in the essay? Provide specific evidence for your answer.
7. Using three to five adjectives, describe the author's tone.

Discussing/Writing Suggestions

1. Do you agree with Sen that the world should not and cannot be neatly divided according to people's religious affiliations? Write an essay to support or to refute his argument based on your experience and research.
2. Sen argues that we should pay greater attention to "the plurality of our identities" rather than "imagined uniformity." Discuss the pros and cons of Sen's argument and predict whether it will surely lead to harmony in the world.

- Other essays with similar themes are by Hugh MacLennan (p. 5), Pico Iyer (p. 96), David Suzuki (p. 88), Wayson Choy (p. 169), Julie-Ann Yoshikuni (p. 140), Derek Cohen (p. 173), Charlie Angus (p. 180), Pier Giorgio Di Cicco (p. 196), Rosie DiManno (p. 211), and Pat Capponi (p. 158).

6

Writing a Research Paper

"A man will turn over half a library to make one book." (Samuel Johnson 1709–1784)

Research Paper: What? Why? How?

A research project is frequently the culminating and most challenging assignment in a reading/writing course. A research paper, as its name suggests, consists of two parts: doing research + writing the paper. Because it requires you to demonstrate skills in research and documentation, as well as the ability to compose an organized and coherent essay with a clear thesis statement and concrete supporting details, it is a test of your combined skills as an effective reader and writer. Tackling a research paper is also a procedure that will prepare you for your future career.

Students often wonder how the kind of work life they have planned for themselves will have anything to do with research. Today, people across the world are connected in the "web" of modern technology, and no human pursuit is isolated from any another. As a result, research is no longer confined to academic or specialized research institutes; rather, it permeates all walks of life and concerns the entire workforce. Every college or university graduate is therefore expected to master those necessary, rather than optional, skills.

While you undertake your research, it is vital to document where you found your information, though many find documentation tedious. There are primarily four reasons for referring to and citing from your research results:

1. To support and strengthen your thesis (to borrow from authority)
2. To set up an anti-thesis or to find a target to attack or a position to counterargue
3. To show the depth and width of your knowledge about the subject area
4. To acknowledge your sources of borrowings in a standard and scholarly manner

Writing Strategy

Because of the more extensive scope of a research paper, the process of writing it is more complex than writing a non-documented essay or even a documented essay. It involves the following nine steps:

Step 1: Choose a topic and narrow it down. If possible, focus on a thesis or a preliminary hypothesis.
Choose a topic that interests you. It may be a subject that you encountered in your study and want to examine in depth on your own or a subject that is of special interest to you because of personal reasons. Consider the length of the assignment and think about how much you can cover within that scope.

Step 2: Brainstorm on the topic and try to come up with as many research leads as possible.
Frequently the name(s) of author(s), title(s) of work(s), or key words in the topic or topic-related areas serve as the initial leads for your research. For more tips, read the section called How to Search and Research (page 260).

   One point that cannot be stressed too much is this: *do not* procrastinate! Time flies by much faster than you think, and the due date can sneak up on you before you realize it. Take Steps 1 and 2 as soon as the project is assigned. Background research at an early stage not only helps you to make sure that you can find sufficient sources for your topic, but it may also influence your choice of subject and focus. You don't want to wait to find out two days before the paper is due that you can't find enough material.

Step 3: Make a preliminary outline or a rough plan of areas to explore.
A sketchy plan of the areas you want to explore will direct your research and note taking. However, you may find it difficult to construct a preliminary outline until you have done some research on your topic. As you become familiar with your subject through research, you will find your thesis becoming clearer, and it will be easier to make the preliminary outline.

Step 4: Read, take notes, and organize your information.
Once your research has led you to something interesting, begin to read—but don't forget to take notes. With books or any other lengthy items that you can't read from cover to cover, use the table of contents and index to guide you to the sections that interest you. Since the first sentence of a paragraph tends to be the topic sentence, you can get a good idea of the content of a paragraph by skimming its opening sentence. Scanning techniques are also helpful for locating information quickly. When you hit upon anything relevant, slow down to read the section carefully and take notes if you think it will be useful later.

   When you take notes, it is a good idea to use index cards as they will allow you greater flexibility than a notebook. Label each card and arrange the cards in the order that you will organize your ideas. Make a separate card for each quotation or main point and label the card by topic at the top left and put the source of the information at the top right.

   Carefully record, either on index cards or in a notebook, all the important details you will need for your list of sources at the end of your paper. If you photocopy or download any pages, make sure you record on the top of paper the exact source and page number from which you have taken the data.

The information you should write down as you research includes the following:

- For a book, record the author's name, the full title, place of publication, name of publisher, date of publication, and page numbers of the references or quotations.
- For an article in a magazine or newspaper, record the author's name, the full title of article, title of publication, date of publication, and page numbers of the quotations.
- For an article from an electronic source, record the title, the author, and the directory path you followed to locate the information, such as the author's name, title of the article and the book, edition, detailed information about the publisher, and the date you access or download any material.

Form a habit of double-checking everything you have copied down, so that you don't need to search for the source material again if you suspect a mistake or query something later.

Step 5: Craft your thesis statement to reflect the refined focus after research and construct a working outline that shows the development of your discussion and allocation of quotations.

Making a working outline is a crucial step in writing a research paper. The greater care you take in constructing the outline, the greater ease you will experience in writing the final draft of your paper. Sharpen your thesis statement to make sure that it clearly informs the reader of the purpose of your paper. As you organize your ideas and material in the outline, note in parentheses the source material or quotations you want to use. You need to have a clear reason for why you are referring to or quoting from a source. If you used index cards to take notes, you could even number the cards or quotations in the order in which you want to develop your thesis. You need to remember, however, the centre of your outline should be *your* opinion and *your* ideas, so don't ever overload the outline with borrowings from your research.

Step 6: Write the first draft, putting your paper in shape.

Just as with the non-documented essays, the research paper writing requires unity, coherence, and clarity. You need to write for your audience while striving to achieve your purpose. All the rules and principles you have learned about effective writing remain valid. Your major challenge, however, lies in how you will combine your thoughts with other people's ideas on the topic (your research results) and document your information sources correctly in the required documentation style. Your initial draft will show you your research paper in a concrete form for the first time. Allow yourself enough time to complete it and stay focused until the draft is completed. Remember: nothing is carved in stone at this stage, so don't expect perfection.

Step 7: Reread your draft carefully, revise, and improve your paper.
Ideally, you should put your draft aside for a few days. When you revisit it, you will have a sense of detachment that will allow you to reread your own writing objectively. Revise and improve your paper using the following checklist:

1. Check your paper for organization and coherence. Make sure your ideas are presented clearly to the intended audience.
2. Check for effective use of source material. Make sure you have not included too many quotations, you have properly acknowledged all borrowings, and you have smoothly integrated all the quotations into your discussion.
3. Check the accuracy of all quotations (direct, paraphrased, and summarized) against your notes or, if necessary, against the original sources.
4. Edit your paper carefully to avoid errors in grammar, sentence structure, spelling, and punctuation.

Step 8: Prepare a list of research sources in the required documentation style.
Many detailed rules govern the way you present your sources; they outline the style—the format and content—you should follow. Apply these rules precisely. List all the sources you have quoted from or consulted in your research exactly as the rules prescribe. Once you have prepared your sources list, check it against the notes the list is based on; double-check and triple-check the format (including punctuation) against the rules. You can never be too careful in documentation.

Step 9: Print out and proofread the final draft of your paper before submission.
Give your entire paper and your list of references another careful reading. Check it carefully against your instructor's directions to make sure that all the requirements, including those regarding the title page, the format of the paper, and the font sizes, have been met. Remember that your teacher is not your proofreader or your copy editor, so your final draft should be free of typographical errors, misspellings, faulty punctuation, and definitely free of mistakes in grammar and sentence structure. Make sure that you keep all the research notes and computer printouts until your paper is returned. It is also advisable to save the original version of your paper.

Plagiarism

Plagiarism occurs when you copy or borrow ideas, words, or work from other people without acknowledging your sources in a standard documentation style. It is also known as "academic theft," a criminal act of stealing another person's intellectual property by pretending it is your own.

Nonetheless, some writers are still tempted to commit this darkest of academic crimes. Although there are different reasons behind each case, plagiarism falls into two general categories: intentional cheating and unintentional dishonesty. Most of the intentional cheaters on college and university campuses choose to ignore the moral and ethical implications of cheating either because they think they are too smart to be caught or because they don't have the time or the ability to write their own research papers. Although the unintentional cheaters don't *intend* to be dishonest, they also violate the principle of academic integrity by failing to credit the real authorship of their borrowings in a standard and scholarly manner. The consequences of plagiarism are serious, and the penalties for it are severe, ranging from a grade of zero on the research paper to failure in the course or even expulsion from college or university.

How do you avoid plagiarism? The answer is simple: (1) be honest and (2) be skillful in documentation-related areas. First, begin your research early and allow yourself sufficient time to solve unpredictable problems. Make all the necessary improvements before submitting your paper. No matter how hard the process is, it is better to be honest. Second, keep a copy of the prescribed documentation rules handy, so that you can always refer to them in order to acknowledge accurately your information sources and avoid running the risk of plagiarizing and being dishonest.

How to Search and Research

In order to begin a search for sources of information related to your topic, you need to derive as many search *leads* as possible from your topic as outlined in Step 2 above. Generally speaking, libraries, CD-ROM publications, and Internet search engines accept similar keywords as search leads, so do a search on all the possible channels to make sure your leads help you discover some interesting titles and provide new leads for further research. Some useful tips on how to search and research follow:

- It is better to begin your search at a library, preferably at the library or resource centre of your college or university. Remember, the reference librarians are resourceful and friendly, so don't hesitate to consult them before beginning your research. They will help you to locate information in subject catalogues, encyclopedias, indexes, periodicals, books, and CD-ROMs. If they are not busy, they might even teach you how to conduct a search, but it is up to you to ask for help.
- If you find some interesting titles in the library online catalogue, use their call numbers—the books' "addresses"—to try to locate them on the shelves. Once you have located the books, remember to look around. You may very well hit upon some "pleasant surprises" nearby that didn't turn up in your research.
- As you read through the books, don't forget to look at their lists of references or bibliographies at the back. Using cross-references, you may find more interesting titles or more leads to useful information.
- Encyclopedias, specialized dictionaries, and reference tools, such as *A Dictionary of Literary Terms*, *The Dictionary of Psychology*, and *The Oxford Companion to English Literature*, are warehouses of valuable background information and useful quotations. Besides, encyclopedia entries often provide reliable bibliographical leads to other works on the same topics. This is why it is wise to look up terms related to your topic area in encyclopedias and other reference tools. You may even want to begin your research with this type of reference books.

- Periodicals, which include magazines and journals, and newspapers provide more up-to-date and better focused information than books. Most of them are available online and are therefore easier to search. Most libraries have online periodical indexes (where you may find more search leads, such as titles of articles, detailed information about where to find them, and a brief summary of their contents) and licensed access to full-text databases (which allow you to download or print out entire articles). To take full advantage of these "short cuts" in your search, seek professional help from library staff, who will save you a great deal of hassle.

- Many students are equipped with computer savvy and sometimes, due to their lack of experience in "human interfacing," prefer the Internet search and wish they could do all their search and research online. To them, the information they need is only a few clicks away on the Net. Why would anyone bother to do the old-fashioned and troublesome search in the library? However, most teachers specify that students must combine the online search with the traditional "offline" research in order to complete the project. It is important to be proficient with research channels other than a few Internet search engines. Get used to accessing recognized educational websites because they monitor and evaluate the reliability and quality of the material on their websites.

- For the most part, information found through the Internet is unregulated, so don't presume everything you find online or in print is reliable, Research involves not only searching and selecting, but also assessing and rejecting. Be especially cautious about the information you have retrieved from the Internet, which, unlike books, periodicals, and other types of printed publications, provides free publishing for everyone, yet with no editors or reviewers to implement quality control. Therefore, it is very important to find out and evaluate the source of the information you find on websites before deciding to use it. It is also important to reject the dubious items that do not bear names of the authors, founding organizations, and dates or places of publication. Likewise, if your search takes you to pages riddled with mistakes in grammar and spelling, you should never take them seriously. In every way, research is a thinking process in which you make decisions constantly based on your knowledge and judgment.

By following these guidelines, you will reap a bumper harvest in your search and research.

Using Quotations in a Research Paper or Documented Essay

Three Types of Quotations

There are three different ways of borrowing information from other sources: direct quotations, paraphrased quotations, and summarized quotations. Each one must be cited properly.

Direct Quotation

When you quote directly, you *accurately* present the exact words and punctuation marks used in the original text. You must not make any changes without acknowledging them. A direct quotation shows readers the tone and wording of an author, which you believe is helpful to build a stronger argument in your own writing. When borrowing directly from your source, use direct quotations *appropriately*. Sometimes students think that stringing together a bunch of lengthy quotations is sufficient proof of their thorough research and that by quoting profusely they will impress their immediate reader, the teacher. Little do they realize, however, too many unconnected and unedited quotations could indicate that the writer is either intimidated or confused by the reference sources. From an instructor's point of view, this kind of "padding" often serves to show that the writer has not thought out the thesis, so he or she decided to use quotations to fill out the length of the paper. Remember: Use direct quotations only when they express what you can't in your own words and quote only the part that is needed to support your point. Beware of meaningless overquoting.

Paraphrased Quotation

Other terms for paraphrase are "rephrase" and "reword." When you paraphrase, you express the ideas or opinions of another in your own words.

In many situations you may simply want to borrow the ideas instead of the exact words from your reading or research. Those are the times when your paraphrasing skills are needed to execute "indirect borrowings." Paraphrasing skills are not only essential for summary writing, which requires you to extract and rephrase the key information in the source text, but they are also crucial to any kind of analytical writing based on material you have read and researched. Paraphrased quotations are used when you need to explain difficult ideas, specialized and technical concepts or jargon, or to simplify for your reader the sophisticated vocabulary in the source text.

To produce an accurate paraphrased quotation, your first step should be to understand what is said in the original. Then you need to figure out how to say it in your own words. It is always advisable to keep a college-level dictionary and a thesaurus handy when you tackle a paraphrasing task. They will give you the rich array of synonyms and synonymous expressions that exist in the English language. When you paraphrase, your intention should always be to simplify. Whatever you do, don't make your words difficult and convoluted: use plain language and short sentences.

Summarized Quotation

A summarized quotation contains a condensed version of the original. Its main purpose is to borrow another author's ideas without giving them so much space as they are allowed in the source text.

The key to effective summarized quotations lies in adherence to the rules regarding summary writing. Undoubtedly you need to understand the source text first, and then (and *only then*) you should try to summarize the original ideas in your own words. Like paraphrased quotations, summarized quotations should remain accurate and faithful to the original. Therefore, you should check your summarized quotation against the original in order to ensure that you have not changed the meaning inadvertently. As a rule, a summarized quotation should be much shorter than the original whereas a paraphrased quotation remains more or less the same length although the original words and syntax are changed.

Primary Sources and Secondary Sources

When writing a research paper, especially on a literary topic, you may be asked to use quotations from both primary sources and secondary sources.

By definition, **primary sources** refer to the original works that form the subject of your research and your paper. For example, if your topic is to compare and contrast the plotting skills used in "The Story of an Hour" by Kate Chopin and "How I Met My Husband" by Alice Munro, the two short stories are your primary sources. To support your argument, you need to make references to the primary sources from time to time and document your citations in the required documentation style. In fact, most in-class documented essays ask for references to primary sources only because of the limited time and resources at hand.

Secondary sources are defined as the materials that analyze, critique, or discuss the works or authors of your choice. In other words, if primary sources are works *by* Kate Chopin and Alice Munro, secondary sources are the writings, which could be books, essays, newspaper articles, postings on the Internet, etc., *about* your two authors and the two short stories or their works in general. When secondary sources are required, your research has to go beyond your textbook and the classroom, and your project could be time-consuming.

Integrating Quotations into Your Writing

No matter what method you use to present your borrowings, you need to integrate the quotations seamlessly into your own writing. It would be confusing and counterproductive if you simply unloaded the quotations the way you found them in the middle of your discussion without linking them with the context. Therefore, you need to introduce each quotation and properly fit it into your discussion. Improperly introduced quotations could weaken your argument and ultimately your essay. Here are some suggestions on how to integrate quotations into your writing:

- *Introducing Quotations:* When introducing quotations, use a variety of verbs that carry similar meanings. Thus, instead of always beginning your sentences with "as so-and-so *says*," try other verbs, such as *state, remark, comment, argue, note, indicate, observe, point out, agree, assert, claim, contend, indicate,* and *conclude*.
- *Citing the Author's Name:* When referring to an author, mention the full name the first time you use it, but only the family name on subsequent occasions. Never use the first name only when referring to an author. For example, the author of *Romeo and Juliet* is *William Shakespeare* (for your first reference), and *Shakespeare* when you refer to him for the second and subsequent times, but never *William*. When the author's name is not known, introduce your quotation with a phrase such as "According to the author/researcher/editor. . . ."

- *Connecting Quotations with Your Discussion:* Quoting is useful only if it is backed up by analysis. Frequently, when student writers use quotations, they assume their readers will draw connections automatically between the thesis of the paper and the quotations. In fact, quotations are only recorded references, and they do not stand alone. As the writer, you are expected to explain the meaning of the quotation and connect it to your point in the paper. Sometimes you need to be explicit about why you are quoting this particular passage to help the reader see the connection.
- *Quoting a Phrase:* If the words you want to quote are not a complete sentence, build a sentence to accommodate the quotation, which should be placed inside quotation marks. For example,

> According to Rick Groen, the true magic of moviegoing is the way in which isolated individuals are transformed into "the archipelago of a rapt audience" (E1).

- *Reshaping a Quotation to Suit Your Needs:* Although as the *borrower* or the user of *borrowed* words or ideas, you don't have the right to change the content of any quotation, you do hold the licence to tailor the form of quotations to your needs.
  a. Removing words from a quotation:
  To indicate that you have cut words from the middle of a quotation, use three *spaced* dots (an ellipsis). However, four dots are needed to indicate any omission up to the end of a sentence or at the beginning of the next sentence. For example,

> To quote from "The Magic of Moviegoing," an essay by Rick Groen, "Although where we watch and what we watch have changed radically over time, how we watch [a movie in a theatre] has stayed relatively constant. . . . [T]he ritual of moviegoing is a large part of the allure, every bit as appealing as the movies themselves" (E1).

Note that the sentence should still make sense even with words removed.
  b. Making changes to a quotation:
  Sometimes to make a quotation clearer to the reader, you need to explain the original context in the source text or to make changes to the quotation in order to fit it into the context of your discussion. In these situations, use square brackets ([ ]) as in the example above to indicate changes you have made.
  To continue the example, the original version of the quote from Rick Groen is presented as follows:

> Although where we watch and what we watch have changed radically over time, how we watch has stayed relatively constant. Indeed, for many, the ritual of moviegoing is a large part of the allure, every bit as appealing as the movies themselves.

Documentation

Documentation refers to the act of documenting or acknowledging the sources of your borrowings. No matter what form your quotations take—direct, paraphrased, or summarized—you need to indicate where you found them. Documentation is required for *all* of your borrowings mainly for two reasons: to acknowledge your sources and to provide detailed information for those who may be interested in locating your source material for their own interests, further study, or research.

How sources are documented varies by discipline and documentation style. Here we focus on two of the most frequently used documentation styles: the MLA (Modern Language Association) style and APA (American Psychological Association) style. Although the two styles serve to achieve the same purpose, the differences between them are numerous and significant enough to deserve careful attention and separate explanation.

MLA Documentation Style

Developed by the Modern Language Association, the **MLA style** is primarily used in disciplines related to the arts and humanities. It consists of two connected and equally important parts:

1. Parenthetical references after each of your quotations
2. A Works Cited or Works Consulted list at the end of your paper

These two parts need to work together to provide the necessary information about your sources. Remember: The key to successful documentation is to follow rules *closely* and *carefully*. Documentation never requires imagination or creativity. When in doubt, consult your style guide or your instructor.

1. Parenthetical References

Parenthetical references consist of parentheses ( ) and the required documentation details included between the two rounded brackets. They appear at the end of each quotation to replace the cumbersome footnote system. To provide the reader with concise and necessary leads (*highway signs*) to "Works Consulted/Cited" list at the back of your paper, follow these rules where applicable:

a.   Put in parentheses the author's family name or the first few content words in the title (where the author's name is not available) and the page number(s).
Example 1 (using author's family name): ". . . let it be said that of all who give gifts these two were the wisest" (Henry 153).
Example 2 (author's name not available, using first few content words in title): "In an historic agreement, midwives will be allowed to deliver babies in a Quebec hospital" ("Midwives to Deliver" A3).

b.   Put in parentheses the page number only if the author's name or the title is mentioned in your paper already. For example,

This is how Rick Groen expresses the paradox of watching a movie in a theatre rather than at home: "When we are most truly alone, we are most truly an audience" (E1).

c. Direct quotations are formatted and punctuated differently depending on whether they are short quotations and long quotations.
    For short quotations (ranging from one word to four typed lines in the original), use quotation marks to enclose the quoted words or sentences, make a parenthetical reference at the end of the quotation, and place the ending punctuation after the parenthetical reference. For example,

> Groen argues that "the theatre becomes simultaneously a public and a private space, with people striving to get the balance right and keep the boundaries straight" (E1).

For a long quotation (longer than four typed lines in the source text), introduce it with a statement ending in a colon (:). Then set it off in block style from your own writing (by blocking the quotation first and then press the "Tab" key on the computer). No quotation marks are needed for the quoted passage. Place the ending period after the quotation followed by a parenthetical reference. For example,

> Patrick O'Flaherty castigates the impact of TV on the mind: But the essence of TV watching, the continual passive receiving and rejecting of images, together with the low level of exertion such a process entails, is so destructive of alertness and retentive faculties demanded by the study of books that it constitutes a real handicap. (169)

d. If you quote from two or more articles by the same author in your paper, you should indicate in the parenthetical reference which one you are referring to by including the author's family name followed by a comma, then the first few words of the title of the specific article you are referring to, and the page number. For example,

> "The forum, organized by the Ministry of Education and Training . . . called for change in math content, teaching methods and testing" (Lewington "Math Myths" A1).

2. Works Cited or Works Consulted List

This list appears as a separate item on a new page after your research paper ends. If it contains only the works referred to or quoted in your essay, it is called *Works Cited*; if it contains all the items you found useful in researching your essay even though you didn't refer to or quote from them in your paper, it is called *Works Consulted*.

With "Works Cited" or "Works Consulted" centred on top of the page, the list should follow these rules:

a. Entries are listed in alphabetical order according to the family name of the (first) author, editor, and first word of the title (excluding the articles *a, an,* or *the*) where no author's name is available.

b. Don't number the entries.

c. Include author, title, and publication information for each entry, if available. Use a period to set off each of these elements from the others as every element is treated as a separate unit. Leave one space after the periods.

d. The first line of an entry begins at the left margin, and subsequent lines of the entry are indented five spaces (by using the "Tab" key on the computer). This format is known as "hanging indent."

e. The entire list is double-spaced.

f. Capitalize the first and last and all content words in all titles and subtitles. Don't capitalize articles, prepositions, coordinating conjunctions, and the *to* in infinitives.

g. In the publication data, abbreviate publishers' names and months (e.g., *Dec.* rather than *December*; *Oxford UP* instead of *Oxford University Press*), and indicate the name of the city where the publisher is located rather than the province or state or country (e.g., *Toronto: McGraw-Hill Ryerson*). Use the first city if several cities are listed. For the year of publication, use the year on the title page; if it doesn't appear on the title page, use the latest copyright date shown at the back of the title page.

h. Don't use *p., pp.,* or *page(s)*. Numbers alone will be enough to indicate page number(s). When page spans over 100 have the same first digit, use only the last two digits of the second number (e.g., 243–47).

i. Italicize or underline titles of works that were published as *separate items,* such as books, magazines, newspapers, and movies. The period comes *after* the underlined or italicized title, but it is not underlined. Place subtitles after titles, but you should separate them with a colon and one space. Other punctuation marks ("?" or "!") should be italicized or underlined when they are part of the title (e.g., *Alias Grace.* [a book], *Maclean's.* [a magazine], *Who's Afraid of Virginia Woolf?* [a movie]).

j. For works that were not published as separate items, such as a short story, a chapter in a book, and a magazine or newspaper article, use quotation marks ("") around the titles. End punctuation should be inside the final quotation mark (e.g., "Swimming Lessons." [a short story] and "Isn't It Ironic?" [a magazine article]).

The basic model for a book entry in a Works Cited/Works Consulted list is presented below. Note the spacing, capitalization, punctuation, and indentation that reflect the rules of the MLA style.

Family name of author, First name. *Title of Book*. City of publication: Publisher, Year

of publication.

In addition to this basic model, there are many other models showing specific rules that govern the variety of sources cited. When constructing your Works Cited/Works Consulted list, first determine the specific type of each of your sources (for example, "book with one author") and then follow the pattern *very closely,* literally *to the letter* and *to the punctuation mark.* Below are listed the most common models you may encounter in your research. It is possible to underline rather than italicize the titles, but if your word processor allows you to italicize, this is the preferred method.

I. Non-Electronic Sources

Book with one author:

van Dijk, Margaret. *Basics and Beyond: Paragraph and Essay Strategies.* Toronto:

Pearson, 2003.

Book with two authors:

Engkent, Garry, and Lucia Engkent. *Fiction/Non-Fiction: A Reader and Rhetoric.*

Toronto: Harcourt, 2001.

Book with three authors:

Flachmann, Kim, Michael Flachmann, and Alexandra MacLennan. *Reader's Choice.*

3rd Canadian ed. Toronto: Prentice Hall, 2000.

Book with more than three authors:

Lipschutz, Gary, et al. *The Canadian Writer's Workplace.* 5th ed. Toronto:

Nelson, 2004.

Book with one editor:

Markham, E. A., ed. *Caribbean Short Stories.* London: Penguin, 1996.

Book with two editors:

Waldman, Nell, and Sarah Norton, eds. *Canadian Content.* 5th ed. Toronto:

Thomson, 2003.

Book with an author and an editor:

Tennyson, Alfred. *In Memoriam*. Ed. Robert H. Ross. New York: Norton,

1973.

Book with no author named:

75 Thematic Readings: An Anthology. New York: McGraw-Hill, 2003.

An edition of a classic text:

Shakespeare, William. *Othello*. Ed. Alvin Kernan. New York: Penguin, 1963.

Book by group or corporate author:

Canadian Human Rights Foundation. *Guide for Teaching Human Rights*. Montreal:

CHRF, 1986.

Government publication:

Canada. Revenue Canada. *Canada Income Tax Guide*. Ottawa: CCH Canadian

Ltd., 2002.

Two or more works by the same author(s):

Davis, Flora. *Eloquent Animals: A Study in Animal Communication*. New York:

Coward, 1998.

———. *Inside Intuition: What We Know About Nonverbal Communication*.

New York: McGraw-Hill, 1973.

Edition:

Goshgarian, Gary, ed. *Exploring Language*. 5th ed. Glenview, Illinois: Scott,

Foresman, 1989.

Translation:

Hesse, Hermann. *Siddhartha*. Trans. Hilda Rosner. New York: Bantam, 1976.

Work in several volumes or parts:

Blackwood, Paul E., ed. *The Science Library*. 6 vols. Chicago: J.G. Ferguson, 1987.

Anthology or collection:

Dasgupta, Geri, and Jennifer Jiang-hai Mei, eds. *Stories about Us*. Toronto:

Nelson, 2005.

One selection from an anthology or collection:

Rhys, J. "Fishy Waters." *Caribbean Short Stories*. Ed. E.A. Markham. London:

Penguin, 1996. 81–94.

Signed encyclopaedia entry:

Shadbolt, Doris. "Emily Carr." *The Canadian Encyclopedia*. 2nd ed.

Unsigned encyclopaedia entry:

"Stellar Structure." *The Columbia Encyclopedia*. 6th ed.

Introduction, Preface, Foreword, or Afterword:

Weintraub, Stanley. Introduction. *Great Expectations*. By Charles Dickens.

New York: Penguin, 1998. v–xii.

Signed article from a scholarly journal:

Nichols, Randall, et al. "Word Processing and Basic Writing." *Journal of Basic*

Writing 5.2 (1986): 81–97.

Signed article from a monthly magazine:

Farber, Celia. "Out of Control: AIDS and the Corruption of Medical Science."

Harper's Magazine Mar. 2006: 37–52.

Unsigned article from a weekly magazine:

"Palace Rebellion." *People* 28 Jan. 2002: 82–88.

Signed article from a daily newspaper:

Galloway, Gloria. "Ottawa Eyes Expanded Benefits." *The Globe and Mail* 29 Dec.

2006: A1.

Unsigned article from a daily newspaper:

"Harper's Christmas Carol." *The Toronto Star* 23 Dec. 2006: F1.

Editorial, letter to the editor, review:

"A Black Mark on Local Government." Editorial. *London Free Press* 27 July 1994: B8.

Interview:

Singh, Kulwant. Personal interview. 18 March 2006.

Lindsay, Freda. Telephone interview. 30 June 2006.

Film or videotape:

Casablanca. Dir. Michael Curtiz. Perf. Humphrey Bogart, Ingrid Bergman and

Claude Rains. Warner Bros. Film, 1942.

TV or radio program:

"Asha Bhosle." *Pearls of Wisdom.* CBC Radio Two, Ottawa. 10 Sept. 2006.

II. Electronic Sources
The abundance of electronic sources has made research easier, but it has also added to the complexity of documentation because of its largely non-regulated nature. On your Works Cited/Works Consulted list, document all your electronic or online sources according to a set of specific rules as well as the general principles that govern the documentation of non-electronic sources, such as alphabetical order of all entries, double-spacing, hanging indentation, and rules on capitalization and punctuation. The basic model for online source entries in a Works Cited/Works Consulted list is presented below. Note the spacing, capitalization, punctuation, and indentation that reflect the rules of the MLA style.

Author's Family Name, First Name [if known]. "Title of Document or File."

Title of Complete Work or Site. Version [if applicable]. Document date of last

revision. <Protocol and URL address>. (date of access).

Here is an example of the model shown above:

Horsley, Carter B. "Vermeer and the Delft School." *The Metropolitan Museum of*

Art. March 8 to May 27, 2001. <http://www.thecityreview.com/vermeer.html>.

(6 Feb. 2001).

Online book:

Morgan, Harry. *Cognitive Styles and Classroom Learning*. Westport: Praeger

Publishing. 1997. *Questia.com*. 13 Sept. 2006. <http://www.questia.com/

PM.qst?a=o&d=23386427>. (27 Mar. 2006).

Work in an online book:

Shakespeare, William. "Hamlet." *The Complete Works*. <http://www-tech.mit.edu/

Shakespeare/works.html>. (10 Sept. 2006).

Article in an online periodical:

"Bulletin Board: Louis Armstrong Centenary." *New York Times on the Web*. 7 Nov.

2001. <http://www.nytimes.com>. (10 June 2006).

CD-ROM:

"Drama." *Microsoft Bookshelf 2000*. CD-ROM. Redmond: Microsoft, 1998.

Professional or personal website:

Rowling, J.K. *J.K. Rowling Official Site*. 2006 Warner Bros. Ent.

<http://www.jkrowling.com>. (17 May 2005).

E-mail:

Allen, Janet. "Re: My Research Assignment." E-mail to L. Francks.

(28 May 2006).

Computer software:

AllWrite! 2.1 with Online Handbook. CD-ROM. Vers. 2.1. New York: McGraw-Hill,

2003.

If you need other models than what is provided here, visit http://www.mla.org or consult the sixth edition of Joseph Gibaldi's *MLA Handbook for Writers of Research Papers* (New York: MLA, 2003).

APA Documentation Style

Developed by the American Psychological Association, the **APA style** is primarily used in subjects related to social sciences and also in professional fields, such as education and business. Like the MLA style, it consists of two connected and equally important parts:

1. In-text citations after each of your quotations
2. A list of references at the end of your paper

These two parts need to work together to provide the necessary information about your sources.

Remember: The key to successful documentation is to follow rules *closely* and *carefully*. Documentation never requires imagination or creativity. When in doubt, consult your style guide or your teacher.

1. In-Text Citations

In-text citations appear at the end of each quotation to replace the cumbersome footnote system. To provide the reader with concise and necessary leads (*highway signs*) to the "References" list at the back of your paper, follow these rules where applicable:

a. Identify the author(s) of the source, either in your introductory sentence or in a parenthetical citation.

b. Indicate the year of publication of the source, as the APA style emphasizes the author and the year of publication. Place the year of publication after the author's name either in parentheses if the author's name is part of your introductory sentence, or, if the author is not named in your text, after the author's name and a comma in a parenthetical citation.

c. Include a page reference for a direct quotation or a specific reference. Put "p." and a space before the page number (e.g., p. 18); however, put "pp." and a space to introduce a range of page numbers (e.g., pp. 18–19). If the author is named in the text, only the page number is needed in the parenthetical citation following the borrowed material.
    Remember: Page numbers are **not** necessary when you are summarizing the source as a whole or paraphrasing an idea found throughout a work.

Example 1 (summarized quotation—author named in sentence):

> According to Lewington (1994), Quebec outperformed the other provinces on the national math test.

Example 2 (paraphrased quotation—author named in parentheses):

> Math education needs to improve its image in the public's mind (Lewington, 1994).

↳ name of article, if no author.

Example 3 (direct quotation—author named in sentence):

> As Lewington points (1994), "Math education in Canada must become more relevant, rigorous and fun . . ." (p. B1).

d. The APA *Publication Manual* recommends that if you refer to a work more than once in a paragraph, the author's family name and year of publication are given the first time you mention the work; thereafter give only the name. There is one exception: If you are citing two or more works by the same author, each citation must include the year of publication so that a reader knows which work is being cited.

e. i. If a source has five or fewer authors, name all of them the first time you cite the source. For example,

> As Celce-Murcia, Brinton and Goodwin (1996) indicate, fossilization is used to describe "a plateau in language learning beyond which it is difficult for learners to progress without exceptional effort or motivation" (p. 21).

ii. After the first time you cite a work by three or more authors, use the first author's name plus *et al.* However, always use both names when citing a work by two authors. For example,

> Pronunciation practice is most effective when sounds are rehearsed as part of a word or phrase rather than in isolation (Celce-Murcia et al., 1996, p. 71).

iii. If you put the names of the authors in parentheses, use an ampersand (&) instead of *and*. For example,

> "Suffixes can also cause a shift of stress in the root word"; for example -eous changes the stress pattern of adVANtage to advanTAgeous (Celce-Murcia, Brinton & Goodwin, 1996, p. 468).

f. In all in-text citations of a work by six or more authors, give the first author's name plus *et al.*

> As Tennison et al. (2005) have argued, anecdotal evidence is a useful first step.

g. Treat an organization or group as the author and spell out its name the first time the source is cited. If the organization is well known, you may use an abbreviation thereafter. For example,

> Public service announcements were used to inform parents of these findings (Social Development Canada [SDC], 2005).

In subsequent citations, as long as you are sure that readers will know what the abbreviation stands for, only the abbreviation and the date need to be given. For example, (SDC, 2005).

h. When no author or editor is listed for a work, use the first one or two important words of the title. Use quotation marks for titles of articles or chapters and italics for title of books.

> The proliferation of high-rise buildings in our major cities "has created veritable wind tunnels in downtown streets" ("Ill winds," 2006, p. A8).

i. If the authors of two or more sources have the same last name, always include the first initial, even when the year of publication differs.

> D. Smith (1999) argues that cooking with gas is more efficient as well as less costly.

j. When referring to a source that you know only from reading another source, use the phrase *as cited in,* followed by the author of the source you actually read and its year of publication. For example,

> The Ministry of Education and Training Forum on Math Education (as cited in Lewington 1994, p. B1) recommended that the math requirements of elementary teachers be raised.

Note: The work by the Ministry of Education and Training Forum on Math Education would not be included in the reference list, but the work by Lewington would.

k. Cite an electronic source the same way you would a print source, with the author's last name and the publication date. If the document is a pdf (portable document format) file with page numbers, cite the page numbers as you would a print source. If the source has paragraph numbers instead of page numbers, use *para.* or ¶ instead of *p.* when citing a specific part of the source. For example,

> According to Environment Canada (2002), "Reducing the use of fossil fuels therefore, including the use of electricity generated by coal- and oil-fired power plants, will help reduce acid rain-causing emissions" (para. 3).

Direct quotations are formatted and punctuated differently for short quotations and long quotations.

l. For short quotations (ranging from one word to thirty-nine words in the original), use quotation marks to enclose the quoted words or sentences, make an in-text citation at the end of the quotation, and place the ending punctuation after the closing parenthesis. For example,

> Groen argues that "the theatre becomes simultaneously a public and a private space, with people striving to get the balance right and keep the boundaries straight" (2002, p. E1).

m. For a long quotation (longer than forty words in the source text), introduce it with a statement ending in a colon (:). Then set it off in block style from your own writing (by blocking the quotation first and then press the "Tab" key on the computer). No quotation marks are needed for the quoted passage. Place the ending period after the quotation followed by a parenthetical citation. For example,

> Patrick O'Flaherty (1988) is critical of the impact of TV on the mind:

> But the essence of TV watching, the continual passive receiving and rejecting of images, together with the low level of exertion such a process entails, is so destructive of alertness and retentive faculties demanded by the study of books that it constitutes a real handicap. (p. 169)

2. List of References

This list appears as a separate item on a new page after your research paper comes to an end. It carries the title "References," which is centred on top of the page. The list should follow these rules:

a. Put references in alphabetical order by the family name of the (first) author or editor, and, where no author's name is available, the first word of the title (excluding the articles *a, an,* or *the*). Give the family name and first or both initials for each author.

b. Don't number the entries.

c. Place the publication year in parentheses following the author's or authors' names.

d. Separate the author's or authors' names, date (in parentheses), title, and publication information with periods. Leave one space after the periods.

e. Capitalize only the first word and proper nouns in titles. Also capitalize the first word following the semicolon in a subtitle.

f. Use a hanging indent. Begin the first line of each entry at the left margin, and indent all subsequent lines of the entry by five spaces (by using the "Tab" key on the computer).

g. The entire list is double-spaced.

h. Use italics for titles of books but not articles. Do not enclose titles of articles in quotation marks.

i. Include the city and publisher for books. If the city is not well known, include the state or province and/or country.

j. Include the periodical title and volume number (both in italics) as well as the page numbers for a periodical article.

The basic model for a book entry on a references list is presented below. Note the spacing, capitalization, punctuation, and indentation that reflect the rules of the APA style.

Family name of author, His/her initials. (Year of Publication). *Title of Book.*

Location: Publisher.

In addition to this basic model, there are many other models showing specific rules that govern the variety of sources cited. When constructing your references list, first determine the specific type of each of your sources (for example, "book with one author") and then follow the pattern *very closely,* literally *to the letter* and *to the punctuation mark.* Below are listed the most common models you may encounter in your research. All titles in these examples are shown using italics but if the machine on which you are preparing your list does not allow for italics, substitute underlining. Also, underline the titles of individual publications (e.g., books, magazines, movies) when italicizing is not possible in handwritten pieces.

I. Non-Electronic Sources

Book with one author:

van Dijk, M. (2003). *Basics and beyond: Paragraph and essay strategies.* Toronto:

Pearson.

Trudeau, P. (1968). *Federalism and the French Canadians.* Toronto: Macmillan.

Book with two authors:

Engkent, G., & Engkent, L. (2001). *Fiction/Non-fiction: A reader and rhetoric.*

Toronto: Harcourt.

Fromkin, V., & Rodman, R. (1974). *An introduction to language.* New York: Holt.

Book with three authors:

Flachmann, K., Flachmann, M. & MacLennan, A. (2000). *Reader's choice.* 3rd

Canadian ed. Toronto: Prentice Hall.

Ward, G., Burns, R., & Burns, K. (1992). *The Civil War: An illustrated history.*

New York: Knopf.

Two or more books by the same author:

List the works in publication order, the earliest first.

Davis, F. (1973). *Inside intuition: What we know about nonverbal communication.*

New York: McGraw-Hill.

Davis, F. (1998). *Eloquent animals: A study in animal communication.* New York:

Coward.

Organization or group as author:

American Psychological Association. (1994). *Publication manual of the American*

Psychological Association (4th ed.). Washington, DC: APA Press.

Book with no author named:

75 thematic readings: An anthology. (2003). New York: McGraw-Hill.

Book with an author and an editor:

Tennyson, A. (1973). *In Memoriam.* Ed. Ross, R. H. New York: Norton.

A selection from an anthology or collection (with an editor):

Mistry, R. (1987). Swimming lessons. In G. Dasgupta & J. Mei (Eds.) *Stories*

about us. (pp. 214–234). Toronto: Thomson.

Book with one editor:

Markham, E. (Ed.). (1996). *Caribbean short stories.* London: Penguin.

Book with two editors:

Waldman, N., & Norton, S. (Eds.) (2003). *Canadian content. 5th ed.* Toronto:

Thomson.

Article in a scholarly journal:

Helson, R., & Pals, J. (2000). Creative potential, creative achievement, and

personal growth. *Journal of Personality. 68 (1)*, 1–27.

Article from a monthly magazine:

Farber, Celia. (2006, March). Out of control: AIDS and the corruption of

medical science. *Harper's Magazine*, 37–52.

Article in a newspaper:

Galloway, G. (2006, December 29). Ottawa eyes expanded benefits. *The Globe

and Mail*, p. A1.

Translation:

Hesse, H. (1976) *Siddhartha*. (H. Rosner, Trans.) New York: Bantam.

Government publication:

Indian and Northern Affairs Canada. (1986). *The Inuit*. Ottawa: Supply and

Services Canada.

Edition other than the first:

Dasgupta, G., & Redfern, J. (1998). *Reading writing* (2nd ed.). Toronto:

Nelson.

Work in several volumes or parts:

Blackwood, P. F. (Ed.). (1987). *The Science library* (Vols. 1–6). Chicago: J. G.

Ferguson.

One selection from an anthology or collection:

Rhys, J. (1996). Fishy waters. In E. A. Markham (Ed.) *Caribbean short stories*.

(pp. 81–94). London: Penguin.

Signed encyclopaedia entry:

Shadbolt, D. (1988). Emily Carr. In *The Canadian encyclopedia* (2nd ed.) (Vol. 1,

p. 366). Edmonton: Hurtig.

Unsigned encyclopaedia entry:

Stellar structure. (2000). In *The Columbia encyclopedia* (6th ed.) (p. 2712).

New York: Columbia University Press.

Introduction, preface, foreword, or afterword:

Weintraub, S. (1998). Introduction. In *Great expectations.* (pp. v-xii). New York:

Penguin.

Unpublished dissertation or essay:

Buckley, J. (1991). *An assessment of Kieran Egan's theory of educational development.*

Unpublished dissertation, University of Western Ontario, London.

Interview:

Kulwant Singh (personal communication, March 18, 2006).

Film or videotape:

Curtis, M. (Director). (1942) *Casablanca.* [film]. Hollywood: Warner Bros.

II. Electronic Sources

On your References list, all the electronic or online sources should be documented
according to a set of specific rules as well as the general principles that govern the
documentation of non-electronic sources, such as alphabetical order of all entries,
double-spacing, hanging indentation, and rules on capitalization and punctuation.
The basic model for online source entries in a references list is presented below.
Note the spacing, capitalization, punctuation, and indentation that reflect the rules
of the APA style.

Author's Family Name, and Initials [if known]. (Date of publication) [if known].

Title of Document. *Title of Complete Work or Site.* Retrieved (date of access:

m d, y), from Protocol and URL address.

Here is an example of the model shown above:

Raeburn, B. B. (June 21, 2000). An Introduction to New Orleans Jazz. *William*

Ransom Hogan Archive of New Orleans Jazz. Retrieved August 28, 2006, from

http://www.tulane.edu/~lmiller/BeginnersIntro.html.

An online book or literary work:

Chekhov, A. (1910). The three sisters. *Bartleby.com: Great books online*. Retrieved

March 7, 2005, from http://www.bartleby.com/195/20/html.

An online information database:

Goofs browser. (1997–2002). *The Internet movie database*. Retrieved March 18,

2006, from http://us.imdb.com/Sections/Goofs.

An article in an online periodical:

Smith, G. (April 20–24, 2004). Parenthood. *Shift.com*. Retrieved June 14, 2005,

from http://www.shift.com.mag/10.1/html/10.licon.asp.

CD-ROM:

"Drama." (1998). *Microsoft Bookshelf 2000*. [CD-ROM]. Redmond: Microsoft..

Retrieved September 6, 2006, from Microsoft database.

Professional or personal website:

Rowling, J. K. (2006). *J. K. Rowling Official Site*. 2006 Warner Bros. Ent.

Retrieved May 16, 2005, from http://www.jkrowling.com.

E-mail:

Allen, Janet. (2006, April 6). "Re: My Research Assignment." E-mail to L.

Francks.

Computer software:

AllWrite! 2.1 with Online Handbook. (2003). [Computer software]. New York:

McGraw-Hill.

An article in an online newspaper:

Klein, M. (2003, October 5). Colonialism and Africa. *Toronto Star Online.*

Retrieved May 7, 2004, from http://www.torontostar.ca/NASApp/cs/

ContentServer?pagename=thestar/Layout/Article.

A government document:

Statistics Canada. (2005, May 28). *Population.* Retrieved July 3, 2006, from

http://www.statcan.ca/english/pgdb/People/Population/demo02.htm.

An article on CD-ROM:

Gas, Natural. (1992). *Oxford Junior Encyclopaedia.* [CD-ROM]. Oxford: New Media,

Inc.

An article from a computer service:

Price, R. (1991, January). Full Day. *Harper's Magazine,* pp. 56–61. *Magazine*

Database. Online. CompuServe.

An article taken from microfilm:

Alberta Department of Agriculture. (1981). Services and Programs 1980–81.

Edmonton. Microfiche: ER Document Service ED90.

An article from the World Wide Web:

National Park Service. (1996). Waterton Lakes Eco-System Renewal. (On-line).

Retrieved June 17, 2005, from http://www.prk.nat/~19endsp/programs.

If you need other models than those provided, visit http://www.apastyle.org or consult the fifth edition of the American Psychological Association's *Publication Manual* (Washington: APA, 2001).

Whichever style you choose, check your work to be sure you have been consistent and accurate.

Sample Research Paper/Documented Essay

Formatting Your Paper

Often instructors have specific requirements on how to format a research paper. If that is the case, make sure you follow those instructions carefully. However, when no specific requirements are provided by your teacher, follow the formatting guidelines specified by the documentation style you are using. Below are the guidelines for formatting according to the MLA and the APA documentation styles respectively.

1. MLA Documentation Format

Title Page

A research paper or documented essay does not require a separate title page. However, you need to type on separate lines your name, the instructor's name, the course number, and the date of submission at the top left margin of the first page of your essay. After that the title of your essay should be centred. All the key words in your title should be capitalized, but the title should not be underlined, italicized, or placed within quotation marks. Right under the title type the first paragraph of the essay, with its first line indented. The entire paper should be double-spaced. Below is an example of the top part of the first page of a research paper.

Ellis 1

Steve Ellis

Professor Chen

GNED 123

16 September 2006

A New Aspect of Heroism in Canada

[Text follows. . . .]

Header, Page Numbers, and Spacing

All pages, including the Works Cited/Works Consulted list at the end of the paper, should be numbered. Use the "header" function of your computer to make your name and the page number appear in the top right margin (see above) of every page. In the header type your family name and numeral "1" with a single space in between, but no punctuation or *p.* is needed. All paragraphs are double-spaced and indented five spaces (using the "Tab" key on your computer).

2. APA Documentation Format

Title Page

In the APA style a separate title page is needed for a research paper or documented essay. You need to create a header that includes a shortened version of the title and the page number and have it appear in the top right margin of all pages, including the title page. The shortened title in the header should indicate your topic. Use the "Enter" key on your computer to set a space of two double spaces or five single spaces between the header and the title. Here is an example of the title page in the APA style:

Heroism in Canada 1

A New Aspect of Heroism in Canada

Steve Ellis

GNED 123

Professor Chen

16 September 2006

All key words in your title should be capitalized, but the title should not be underlined, italicized, or put within quotation marks. The title should be centred and placed in the top half of the page (approximately four double-spaced lines down from the top of the page). Use the "Enter" key on the computer to locate the spot.

Type your name, the course code, the instructor's name, and the date of submission on separate lines below the title. All these elements should be centred and double-spaced.

Header, Page Number, and Spacing

All the pages, including the title page and the References at the end of the paper, should be numbered in the header, with number "1" appearing in the top right margin on the title page (see sample above). All lines of the paper should be double-spaced, and all paragraphs should be indented five spaces (using the "Tab" key on your computer).

First Page of Text

The first page of your paper should begin with your complete title centred at the top and followed by the text of your paper.

Outlining

An outline is like a skeleton. It forms the "bare bones" of your research paper, making the project less daunting and more manageable. Therefore, it is always helpful to spend some time outlining and charting out the development of your thesis before you begin to write. Outlines can be written in point form or short sentence form; their main purpose is to provide a blueprint at an early stage. Although nothing is carved in stone yet, what is laid out helps you to envision the organization and structure of your paper. Below are presented a brief outlining process and a sample outline for research paper.

Outlining Process

1. Write your chosen topic and focused subject on a piece of paper.
2. Present a clear and well-crafted thesis statement in your introductory paragraph.
3. Provide contents for your body paragraphs, indicating what key ideas will be discussed and, if possible, what quotations are to be cited and what examples to be used. Make sure ideas connect with each other and they all relate to the thesis statement.
4. Bring your discussion to a well-supported conclusion.

Sample Research Outline

Topic: Multiculturalism in Canada

Introductory Paragraph—Thesis Statement: It requires respect, mutual understanding, and willingness to compromise to preserve and enhance multiculturalism in Canada.

- definition of multiculturalism
- a quote from *Canadian Multiculturalism Act*

1. First body paragraph:
Respect is the basis of multiculturalism.

- examples in real life
- a quote on respect for other cultures

2. Second body paragraph:
Mutual understanding is important for multiculturalism.

- examples in neighbourhood
- one or two suitable quotes

3. Third body paragraph:
When conflicts arise, people should also learn to compromise for the sake of multiculturalism.

- examples and one quote or two

Concluding Paragraph: Restate the thesis: Without respect, understanding, and the ability to compromise, multiculturalism is not possible.

- find a good quote to end the essay

List possible sources of quotations

Below we present a sample research paper (a documented essay) composed on the basis of the outline. It has two versions: one documented in the MLA style and the other in the APA style. Note how the in-text citations and the list of sources at the end of the paper depend on each other and how the documentation rules are carefully put into practice.

Sample Research Paper (documented in the MLA style):

Name

Instructor's Name

Course Number

Date of Submission

Multiculturalism in Canada

direct and long quotation

In *The Columbia Encyclopedia,* "multiculturalism" is defined as

> A term describing the coexistence of many cultures in a locality,
> without any one culture dominating the region. By making the
> broadest range of human differences acceptable to the largest
> number of people, multiculturalism seeks to overcome racism,
> sexism, and other forms of discrimination. ("Multiculturalism")

I believe it was based on this general principle of "multiculturalism" that the

direct and short quotation

Canadian Multiculturalism Act was enacted in 1988. According to the
Canadian Multiculturalism Act, the "Constitution of Canada recognizes the
importance of preserving and enhancing the multicultural heritage of
Canadians" (Hutcheon 369). To me, this sentence sets the tone for multiculturalism in Canada. While living in Canada, I have come to know so many
people from so many different cultures. It is an experience, which I had
never had before I immigrated to Canada with my family. I believe this multicultural experience has opened my eyes to what lies beyond the surface of
life in my adopted country. Now I feel more like I am a part of Canada than

thesis statement

ever before. In my opinion, it takes respect, mutual understanding and willingness to compromise to preserve and enhance multiculturalism in Canada.

topic sentence

First of all, respect is the cornerstone of multiculturalism. Even though
the author of "The Myth of Canadian Diversity" argues strongly against
what he calls "the three myths" about Canada, he cannot deny that Canada

summarized quotation

is a country composed of immigrants from all over the world ("Myth"). As a matter of fact, the "Canadian mosaic" is becoming more and more multi-cultural and multicoloured as more and more immigrants are choosing Canada as their new homes. I am always amazed at the large number of cultures represented by people living in my neighbourhood. Although we go to the same shopping malls to shop, use the same hairdressers for haircuts, and send our children to the same schools, we all value and, in most cases, practise our own cultures (and/or religions) and customs, which could be as different as black and white. In spite of the differences, however, we should respect other cultures as well as our own. We should also respect others' ways of doing things no matter how different they seem. Without respect, life would be impossible, and multiculturalism would be empty talk only. You cannot expect a new immigrant to assimilate overnight. By not respecting the cultural differences, we are actually forcing the new immigrants to avoid interactions with other Canadians.

topic sentence

Second, we need to realize that only respect or tolerance of the cultural differences is not enough; we must also educate ourselves to correctly understand other cultures. Neil Bissoondath states in his essay entitled "I'm not Racist But . . ." that true racism is frequently a product of ignorance and prejudice based on racial and cultural stereotypes (212). To truly preserve and enhance our cultural heritages, we Canadians, old as well as new, must actively educate ourselves about the common misconceptions of other cultures. Every Canadian deserves equal rights and an equal chance in life. Unfortunately, racial stereotypes often create unfair images and hard feelings among members in the Canadian society. Only with good education can we achieve good and thorough understanding of other people's cultural values and customs. That is undoubtedly the true base for implementation of multiculturalism.

paraphrased quoation

Name 3

topic sentence

Finally, based on respect and mutual understanding, we should also learn and try to compromise when conflicts arise. In a way Canada is like a big family of many members with different opinions and habits. As in a traditional Chinese family where married sons all live under the same roof with their parents, conflicts and disputes are bound to happen among the family members. The most important thing is that we should not forget that we all belong to one family and to keep our family in harmony is our No. 1 job. If we always keep that in mind, we will definitely find nothing is too hard to compromise on, and no pride cannot be swallowed or tucked away. In other words, we should all look at Canada as what it is, a multicultural nation, so, despite our differences, every one of us can be a part of what makes Canada.

direct, short quotation

"For all our dispute about language and ethnicity and regional rights, our differences shrink beside our similarities, and the things that unite us dwarf those that divide us" ("Myth").

thesis restated

The value of respect, understanding, and compromise will show itself most clearly when a truly multicultural Canada keeps progressing and prospering for many generations to come. The benefits of preserving and enhancing multiculturalism in Canada are that eventually we can all share a rich cultural heritage, which we can all call our own Canadian heritage, one of its own kind in the whole, wide world. No matter what happens, we must unite this country by familiarizing ourselves with what makes us unfamiliar to each other.

thesis restated

In a country like Canada, the only way to survive and thrive is to respect, understand, and be willing to compromise for multiculturalism.

Name 4

Works Cited

Bissoondath, Neil. "I'm not Racist But . . .". *Canadian Content*. Eds. Nell

Waldman and Sarah Norton. Toronto: Nelson, 2003. 211–213.

Hutcheon, Linda, and Marion Richmond. *Other Solitudes*. Toronto: Oxford

University Press, 1990.

"Multiculturalism." *The Columbia Encyclopedia*. 6th ed.

"The Myth of Canadian Diversity." Editorial. *The Globe and Mail* 13 June,

1994: A9.

Works cited appears on
separate page

Sample Research Paper (documented in the APA style):

Multiculturalism 1

Multiculturalism in Canada

Name

Course Number

Date of Submission

Multiculturalism 2

direct and long quotation

In *The Columbia Encyclopedia,* "multiculturalism" is defined as

> A term describing the coexistence of many cultures in a locality,
> without any one culture dominating the region. By making the
> broadest range of human differences acceptable to the largest
> number of people, multiculturalism seeks to overcome racism,
> sexism, and other forms of discrimination. (Multiculturalism,
> 2000, p. 1923)

I believe it was based on this general principle of "multiculturalism" that
the *Canadian Multiculturalism Act* was enacted in 1988. According to the
Canadian Multiculturalism Act, the "Constitution of Canada recognizes the

direct and short quotation

importance of preserving and enhancing the multicultural heritage of
Canadians" (Hutcheon, 1995, p. 369). To me, this sentence sets the tone for
multiculturalism in Canada. While living in Canada, I have come to know
so many people from so many different cultures. It is an experience, which
I had never had before I immigrated to Canada with my family. I believe
this multicultural experience has opened my eyes to what lies beyond the
surface of life in my adopted country. Now I feel more like I am a part of

thesis statement

Canada than ever before. In my opinion, it takes respect, mutual understanding, and willingness to compromise to preserve and enhance multiculturalism in Canada.

topic sentence

First of all, respect is the cornerstone of multiculturalism. Even though
the author of "The Myth of Canadian Diversity" (1994) argues strongly
against what he calls "the three myths" about Canada, he cannot deny that

summarized quotation

Canada is a country composed of immigrants from all over the world. As a
matter of fact, the "Canadian mosaic" is becoming more and more multicultural and multicoloured as more and more immigrants are choosing
Canada as their new homes. I am always amazed at the large number of cultures represented by people living in my neighbourhood. Although we go to

Multiculturalism 3

the same shopping malls to shop, use the same hairdressers for haircuts, and send our children to the same schools, we all value and, in most cases, practise our own cultures (and/or religions) and customs, which could be as different as black and white. In spite of the differences, however, we should respect other cultures as well as our own. We should also respect others' ways of doing things no matter how different they seem. Without respect, life would be impossible, and multiculturalism would be empty talk only. You cannot expect a new immigrant to assimilate overnight. By not respecting the cultural differences, we are actually forcing the new immigrants to avoid interactions with other Canadians.

topic sentence

Second, we need to realize that only respect or tolerance of the cultural differences is not enough; we must also educate ourselves to correctly understand other cultures. Neil Bissoondath (1989) states in his essay entitled "I'm not Racist But . . ." that true racism is frequently a product of

paraphrased quotation

ignorance and prejudice based on racial and cultural stereotypes. To truly preserve and enhance our cultural heritages, we Canadians, old as well as new, must actively educate ourselves about the common misconceptions of other cultures. Every Canadian deserves equal rights and an equal chance in life. Unfortunately, racial stereotypes often create unfair images and hard feelings among members in the Canadian society. Only with good education can we achieve good and thorough understanding of other people's cultural values and customs. That is undoubtedly the true base for implementation of multiculturalism.

topic sentence

Finally, based on respect and mutual understanding, we should also learn and try to compromise when conflicts arise. In a way Canada is like a big family of many members with different opinions and habits. As in a traditional Chinese family where married sons all live under the same roof with their parents, conflicts and disputes are bound to happen among the family members. The most important thing is that we should not forget that we all belong to one family and to keep our family in harmony is our No. 1 job. If we always keep that in mind, we will definitely find nothing is too hard to compromise on, and no pride cannot be swallowed or tucked away. In other words, we should all look at Canada as what it is, a multicultural nation, so, despite our differences, every one of us can be a part of what makes Canada. "For all our dispute about language and ethnicity and regional rights, our differences shrink beside our similarities, and the things that unite us dwarf those that divide us" (Myth, 1994, p. A9).

The value of respect, understanding, and compromise will show itself most clearly when a truly multicultural Canada keeps progressing and prospering for many generations to come. The benefits of preserving and enhancing multiculturalism in Canada are that eventually we can all share a rich cultural heritage, which we can all call our own Canadian heritage, one of its own kind in the whole, wide world. No matter what happens, we must unite this country by familiarizing ourselves with what makes us unfamiliar to each other. In a country like Canada, the only way to survive and thrive is to respect, understand, and be willing to compromise for multiculturalism.

direct, short quotation

thesis restated

thesis restated

Reference list appears on
separate page

Multiculturalism 5

References

Bissoondath, Neil. (1989). I'm not racist but. . . . In Neil Waldman & Sarah

Norton (Eds.), *Canadian content*. (pp. 211–213). Toronto: Nelson.

Hutcheon, Linda, & Richmond, Marion. (1995). *Other solitudes*. Toronto:

Oxford University Press.

Multiculturalism. (2000). In *The Columbia encyclopedia*. (6th ed.)

(p. 1923). New York: Columbia University Press.

The myth of Canadian diversity. (1994, June 13) [Editorial]. *The Globe and*

Mail p. A9.

Reading Your Own Writing

A1. Proofreading, Editing, and Revising

Before you submit any piece of writing, whether to a teacher, a supervisor, or a colleague, you must take the time to ensure there are no errors in facts, meaning, grammar, or spelling. The following article, by Patty Martino Alspaugh, is taken from a professional journal called *The Secretary*. It contains sound advice on reading your own writing.

Win the War against Typos

Patty Martino Alspaugh

"I can't proof my own work; I'm too close to it . . . I always find someone else's mistakes more easily than my own."

These are the familiar laments of nearly everyone who writes, even professional writers and editors. And, unfortunately, most people *do* spot others' typos more easily than their own. It's as if the typos are camouflaged—until they get into someone else's hands, that is.

Secretaries often are the ones on the frontlines of the typo battle—whether it's proofreading their executives' correspondence, departmental reports, or corporate publications. They're also the people who may have input the text of the communication in the first place, making it far more difficult to catch every typo—despite those handy spell-check programs, which are *not* foolproof in catching every type of error.

To make sure you're proofreading thoroughly and accurately, here are some tried-and-true guidelines.

Basic Training

Here are the basics for every office professional whose aim is flawless proofing:

Read through the material you are proofing twice. It's easy to overlook something in the first reading. By reading it twice you are, in effect, doubling your odds of finding all the typos.

Place a check mark next to executed edits. Checking off each edit on the marked-up version as you proof it against the cleaned-up version is about as foolproof as you can get.

If in doubt, look it up. If you have any doubt about the use of a word—grammar, syntax, etc.—consult the appropriate source.

Use the standard proofreading marks. Just as nations have universal languages, editors have standard editing marks. And just like languages, these marks are necessary for effective communication. You can find these standard proofreading marks in style manuals and in some dictionaries.

Make all edits in a *contrasting* color. This will help ensure the edits are seen. It's also a good idea to put an "x" or to repeat the proofreading mark in the right-hand margin, as well. Circle the edit if it's easily overlooked, like a comma or a hyphen— especially if you are planning to fax the edits. And, if you're making lengthy edits, use an erasable pen—you'll appreciate being able to rethink (erase) your own edits.

Take pride in your work. If you care about your work, you'll do a better job. It takes a dedicated and somewhat compulsive individual who strives for uniformity and perfection to be an editor.

Always, always use a spell-check program. This applies to anyone using a word-processing program. Never leave a file without spell-checking it—even if you are only making a few edits. But, remember, spell-check programs will not catch improper word uses, grammar errors, punctuation, and so forth.

Read good writers. Over time, you'll assimilate some of the writers' styles and more easily recognize awkward or ineffective language use when you're proofing.

Enlarge your vocabulary. Increasing your vocabulary increases your understanding of the things around you. And, the more well-rounded your thinking is, the more help you can be to the writer. If you don't understand what's being said, how can you know if it's being said *properly?* When reading, don't ignore unknown words—look them up, write them down, and refer back to them. Buy vocabulary books. Listen to vocabulary-building cassette tapes. You'll find the challenge will not only improve your depth of understanding, but will improve your verbal and written skills, too.

Use a systematic approach. For instance, if you are executing someone else's edits, first make all the edits without really paying attention to anything else. Next, check to make sure you made all the edits. Finally, read through the document to check for errors not picked up by the other proofreader(s).

First Aid

Keep these supplies on hand for every proofreading job:

A dictionary—preferably a comprehensive one. Become familiar with how your particular dictionary works, because they aren't all alike. The front of the dictionary explains how you should interpret it.

At least one style manual—This is a must—especially if you are proofreading something for publication in the print media. Style books answer such questions as: Do I put a colon before or after the quotation marks? Is *north* capitalized when it's used as a region?

Grammar books—As a reference book, a good college handbook is great. A comprehensive index makes looking up anything easy. A good grammar review book is also useful giving you a *simple* way to figure out the proper way.

A secretarial handbook—The indexes generally are laid out well, the material is up-to-date, and they include a wide variety of information geared specifically to the office person. Professional Secretaries International® (PSI®) is among publishers of secretarial handbooks.

Condensed encyclopedia-type books—These books don't cover the breadth that encyclopedias do, but they're a handy and compact source you can keep nearby. They reference everything from people to events to historical data. There are many to choose from. . . .

Additionally, don't forget these resources:

Your local library—The literary sections of most libraries are great sources for grammar questions. Most grammar hotlines are located at libraries.

Seminars—Many offer great one-day refresher courses. There are seminars specifically on editing and proofreading, including those often conducted at the PSI International Convention. Most cost around $100.

Anticipation Wins the War

Here are common—yet frequently missed—writing errors that you should anticipate every time you proof: Watch out for job jargon. Many of your industry's bywords probably aren't known to the general public. If addressing an audience outside of your own, explain (in parentheses) the first use of industry vernacular if the universality of a word or expression is in doubt.

Be on the lookout for domino-type changes. For example, figure changes that affect cumulative figures elsewhere; changed headings that require changes in the table of contents; noun number changes that will affect verb tenses.

Make sure the dates on letters are current. Sometimes letters sit for a few days because of rewrites or routing. Take an extra second to double-check the date before sending out any letters.

Verify names. This is critical if it's an important piece of correspondence. No one likes to see her name, or even her company's name, spelled wrong.

Don't get sidetracked. Sometimes the same sentence will have two typos, but you get so caught up in finding the solution to one, that you bypass the other. Read the sentence over again after fixing a typo.

Make it attractive. How it looks—the layout is an important aspect of making the final text presentable. It might be typo-free, but if it looks shoddy (correction fluid globs, jagged edges), it's not presentable. Even the spacing between words—and lines—is important. Because, in the editing world, looks *do* count.

Be on the alert for double meanings. One classic example is the Chevrolet Nova automobile. When the company tried to market the car in Mexico, they discovered that the name means "no go" in Spanish.

Slow down. More mistakes are made because someone is in a big hurry to get something done and doesn't double-check the work. To paraphrase an old proofing expression: They can have it now, or they can have it right.

Don't assume. If, when making edits, you have any contextual questions, flag those areas on the hard copy; don't assume if you're not sure. If it's a grammatical or spelling edit, go for it; but if it's a matter of making sense, always verify changes with the writer.

Make sure the punctuation is correct. Punctuation marks are there to help guide the reader's comprehension. Missing and misused punctuation only confuses the reader. Keep an especially vigilant eye out for missing question marks and quotation marks, and misplaced commas.

Proof in pairs if it's really important. If you are proofing something *really* important—for instance, a brochure that is ready to go to the printer and will ultimately become a printed piece sent to thousands—get someone to proof with you. One method of proofing in pairs involves having one proofer read every word aloud, indicating spaces, punctuation, capitalization, and so forth, while the other proofer follows with original copy. This is particularly effective when proofing names or figures that have been entered onto a computer from another source.

Proof the printout. If proofing a file on a computer, print it out and proof it again. Mistakes are easier to spot on a hard copy.

Double-check all math. Not only should you double-check the math, but you should attach an adding machine tape for verification (if you use the computer's math program to do your calculation, put a check mark next to the totals to let the writer know).

Be consistent. Whatever you do, however you do it, do it consistently; for instance, parallel construction. If you list things beginning with verbs, don't change midway to nouns. And watch out for inconsistent bullet-point styles, i.e., beginning some bullet points with capitals and others without; ending some bullet points with periods and others without.

But remember, a typo may escape even your most thorough proofreading; they elude even the most experienced editors. So next time you find one after the fact, don't be too upset; just put yourself through the drills and prepare for your next battle.

A2. Checklist for Revising, Editing, and Proofreading

Structure

1. Is there a clear thesis statement written in correct parallel form?
2. Does each paragraph have a topic sentence that contains *one* idea and that relates to the *key ideas* expressed in the thesis statement?

3. Do the supporting details in each paragraph develop the idea stated in the topic sentence?
4. Does each paragraph have unity and coherence? (See pages 59–63.)
5. Are transitional words and phrases used correctly? (See pages 59–63.)
6. Are there a proper introduction and conclusion? (See pages 51–53.)

Sentences

1. Does each sentence have a subject and a verb? Are the verb tenses used correctly and consistently?
2. Are there any sentence fragments or run-ons (including comma splices)?
3. Is word order—syntax—correct and clear?
4. Do verbs agree with subjects?
5. Do pronouns agree with their antecedents? (Note: Watch out for the use of *their* when referring to a single subject such as *everyone, someone,* and *nobody.*)
6. Are words appropriately used to express the idea in the sentence?
7. Are the sentences of varied types and lengths?
8. Are there any dangling modifiers or incomplete dependent clauses?
9. Do all sentences have correct verb forms?
10. Are there any shifts in person (from first to second, for example)? Is the second person *you* overused?

Words

1. Are all words correctly spelled?
2. Are there any errors in "mismatched" words that sound alike but are spelled differently, or that are similar in spelling (e.g., *there* vs. *their* vs. *they're, then* vs. *than* vs. *that,* and *affect* vs. *effect*)?
3. Are countable (C) nouns and uncountable (U) nouns properly used (e.g., *much help* [U], *a lot of information* [U], *many friends* [C])? Are plural forms of nouns correctly spelled (e.g., *sheep/sheep, criterion/criteria, dish/dishes*)?
4. Are adjectives and adverbs correctly used and spelled? (Be careful with popular confusions such as *good/well, real/really,* and *more easier.*)
5. Is there any jargon or unclear use of terms? Are there incorrect or awkward choice and usage of words, or inappropriate "big" words?

Punctuation

1. Does every complete sentence (statement) end with a period?
2. Are commas used to separate list items, introductory dependent clauses, short phrases, and interjections only?
3. Is the semicolon confused with the comma or the period?
4. Are apostrophes used correctly for possessives and contractions? (Be careful with confusions such as *its/it's* and *your/you're.*)

5. Is the colon used correctly to introduce a series? Make sure the colon is *not* used after any form of the verb *to be*. A colon properly follows an independent clause.
6. Is capitalization correctly used? Are first words of sentences and all proper nouns in capitals?
7. Are quotation marks placed correctly? (See Unit Six for use of quotations in essays and research papers.)
8. Do all questions end with question marks?

Presentation

1. If there is a title page (for a report or a major paper), is it in the required format? Is the teacher's name spelled correctly? Are the numbers for sections and courses correct? Is your student number correct?
2. Are pages numbered clearly and consecutively?
3. In a research paper, is the use of the MLA or APA style correct and consistent? (See Unit Six.)
4. If an essay or research paper is word-processed, are there any errors in the typing? Use the spell-check function.
5. Is the essay or research paper double-spaced?
6. If an essay is handwritten, is the handwriting readable?
7. If an essay is hand-printed, is it done in upper- and lower-case letters?

A3. Useful Transitional Words and Phrases

Below are some transitional words and phrases organized by their use.

1. **Adding a Point**

and	again	also	another	as well as
in comparison	further	furthermore	in addition	besides
in the same way	likewise	moreover	next	secondly

2. **Showing Connections in Time or Sequence**

first (second, . . .)	next	also
in the first place	then	finally
before	later	when
previously	immediately	thereafter
while	lately	once
soon	eventually	then
now	in the future	ultimately
subsequently	presently	meanwhile
at this time	at present	nowadays
simultaneously	after	afterward

3. **Emphasizing a Point**

above all	in fact	especially
certainly	to be sure	chiefly
in particular	without doubt	surely
doubtless	unquestionably	indeed
primarily	obviously	undoubtedly
of course	truly	for sure

4. **Showing Similarities**

in like manner	in the same way	similarly
like	in comparison	likewise
also	to compare	in the same manner

5. **Showing Differences**

but	nevertheless	yet
however	on the contrary	otherwise
on the other hand	despite	in contrast
unlike	contrary to	still
instead	although	whereas
conversely	nonetheless	in spite of
while	even though	although

6. **Introducing Examples or Details**

for example	for instance	namely
as you can see	for one thing	in fact
in particular	to illustrate	that is

7. **Restating a Point**

in other words	to put it another way	that is
in effect		in fact
	that is to say	in short

8. **Showing Cause and Effect**

as	then	accordingly
because	therefore	hence
as a result	for	thus
consequently	for that reason	since
so	thereby	as a consequence

9. **Concluding**

in brief	in conclusion	therefore
to sum up	on the whole	thus
to conclude	accordingly	briefly
finally	as we have seen	

A4. Common Prefixes and Suffixes

Many words in English begin with prefixes. The meanings of prefixes remain consistent—when you encounter two words starting with the same **prefix,** you know the words are related in meaning. For example, in these two words *prearrange* and *prefix,* pre- means *before* or *ahead of time.* So *prearrange* means to organize or set up something beforehand, in advance. And *prefix* refers to the affix that is placed before a whole word or word stem.

1. Common Prefixes

Prefix	Meaning	Example
ab-	away from	absent, abnormal
an-	without or not	anarchy
ant-, anti-	against	antacid, antiwar
bi-	two	bicycle
bio-	life	biography, biology
co- (col-, com-, con- cor-)	together, totally, with	colleague, complete, contact, co-pilot, correspond
de-	down, away, opposite of, remove	decline, defoliate depart, deplete
dec-	ten	decade, decathalon
di-	two	carbon dioxide
dia-	through, not, opposite	diameter
dis-	remove	disable, disinfect
du-	two	duet
en-	to make or cause	enlarge, enrage
ex-	out of	expel, extract
inter-	among, between	interview
intra-	within	intramural
il-, im-, in-, ir-	not	illegal, impossible, inexact, irregular
im-, in-	into	immigrate, install
mal-	evil, bad	malfunction, malignant
mis-	wrong	misplace, misspell
mono-	single	monotone
multi-	many	multiply
non-	not	nonviolent
ob-	against or toward	obstruct
pre-	before	preschool, preseason,
pro-	before or forward	progress
re-	back or again	regress, recall, redo
retro-	backward	retrograde

semi-	half	semicircle
sub-	under	submarine, subordinate
super-	above	superhuman, superior
sym-, syn-	with, together	sympathy, synonym
tele-	far, distant	telephone, television
trans-	across	transport
tri-	three	triangle
ultra-	beyond	ultraviolet
un-	not, opposite	unlock, unkind

2. Suffixes

Suffixes, or word endings with fixed meanings, can tell you the part of speech of a word.

Common Noun Endings

Noun Endings	Meaning	Example
-acy	state of being	democracy
-age	state of being	marriage
-ance, -ancy	state of being	attendance, pregnancy
-ar	one who	liar
-arian, -ian	one who	librarian, dietitian, Italian
-ary	a place	library
-ate	one who	delegate
-cy	state of being	normalcy
-dom	area, state of	kingdom
-ence, -ency	state of being	difference, presidency
-er, -or	one who does	teacher, professor
-ery	place where	bakery
-hood	state of being	childhood
-ing	process, action	reading
-ion	state of being, doing	procession
-ism	system of, state of	nationalism, alcoholism
-ist	one who	cyclist
-ity	state of being	gravity
-ment	state of being	argument
-ness	state of being	happiness
-ology	study of	psychology
-onomy	rules of, study of	economy
-tory	place where	laboratory
-ship	state of being	friendship
-sion, -tion	state of being, doing	depression, attention
-tude	state of being	attitude

Common Adjective Endings

Adjective endings	Meaning	Example
-able, -ible	can do, able, fit for	readable, edible
-al, -ial	within or related to	natural, special
-ant, -ent	related to, state of being	vacant, independent
-ar, -ary	related to	regular, secondary
-ate	related to, full of	passionate
-ful	full of	helpful
-ic	related to	acidic
-ine	related to	feminine
-ing	process or action	entertaining
-ish	like	foolish
-ive	relating to or causing	inventive, digestive
-less	without	careless, hopeless
-ly	in a way that is	lovely, friendly
-oid	in shape of	humanoid,
-ous	full of	famous, harmonious
-y	full of, covered with	icy, funny

A5. Grammar Review

A college handbook on grammar is useful, so you should form a habit of consulting it whenever you are not sure about your grammar. The following *basic* grammatical rules, however, are meant to help you recognize and beware of some very common errors in writing.

Verbs

Consistency of Tenses

Be consistent in your use of verb tenses. If you begin writing a piece in the past tense, don't suddenly jump to the present tense, unless the meaning requires you to do so. Notice the verb tenses in the following passage:

> I learned respect for preparation when I helped my mother make my wedding dress. My mother was precise about measuring and allowing for alterations in the future. Before she cut out the material, we discussed whether the dress would have another life after my wedding. I decided I wanted a dress that I could use on other occasions. With this in mind, my mother made "two dresses in one." The dress she made for my wedding was altered afterwards and I wore it to formal functions like my sister's wedding and my aunt and uncle's fiftieth anniversary party. All my mother does to make my wedding dress new again is add a bit of lace or shorten the hem and sleeves. I will wear the dress to my office's first formal Christmas party.

The shifts in tense in the above passage are correct. The author moves from the past to the present and then to the future as required by the content, changing tenses logically.

Agreement between Subject and Verb

1. In sentences beginning with *here* or *there*, the real subject is NOT *here* nor *there;* rather it is the noun following the form of the verb *to be* used in the sentence.

    There *are* three *trees* in my yard.
    There *is* a big *parade* scheduled for today.
    Here *are* several *books* for you to read.
    There *are* many *players* who cheat.
    There *are lots* of students in the cafeteria.

2. When the following words are used as subjects, they are always singular in concept; therefore, they always require singular verbs.

everyone	someone	anyone	no one	each
everybody	somebody	anybody	nobody	either
everything	something	anything	nothing	neither

    Everyone is happy to see you.
    Neither of the twins likes ice cream.

3. When *each* or *every* comes before singular subjects joined by *and*, a singular verb is required.

    Every man and woman has the right to vote.
    Each student and teacher has a book.

4. The emphatic *it* in the following structure is singular, so *it* is always followed by a singular verb even when its referent is plural.

    It was the noisy children who always disturb me.
    It is his final exams that worry him.

5. Words that come between a subject and its verb do not change the number of the subject.
    Be especially careful with prepositional phrases that are placed in such a position.

    A woman, along with her thirty-seven cats, lives on that farm.
    Everyone *except Sheila and Mike* has a book.
    Daniel, together with his family, is visiting Ottawa.
    The teacher, along with her students, is viewing a film.
    One of the most enjoyable books published this year was written by Margaret Atwood.

6. Subjects joined by *and* or *both* take a plural verb (but see rule 2).
    A loud bang and sudden scream are enough to startle anyone.

    A red Honda and a blue Ford are parked outside.
    Both Jane and Michelle are coming to the party.

7. *Several, many, both,* and *few* are plural words and always take a plural verb.

    Both are going to Halifax next week.
    Only a few have failed the test.

8. Some nouns are always plural in form and always take plural verbs.
    clothing and accessories: jeans, pants, sunglasses, trousers
    tools: scissors, pliers, tweezers
    However, some of them are followed by a singular verb when used together
    with phrases such as a *pair of*.

    Her jeans are very tight.
    That pair of jeans is old.

9. When subjects are joined by the following structures, the verb must agree
    with the closer subject.

    Neither the students *nor* the teacher likes the classroom.
    Either the teacher *or* the children are making the sets.
    Not only the mother *but also* the children are coming soon.

10. Some words may be singular or plural depending on what they refer to: *lots,
    all, some, any, most, half,* etc. When these words are followed by a preposi-
    tional phrase, the noun in the phrase will determine whether the verb is
    singular or plural.

    All of the books have been destroyed.
    All of the book has been damaged.
    Lots of the books were torn.
    Lots of the book was torn.

11. The expression *a number of* is plural, but the look-alike expression *the
    number of* is singular.

    A number of cars were stolen from the lot.
    The number of children at home is amazing.

12. Expressions stating an amount of time, money, weight, and volume are
    plural in form but take singular verbs.

    Three weeks is not enough time for a visit to Italy.
    Six hundred dollars is needed as a deposit.
    Thirty extra pounds is too much to lose in a week.
    Four gallons of gasoline costs over thirty pesos.

13. Some words seem to have plural endings, but they are singular in meaning. These words require singular verbs.

    mathematics, physics, economics, statistics . . .
    measles, mumps, herpes . . .
    news, ethics, politics . . .

Mathematics is an easy subject.
The news was always depressing.

14. Titles of books and movies, even if plural in form, take singular verbs.

The Globe and Mail is a fine newspaper.
Star Wars is an action-packed adventure.

15. Collective nouns are usually singular, but may be plural if the members are functioning independently. Watch the pronouns for clues to the singular or plural nature of the subject. Some of these words are *class, team, police, committee, audience, family, faculty,* and so on.

The class takes its final exam next Wednesday.
The class are finishing their spring projects.

16. Some nouns use the same form for both singular and plural meanings. The pronouns and modifiers with these words will indicate whether they are singular or plural in meaning.
    s: *species, series*

That species is extinct. Those species are unusual.

    no s: *sheep, deer, fish*

That deer is graceful. Those deer are young.

17. a. A noun for a nationality that ends in *ese, ch,* or *sh* refers to the *people of the country,* so it is plural and takes a plural verb; it is preceded by the article *the.*

The Chinese are looking forward to hosting the Olympic games in 2008.
The French are famous for their wines.
The English adore sweet puddings.

    b. When a singular individual is intended, the noun is used adjectively and often a noun is required after it.

That Japanese student is studying in Vancouver.
Peter O'Toole is an Irish actor.
Penelope Cruz is Spanish.

    c. A noun for nationality that ends in *an* or *ian* is singular and takes "s" in its plural form.

The Italians won the World Cup in soccer in 2006.
Mahatma Gandhi is a famous and influential Indian.
Jamaicans created reggae music.

Sentence Structure

Fragments

A sentence has a subject and a verb and conveys a complete thought. However, a sentence fragment looks like a sentence in that it starts with a capital letter and ends with an ending punctuation (the period, the question mark, or the exclamation mark), but the reader knows something is missing. In most writing, sentence fragments are not acceptable. There are six types of fragments.

1. **Prepositional phrase fragment:** A prepositional phrase has no subject or verb and begins with a preposition. Correct the fragment by joining it to the rest of the sentence.
   a. I love skiing. *In the mountains.*
      I love skiing in the mountains.
   b. Luke was so anxious during the accounting exam. *In spite of his good study habits and excellent preparation.* He only got a D.
      Luke was so anxious during the accounting exam that in spite of his good study habits and excellent preparation, he only got a D.

2. **Missing verb fragment:** There is no main verb. Correct the following by adding an appropriate verb.
   a. The annual George Wicken Award *given* by the college for teaching excellence.
      The annual George Wicken Award *is given* by the college for teaching excellence.
   b. The moon *seen* to have a pitted surface of craters and volcanoes.
      The moon *can be seen* to have a pitted surface of craters and volcanoes.

3. **Infinitive fragment:** The infinitive is used incorrectly as a complete verb in the sentence. Correct the fragment by combining the infinitive phrase with the sentence it belongs to or by changing the infinitive to a complete verb.
   a. You should always proofread your work carefully. *To be sure you have completed the requirements and to feel you've produced a piece you can be proud of.*
      You should always proofread your work carefully to be sure you have completed the requirements and to feel you've produced a piece you can be proud of.
      You should always proofread your work carefully. Then you can be sure you have completed the requirements and feel you've produced a piece you can be proud of.

4. **Participle fragment:** The *ing* participle is used alone as a complete verb, without the helping verb.
   Correct it by adding a subject and a correct form of the verb, or by joining the participle fragment to the sentence it belongs to.
   a. He enjoyed travelling to school on the bus each day. *It being his only opportunity to daydream.*

He enjoyed travelling to school on the bus each day. It was his only opportunity to daydream.

He enjoyed travelling to school on the bus each day, it being his only opportunity to daydream.

   b. *Growing up in a vociferous family.* He became a great debater.

Growing up in a vociferous family, he became a great debater.

5. **Missing subject fragment:** Correct the fragment by adding a subject to create a new sentence, or attach the fragment to the appropriate sentence.

   a. Many teachers offer help outside of the classroom. *Also assign extra work for the better students.*

Many teachers offer help outside of the classroom. They also assign extra work for the better students.

Many teachers offer help outside of the classroom and also assign extra work for the better students.

6. **Dependent clause fragment:** A dependent clause cannot stand alone. It is easily recognized by the conjunction that introduces it. Correct the fragment by joining the dependent clause to an independent clause, or by removing the conjunction and creating a new independent clause. You may need to replace the conjunction (if the conjunction is *who, which,* or *that*) with a subject.

   a. I decided to jog home. After I had finished my workout.

I decided to jog home after I had finished my workout.

   b. As a boy he enjoyed watching air shows. Which may account for why he chose to be a pilot when he grew up.

As a boy he enjoyed watching air shows. This may account for why he chose to be a pilot when he grew up.

Run-On Sentences

Unlike sentence fragments, which contain too little to be a sentence, run-on sentences contain too much. There are three basic types: the comma splice, the fused sentence, and the cluttered sentence.

1. **The comma splice:** In this error two independent clauses are united with nothing but a comma between them.

Roses are red, violets are blue.

There are several ways to fix a comma splice:
   a. Correct it by writing the comma splice as two distinct sentences.

Roses are red. Violets are blue.

   b. Correct it by replacing the comma with a semicolon, which acts as a balancer between the two clauses.

Roses are red; violets are blue.

   c. Correct it by placing a coordinating conjunction after the comma, thus creating a compound sentence. A coordinating conjunction is sometimes

referred to as a "short" connector. There are only seven of them and a handy mnemonic is to call them the FANBOYS, which stands for *for, and, nor, but, or, yet,* and *so.* Then the formula to remember is
, + one of FANBOYS (as required by the meaning).

Roses are red, but violets are blue.

d. Correct it by using a "long" connector (e.g., *however, therefore, nevertheless, as a result, in fact, consequently,* and *in addition*) after the semicolon and placing a comma after the connector. Then the formula to remember is
; + however etc. (as required by the meaning) + ,

e. Correct it by making one of the two clauses dependent, thus creating a complex sentence.

Although roses are red, violets are blue.
Roses are red whereas violets are blue.

2. **The fused sentence:** This error, like the comma splice, puts two independent clauses side by side without using any punctuation.

I am glad March break has finally arrived I certainly need a chance to relax.

Correct it by recognizing the two independent clauses and then apply the same techniques as for the comma splice.

I am glad March break has finally arrived. I certainly need a chance to relax.
I am glad March break has finally arrived; I certainly need a chance to relax.
I am glad March break has finally arrived, for I certainly need a chance to relax.
I am glad March break has finally arrived; in fact, I just need a chance to relax.
I am glad March break has finally arrived because I certainly need a chance to relax.
Since I need a chance to relax, I am glad March break has finally arrived.

3. **The cluttered sentence:** The cluttered sentence may be grammatically correct, but it is difficult for the reader to understand. One kind of cluttered sentence contains too many ideas and clauses.

In the last two years, I have had the sense that the weather patterns have changed because the winters have been relatively mild with as much rain as snow, which has in turn led to the ice storms that caused so much damage, and we have experienced the hottest days on record in the summer, but whether this is due to global warming or whether it's simply a coincidence I really don't know.

Correct this type of cluttered sentence by dividing it into several sentences based on the clusters of ideas contained in the sentence.

In the last two years, I have had the sense that the weather patterns have changed. The last two winters have been relatively mild with as much rain as snow, which has in turn led to the ice storms that caused so much damage. Also each summer we have experienced the hottest days on record. However, I really don't know whether this is due to global warming or whether it's simply a coincidence.

Another kind of cluttered sentence contains incongruous ideas, or the relationship between ideas is not clearly stated for readers.

Even with OSAP, students find the financial demands of college difficult to manage and having a social life is something a lot of students don't have time for because they have to work part-time and complete their college assignments.

Correct it by sorting out the ideas and making them clearer.

Even with OSAP, students find the financial demands of college difficult to manage. In addition, having a social life is something a lot of students don't have time for because they have to work part-time and complete their college assignments.

Correct Use of Pronouns

1. **Agreement in number:** Pronouns, being replacements of nouns, should agree in number with the nouns they replace (their antecedents). If the antecedent is singular, the pronoun is also singular; if the antecedent is plural, so is the pronoun. One common problem that occurs relates to the use of *each, every, any, some, no, either,* and *neither.* (See pages 307–309 on "Agreement between Subject and Verb.") These words seem to be all inclusive, but they are always singular in concept. Many of the rules of agreement dealing with pronouns are the same as those that deal with verbs, namely singular nouns to be replaced by singular pronouns and plural nouns to replaced by plural pronouns.

Every student has to bring *their* own lunch.

Correct the wrong use of pronoun by making the pronoun agree with its antecedent noun (here the noun is *student*).

Every student has to bring *his or her* own lunch.
All students have to bring *their* own lunches.

Note: If you change the noun (the antecedent) to the plural, you must make all other parts of the sentence agree.
If you find *his or her (his/her)* too cumbersome, try to find a way to avoid using it.

Every student has to bring a lunch.

Collective nouns and their pronouns also create problems for writers. (See page 309.) When members of a group act individually, the pronoun is plural; when members act collectively as a unit, the pronoun is singular.

a. The team are picking up their new helmets. (Here each member of the team has his/her own helmet.)

b. The committee reached its unanimous decision to suspend trading yesterday. (Here the committee acts as a unit.)

2. **Agreement in person:** Pronouns should agree in person with their antecedents. *Person* refers to the one speaking (first person—*I, me, my, mine; we, us, our, ours*), the one spoken to (second person—*you, your, yours*), and the one spoken about (third person—*he, him, his; she, her, hers; it, its; they, them, their, theirs*). Mistakes occur when point of view is changed or when writers begin in the singular and move to the plural for no reason. Correct the improper use of pronouns by making all singular or plural.

a. *The prospective employee must have their résumé when they go to an interview.*

The prospective employee must have a résumé when he or she goes to an interview.

Prospective employees must have their résumés when they go to an interview.

The prospective employee must have a résumé when going to an interview.

b. *I know that to write a good paragraph you have to have a topic sentence.*

I know that to write a good paragraph I have to have a topic sentence.

You know that to write a good paragraph you have to have a topic sentence.

c. *The person who repaired my VCR did a good job and they didn't charge me much.*

The person who repaired my VCR did a good job and didn't charge me much.

The person who repaired my VCR did a good job, and she didn't charge me much.

3. **Vague pronoun references:** Pronouns depend on antecedents to give them meaning. If an antecedent is not identified or is unclear, the sentence is confusing for readers.

Kieran loves to play soccer, baseball, and hockey, and he would like to be a professional one when he grows up.

The problem is with the pronoun *one:* which doesn't replace any of the nouns used in the early part of the sentence. The readers are left wondering: A professional what? One solution is this:

Kieran loves to play soccer, baseball, and hockey, and he would like to be a professional athlete when he grows up.

Identify the vague pronoun in this example:

Lucia won so many local swimming meets that she decided to do it at the national level.

> The problem is with the pronoun *it,* which is vaguely used without a clear antecedent. What did she decide to do?

Lucia won so many local swimming meets that she decided to compete at the national level.

> Here's another easily missed problem with a vague pronoun:

Zazu's hobbies are reading and collecting rocks. Doing it makes her happy.

> The problem is with *it,* another pronoun vaguely used. There are two antecedents *it* could refer to (reading and collecting), but the writer didn't make it clear which one was the antecedent.

Zazu's hobbies are reading and collecting rocks. Both of them make her happy.

Parallel Structure

Whenever you write a series of items in a sentence, you should present them in a parallel structure. Parallel structure means all the items in the list have the same grammatical form. As a technique, parallel structure is useful because it shows a clear connection between ideas and adds coherence.

1. Single words:

    A successful student must be intelligent, diligent, and persistent.

2. Phrases:

    A first date can be either a romantic adventure or a horrendous bore, but it is always a nerve-wracking experience.
    If you want to be a good photographer, you need good-quality, superior equipment, artistic vision, and suitable subjects.

3. Clauses:

    My parents did some things that I will never do: they married too young, they created a large family, and they scrimped to save every penny.
    The prime minister claimed that he would reduce the deficit, that he would increase job prospects, and that he would get tough on crime.

Placement of Modifiers

A modifier adds detailed information about a component of a sentence. Adjectives *modify* nouns. Adverbs *modify* verbs, adjectives, and other adverbs. Modifiers can be single words, phrases, and clauses. There are two problems associated with modifiers: *misplaced modifiers* and *dangling modifiers*.

1. **Misplaced modifiers:** A misplaced modifier is placed too far away from the word to which it applies.

   To correct a misplaced modifier, determine the word(s) to which the modifier relates and then place the modifier as close to the word(s) as possible.

   a. The publishing company needed someone to type *badly*.
      The publishing company *badly* needed someone to type.
   b. He chased the thief out of the locker room *wearing only a towel.*
      Wearing only a towel, he chased the thief out of the locker room.
   c. Barry ate a doughnut at the shop *that was full of Boston cream filling.*
      At the shop, Barry ate a doughnut *that was full of Boston cream filling.*
   d. Sarah fed a fresh mango to Ed *dipped in cream.*
      Sarah fed Ed a fresh mango *dipped in cream.*

2. **Dangling modifiers:** A dangling modifier has no word to relate to in the sentence. As a result, the modifier "dangles" and accidentally modifies an unintended word, often with ludicrous consequences.

   Rollerblading down the hill at dusk, the raccoon streaked in front of me.

   To correct this error, use one of the two methods:
   i. Add information so that the meaning is clear.

   As I was rollerblading down the hill at dusk, the raccoon streaked in front of me.

   ii. Make sure both parts of the sentence share the same subject.

   Rollerblading down the hill at dusk, I saw the raccoon streak in front of me.

How to Punctuate

Russell Baker

The following article by Russell Baker treats the subject of punctuation in a light-hearted manner.

When you write, you make a sound in the reader's head. It can be a dull mumble—that's why so much government prose makes you sleepy—or it can be a joyful noise, a sly whisper, a throb of passion.

Listen to a voice trembling in a haunted room:

"And the silken, sad, uncertain rustling of each purple curtain thrilled me—filled me with fantastic terrors never felt before . . ."

That's Edgar Allan Poe, a master. Few of us can make paper speak as vividly as Poe could, but even beginners will write better once they start listening to the sound their writing makes.

One of the most important tools for making paper speak in your own voice is punctuation.

When speaking aloud, you punctuate constantly—with body language. Your listener hears commas, dashes, question marks, exclamation points, quotation marks as you shout, whisper, pause, wave your arms, roll your eyes, wrinkle your brow.

In writing, punctuation plays the role of body language. It helps readers hear you the way you want to be heard.

"Gee, Dad, Have I Got to Learn All Them Rules?"

Don't let the rules scare you. For they aren't hard and fast. Think of them as guidelines.

Am I saying, "Go ahead and punctuate as you please"? Absolutely not. Use your own common sense, remembering that you can't expect readers to work to decipher what you're trying to say.

There are two basic systems of punctuation:

1. The loose or open system, which tries to capture the way body language punctuates talk.
2. The tight, closed structural system, which hews closely to the sentence's grammatical structure.

Most writers use a little of both. In any case, we use much less punctuation than they used 200 or even 50 years ago. (Glance into Edward Gibbon's "Decline and Fall of the Roman Empire," first published in 1776, for an example of the tight structural system at its most elegant.)

No matter which system you prefer, be warned: punctuation marks cannot save a sentence that is badly put together. If you have to struggle over commas, semicolons and dashes, you've probably built a sentence that's never going to fly, no matter how you tinker with it. Throw it away and build a new one to a simpler design. The better your sentence, the easier it is to punctuate.

Choosing the Right Tool

There are 30 main punctuation marks, but you'll need fewer than a dozen for most writing.

I can't show you in this small space how they all work, so I'll stick to the ten most important—and even then can only hit highlights. For more details, check your dictionary or a good grammar.

Comma [,]

This is the most widely used mark of all. It's also the toughest and most controversial. I've seen aging editors almost come to blows over the comma. If you can handle it without sweating, the others will be easy. Here's my policy:

1. Use a comma after a long introductory phrase or clause: After stealing the crown jewels from the Tower of London, I went home for tea.
2. If the introductory material is short, forget the comma: After the theft I went home for tea.
3. But use it if the sentence would be confusing without it, like this: The day before I'd robbed the Bank of England.

4. Use a comma to separate elements in a series: I robbed the Denver Mint, the Bank of England, the Tower of London and my piggy bank.

Notice there is no comma before and in the series. This is common style nowadays, but some publishers use a comma there, too.

5. Use a comma to separate independent clauses that are joined by a conjunction like and, but, for, or, nor, because, or so: I shall return the crown jewels, for they are too heavy to wear.

6. Use a comma to set off a mildly parenthetical word grouping that isn't essential to the sentence: Girls, who have always interested me, usually differ from boys.

Do not use commas if the word grouping is essential to the sentence's meaning: Girls who interest me know how to tango.

7. Use a comma in direct address: Your majesty, please hand over the crown.

8. And between proper names and titles: Montague Sneed, Director of Scotland Yard, was assigned to the case.

9. And to separate elements of geographical address: Director Sneed comes from Chicago, Illinois, and now lives in London, England.

Generally speaking, use a comma where you'd pause briefly in speech. For a long pause or completion of thought, use a period.

If you confuse the comma with the period, you'll get a run-on sentence: The Bank of England is located in London, I rushed over to rob it.

Semicolon [;]

A more sophisticated mark than the comma, the semicolon separates two main clauses, but it keeps those two thoughts more tightly linked than a period can: *I steal crown jewels; she steals hearts.*

Dash [—] and Parentheses [()]

Warning! Use sparingly. The dash SHOUTS. Parentheses whisper. Shout too often, people stop listening; whisper too much, people become suspicious of you. The dash creates a dramatic pause to prepare for an expression needing strong emphasis: *I'll marry you—if you'll rob Topkapi with me.*

Parentheses help you pause quietly to drop in some chatty information not vital to your story: *Despite Betty's daring spirit ("I love robbing your piggy bank," she often said), she was a terrible dancer.*

Quotation marks [" "]

These tell the reader you're reciting the exact words someone said or wrote: Betty said, *"I can't tango."* Or: *"I can't tango,"* Betty said.

Notice the comma comes before the quote marks in the first example, but comes inside them in the second. Not logical? Never mind. Do it that way anyhow.

Colon [:]

A colon is a tip-off to get ready for what's next: a list, a long quotation or an explanation. This article is riddled with colons. Too many, maybe, but the message is: "Stay on your toes; it's coming at you."

Apostrophe [']

The big headache is with possessive nouns. If the noun is singular, add 's: *I hated Betty's tango.*

If the noun is plural, simply add an apostrophe after the s: *Those are the girls' coats.*

The same applies for singular nouns ending in s, like Dickens: *This is Dickens's best book.*

And in plural: *This is the Dickenses' cottage.*

The possessive pronouns *hers* and *its* have no apostrophe.

If you write *it's,* you are saying *it is.*

Keep Cool

You know about ending a sentence with a period (.) or a question mark (?). Do it. Sure, you can also end with an exclamation point (!), but must you? Usually it just makes you sound breathless and silly. Make your writing generate its own excitement. Filling the paper with !!!! won't make up for what your writing has failed to do.

Too many exclamation points make me think the writer is talking about the panic in his own head.

Don't sound panicky. End with a period. I am serious. A period. Understand?

Well . . . sometimes a question mark is okay.

Glossary of Terms

Active reading: a type of reading that requires the reader to interact constantly with the reading material—it, unlike casual reading, involves active and analytical thinking

Alliteration: the repetition of identical sounds, particularly at the beginning of words close to one another (e.g., safe and sound, fine feathered friend)

Allusion: a reference to something or someone in history, mythology, religion, or other literary works that brings added information or emotional meaning to the present work

Analogy: an extended comparison of two things, similar to one another in certain aspects, usually to explain complicated or unfamiliar concepts by comparing them to simple or familiar ones

Analysis (analyze [v], analytical [adj]): detailed study or examination of something in order to understand it better

Anecdote: a short, interesting, or amusing story about a real person or event.

Antonym: a word that means the opposite of another word

APA style: a documentation system developed by the American Psychological Association (APA) and widely used in the social sciences

Argument: See *Argument/Persuasion*

Argument/Persuasion: one of the rhetorical modes in writing that consists of *argument* (aimed at arguing for or against a certain point) and *persuasion* (efforts to win over readers and persuade them to take action on the author's belief)—most authors choose to be both argumentative and persuasive

Audience: one of the key concepts that a writer should be clear about before beginning to write—the intended *audience*, together with *purpose*, determine the author's level of language, tone, etc.

Audience and purpose: the two key concepts that a writer should keep in mind while writing as they determine the author's level of language, tone, etc.

Brainstorm: the initial stage of the pre-writing procedure that involves thinking freely about ideas related to the chosen subject and generating content for the piece to be written

Causal analysis: also known as analysis of *cause and effect,* a type of organizational pattern for developing essays and paragraphs—it is focused on analyzing the reasons for a certain situation (looking for the cause) or explaining how something happened or will happen (analyzing the effect)

Cause and effect: See *Causal analysis*

Chronological order: also called *time order*—information and ideas introduced *chronologically* are presented in order of time sequence

Classification: a type of organizational pattern in writing that involves dividing or classifying subjects or items into different categories based on the traits discussed

Cliché: a phrase or an idea that has been used so often it becomes meaningless and boring

Climactic order: an arrangement of key ideas in order of importance so that the most important idea is presented last, leading the reader to a climax

Coherence: one of the key concepts in effective writing that, meaning literally *sticking together,* requires all parts of a piece of writing to be organized according to an order appropriate to its subject and purpose and to be connected with appropriate methods of transition

Colloquialism: a word or phrase that is used in conversation but not in formal speech or writing

Comparison and contrast: one of the organizational patterns in effective writing, which involves *comparing* and/or *contrasting* two and more objects or persons— in this particular context, *comparison* refers to searching for similarities in the objects/persons in question and *contrast* refers to searching for differences

Complex sentence: a type of sentence that consists of one independent clause connected by a subordinate conjunction to one or more dependent clause(s)

Compound sentence: a type of sentence that consists of at least two independent clauses connected by a coordinate conjunction

Conclusion: the part of a piece of writing where the author presents his or her final or conclusive remarks—in an essay it could be in the form of one (or more) paragraph(s) at the end; in a paragraph it is normally the last few sentences

Connotation: the associations, suggestions, or overtones of a word or expression, in addition to its *denotation,* or dictionary meaning—a scientist normally holds words to their denotative meaning but a writer of literary works relies on connotation to carry deeper meanings. (See *Denotation*)

Context: the words that come just before and after a word, phrase, or statement that help you to understand its meaning

Contraction: a short form of a word: for example, *he's* is a contraction of *he is* or *he has*

Critique: to write or give your opinion of, or reaction to, a set of ideas, a work of art, etc.

Deduction: a logical reasoning process that involves using knowledge about things that are generally true in order to think about and understand particular situations or problems

Definition: an explanation of the meaning of a word or phrase, the act of stating the meanings of words and phrases

Denotation: the specific, exact dictionary meaning of a word, without any of its emotional associations. (See *Connotation*)

Description: one of the rhetorical modes that is used mainly to recreate a sensory picture or experience by appealing to the reader's senses

Diction: the choice of vocabulary and of level of language, whether formal, informal, or colloquial

Documentation: the act of recording and acknowledging sources of borrowed information or quotations according to a standard documentation style such as the MLA style or the APA style

Documented essay: an essay that cites information or quotations according to a standard documentation style as part of its supporting details; it is often a personal, critical response to a reading

Draft: rough written version of something that is not yet in its final form

Editing: the process of correcting mistakes and making improvements to a piece of writing

Epigram: a short poem or phrase that expresses an idea in a clever or amusing way

Equivalent order: a way to arrange details in any order, as each one is of equal importance

Eulogy: a speech given at a funeral to praise the person who has died

Evidence: the information that is used to support an argument or theory

Examples, use of: one of the commonly used organizational patterns, which involves using specific cases or situations to back up an idea or opinion

Exposition: one of the rhetorical modes that is used mainly to explain or inform—major types of expository writing include process analysis, definition, classification and division, cause and effect, and comparison and contrast

Expository prose: a type of writing that explains ideas and concepts by presenting information in an organized manner

Fallacies: a false way of thinking or reasoning about something; a false idea that many people believe is true

Fiction: a major literary genre, which includes a variety of narrative writing, either in prose or in verse, drawn from the imagination of the author rather than from history or fact—along with drama and poetry it forms one of the three major genres of literature

Figure of speech: a word or phrase used in a different way from its usual meaning in order to create a particular mental image or effect (e.g., metaphor, simile)

Flashback: an interruption of the chronological sequence of events to present an event that occurred earlier

Idiom: a group of words whose meaning is different from the meanings of the individual words put together; for example, *Let the cat out of the bag* is an idiom meaning to *tell a secret by mistake*

Imagery: literally, the collection of images in a piece of writing. Imagery, often contributing to the mood or atmosphere of a writing, may provide keys to the deeper meaning of the piece or pointers to the unconscious motivations of its author

Immediate cause: a phrase used in a causal analysis that refers to the cause that has a direct effect on the case in hand

Induction: a way of logical reasoning that involves using particular facts and examples to form general rules and principles

Introduction: the beginning part of a piece of writing where the thesis is likely stated or implied

Ironic: adjectival form of *irony*. (See *Irony*)

Irony: a broad term referring to the contrast between reality and appearance or what is said and what is meant by an author in a piece of writing

Jargon: words or expressions that are used by a particular profession or group of people and are difficult for others to understand

Levels of language: different registers and styles of a piece of writing ranging from formal to informal, mainly reflected in choice of words, sentence and paragraph structure, and syntax

Logical fallacy: See *Fallacies*

Logical order: one way to arrange supporting details in a piece of writing that shows how one idea leads to another, or how one idea causes another to occur

Metaphor: a figure of speech that imaginatively identifies one object with another and ascribes to the first object qualities of the second

MLA Style: also called the MLA Documentation Style, developed by the Modern Language Association, mainly used for papers or publications in the arts and humanities

Narration: one of the rhetorical modes of composition, the purpose of which is to recount an event or a series of events, a story

Neologisms: the creation of new words and expressions

Order: referring (in the context of writing) to the ways information is arranged to support the thesis

Organizational patterns: also called structural or rhetorical patterns, referring to the major techniques used in organizing a piece of writing, such as the use of examples, cause/effect, and comparison/contrast

Outline: sketchy plan of a piece of writing that lays out the structure or development of the author's ideas—an outline could be formal or informal, in point form or in complete sentences

Paradox: a statement that seems to be contradictory or absurd but, upon deeper analysis, contains a profound truth (e.g., more haste, less speed)

Paragraph: a section of a piece of writing, usually consisting of several sentences dealing with a single subject—a well-developed paragraph usually contains a topic sentence

Parallelism: a principle in writing that requires the presentation of equally important ideas in the same grammatical form

Parallel structure: a stylistic technique that consists of repetitive use of the same sentence structure for a special effect in style

Paraphrase: to express or state something that is said or written using different words, especially to make it easier to understand

Parody: a piece of writing, music, or art that deliberately copies the style of someone in order to be amusing

Parts of speech: one of the classes into which words are divided according to their grammatical function: e.g., noun, verb, adjective

Personification: a figure of speech that endows animals, ideas, abstractions, and inanimate objects with human form, character, or sensibilities

Persuasion: See *Argument/Persuasion*

Plagiarism: the act of copying another person's ideas, words, or work and pretending they are your own

Point of view: the perspective from which a piece of writing is written

Prefix: the affix (e.g., pre- and re-) placed before a whole word or word stem

Primary sources: also called *primary evidence*, referring to the written works that form the subject of your essay or paper

Process analysis: a type of *exposition* used to explain how to do something or how something happened

Pun: a play on words based on the similarity of sound between two words with different meanings

Purpose: one of the two important concepts (the other being *Reader*) that a writer should keep in mind while writing—he/she may choose to inform, to persuade, or to entertain

Quotation: words borrowed from other sources used to support your own point—quotations could appear in your writing as direct quotations, paraphrased quotations, and summarized quotations, but they all should be properly documented

Refutation: a type of argumentation whose major purpose is to counterargue an existing theory and prove it is wrong, untrue, or unfair

Revision: the process of making changes to your writing in order to improve it both in form and content

Rhetorical mode: major types of writing that include narration, exposition, description, and argumentation—different rhetorical modes are used for different purposes

Rhetorical question: a question asked only to make a statement or to produce an effect rather than to get an answer

Satire: a literary manner that blends a critical attitude with humour and wit, frequently to point out how human institutions or humanity should be improved

Scan: to read to search for a detail or fact

Secondary sources: writings that analyze, critique, review, or discuss the works or authors that you choose to write on in your research paper

Sensory details: supporting details (mainly used in descriptive writings) that appeal to the reader's senses (of sight, sound, smell, taste, and touch) in order to recreate the effect of the original experience

Simile: a figure of speech in which two essentially unlike objects are directly compared (usually introduced by *as* or *like*) to express a resemblance in one aspect (e.g., *as warm as toast, a smile like a spring day*)

Skim: to read a text rapidly to get a general understanding of its content

Slang: very informal words and expressions that are more common in spoken language, especially used by a particular group of people

Spatial order: a way to arrange supporting details according to the order of relationships in space, e.g., from top to bottom, from front to back—it is frequently used in descriptive writing

Stereotype: a fixed idea or image that many people have of a particular type of person or thing, but which is often not in reality

Structural pattern: See *Organizational patterns*

Style: the manner of expression displayed through selection and arrangement of words and sentence structure

Subject: an idea that is being discussed or is worth writing about

Suffix: a word-ending affix that indicates the part of speech of a word (e.g., -able and -ment)

Summary: a shorter and condensed form of a longer work that gives only the main points, not the details

Synonym: a word or expression that has the same or nearly the same meaning as another, for example, *big* and *large*

Syntax: the way that words and phrases are put together to form sentences

Thesis: the main idea of a piece of writing, either stated or implied

Thesis statement: the sentence(s) in which the main idea and sometimes the major supporting arguments are presented—normally it appears in the introductory paragraph of a piece of writing

Tone: the writer's attitude toward the subject or audience as shown in the choice of language, imagery, and rhythm—the author's tone may be formal, informal, intimate, solemn, sombre, playful, serious, ironic, or any of many other possible attitudes, and may shift during the narrative

Topic sentence: the sentence(s) in which the central idea of a paragraph is stated—normally it begins a paragraph

Transitions: devices, either implied or stated by means of words or phrases, that are used to connect sentences and paragraphs and to achieve coherence in a writing

Ultimate cause: a phrase used in causal analysis to refer to the key reason for the phenomenon in discussion

Unity: one of the most important principles in effective writing, which requires the *oneness* of a paragraph or an essay, i.e., all words and sentences working together to support the main idea and to serve the author's purpose

Credits

Unit 1

p. 5: From *My Canada,* edited by Glenn Keith Cowan, Irwin Publications, 1984. Reprinted with permission from McGill-Queen's University Press; **p. 14:** Excerpted from *Notes from a Big Country* by Bill Bryson. Copyright © 1998 by Bill Bryson. Reprinted by permission of Doubleday Canada; **p. 19:** From *The Autobiography of Malcolm X* by Malcolm X and Alex Haley, copyright © 1964 by Alex Haley and Malcolm X. Copyright © 1965 by Alex Haley and Betty Shabazz. Used by permission of Random House, Inc.

Unit 2

p. 28: Nader, Ralph. "Automatic Lubricators—The Real McCoy," from *Canada Firsts,* 1992, McClelland & Stewart, Inc. Reprinted with permission of the author; **p. 33:** Reprinted with the permission of the author; **p. 36:** *Ambition* by Joseph Epstein. Copyright © 1980 by Joseph Epstein. Reprinted by permission of Georges Borchardt, Inc., on behalf of the author; **p. 40:** Reprinted with the permission of the author.

Unit 3

p. 64: From *The Autobiography of Bertrand Russell,* Russell, B., Copyright © 2000 The Bertrand Russell Peace Foundation Limited and Routledge. Reproduced by permisson of Taylor & Francis Books UK; **p. 72:** "How to Write With Style," from *Palm Sunday* by Kurt Vonnegut, Copyright © 1981 by Kurt Vonnegut. Used by permission of Dell Publishing, a division of Random House, Inc.

Unit 4

p. 85: Reprinted with the permission of the author; **p. 88:** Reprinted with permission from Dr. David Suzuki; **p. 92:** "Remembrance," from *Inside Memory: Pages from a Writer's Notebook* by Timothy Findley. Published by HarperCollins Publishers, Ltd. Copyright © 1999 by Pebble Productions, Inc. All rights reserved; **p. 96:** Copyright © 1998 Time Inc. Reprinted by permission; **p. 105:** Reprinted with permission from the *Globe and Mail;* **p. 109:** Reprinted with the permission of the author; **p. 111:** Reprinted with the permission of the author; **p. 114:** Reprinted with the permission of the author; **p. 123:** "A Fable for Tomorrow," from *Silent Spring* by Rachel Carson. Copyright © 1962 by Rachel L. Carson, renewed 1990 by Roger Christie. Reprinted by permission of Houghton Mifflin Company. All rights reserved; **p. 126:** Reprinted with permission from the *Globe and Mail;* **p. 129:** Reprinted with the permission of the author; **p. 132:** Copyright © 1996 by Stephen L. Carter. Reprinted by permission of Basic Books, a member of Perseus Books Group; **p. 142:** Reprinted with the permission of Redbook magazine; **p. 147:** Reprinted with the permission of the author; **p. 150:** Reprinted with the permission of Pendragon Ink; **p. 155:** Reprinted with the permission of the author; **p. 158:** From *Dispatches from the Poverty Line* by Pat Capponi. Copyright © 1997 by Pat Capponi; **p. 166:** From *Contest Essays, 2/E,* by Hookey. 1994. Reprinted with permission of Nelson, a division of Thomson Learning; www.thomsonrights.com. Fax 800 730-2215; **p. 169:** "I'm a Banana and Proud of It," Copyright © 1997 by Wayson Choy. First published in Canada in the *Globe and Mail.* Reprinted with permission of the author; **p. 173:** Reprinted with the permission of the author; **p. 176:** "When Bright Girls Decide That Math Is 'A Waste of Time'" by Susan Jacoby. Copyright © 1983 by Susan Jacoby. Originally appeared in the *New York Times* (1983). Reprinted by permission of Georges Borchardt, Inc., on behalf of the author; **p. 180:** Reprinted with the permission of the author.

Unit 5

p. 191: "The Inner Game of Pinball," first published by the *Atlantic Monthly.* Copyright © 1979 by Anthony J. Lukas. Reprinted by permission of International Creative Management, Inc; **p. 194:** Reprinted with permission—Torstar Syndication Services; **p. 196:** Reprinted with the permission of the author; **p. 202:** "The Shack," from *Heart of a Stranger* by Margaret Laurence © 1976. Published by McClelland & Stewart Ltd. Used with permission of the publisher; **p. 208:** First published in *Parents* magazine, December 1990. © 1990 by Michael Dorris, permission of The Wylie Agency; **p. 211:** Reprinted with permission—Torstar Syndication Services; **p. 218:** From *I Know Why the Caged Bird Sings* by Maya Angelou, copyright © 1969 and renewed 1997 by Maya Angelou. Used by permission of Random House, Inc; **p. 221:** "But a Watch in the Night: A Scientific Fable" by James C. Rettie from *Forever the Land: A Country Chronicle and Anthology,* Edited by Russell and Kate Lord. Copyright © 1950 by Harper & Brothers; Copyright renewed © 1978 by Russell and Kate Lord. Reprinted by permission of HarperCollins Publications; **p. 235:** Reprinted with the permission of the author; **p. 240:** Reprinted with the permission of the author; **p. 244:** Reprinted with permission of the Estate of Northrop Frye; **p. 248:** "The Case for Curling Up with a Book" by Carol Shields, first published in *The Journal,* Spring 1997, is reprinted with the permission of Carol Shields Literary Trust; **p. 252:** "A World Not Neatly Divided" by Amartya Sen for the *New York Times,* November 23, 2001. © 2001, The New York Times Co. Reprinted with permission.

Appendix

p. 287: From *The Secretary,* March 1995; **p. 306:** From *The Power of the Printed Word* series. Reprinted by permission.

Index